Research and Development in Expert Systems VII

THE BRITISH COMPUTER SOCIETY CONFERENCE SERIES

Editor: P. HAMMERSLEY

The BCS Conference Series aims to report developments of an advanced technical standard undertaken by members of The British Computer Society through the Society's conference organization. The series should be vital reading for all whose work or interest involves computing technology. Volumes in this Series will mirror the quality of papers published in the BCS's technical periodical *The Computer Journal* and range widely across topics in computer hardware, software, applications and management.

1:   SE90 Edited by P.A.V. Hall

British Computer Society Conference Series 2

Research and Development in Expert Systems VII

Proceedings of Expert Systems 90, the Tenth Annual Technical
Conference of the British Computer Society Specialist Group
on Expert Systems, London, September 1990

Edited by

T. R. Addis
University of Reading

R.M. Muir
Rolls-Royce plc

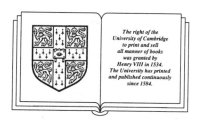

The right of the
University of Cambridge
to print and sell
all manner of books
was granted by
Henry VIII in 1534.
The University has printed
and published continuously
since 1584.

Published by
CAMBRIDGE UNIVERSITY PRESS
on behalf of
THE BRITISH COMPUTER SOCIETY
Cambridge
New York Port Chester Melbourne Sydney

Published by the Press Syndicate of the University of Cambridge
The Pitt Building, Trumpington Street, Cambridge CB2 1RP
40 West 20th Street, New York, NY 10011, USA
10 Stamford Road, Oakleigh, Melbourne, Australia

First published 1990

Printed in Great Britain at the University Press, Cambridge

Library of Congress cataloging in publication data available

British Library cataloguing in publication data available

ISBN 0 521 40403 7

CONTENTS

Preface

The papers in this volume are those presented at Expert Systems 90, the Tenth Annual Conference of the British Computer Society's Specialist Group on Expert Systems.

I would like to take this opportunity to acknowledge the contribution of time and skills from several groups of people.

I wish to thank sincerely my Organising Committee for the time, skills and ideas which they contributed to the overall management of the Conference; the Programme Committee for the formulation and organisation of the technical structure and content of the Conference; the Referees for their time and effort spent in assessing the technical papers with great care and thoroughness, to a tight schedule and all contributors of papers (successful or not) for their efforts in providing the Programme Committee with such a variety of topics from which to choose.

Last, but by no means least, I wish to acknowledge the professional organisation and administration of Clearway International staff, in particular, Fiona Pearson and Raffaella Stubbs, without whom the successful production of these proceedings and Expert Systems 90 would not have been accomplished.

Robin Muir
Conference Chairman

Organising Committee

Prof Tom Addis (Programme Chairman)   Ms Fiona Pearson
Dr Rob Milne   Mr Adrian Wheldon

Programme Committee

Prof Tom Addis (Programme Chairman)   Prof Les Johnson
Mr James Anderson   Prof Peter King
Prof Max Bramer   Mr Robin Muir
Mr Chas Church   Prof Kevin Warwick

Referees

Mr Geoff Alderman   Dr Nancy Johnson
Dr Peter Alvey   Mr Peter Jones (Creative Logic Ltd)
Mr Martin Bennett   Mr Peter Jones (Rolls Royce & Ass. Ltd)
Mr Gary Born   Mr Mike Keen
Prof Max Bramer   Mrs Linda MacAuley
Mr Chas Church   Prof Ken MacCullum
Dr Ken Currie   Dr John Masterson
Mr Mike Dulieu   Dr Robert Milne
Dr Janet Efstathiou   Dr Stuart Moralee
Mr Alex Goodall   Mr Richard Perkin
Prof Peter Hammond   Mr Kevin Poulter
Dr Sheila Hughes   Dr Han Reichgelt
Dr Robert Inder   Dr Nigel Shadbolt
Dr Peter Innocent   Dr Sam Steel
Prof Les Johnson   Mr Brian Ward

Introduction

It has been estimated that it takes on average ten years for a trained person to become an expert in his/her own field and ten years will have now passed since the first Expert Systems Conference. In 1981 there was the excitement of a new technology rich in potential. Since then the industrial stimulus has seized these ideas and converted them into products. This experience has shown that it takes a good ten years for an idea to develop into a product. Ten years have now elapsed in which the experts have matured, products have emerged and a new era has commenced.

One of the principal signs of the new era is the change in vision that knowledge engineering has brought about in the field of computer science and in the arena of industry. The extensive experience that has gone into developing the database can now been harnessed to extend the knowledge-base; to extend the knowledge-base into a system that will have company-wide applicability. The development of computer languages derived from logic and from functional mathematics has created a means of representing complex patterns of thought. The new computer architectures provide a means through which languages can be supported. Knowledge systems development environments are now integrated with the tools for knowledge acquisition and hence provide computer support for model creation.

Work on neural nets, a non symbol-based method of capturing expertise, has been suppressed for over thirty years by the fundamental philosophy that made Artifical Intelligence successful; a philosophy that defined the process of reasoning as being symbol manipulation. The last ten years have stretched this apotheosis of symbol manipulation to its limit. This is because those involved in knowledge engineering have become aware that the real sign of an expert is that he/she <u>breaks</u> the rules rather than always follows them. The expert has a <u>feel</u> for his/her subject that goes beyond mere expression.

This new era will acknowledge the differences between people and machines. We shall see an increasing occurrence of systems that will combine these differences; systems that will eventually function far beyond the performance of human specialists. We shall see machines that will short circuit the activity of symbol processing; machines designed to have the potential to react successfully in a general task domain.

This book reflects these trends by selecting the papers that best represent the field. It is a field that has reached a level of maturity and is in preparation for the current new decade of development and insight.

T R Addis
Programme Chairman
June 1990

MACHINE EXECUTABLE SKILLS FROM "SILENT" BRAINS

Donald Michie, The Turing Institute Glasgow, UK

Our mental business is carried on much in the same way as the business of the State: a great deal of hard work is done by agents who are not acknowledged.

George Eliot in Adam Bede (chapter 16), 1858.

Abstract

Knowledge engineers have generally assumed that the procedural knowledge which drives an expert's skilled behaviour can be elicited by dialogue. The findings of the past decade in brain science, cognitive psychology and commercial software do not support this idea. Evidence is lacking that skills, having once reached the "automatization" stage, can be de-automatized by dialogue so as to make their inner workings accessible to introspective report. Nor do skilled procedures ordinarily originate in the style of Feigenbaum's metaphor of "compiled knowledge", that is, by top-down derivation from pre-existing mental descriptions. Rather, the picture is one of inductive generalization from sensory data gathered in the course of trial and error. The role of higher-level knowledge is then to initiate and steer the learning process, not to participate directly.

The bottom-up path, by inductive inference from sampled data, can be simulated by machine. Even when the trained brain's silence is total, as in some control skills, computer induction applied to recorded behavioural traces can reconstruct rule-based models of the brain's hidden strategies.

Simulators were used to examine this as an approach to automatic control. The first stage, a comparison of rule-based with conventional methods for the stabilization of a space platform, established the adequacy of the production-rule formalism. The second stage employed a controllable inverted pendulum system in simulation. Rules automatically induced from behavioural traces were found to generate performance exceeding in reliability the trained subjects' own. Goals set by previously intractable control problems may now bring computer induction to the fore.

1. Introduction

The Dreyfus brothers (1990) have recently reminded us that Socrates (in Plato's Euthyphro) was the first to propose that experts who cannot articulate their specialist skills can be helped to do so by dialogue. Edward Feigenbaum, whose analogous proposal for knowledge engineering is well known, has acknowledged Plato's and Socrates' priority (Feigenbaum and McCorduck, 1983, p.79), — and also that the Socratic presumption that knowledge is indivisible is wrong. Two main forms of knowledge are usually distinguished, under the names "declarative" and "procedural". They are handled differently by the human brain. For some kinds of skilled task, and for <u>all</u> kinds under sufficiently demanding response-time constraints, involvement of declarative knowledge effectively fades out. The expert brain then becomes a "silent" source of expertise. Inarticulate skills can however be recovered in explicit (and commercially profitable) form by machine learning.

2. Nature of declarative knowledge

Not only in the time of Socrates, but also in today's usage, the single word "knowledge" lumps together the procedural and the declarative. This is unfortunate, since most of what can be said of the one fails to apply to the other, and <u>vice versa</u>. In particular, the retrieval and use of declarative knowledge is ordinarily done in conscious awareness. From a wealth of neurobiological observations concerning the effects of brain lesions on memory, L. R. Squire (1987, chapter 11) distinguishes declarative memory from procedural as "memory that is directly accessible to conscious recollection". By contrast, the hall-mark of a trained brain is to proceed intuitively. "Dialogue elicitation" of rules for building expert systems must therefore critically depend on whether a given expertise involves strategies stored in procedural memory. Inaccessibility to consciousness of even small parts of a targeted expertise could then cause the failure of large knowledge engineering projects. Reliable differentiation of the two forms is thus a matter of some technological urgency.

Declarative knowledge comprises whatever lends itself to logical formulation: goals, descriptions, specifications, constraints, possibilities, hypotheses. The declarative category also includes <u>facts</u>. When these relate to events in the agent's own experience, their place of storage is referred to as "episodic" memory. Another subdivision of declarative knowledge is held to reside in "semantic" memory, which Squire defines as follows:

> Semantic memory refers to knowledge of the world. This system represents organized information such as facts, concepts, and vocabulary. The content of semantic memory is explicitly known and available for recall. Unlike episodic memory, however, semantic memory has no necessary temporal landmarks. It does not refer to particular events in a person's past. A simple illustration of this difference is that one may recall the difference between episodic and semantic memory, or one may recall the encounter when the difference was first explained.

"Knowledge" is used here to denote whatever a given agent uses as knowledge, regardless of whether others see it as necessarily reflecting reality. "My Redeemer liveth" and "Last night I counted up to a million" are possible components of a body of declarative knowledge (respectively semantic and episodic), just as "Switch to black after seven reds in a row" is a possible component of a roulette player's procedural knowledge.

At the higher levels the various declarative constructs are aggregated by the brain into theories and annotated catalogues, and also into __stories__ both personal and communal. The latter can serve various purposes, — for example anecdotal (e.g. Homer's Odyssey), explanatory (e.g. the Flood) or mnemonic (e.g. the fiction of Galileo dropping balls from the Tower of Pisa). In externalised form, declarative knowledge is the stuff of which encyclopaedias are made.

Beyond mankind's external records lie even more challenging compendia, namely those unwritten encyclopaedias held together with folk notions of causality and common sense by means of which ordinary minds assimilate ordinary experience. Note that the latter consists largely of social experience. Hence intelligent agents require predictive models of __each other's__ reactions. When the formalizers finally crack this toughest nut of all, our descendants will possibly wish to apply the J test, proposed by the mathematician I. J. Good (personal communication). The machine is first primed with a sufficiency of background knowledge drawn from a given cultural milieu. It is then fed a succession of jokes from that same culture. Some are translated unchanged into the input formalism. Others have their punch lines subtly altered, — becoming in effect non-jokes. The machine is required to print the letter J whenever it spots a joke.

The point of the J test is that it dramatizes a special difficulty confronting the formalization of common-sense reasoning. Textbook expositions of the problem usually confine themselves to the seemingly trivial level of an isolated agent pitted against an inanimate environment: how should the monkey plan to get the bananas? This class of problem, posed in John McCarthy's 1959 paper "Programs with common sense", remains to this day without agreed generic solutions. Satisfactory logics will be obliged to incorporate consistent and effective means for handling temporal sequence, cause and effect, uncertain inference, incremental modification of beliefs and the notion of possible worlds. All of these today are storm centres of progress, and also of continuing controversy, among logicians. Yet the problems of the real world are far harder than even this list of requirements suggests. The world is __not__ inhabited by just one intelligent agent, but by heterogeneous groupings of problem-solvers with diverse abilities, motives, beliefs, attitudes and powers of dissimulation, in continual inter-communication. A vehicle for understanding how the world works must therefore carry heavier epistemological cargo than the logicians yet envisage. The winning formalism must not only enable a machine to see that the monkey's plan will fail if he climbs the stool in such a way as to stand on the stick which he then needs to use. The system should also be able to explain why an onlooker might find the impasse funny.

A school of Artificial Intelligence founded by John McCarthy in the 1950's aims to extend formal logic to serve as a vehicle for mechanizing declarative knowledge (see a recent collection edited by Ginsberg, 1987). I will say little further about the project, beyond expressing my respect for such work. Its philosophical importance is indeed matched only by its difficulty. My theme, as is proper to this occasion, is closer to the name and nature of expert systems. These are not so much to do with endowing computers with knowledge of the world, as with equipping them with useful know-how. I shall argue that between the procedural form of knowledge and the declarative there is a great gulf fixed. In face of the mountainous difficulties which confront the McCarthy project, this is perhaps just as well. To me the gulf suggests that the mechanization of procedural knowledge can advantageously be encapsulated as a separate problem, all the more tractable if tackled separately. With any luck we should then be able to climb our chosen hill while the logicians' Himalayan expedition is still studying its maps.

3. Nature of procedural knowledge

Procedural knowledge limits itself to the "how to" of skilled tasks, whether physical as in making a chair, or more abstract as in prediction of sterling rates against the dollar or the differential diagnosis of acute abdominal pain. A common synonym for such knowledge is know-how, and its manifestation in observable behaviour is called "skill". One difficulty is that observed task-performance is not enough to determine whether a given expert's behaviour really exemplifies a skill in the procedural sense or whether he or she is using declarative-semantic memory to form action-plans on the fly. Squire's earlier-cited definition supplies a test, namely the ability to render a verbal account of the way in which each decision was made, — possible only for declarative memory. Further evidence, as we shall see, can be obtained from the rate of the recognise-act cycle.

Although brain locations for specialised skills remain generally unknown there is evidence of memory mechanisms separate from those which mediate at least the episodic kinds of declarative knowledge. The ability to lay down episodic memory traces requires the active functioning of a particular complex in the brain, the hippocampal structures. Bilateral destruction of these structures puts a permanent stop to further additions to episodic memory. All but the more recent pre-existing memories remain unaffected, but there is failure of memory for whatever happened after the hippocampal destruction.   Such a person lives entirely with his or her previously existing memories together with short-term memories of duration typically less than a minute. Events are forgotten soon after they have occurred.   Yet know-how can be learned and retained.

In one subject with bilateral hippocampal damage (Milner, 1966, cited by Churchland, 1986, chap. 9.4) a study of mirror-tracing and of rotor pursuit showed that he was able to acquire both skills.   His learning curve was normal or close to normal.   Evidently he had acquired new know-how.   But his defect had long prevented the acquisition of new episodic knowledge. Eccles (Popper and Eccles, 1977) describe the building of "skills in motor performances such as drawing a line in the narrow space between the double line drawings of a five pointed star using only the guidance provided by the view in a mirror of his hand and the double star.   But the subject has no memory of how he learned the skill!"   Neural segregation of procedural and declarative-episodic memory systems was already strongly suggested in the late 1970's by experiments of Weiskrantz and Warrington, and also by studies by Brenda Milner of certain amnesics able to acquire new skills while unable to acquire new episodic knowledge.   This work, together with the current state of understanding in neuroscience of declarative/procedural subdivisions, is treated in depth by Churchland (1986) and by Squire (1987).

Separability between conscious recall expressed in verbal report and the unconscious retrieval of learned patterns applies with equal force to the learning of expert skills by neurologically intact brains.   The more know-how the expert acquires, the less he or she can tell you about it.   In his chapter on cognitive skills Anderson (1980) portrays the progression.

> 1. Our knowledge can be categorized as declarative knowledge and procedural knowledge.   Declarative knowledge comprises the facts we know; procedural knowledge comprises the skills we know how to perform.
>
> 2. Skill learning occurs in three steps: (1) a cognitive stage, in which a description of the procedure is learned; (2) an associative stage in which a method for performing the skill is worked out; and (3) an autonomous stage, in which the skill becomes more and more rapid and automatic.
>
> 3. As a skill becomes more automatic, it requires less attention and we may lose our ability to describe the skill verbally.
>
> 4. Skills can be represented by sets of productions.   Each production consists of a condition and an action.   The condition is a general description of the circumstances under which the production should apply.   The action consists of both the external behaviour and the changes to be made in memory if the production applies.

For those concerned to recover the productions of point 4, as in building expert systems, the lack of verbal accessibility described in point 3 should compel attention. Yet there is widespread faith among knowledge engineers that special methods of "dialogue elicitation" exist which can circumvent the problem. Since I have further evidence to review from clinical and academic psychology, I shall defer assessment of this belief.

4. Knowing how without knowing anything else

Feigenbaum and McCorduck (loc. cit., p. 55) give the example of tying one's shoes as a paradigm of procedural knowledge. It is interesting that once this skill has reached the stage known as automatization it can continue unaffected by massive disruption of the individual's brain mechanisms for acquiring and handling important forms of declarative knowledge. Damasio describes a patient named Boswell. The following summary is from Patricia Smith Churchland (personal communication).

> In addition to losing the hippocampal structures, he has massive damage to frontal cortex. He can identify a house, or a car, but he cannot identify his house or his car; he cannot remember that he was married, that he has children, and so forth. He seems to have no retrograde episodic memory, as well as no anterograde episodic, ... Boswell can still play a fine game of checkers, though when asked he says it is bingo. He cannot learn new faces and does not remember "pre-morbid" faces such as that of his wife and his children... Boswell can play checkers, tie his shoes, carry on a conversation, etc.

Supposing that Boswell can also tie his tie, what will happen if he is asked to tie someone else's tie (as far as I am aware, this experiment has not been done)? Most of us would respond to such a request by dropping what we (procedurally) know about tie-tying and making an eventually successful attempt derived haltingly from "first principles". With such patchily surviving declarative knowledge as Boswell's, one wonders whether such an attempt on his part could succeed, even if not prevented by his 40-second memory span ("Let's see ... What was I trying to do with your tie?"). The antithesis here, of course, is between problem-solving by pattern-match versus problem-solving by planning.

Of considerable interest is the survival of Boswell's checkers skills. What I later term "fast" skills are not the only ones for which the role of procedural knowledge may be so dominant as effectively to eclipse declarative. In contrast to chess skill, checkers was already known not to lend itself to the planning approach and to be essentially "intuitive". When A. L. Samuel was engaged in his classic studies of machine learning using the game of checkers, he had numerous sessions with leading checkers masters directed towards dialogue acquisition of their rules and principles. Samuel reported (personal communication) that he had never had such frustrating experiences in his life. In terms of discernible relationship to what the masters actually did, the verbal material which he elicited contained almost nothing which he could use or interpret. It seems that even Feigenbaum has not been without frustrations. Feigenbaum and McCorduck (loc. cit., p. 82) report such expert responses to the knowledge engineer as "That's true, but if you see enough patient/rocks/chip-designs/instrument readings, you see that it isn't true after all." They conclude "At this point, knowledge threatens to become ten thousand special cases."

The message from clinical studies is that skilled performance of even sophisticated tasks can still be manifested, and learned, when the brain is so damaged that knowledge of new happenings cannot be retained and previously stored facts and relations (declarative-semantic memory) are seriously disrupted. This message is consistent with certain phenomena of trained skill encountered in everyday life. When the normal human learner has no external source of "how-to-do-it" instruction the only means of acquisition may be trial and error. He or she then by-passes altogether item (1) in Anderson's second numbered paragraph, which he terms the cognitive stage. In such a case an expert skill is developed without mediation of declarative knowledge, with a remarkable denouement. Trainees eventually perform the learned task with expert precision without any sign of knowing, in the declarative sense, what they are doing! A well known textbook case is touch-typing, learned by practice under tutorial constraints including the use of typewriters with unlabelled keys.

It is generally, but wrongly, assumed that an expert touch-typist knows which symbols correspond with which keys of the typewriter. This assumption is easily tested by asking the typist to label from memory the typewriter's unlabelled keys. Typically the expert typist cannot do this, except in a halting, slow, uncertain, error-prone and incomplete fashion. The only effective way of responding is for him or her to form an intention to type a symbol and then to note which key is fingered. It is as though the fingers "know" but the brain does not. Of course, that part of the brain responsible for orchestrating the learned behaviour knows perfectly well which movements to make to produce an "a", which to produce a "b" and so on. But this part operates independently of other parts of the brain concerned with storage and management of the conscious knowledge that this key is called an "a", this one is a "b", etc. To extract declarative-semantic specifications from an intuitive skill it seems that one has to guess the logic from the observed behaviour. In the above case the logic-guesser and the performer is one and the same person. Later we will meet cases, where (1) the logic-guesser is another person and (2) where the logic-guesser is a computing system.

It is clear that the skill of touch-typing, just as the mirror-guided drawing of the hippocampal patient, does not depend on the storage and retrieval of declarative knowledge, and can be acquired and executed in its virtually complete absence. Recall that when copy-typing at speed the typist does not need to understand the words as he or she reads them. Indeed, after a speed test little or nothing of the text's content can be recalled. It is, however, a relevant restriction that even the earlier-described mirror-drawing skill is transacted via a fairly rapid recognise-act cycle. H. A. Simon (1990) has recently emphasised that simple recognition of a familiar object takes at least 500 milliseconds. Our observations indicate 1000 milliseconds as a useful bound for differentiating procedural from declaratively-based forms of decision taking. Operations involving reference to a semantic model of the task domain, are to be found only in the slow lane. Here seconds, minutes or even hours are required to incubate a decision. The bare bones of an explicit rationale for a slow-lane decision, when it comes, can usually be elicited from the expert by verbal report. In the fast lane, however, the expert rarely has even bones to offer.

5. Declarative support for procedural skill, and vice versa

But surely, in some at least of these cases, the expert relies purely and solely on declarative knowledge, so that dialogue elicitation of his or her skill may yet be a feasible option? When an expert has all the time in the world, as in selecting a move in correspondence chess or making a long-range weather forecast, he or she does indeed use declarative knowledge, possibly resorting not only to brain-stored knowledge but to colleagues, to case notes or to a library before final decision. None the less, when exploiting his stores of declarative knowledge, including the "what if" use of causal models, the expert is critically supported at every turn by a rich infra-structure of instant pattern-knowledge, — some 50,000 subcognitive chunks in the case of chess masters (Simon and Gilmartin, 1973; Nievergelt, 1977).

It is easy to forget that to have a computing system exercise higher-level skills in many cases one has also to implement this supporting infrastructure, — typically accounting for the bulk of the final code. I have elsewhere (Michie, 1990) cited a case where it would seem on the surface that an expert system could be quickly and easily built by the dialogue method. Johnson-Laird (1988) cites Morris Halle to the effect that all the high-level knowledge required to form expert opinions on the pronunciation of the plurals of concocted English nouns, such as "brell", "snorp" and "platch", can be expressed in the following three short rules:

1. If a singular noun ends with a sound made by raising the blade of the tongue and making a strident hiss, then add the _ez_ sound.

2. If a singular noun ends with a sound that does not involve the larynx vibrating, then add the _ss_ sound.

3. In any other case, add the _z_ sound.

On closer scrutiny it becomes evident that to interpret and apply these rules would require that the machine be endowed with further rules for converting the input character-string representation of singular nouns into conjectured sounds, together with rules for deciding whether particular sounds involve given speech movements. To interpret Halle's rules a plethora of new rules would thus be required. In the end the machine could scarcely avoid a need itself to be endowed with auditory and sensorimotor speech faculties so that (as children do) it could learn experimentally by observing its own behaviour. How else is the machine to know in each case whether a given sound requires raising the blade of the tongue, vibrating the larynx etc.?

Thus for "slow" skills, although substantial stored declarative knowledge may be at the core, transfer of skill to machine depends on combining two classes of methods:

(i) methods suitable for accessing the experts' declarative knowledge, which in general _can_ be articulated, and

(ii) methods suitable for accessing the experts' patterns and heuristics which, as Socrates discovered, they possess little awareness of and cannot explicitly access for themselves.

6. Beyond the Feigenbaum model

With so many considerations and findings running counter to received belief in the power of dialogue, we should now examine the basis. Can some thread of scientific argument, some corpus of experimental observation, or some documented industrial study be set against what has been reviewed? Required is a documented case, preferably many cases, showing that what was formerly automatized and silent in an expert has been brought to articulate life by patient application of the postulated technique. After ten years I do not know of a single such case. Moreover recent commercial history suggests that the long-awaited case may never be found. The two latest (BMT and GASOIL) of the world's three largest expert systems were _not_ constructed from rules obtained in dialogue fashion, but by automated induction from expert-supplied data. In other words, the induction engineer trained the system in the desired skill in exactly the style that the master of a craft trains an apprentice, — by a structured sequence of shrewdly chosen examples. Rates of code production are typically in excess of 100 lines of installed Fortran, C, Pascal etc. per programmer day (_see_ Hayes-Michie 1990 for relevant data on BMT, and Slocombe, Moore and Zelouf 1986 for GASOIL). The methodology allows validation to be placed on a user-transparent basis (Michie 1989), and maintenance costs can in some cases be trivialised, — see Figure 1.

	APPLICATION	NO. OF RULES	DEVELOP. MAN-YRS	MAINTENANCE MAN-YRS/YR	INDUCTIVE TOOLS
MYCIN	medical diagnosis	400	100	N/A	N/A
XCON	VAX computer configuration	8,000	180	30	N/A
GASOIL	hydrocarbon separation system con- figuration	2,800	1	0.1	ExpertEase and Extran 7
BMT	configuration of fire-protection equipment in buildings	>30,000	9	2.0	1st Class and RuleMaster

Figure 1. Tabulation from Slocombe et al. (1986) with 1990 data on BMT added.

7. The "knowledge compilation" metaphor

Returning to Anderson's account of human skill learning, we have
        (i) an opening stage, where the learner launches on his task armed with a conscious "description" of the procedure from a teacher or a written codification, and
        (ii) a final stage, where the learner has acquired an automatized representation, largely subconscious, in a form believed by cognitive scientists to be representable as productions.
        To a computer scientist (i) above seem reminiscent of a declarative specification.   The subconsciously executed production rules of (ii) sound like finally debugged procedures.   So far so good. There seems little harm and some useful clarification to be had from a programming analogy of this kind.   But Edward Feigenbaum has gone further, and postulated that procedural implementations are actually derived from starting descriptions by processes akin to compiling.   This leans a little too heavily on metaphor.
        In citing Socrates and Plato, Feigenbaum was aware that the early philosophers had omitted to separate declarative and procedural forms.   For the Greeks there was only one kind of knowledge, and that was the stuff of which a person can give a coherent account.   Experts, Socrates complained, forget that which they once possessed, retaining only some operational imprint not

to be dignified as knowledge.   To take up the story as told by the
brothers   Dreyfus:

> Plato admired Socrates and sympathised with his problem.   So he
> developed a partial account of what caused the difficulty.   In
> theoretical domains such as mathematics, at least, experts had
> once known the rules they use but then they had forgotten them.
> In these domains, the rules are there functioning in the expert's
> mind whether he is conscious of them or not.   How else could we
> account for the fact that he can perform the task?   The role of the
> philosopher is to help the experts remember the principles on
> which they act.
> S.E.Dreyfus & H.L.Dreyfus (1990) p.396.

Wishing to extend the "knowledge" umbrella to cover the
heuristics of practitioners, while preserving the distinction
between declarative and procedural, Feigenbaum elaborated his
model to present the expert's heuristics as <u>derived</u> from pre-
existing declarative models by a process akin to compiling:

> When we learned how to tie our shoes, we had to think very hard
> about the steps involved ... Now that we've tied many shoes over
> our lifetime, that knowledge is "compiled", to use the computing
> term for it; it no longer needs our conscious attention.
> Feigenbaum & McCorduck (1983), p.55.

Feigenbaum does not express a view on what happens to the
original declarative knowledge after it has been compiled into
know-how, — to what extent it stays around and to what extent it
decays.   Within the idiom of this metaphor we could perhaps speak
of it as "source code".   But since it is declarative I shall call it
"source logic", — a kind of partial specification which the brain
(slowly and with difficulty) can <u>interpret</u>, and which Feigenbaum
believes it can <u>compile</u>.   It is clear from writings by him and by
others of his school, that the source logic's persistence is not
pictured as central either to expert performance or to the
knowledge engineer's task.   The latter is seen as elicitation of
verbal expressions of the compiled rules themselves.   The above-
cited passage also indicates a reason for wishing to elicit compiled
code rather than source logic.   "Now that we've tied many shoes
over our lifetime" implies that the compiled rules <u>contain more</u>.
The source logic is thus only a partial specification.   In any case, as
Plato conjectured, it may have faded from memory.
        Since revision and enhancement through trial and
error manifestly plays a part, more is evidently involved in laying
down know-how than compilation.   It is as though repeated
execution of code were accompanied by corrections, refinements
and extensions interjected by a run-time editor.   According to this
model, incremental effects of repeated shoe-tying would come to be
embedded in oft-revised compiled code.   The latter would diverge
from, and eventually grow far more detailed than, the original

source logic, partly by the filling in from experience of gaps in the original specification and partly by extension.   But would it not then be tempting to omit the postulated compilation step altogether and leave such things entirely to the run-time editor?   The role of source logic supplied by tutor or text could then be restricted to two important, but not indispensable, functions:

(1) top-down decomposition of the planned implementation into modules, which themselves have to be instantiated bottom-up by practice.

(2) execution of the source logic, possibly halting and interpretative in style, as an initial means of generating experiential raw material for learning.

8. Expert skills without expert brains

This is, indeed, a picture which has been taking shape. Functions (1) and (2) have been transplanted into the computational domain (see Shapiro, 1987; Bratko, Mozetic and Lavrac, 1989).   A semi-automatic methodology has been developed to synthesize specific know-how, not from the testimony or performance of expert brains, but by de novo synthesis from compact logical models of domain causality.   These demonstrations lead away from my present topic.   They do, however, show that internally transforming declarative knowledge into expert procedures, mistakenly conjectured by Feigenbaum to be a human capability, can be accomplished by machine, — but only by a two-stage process.

First stage: exhaustive generation of example decision-data from the source logic.

Second stage: Inductive compression of the generated data into rules. Interestingly, application of the term "compiling" to just this second stage would be legitimate, although remote in concept from Feigenbaum's.   This is because the decision-data themselves can be regarded as an (extensional) specification of a procedure's desired behaviour from which computer induction "compiles" executable code.

The success of these two demonstrations leads to the conclusion that although the brain has no mechanism for transforming knowledge into know-how, there is a feasible and powerful process for getting computing systems to do just this. Moreover, industrial applicability has recently been shown.   The same methodology of know-how synthesis from source logic was used to build a complete and correct diagnostic system for the electronics of a space statellite (Pearce, 1989).

9. Postulates of skill acquisition

There seems to be prima facie justification for breaking with the traditional knowledge engineer's picture of the relation between declarative and procedural knowledge. Experimental work which I shall now describe was animated by a point of view about brains, summarised below as a list of postulates. Declarative knowledge is abbreviated to "D" and procedural to "P". To avoid committing to a view about embryonic forms, P designates only procedural knowledge which has already reached the automatized stage.

1.   human agents are able verbally to report their own D;
2.   human agents cannot verbally report their P;
3.   D can be augmented by being told, and also by deduction;
4.   P is built by learning, whether by imitation or by trial and error;
5.   P can be executed independent of D, but not vice versa;
6.   decision-taking via P is fast relative to use of D;
7   hence fast control skills necessarily depend on P alone;
8.   for some skills (including also many slow skills) P is sufficient for expert performance;
9   although the trained brain is silent, rule-induction can extract an explicit form of P from behavioural traces.

Experiments on dynamical control have yielded illustrations of the listed postulates, culminating in a test of no. 9, namely induction of rules from silent brains. Before describing the work, a comment is required on a seeming contradiction between assumption 2 and the undoubted existence of expert systems (EXCON was mentioned earlier) whose rule-bases have, with whatever difficulty, been constructed by dialogue acquisition.

Many observers have noted that experts seek to escape from the requirement of rule-formulation (which they find uncongenial) by supplying "rules" of such low-level form that they constitute no more than concocted sample cases, i.e. specimen decision-data. It is a widely remarked trait of expert practitioners that their inarticulacy when asked to describe is matched only by their readiness to perform. The phenomenon is well described in Sterling & Shapiro's (1986) account of building a credit evaluation expert system.

> The major difficulty was formulating the relevant expert knowledge. Our expert was less forthcoming with general rules for overall evaluation than for rating the financial record, for example. He happily discussed the profiles of particular clients, and the outcome of their credit requests and loans, but was reluctant to generalize.
>
> Sterling & Shapiro (1986) The Art of Prolog, p.357.

Profiles paired with outcomes constitute, of course, the typical form of "training set" used in machine learning. What if these knowledge engineers in search of improvements on raw formulations, were consciously or unconsciously to apply their own powers of inductive inference to such training data? They could then themselves create the kind of high-level rule structures that they had hoped to elicit from the expert. The result, however, would be testimony more to their own powers of inductive generalization than evidence that experts can introspect their own rules. This is no more than conjecture. Perhaps the builders of EXCON and other products of dialogue acquisition will be able to correct me. None the less, in a recent aerospace application two knowledge engineers were able, by deliberately exploiting this style of "rule-conjecture and test", to construct a rule-based solution with no more than a black-box simulator of the task to provide corrective feed-back. No set of rules pre-existed, either in an expert's brain or anywhere else.

10. Rule-based control of the attitude of a space platform

The role of the systems developer postulated above requires only a reactive oracle from which he or she can elicit verdicts. This source need not be a human expert. Indeed, it need not be human. As will be described it could be a simulator on which the developers can play "what-if" games with their latest conjectured rules ("what if we modify the rules like this? ...what would result from that adjustment? ... etc."). In an R & D contract for a US space consortium (Sammut and Michie, 1989), Dr Claude Sammut and I were given access to just such an interactive oracle.

When building a controller for a physical process, traditional control theory requires a mathematical model to predict the behaviour of the process. Many processes are either too complicated to model accurately or insufficient information is available about the process environment. Space-craft attitude control is an example of the latter, and was the subject of an early study of the applicability of machine learning techniques by Barron, Davies, Schalkowsky and Snyder (1964, 1965). Our client was interested in the development by machine learning of a rule-structured controller. A check was desirable as to whether dynamical control tasks can be satisfactorily handled by production rules at all, whether these are captured by learning algorithms or developed in some other way.

If the attitude of a satellite in low Earth orbit is to be kept stable by means of thrusters, the control system must contend with many unknowns. For example, although very thin, the Earth's atmosphere can extend many hundreds of kilometres into space. At different times, the solar wind can cause the atmosphere's density to change, thus altering the drag and aerodynamic torques on the vehicle. These are factors which earthbound designers cannot predict and even after three decades of space flight, attitude control is still a major problem.

We were asked to make a trial of rule-based control, using a computer simulation of an orbiting space-craft under "black box" conditions. By this we mean that knowledge of the simulation's structure and parameters was unavailable to us and hence to the controller. Constraints and assumptions built into the client's specification of requirement included minimal human supervision. Only one ground station is to be used for control. The ground crew therefore have only a 16-minute window in each 90-minute orbit during which they can communicate with the space-craft. A premium is thus placed on the controller's aptness for generating intelligible reports.

The client's "black box" simulated three-axis rigid body attitude control with three non-linear coupled second order differential equations, and was supplied as Fortran object code. The use of pseudo-random generators introduced various time-varying disturbances, not only concerned with aerodynamic effects of solar wind variations and of atmospheric density and altitude changes, but also effects of propellant expenditure, payload redistribution, solar array articulation, extension and retraction of the gravity gradient boom and the motion of robotic and other on-board manufacturing appliances. Due to such unpredictabilities and to the possibility of a failure while out of communication with the ground, interest in a rule-based controller as possible back-up centred on robustness, simplicity and conceptual transparency.

We already enjoyed familiarity with the BOXES adaptive rule-based control algorithm (Michie and Chambers, 1968; Chambers and Michie 1969). A laboratory problem of learning to balance a pole was recently the subject of new work by Sammut (1988) who also reviewed trials of other algorithms for learning rule-based solutions to the problem. A rigid pole is hinged to a cart which is free to move along a track of fixed length. The learning system attempts to keep the pole balanced and the cart within the limits of the track by applying to the cart a force of constant magnitude but variable sign, either right or left ("bang-bang" control). The pole and cart system is characterised by four state variables which make up a four-dimensional space. By dividing each dimension into intervals, the state space is filled by four-dimensional "boxes". With each box (i.e. local region of state-space, or "situation" in the terminology of situation-action rules) is associated a setting which indicates that for any point within the given box the cart should be pushed either to the left or to the right. We set out to test essentially this representation on the client's simulated space-craft.

11. The black box

The task is to drive the system from its initial state to the specified final state and maintain that state. Included in the black box is a fourth order Runge-Kutta numerical algorithm which integrates the dynamics of the equations of motion. The time step has a fixed value of 10 seconds. The black box keeps track of time and randomly injects various time-dependent disturbances as earlier described.

The state variables:

Attitudes: yaw (x), roll (y), pitch (z)

Body rates: $\omega_x, \omega_y, \omega_z$.

Initial values of the state variables:

$x = y = z = 10$ deg

$\omega_x = \omega_y = \omega_z = 0.025$ deg/sec.

The desired state:

$x = 0 \pm y = z = 0 \pm 3$ deg

$\omega_x = \omega_y = \omega_z = 0.005$ deg/sec

Failure condition

x or y or z exceeds ± 30 deg

ω_x or ω_y or ω_z exceeds ± 0.05 deg/sec

A flag is turned on if any of these go out of bounds.

Available control inputs

Torques: T_x, T_y, T_z.

Torque is applied by the firing of thrusters which are aligned to the body axes. Although other attitude control devices (momentum exchange systems) will be used on the satellite in addition to thrusters, this work only addressed the use of thrusters. The following are minimum and maximum torques which can be applied by the thrusters:

$T_x(\text{Min}) = T_y(\text{Min}) = T_z(\text{Min}) = 0$ ft-lbf

$T_x(\text{Max}) = \pm 0.5$ ft-lbf; $T_y(\text{Max}) = T_z(\text{Max}) = \pm 1.5$ ft-lbf.

A flag turns on if the torque command is out of bounds.

12. Control rules for a black box

The first trial was made by directly adapting a set of BOXES-derived rules from the pole-and-cart domain to a sequential logic suggested by hand-derived rules due to Makarovic (1987). In each recognise-act cycle rule-matching follows a certain priority order, cycling through the state variables until an action is selected. For each in turn the rule first checks that the first derivative does not exceed certain bounds. If it does, then a force is applied to oppose it. If it does not, then with respect to the same variable check its magnitude. If it exceeds given bounds then a force is applied accordingly.

In the case of the pole and cart, there was a clear priority to the order in which dimensions were checked. It was critical that the angular velocity and the angle of the pole were considered before the cart variables, since neglect of the pole leads to failure much more rapidly than neglecting to keep the cart away from the ends of the track. If this principle is applicable to the case of the space-craft then it is necessary to determine which of the state variables changes most rapidly. This was done, yielding rules expressible in "if-then-else" form, thus:

if ω_z < -0.002 then	apply a T_z of +1.5
else if ω_z > 0.002 then	apply a T_z of -1.5
else if z < -2 then	apply a T_z of +1.5
else if z > 2 then	apply a T_z of - 1.5
else if ω_y < -0.002 then	apply a T_y of +1.5
. . . and so on.	

Note that we are using "bang-bang" control, i.e. the torquers are either fully positive or fully negative just as in the pole-balancing experiments. The thresholds for the variables were determined by choosing an arbitrary value slightly within the bounds given for the desired values of the variables.

This control strategy proved to be successful but slow, requiring 8,700 seconds to bring the vehicle within desired bounds, and it also consumed 11.2 units of propellant. The question arose whether the control of each dimension could be decoupled. The cited rule only allows one thruster to be fired at any one time. If each axis of the craft were considered separately then all three thrusters could be fired simultaneously. This modification resulted in rules which brought the vehicle under control very quickly, requiring only 4,090 seconds. But propellant consumption, although improved, was still too high, using 7.68 units before the vehicle became stable. Therefore we decided on a partial retreat from pure "bang-bang", with a view to replacing it with finer control of the thrusters.

The resulting strategy is best understood by a decision array. For example, yaw control can be displayed as in Figure 2. Each of the 15 boxes corresponds to one control rule. Thus the box in the top left hand corner states that if the yaw is positive (i.e. above the bounds on the desirable yaw) and the yaw rate, ω_x is well below the bounds of desirability then apply a quarter of the full torque in the positive direction. Thresholds were set for angles at $\pm$ 2 deg and for angular velocities they were $\pm$ 0.002 and $\pm$ 0.003. The decision arrays for roll and pitch dimensions were of the same form. The resulting control behaviour was highly satisfactory. The pitch dimension, which was slowest of the three to be brought within the desirability zone, is shown in Figure 3.

Yaw too-positive	Tx/4	0	-Tx/4	-Tx/2	-Tx
Yaw OK	Tx/2	0	0	0	-Tx/2
Yaw too-negative	Tx	Tx/2	Tx/4	0	-Tx/4
	Yaw-rate too-neg.	Yaw-rate negative	Yaw-rate OK	Yaw-rate positive	Yaw-rate too-pos.

Figure 2.   A decision array for control of the yaw dimension.

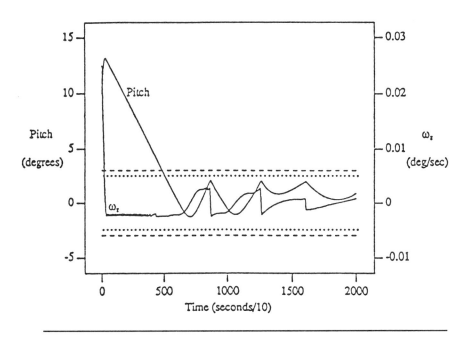

Figure 3.   Plot over time of vehicle's pitch behaviour, before final rule-adjustment for this dimension (see text).

The client's engineers informed us that both in speed of recovery and in propellant expenditure our results were close to calculated optima. Since however it appeared that the satellite had greater inertia in the z-axis (pitch) than in the other two we decided to increase somewhat the thrust of the z-torquer.   This brought the vehicle under control in 5,290 seconds, somewhat more slowly than the previous controller.   But it only required 1.7 units of propellant, a substantial saving.   Also calculations and numerical simulations by the client's engineers made our result appear slightly better than optimal! This doubtless arose from minor approximations and/or distributional assumptions made in their numerical work. Time did not permit the point to be elucidated. But the broad conclusion was seen by both client and contractor as encouraging. An industrial-strength problem had shown that the simplicity, robustness and conceptual transparency of rule-based control does not have to be purchased at the cost of significant degradation of performance.

13. Control rules from silent brains

Supported by the freedom interactively to test each conjectured modification on the simulator, Sammut and I found our own powers of rule conjecture adequate. But tasks of higher complexity, such as remote control of pilotless aircraft, would demand a less primitive approach. Present ideas are oriented towards the industry's use of interactive simulators for training pilots. A simulator-trained performer cannot tell you his or her strategy, but can demonstrate it. What is demonstrated can be automatically recorded. What is recorded can be inductively analysed. With my psychology-trained colleagues, Michael Bain, Jean Hayes-Michie and Chris Robertson I have embarked on an investigation into the use of Quinlan's rule-induction algorithm C4.5 to uncover effective control rules from the behavioural records of trained brains. Experimental subjects were trained on an interactive simulation of a task illustrated in Figure 4. New results together with early findings with this experimental system (Chambers and Michie 1969) lead to conclusions which I will summarise (details are available in Michie, Bain and Hayes-Michie, 1990).

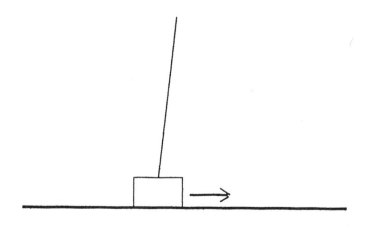

Arrow indicates current direction of motor

Figure 4.   Diagram of the pole and cart task.

First conclusion: role of problem representation. Chambers and Michie used two regimes of training, identical except for the graphical animation seen by the subject. In one variant the picture was as shown. In the other the subject saw only a display of four separate horizontal lines, along each of which a pointer wandered to and fro. The subjects in this second variant were kept in ignorance of the nature of the simulated physical system. Unknown to them, the pointers actually represented the current status of four state variables, namely position of cart, velocity of cart, angle of pole and angular velocity of pole. Our hypothesis was that when the system is run fast, leaving only time for use and up-dating of procedural memory, then there will be no difference in the learning curves of subjects using the two different representations. An indication of this was observed by Chambers and Michie. In our recent work we additionally used a rate sufficiently slow for subjects to report the task as having a major "planning" component. This slow-trained group learned more slowly, at least in the initial stages. Our provisional explanation is that they had the additional burden of managing and up-dating declarative memory in addition to acquiring a purely pattern-driven procedural model. In the new work trials have not yet been made of the scales-and-pointers representation.

Second conclusion: induction of rules from behaviour. Machine learning by imitation of a trained human was first shown for the inverted pendulum by Donaldson (1960) and reproduced under bang-bang conditions by Widrow and Smith (1964). Our concern was to test the ability of modern induction algorithms to extract from the behavioural record the kinds of rules believed to accumulate in procedural memory during skill-learning (see the passage from Anderson quoted earlier). Results have been positive. A task was investigated where the object was to cross the centre of the track as often as possible in an allotted time-span without dropping the pole or crashing the cart. When induction-extracted rules were installed in the computer as an "auto-pilot", performance on the task was similar to that of the trained human who had generated the original behavioural trace.

Third conclusion: the clean-up effect. Rules induced from a behavioural record can be assessed in two different ways. Predictive mode tests the ability of a rule-set correctly to describe other behaviour sampled from the same source. Performance mode tests the ability of the rules to substitute for the human source in executing the skilled task.

We were at first puzzled to find that induced rule-sets performed satisfactorily in the second mode while consistently showing high error rates, in the range 20% — 30%, in predictive mode. My co-worker Mr. Michael Bain then pointed out that when watching a machine-generated rule-set's performance on the screen one is struck by the almost superhuman precision and stability of its behaviour. We surmised that a trained human skill, although controlled by an equally precise and stable set of productions, is obliged to execute _via_ an error-prone sensorimotor system. The superimposition of inconsistencies and errors of inattention would then be stripped away by the averaging effect implicit in inductive generalization, thus restoring to the experimenters a cleaned-up version of the original production rules. When tested in predictive mode, such a rule-set can do no better than the cumulative sum of human perceptual and execution errors allow. But in performance mode one might expect a super-reliable stereotype of the behaviour of the human exemplar.

Direct confirmation of this idea was obtained by calculating the magnitude of the pole and cart's excursions during a control session along each of the four dimensions of the state space. Calculated ranges tabulated in Figure 5 were obtained from a behavioural trace recorded from Mr. Bain's own performance as a trained exemplar.

	x	xdot	theta	theta-dot
Trained human (ranges)	2.79	4.85	0.562	5.021
Induced rule (ranges)	0.46	1.83	0.134	2.276
Range differences	2.33	3.02	0.428	2.745
"Clean-up"	83%	62%	76%	55%

Figure 5.   Clean-up effect shown by induced control rules.
            x = position, theta = angle: "dot" denotes first derivatives.

The indications are that "skill-grafting" from behavioural traces may be possible. The key idea is that if we could look inside the head of the ground-based pilot of a remotely controlled aircraft, or indeed of the on-board pilot of a difficult vehicle such as a helicopter, we might see an encoding of a fully sufficient skill — degraded in real-time execution by sensorimotor delays and errors. Recovery of the postulated rule structure and its transplantation to an error-free device (i.e. a control computer) then offers a source of enhanced and more reliable performance. We see prospects of developing into a systematic technology the automatic extraction and grafting of machine-executable skills from "silent" brains.

14. Concluding remarks

In the early days of the horseless carriage, neither scientific knowledge of the thermodynamic advantage of internal combustion nor even the evidence from road trials were sufficient to overturn time-hallowed preferences for steam propulsion. An arresting historical parallel is presented today by the persistence of methods of which Feigenbaum has given a vivid and clear account:

> ...knowledge is currently acquired in a very painstaking way; individual computer scientists work with individual experts to explicate the expert's heuristics — the problem of knowledge acquisition is the critical bottleneck in artificial intelligence.
> Feigenbaum & McCorduck (1983) pp. 79-80.

To bring the petrol engine technology to the fore, a goal was needed for which the old methodology was not applicable at all, — a goal providentially brought into ·focus by the Wright brothers. For computer induction I have sought a task for which the old rule-acquisition methods are similarly inapplicable, namely rule-based dynamical control. The material already gathered is proving scientifically rewarding. In the longer term this goal could act as a focus for a significant extension of expert systems technology.

The commercialization of machine learning has been a largely European phenomenon, with Britain as a main innovative source. This is also true of logic programming, and some other areas. Yet on the broader software scene, European markets are succumbing to the domination of American suppliers. Research published in the summer of this year by Ovum Ltd showed that of the 40 leading suppliers to Europe more than half are American and only three British. Should Governmental encouragement be targeted to application areas where the establishment of niches for the British software industry still remains a possibility?

The idea needs to be handled with care. Government departments may best succeed by manipulating market pull, which they understand, rather than by bringing in technical advisors from other disciplines. If it is desired to capitalize on a current British commercial lead in rule-learning, — or qualitative modelling, or program validation or whatever it may be, — then tax policies, or other government-controlled inducements, should be used to promote the purchase by companies and public institutions of targeted software categories. A specifically British thrust would complement instruments such as ESPRIT, and should be aimed to stimulate rather than distract. The natural habitat of scientists and engineers is not the world of airports, commmittee rooms and lobbies. It is the world of discovery and invention by which this country's industrial destiny was shaped.

15. Acknowledgements

The experimental work summarised here was made possible by research contracts from Westinghouse Corporation, USA, British Aerospace, UK, and The National Engineering Laboratory, UK. The preparation of the paper greatly benefited from critical comments by Mrs J. E. Hayes-Michie and by Dr Patricia Smith Churchland. Dr Churchland also gave me valuable pointers to the relevant neurobiological literature.

16. References

Anderson, J.R. (1980) Cognitive Psychology and its Implications, Freeman & Co.

Barron, R.L., Davies, J.M., Schalskowski, S. and Snyder, R.F. (1964) Self-organising adaptive systems for space vehicle attitude control. Presented at SAE-18 Committee Meeting, Miami Beach, Florida, December 1964.

Barron, R.L., Davies., Schalkowski, S. and Snyder, R.F. (1965) Self-organising adaptive systems for space vehicle attitude control. Presented at the AIAA/ION Guidance and Control Conference, Minneapolis, Minnesota, August 1965.
Note: the foregoing two references are cited in C. T. Leondes and J. M. Mendel's "Artificial intelligence control" in Surveys of Cybernetics, London: Iliffe Books, 1969.

Bratko, I., Mozetic, I. and Lavrac, N. (1989) Kardio: a Study in Deep and Qualitative Knowledge for Expert Systems, Cambridge, MA: The MIT Press.

Chambers, R.A. and Michie, D. (1969) Man-machine co-operation on a learning task. In Computer Graphics: Techniques and Applications (ed. R. Parslow, R. Prowse and R. Elliott-Green), London: Plenum.

Churchland, P.S. (1986) Neurophilosophy: Towards a Unified Science of the Mind/Brain, Cambridge, MA: The MIT Press.

Donaldson, P.E.K. (1960) Error decorrelation: a technique for matching a class of functions, in Proc. Third Internat. Conf. on Medic. Electronics, 173-178.

Dreyfus, S.E. and Dreyfus, H.L. (1990) Towards a reconciliation of phenomenology and AI. In The Foundations of Artificial Intelligence (ed. D. Partridge and Y. Wilks), Cambridge University Press.

Feigenbaum, E.A. and McCorduck, P. (1983) The Fifth Generation: Artificial Intelligence and Japan's Computer Challenge to the World, Reading, MA: Addison-Wesley.

Ginsberg, M.L., ed. (1987) Readings in Nonmonotonic Reasoning, Los Altos, CA: Morgan Kaufmann.

Hayes-Michie, J.E., ed. (1990) Pragmatica: Bulletin of the Inductive Programming Special Interest Group, No. 1, Spring 1990, Glasgow: Turing Institute Press.

Johnson-Laird, P.N. (1988) The Computer and the Mind, Cambridge, MA: Harvard University Press.

McCarthy, J. (1959) Programs with common sense. In Mechanization of Thought Processes Vol. 1, London: Her Majesty's Stationery Office. Reprinted in M. Minsky, ed. (1960)

Semantic Information Processing, Cambridge, MA: MIT Press.

Makarovic, A. (1987) Pole-balancing as a benchmark problem for qualitative modelling.   Technical Report DP-4953, Ljubljana: Josef Stefan Institute.   Revised as "A qualitative way of solving the pole-balancing problem" in Machine Intelligence 12 (eds. J.E. Hayes-Michie, D. Michie and E. Tyugu), Oxford University Press (to appear).

Michie, D. (1989) Problems of computer-aided concept formation. In Applications of Expert Systems, Vol 2 (ed. J.R.Quinlan), Addison-Wesley.

Michie, D. (1990) Turing's test and conscious thought, In Proceedings of the Turing 1990 Colloquium, 3-6 April 1990, Brighton, UK, (ed. P. Millican) to appear.   Also available as Turing Institute Occasional Paper TIOP-90-013, Glasgow: The Turing Institute Press.

Michie, D. and Chambers, R.A. (1968) BOXES: an experiment in adaptive control, In Machine Intelligence 2 (eds. E. Dale and D.

Milner, Brenda (1966) Amnesia following operation on the temporal lobes. In Amnesia, (ed. C.W.M. Whitty and O. Zangwill), 109 - 133.   London: Butterworth.

Nievergelt, J. (1977) Information content of chess positions — information for chess-specific knowledge of chess players. Sigart Newsletter, 62, April, 13-15.   Also to appear in revised form in Machine Intelligence 12 (eds. J.E. Hayes, D. Michie and E. Tyugu), Oxford University Press.

Pearce, D. (1989) The induction of fault diagnosis systems from qualitative models.   In Proc. Seventh Nat. Conf on Art. Intell. 1988 (AAAI 88), 353-357, St Paul, Minnesota.

Popper, K.R. and Eccles. J.C. (1977) The Self and its Brain.   London and New York: Routledge and Kegan Paul.

Sammut, C. (1988) Experimental results from an evaluation of algorithms that learn to control dynamic systems. In Proc. Fifth Internat. Conf on Machine Learning (ed. J. Laird), San Mateo: Morgan Kaufmann.

Sammut, C. and Michie, D. (1989) Controlling a "black box" simulation of a space craft. Turing Institute Research Memorandum TIRM-89-039, Glasgow: The Turing Institute Press.

Shapiro, A.D. (1987) Structured Induction in Expert Systems, Addison-Wesley in association with the Turing Institute Press.

Simon, H.A. (1990) Machine as mind, In Proceedings of the Turing 1990 Colloquium, 3-6 April 1990, Brighton, UK, (ed. P. Millican) to appear.

Simon, H.A. and Gilmartin, K.A. (1973) A simulation of memory for chess positions. Cognitive Psychology, 5, 29-46.

Slocombe, S., Moore, K. and Zelouf, M. (1986) Engineering expert system applications.   Presented at the Annual Conference of the BCS Specialist Group on Expert Systems, December 1986.

Squire, L (1987) Memory and Brain, Oxford University Press.

Sterling, L. and Shapiro, E. (1986), The Art of Prolog, Cambridge, MA: The MIT Press.

Widrow, B. and Smith, F.W. (1964) Pattern recognising control systems, in Computer and Information Sciences (eds. J. T. Tou and R. H. Wilcox).   Clever Hume Press.

THE SPECIFICATION OF REAL TIME SOFTWARE

R Threadgold B Sc.
RAMJET Software, Codas House, 54-60 Merthyr Road,
Whitchurch, CARDIFF, South Glamorgan, CF4 1DJ.

Abstract

This paper describes an expert system which has
been implemented by RAMJET Software. The purpose of the
scheme is to assist when a Real Time software system needs to
be specified. Formal methods underpin the scheme. The
expertise which is tapped comes from several sources and
represents many years of experience in all aspects of Real
Time software procurement. The tool is one of several which
are available to help in the development of such systems. A
glossary describes those terms stated in capitals.

1. Introduction

The purpose of the system described is to assist in
the specification of real time software. It is one of an
integrated set of such systems. For example, a specification
produced using it, can be converted into prototype software
code and tested using a second system. A third is able to
cross check aspects of target system quality when the work of
two or more teams is brought together.

The work enhances an earlier documentation
maintenance scheme. This was developed between 1977 and 1987
under an MOD contract awarded to the Plessey Company. Parts
of the earlier work underpin the current scheme (the database
utilities are an example). However, the enhancements mean the
new scheme is totally different from the old.

Experience in the construction of any type of
system reveals 'standards' which can be exploited when
further systems of the same type are built. 'Formal methods'
may exist or be evolved to assist the application of such
standards. 'Real Time' systems are no exception to this. A
number of standards have appeared during the last thirtyfive
years or so. They sum up the expertise of a very large number
of software writers. In addition some formal methods are
available. These help the development of a software system to
meet the standards.

A specification method involving flow diagrams was
used by the earlier scheme. The symbols on the diagrams
contained 'English' descriptions. The enhanced scheme retains
the use of English. It replaces the flow diagram symbols with
a tree structure. This improves visibility of the underlying
logic and gives other advantages which are described.

The most costly phase in procurement of Real Time
software is usually testing and integration. An aim is to
reduce these costs. Earlier work in switching and computer
logic had benefited from using methods based on Boolean
algebra. The reason is because operations of a new circuit

can be completely determined at the specification stage. The
equations specify how the output states depend on the input
states. They permit the use of computer assisted circuit test
specifications and of statistical sampling techniques (to
reduce testing). Using a tree structure allows the same
methods to be applied to software. Rationale is given in the
paper for potential savings which accrue from this.

   The importance of testing has meant that the basic
tree structure has had to be improved. Petri net methods are
used to do this. They mean that 'conflicts' and 'deadlocks'
can be identified easily. This is done in another tool which
'models' the software module. The nets must be capable of
easy construction by a designer. 'Place' screen dialogues are
used to expedite this. Nets are changed one place at a time.

   For practical reasons, information about the target
system is recorded in a database which exploits set theory
methods. The enquiries that are needed when information is
extracted, use methods based on formal logic. 'Rules'
associated with the target system are recorded. They must be
able to be looked at from both of the logical points of view.
The relationship between Boolean algebra and the other kinds
of logic make the dual viewpoints possible. This is not dealt
with in depth but it is felt to be important. The view taken
is that if the target software is to be of high quality, then
it must always be traceable to its logical roots.

   Most real time systems are complex. This means that
there will be more than one page in the specification. The
effect is that a method is needed which controls such
partitioning. The one used is based on properties of tree
structures. A closely allied subject is the position of the
specification component in the system documentation
hierarchy. The use of system procurement lifecycle rules is
advised. These have to be applied manually. They need to be
obeyed if automatic code conversion is wanted later.

   No Real Time system can be specified without some
thoughts about the operating system. The specifications
produced by the scheme assume that the MOD sponsored MASCOT
method is typical. Where words associated with the operating
system interface are needed, the MASCOT ones are used. They
do not, in any case, affect what it is the user specifies.

   One aim of the scheme is to make things simple for
the user. To assist, the number of screen types is kept down
and comprehensive 'help' facilities are provided. The
organisation of the database helps restrict lists to relevant
items. If the code conversion scheme is used, some
constraints on the content of texts may be needed. Otherwise
the user is free to specify any text which is suitable.

   A section is included which describes how the
system operates. It takes the viewpoint of a user looking at
screens generated during operation.

2. Logic and the use of trees

   The earlier work showed that the flow diagram
method suffered from disadvantages. The most important was

that system jobs were hard to determine. Some work done at
RSRE Malvern by the late Dr C S E Phillips was exploited.
This produced tree diagrams (from the flow diagram database).
These disclosed jobs in the form of threads. The current
scheme has developed this idea further. The flow diagrams
have been replaced by trees. The tree vertices and edges have
textual annotations added adjacent to them. Using trees has
other advantages. For instance, users get the benefits of an
approach to software engineering based on formal logic
without having to learn anything about the logic itself.
          In brief when control threads a particular tree, a
system state must be in existence. If this is valid for the
tree, control will track a complete thread. CONFLICT and
DEADLOCK are reasons for invalidity. Each thread corresponds
to just one valid system state. This means that relationships
between system states and CONTROL THREADS can be represented
as a logical formula: 1st condition state (TRUE or FALSE) AND
2nd condition state AND etc. implies 1st thread. The formula
can be deduced automatically from the tree. An extension is
that a group of threads can be combined into one formula
using logical OR's. This helps check if a state is valid.
Once a thread is known, it is possible to determine the
results (ie what happens to the output state when the thread
is run). Further analysis can be used to differentiate
between conflict and deadlock when an invalid state occurs.
Such analyses are helped by the use of a database which just
contains facts. These map onto the formulae in a natural way.
          What has been done is to note earlier work in
switching and computer logic circuits. This used formulae in
Boolean algebra to specify the states and results for a
circuit. In the software case, a control thread mediates one
input state to output state transformation. The significance
is that module testing can be reduced. Similar techniques to
those employed by circuit testing are used. For example,
statistical sampling could replace 100% testing. Large
reductions are possible if this is done. It is viable
because, like circuits, the tree is a complete specification
of the software. Independent confirmation is possible. This
is because implemented code produced using the scheme is
always logically valid to its requirements. The confirmation
is helped by an associated scheme which is able to generate
and classify test patterns associated with the module.

3. Simplified Petri nets

3.1. Improved specification clarity

          The scheme is designed to help the user when he
creates or alters a specification. This brings us to the
PETRI NET formal method. Each tree is thought of as a
simplified form of net. Tree vertices are replaced by PLACE
symbols, tree edges by TRANSITION symbols. This improves the
layout of trees. The transition symbols simplify referencing
to dataflow information with enabling conditions on the left
and generated events on the right. This improves clarity and

reduces ambiguity. Control flow places have the associated
software module identity on their right. Clutter is removed
from the nets by omitting connectors and symbols.
        In real time systems dataflow STIMULI are
important. Putting one on the left of an action layer place
symbol shows that it could FIRE an associated transition.
        The stimulus concept has been generalised. Stimuli
are used to call named modules and to name assignment
variables as well as to start/restart a process (see MASCOT).

3.2. All specification material as nets

        Experience of generating flowtrees in the original
work showed that they needed to be split up. This has been
done by seperating the configuration, decision and action
aspects. It is used to ensure orderly capture of the design.
All publishable diagrammatic specification material takes one
of these three forms. All nets are able to be viewed on a NET
SCREEN as well as printed.

3.3. All specifications composed using net places

        The idea of constructing a specification element by
element where each corresponds to a Petri net control flow
place is exploited. All places on all nets are constructed by
the technique. As the information about a place is added, the
CONJUNCTION rule of inference is used. It assists the
recording of the information. It sets up underlying Boolean
formulae. PLACE SCREENS are highly interactive with net
screens. This assists the user. He is able to see how the end
result is looking as he builds up each piece of his net.
        These dialogues are the focus of the expertise
built into the scheme. The list screens which are called down
during each such dialogue reflect the users own expertise
back to him. He defines target system objects and can use
them if they are suitable when a further object is specified.

4. Set theory and formal logic

        The third formal method is set theory. A number of
aspects of this subject are exploited.
        RELATIONS are used, each of which links two SETS
together. Data about a specification is recorded in files
which mirror this. The CARTESIAN PRODUCT (CP) idea is useful.
Think of the elements in the first set as abscissae and those
in the second set as ordinates. The marks in the CP graph
each define an individual relationship (or 'fact') between an
X element and a Y element. The record of these relationships
is a set of pointer pairs. All relation files are like this.
All sets are files of descriptive texts, one per element.
This sort of file organisation is called BINARY RELATIONAL.
        One set can be connected to several other sets via
relations. The whole structure of set and relation files

forms a DATABASE. A file structure suitable for recording a
software specification is used.

Logical rules of inference are used to transform
relational data back into specification form. If an element
of a set is chosen, the group of pointer pairs connecting to
it deliver related set elements from a connected set. This is
analogous to using the MODUS PONENS rule of inference. The
exploitation is visible directly in the form of LIST SCREENS.
These appear in support of many of the application programs.

When a section of specification is rebuilt from the
database other rules of inference are needed. Among these is
HYPOTHETICAL SYLLOGISM. This rule is useful for other reasons
as well. Thus given a JOB that the software has to perform,
the SYSTEM STATE which controls its running can be deduced.

Boolean algebra maps onto formal logic. For example
the TRANSITIVE LAW is equivalent to hypothetical syllogism.

5. Top down design

The scheme is designed to assist the specification
of a software system FROM THE TOP. This is not to the
author's knowledge, a formal method. Its application does
however make use of formal techniques. In total these define
a series of stepwise refinements. The designer can use them
when a specification is developed. A place screen dialogue
controls data acquisition for each refinement type.

5.1. Capturing the configuration aspects of a specification

Three types of Petri net have been noted. The user
will start with a CONFIGURATION NET. This causes him to
identify jobs which the system must perform (or additional
jobs in a maintenance scenario). It also causes him to
identify dataflow paths which the jobs need for signalling.

Jobs which start at the same place are grouped as a
JOB TYPE. Each will generate two skeleton nets. The upper is
a DECISION NET. The lower is an ACTION NET. These are fleshed
out by the user in the later stages of design or redesign. To
ensure that decision and action nets are relatable to their
parent configuration net, the terminal ACTIVITY (see MASCOT)
names match those of the corresponding job type and job.
Subsequent alterations retain this relationship.

5.2. Capturing the decision making aspects of a specification

The purpose of decision nets is to record the
relation between system states and jobs. To do this, it may
be necessary to introduce DECISION MODULE activities onto the
skeleton net. Each job can be fleshed up by making it thread
a group of such modules. As this is done CONDITIONS which
control (or in Petri net terms ENABLE) the job thread are
requested. Each new decision module generates a new action
net skeleton automatically. The start activity is given the

name of the parent decision module. The end activities are given the names of the modules which follow it. This ensures that the action nets are relatable to their parent module in the decision layer. Alterations retain this relationship.

Two concepts are important to decision nets. The first is the concept of the Immediate Post Dominator. This was developed during pioneering work by C S E Phillips. He used a technique called directed graphs to analyse programs. As a result, he realised that all programs contained natural partitioning points within themselves. He called them IPD's. They are convergences in the software control structure.

IPD's are useful if a minimum control structure for a decision net is needed. Another use is described below under the PARTITIONING heading. An implication of IPD's is that one or more of the formally defined jobs will terminate on them. This needs to be remembered when nets are used. The 'actual' jobs will outnumber the 'formal' jobs. This is because an actual job thread will usually travel on through the IPD. The theoretical significance is that while decision net control structures are tree like, they are GRAPHS.

The second concept concerns the necessity of adding dummy nodes to a decision net control structure. This has to be done if two control threads pass between the same pair of decision modules but imply different actions.

5.3. Capturing the action taking aspects of a specification

Action nets record relationships between job transitions and the actions which the jobs undertake.

Top down includes reuse of net creation techniques in several levels of system detailing. For example, a system development might involve four levels of specification. At the top the scheme would assist specification of the system SIGNALLING SEQUENCES. These specify communications between independent processes. This includes users as if they too are processes. Next come OPERATIONAL SEQUENCES used to implement the signalling. Then come the CONTROL SEQUENCES. These detail up the steps between signal interaction WAITPOINTS. Finally there are the PROGRAM SEQUENCES which amplify the control sequences (or higher level program sequences).

In the SS and OS levels, actions are one/one with system waitpoints. A stimulus will release control after a wait. The stimuli appear on the action nets. When control flows between a pair of actions, it generates signals in the form of EVENTS. Signals may be formatted and contain fields.

CS's detail up the steps between OS waitpoints giving rise to a job type per waitpoint. Each of its jobs is a control thread to another waitpoint. When a stimulus which is legal for the waitpoint occurs, control flows in an enabled job thread of the CS. Calling of a lower level procedure (including parameterisation) can be specified.

PS's are common modules which are called in the first instance by control sequences. They must also be able to call each other hierarchically. Development accompanies that of the system data pathways and their support records.

In the higher levels, the pathways are concerned with inter process communication. Lower down, detail is added, for example: specification of communication message structures.

5.4. Data types

Typing has become important to real time systems in the last few years. A TYPE is an attribute attached to an element in a data structure. Dataflow paths in the scheme are just types. MASCOT CHANNELS and the formatted messages which traverse them are associated with types. This links naturally to the files, records, arrays etc. which hold message data and which are specified by types. MASCOT POOLS are implicit in the data structures. The development of the types used to specify the data structures parallels that of the module hierarchy. In practical terms, events specify the variable part and the events' path specifies the variables' type.

5.5. Trusted code modules

Most software houses possess libraries of existing, well proved and trusted, code modules. Such code must be able to be used within the scheme with a minimum of analysis.

Calls on such code can be specified. Exploitation varies. If the code is in Pascal, its source can be captured using a word processor. The capture process includes getting auxilliary data such as called modules and declarations. If some other language is used, calls on the executable binary files can usually be embedded in the high level Pascal. Extra analysis will be necessary to get the declarative material. Ultimately, full reverse engineering may be needed.

At some stage, the top down design progression will define events which are closely akin to ordinary programming statements. When it happens, Pascal like function calls and assignments appear. These may include algebraic formulae. On the control side, condition expressions may appear.

5.6. Partitioning

When C S E Phillips invented IPD's, one of his motivations was that the real time programs he dealt with produced very large directed graphs. Some were so big that they were nearly as difficult to follow as the original program itself. He found that determining the IPD's in such a program, gave a reduced graph which disclosed the programs essential structure. Thus he found that IPD's rendered the task of understanding someone elses program easier.

Phillips noted that IPD's have a second use. They mark potential boundary points in a restructured program. The chunks of program within such boundaries are able to be turned into modules. A reduced graph is built corresponding to an overview program which calls on the new modules.

Turning this idea on its head is useful. Operational sequences are potential scheme processes. They overview the next level, the control sequences. These in turn overview the top level of the program sequences. A series of natural IPD's (such as waitpoints) have been identified. They are exploited in a top down design progression and give manageable sized graphs (ie nets) at all times.

6. Mascot

The words ACTIVITY, STIMULUS, CHANNEL and POOL have been noted. They are from MASCOT, a philosophy for real time systems sponsored by the Ministry of Defence.
Activity is the MASCOT name for a software module. Stimulus is the name given to a transmitted signal whose purpose is to awaken or reawaken a process. Channels and pools are two types of dataflow path. Channels imply immediate transfer of data. Pools imply use of a store for data communication. The implementation of a channel may involve a type of data store called a queue. Stimuli are stacked in this awaiting their turn for processing by the operating system. This doesn't concern us here.
What is of concern about MASCOT is its impact on the scheme. It means decision modules and actions are activities. It means data pathways are channels or pools. It means activities can be awoken or reawoken by a stimulus. The aim is compatibility with MASCOT. In the case of pools a particular implementation is assumed. It uses FORMATTED MESSAGES through channels. This is done to assist standardisation when data is passed to another processing module. It allows an across the system stimulus to be treated as if it were part of a parameterised procedure call.

7 Operation of the scheme

Besides the net, place and list screens which have been mentioned, there are access screens. These may be simple menus or may be similar to list screens.
At entry, a sector of the database is loaded and searched to define a wanted net. This is reconstructed and displayed as a net screen. Alterations may be done. The cursor is placed on an entity and A (for amend), 'Del' (for delete) or 'Ins' (for insert) is pressed. During the place screen dialogue which ensues, relevant list screens are extracted from the database and displayed. The definition of new information is associated with the list screens. Once alterations are complete, an escape can be made to the entry screen. This includes provision for saving the work.

7.1 Place screens

The screen layout is in two parts. Information about a cursor selected activity (ie a job type, decision module or action) is at the top. Beneath is data about the transitions leading out of this place. A section lists the set of next activities (jobs in the case of the configuration layer). Another section handles data flow information. This treats the paths as dataflow places. It lists conditions in the decision layer and events in the action layer. The configuration layer names the literal paths here. These are the English names of system dataflow paths.

Place screen sequences are able to be used in part or in whole. It means all types of system entity can be inserted with their aid. These include events, paths, transitions etc.. As the sequences proceed, the user is reminded where he is up to with the help of a reverse video highlight. As information is added to the screen, it accumulates. This is helpful if an abort is needed. A zoom feature is provided which allows a peek at the parent net screen. This can be used at all steps in the sequence.

7.2 Net screens

The layout of the nets is simple and is easily comprehended. The formats of the three types of net screen will be found in the explanatory information of the screen.

Nets will often exceed the size of the net screen. If so the page display aperture can be moved about the net.

7.3 List screens

When inferences are drawn, a screen may be composed and displayed in the form of an option list.

For example the name of a dataflow path may be known. It is used to get names of all signals that traverse it. This assists the user in a design situation. He can see whether or not a new signal needs adding. List screens are composed at many points in the place screen dialogues. They assist the user by telling him all pertinent options.

Lists may exceed the size of the list screen aperture. If so page turning is available.

Conclusion

The expert system described, is based on formal methods and is available for use. Its purpose is to assist in specification of Real Time software systems. The methods are integrated into a seamless whole. The scheme's motivation was the realisation that the ability to trace code back to its logical roots meant testing could be controllably reduced.

Specifications produced by the scheme are Petri net compatible. Petri nets are a well defined modelling technique. They have formal animation properties. It means specifications are able to be converted to executable code with the help of a sister scheme, and can have potential test patterns generated.

The formal methods were developed as the result of long experience in definition of standards for Real Time systems. These are the source of the expertise which is exploited. In use the scheme reflects the users own expertise back to him by displaying relevant options at choice points.

Particular attention has been paid to speed of response. The binary relational database has all its files fully sorted. This means that searches are normally extremely fast. It allows specification diagrams to be calculated direct from the database when they are wanted.

Another important operational aspect is ease of use. The alteration sequences are all organised to this end. They are supported by a comprehensive 'help' facility.

Glossary of terms

ACTION NET: portrays the control structure of a decision module. Shows relationships between net control threads and stimuli and events which occur during execution.

ACTIVITY: A term for a real time software module.

CARTESIAN PRODUCT: An aspect of set theory, useful when a binary relational database structure is defined.

CHANNEL: Mechanism for communication of data between independent processes in a real time system.

CONDITION: used to help enable a transition. Is set or reset by an event and recorded in a variable.

CONFIGURATION NET: portrays relationships between job types, jobs and data paths in a real time system sector.

CONFLICT: occurs when a MARKING is reached in which at least two transitions are enabled and in which the firing of one will disable the other.

CONJUNCTION: Logical rule of inference used when a database is built. Is expressed: p, q, therefore p AND q.

CONTROL SEQUENCE: is a system specification level. Once operational sequences are endorsed by the customer, detailing is begun. CS's amplify steps between OS waitpoints,

CONTROL THREAD: Term describing the path used by control when it traverses a net.

DATABASE: A collection of set files connected by relation files.

DEADLOCK: occurs when a marking is reached in which no transition is enabled.

DECISION MODULE: is a control flow place on a decision net which identifies a control thread convergence and/or a divergence. Each one overviews an action net.

DECISION NET: portrays the control structure of jobs grouped by a job type. The net shows relationships between modules threaded by a job and conditions enabling it.

ENABLE: If all input places on a transition contain at least one TOKEN, the transition is said to be enabled.

EVENT: Each specifies something which is expected to happen in a software system. Is done in the action layer. Control flows through a transition in response to the need to perform a system job. The firing of the transition generates tokens (as events). They traverse dataflow places.

FIRE: An enabled transition is fired at the users discretion to animate a net. It means one token is removed from each input place and one put in each output place.

FORMATTED MESSAGE: An implementation of the MASCOT 'pool' concept for sharing data between processes. Messages traverse a channel. Data is passed through the channel queues from stores at the transmitting end into stores at the receiving end. The messages can have a field structure.

FROM THE TOP: A philosophy which assumes a software system is specified from the topmost level downwards.

GRAPH: A collection of vertices connected by edges.

HYPOTHETICAL SYLLOGISM: Logical rule of inference used when a Petri net database is exploited. Is expressed: p implies q, q implies r therefore p implies r.

IPD ('immediate post dominator'): A point where control threads converge. It 'dominates' these threads. It is also 'immediately' after (or 'post') each of them.

JOB: specifies a control thread in a decision net.

JOB TYPE: A control flow place in a configuration net. It groups up jobs which start at the same place and links to dataflow paths implied by them.

LIST SCREEN: displays a subset of system elements which are relevant to the current net editing operation.

MARKING: The use of 'tokens' to represent a system state on a net specification. These are put onto net 'places' and Petri net modelling rules are used to determine the consequences of an initial marking. (see 'enabled' & 'fire')

MASCOT: Modular Approach to Software Coding Operation and Test.

MODUS PONENS: Logical rule of inference used when a Petri net database is exploited. Is expressed symbolically: p implies q, p, therefore q.

NET SCREEN: displays system specification material in the form of a simplified Petri net. Three types of net cover the aspects of: configuration, decision and action.

OPERATIONAL SEQUENCE: Contractors response to part of the customers signalling sequences. Specifies a potential independent process in the target real time system.

PARTITIONING: The use of requirement attributes (such as signalling points) to define software partitions.

PETRI NET: A network of places and transitions which can be used to help specify software. Nets are simplified (eg connectors are implied). Each is based on the graph of the reachability tree from the (assumed) net control start place.

PLACE: The schemes nets are bipartite directed graphs in which two types of symbol are connected together by directed lines. One of the types of symbol is called a place. It is represented by one or more circular symbols in a row.

PLACE SCREEN: Mechanism used to assist the user when new data about a software system is inserted.

POOL: A mechanism for the communication of data between independent processes using storage of data.

PROGRAM SEQUENCE: Pictorial specification of a program

RELATION: A mechanism for recording database facts.

SET: A record of system entity descriptions. Each descriptive text is associated with one or more database facts. Relation files determine the associations.

SIGNALLING SEQUENCE: The customer signalling plan includes a definition of all system signalling. Both inter process and man/machine signalling are covered.

STIMULI: A term describing messages sent between processes in a real time system. The usual purpose of such a message is to start or restart a remote process. The term has been broadened to cover calling a procedure and assignment.

SYSTEM STATE: A term used to describe the current setting of conditions used to enable the actual job threads.

TOKEN: An item used to help animate a Petri net.

TRANSITION: Hyphens are used to denote transitions on nets. They indicate a control flow relationship between two activity place symbols. They may also indicate one from a dataflow path place on the left and/or to one on the right.

TRANSITIVE LAW: The name given in Boolean algebra to the equivalent of logical hypothetical syllogism.

TYPE: An attribute associated with stored data. Is an idea from the computer language Pascal. Is helpful when dataflow requirements and data structures are defined.

WAITPOINT: An attribute of a real time system. It is associated with a signalling interchange. 'Expected' signals step control through an operational sequence. Specified 'unexpected' signals can occur. They cause a new operational sequence to begin. Its aim will be to recover the system to a starting state. Other signals will be ignored.

Background reading

Copi, I. M. Introduction to logic. The MacMillan Company, New York. Collier-MacMillan Ltd. London.

Petersen, J. L. (1981). Petri net theory and the modelling of systems. Prentice Hall.

Petersen, J. L. (1977). Petri Nets, in ACM Computer Surveys, vol 9, pp. 223-252, Sept 1977.

Lipsshutz, S. Theory and problems of set theory and related topics. Schaum Publishing Co. New York.

Horowitz, E. and Sahni, S. Fundamentals of Data Structures in Pascal. Pitman (has some notes on graphs and trees).

Computer Division, N Building, RSRE, 29 St. Andrews Rd., Gt. Malvern, Worcs., for the official MASCOT handbook.

ACCESSING EXTERNAL APPLICATIONS FROM KNOWLEDGE BASED SYSTEMS

Richard W. Southwick and Yannis Cosmadopoulos
Logic Programming Group, Imperial College, London.

Kostas Stathis
Knowledge Based Systems Group,
Numerical Algorithms Group, Oxford.

Abstract

This paper addresses the problem of interfacing knowledge-based systems (KBS) to external software packages. We describe a methodology for building tightly-coupled interfaces between logic-based KBS front-ends, and back-end application packages. These methods have been implemented in the form of a Back End Manager (BEM), a KBS component that is designed to handle the flow of information between problem solvers and back-end applications.

The system proposed here offers several advantages in KBS design. First, it allows a logical treatment of data from back-end applications. The back-end is treated as an external database — all knowledge of the operation of the back-end is kept local to the the BEM. Second, it provides a modular approach to system construction. The result of this is a sharp conceptual division between problem solving, and controlling back-end applications. Finally, it requires no modification to existing back-end applications.

We discuss techniques for controlling back-end processes, for translating front-end goals into back-end commands, and for extracting pertinent information from the back-end for use by the front-end. We give an example taken from a BEM for a statistical modelling package.

1 Introduction

In this paper we discuss the problem of interfacing knowledge-based systems (KBS) to existing software packages. Such KBSs can be thought of as *front-ends* to application packages, which are known as *back-end* applications.

There are two main reasons why this activity is a desirable one. First, it is unreasonable to expect that all necessary information for a problem solving domain be supplied in advance. If there are external programs that can provide this information to the problem-solving process, this gives us a useful extension to the knowledge available for problem solving. An example of this might be a KBS that has recourse to a database management system, with a large database of information pertinent to the problem.

Second, application packages are often complex, and require a certain amount of expertise to use properly. Examples of software of this type include engineering modelling packages that require complicated patterns of input parameters to operate correctly. Often the people who use these programs are experts in their field (engineering, say), but are sporadic users of the software, and so require assistance in using the software and interpreting the results.

One way to address this problem is through the design of intelligent front-ends for application packages, which provide expert advice both in the use of the software, and in the problem solving domain itself. There is a great deal of investment made in software, and the use of an intelligent front-end to these applications can extend its useful life considerably.

In this paper, we describe a methodology for building tightly-coupled interfaces between logic-based KBS front-ends, and back-end application packages. These methods have been implemented in the form of a Back End Manager (BEM). This is a KBS component that is responsible for the control of back-end processes, and handles the flow of information between problem solvers and back-end applications in a manner transparent to the front-end. The BEM was designed to be a general tool for the development of KBS/back-end links. Use of the BEM gives a KBS developer the basic mechanism for interaction, and a framework for specifying the logical role of back-end information. The domain knowledge base can be developed independently, requiring no knowledge of the specifics of the back-end.

Other work on interfaces to application packages include knowledge based systems that interact with database management systems, which have been described by Vassiliou et al [11] and Torsun and Ng [10]. The use of a KBS as a front-end to a software package has been explored in the GLIMPSE system (Wolstenholme and O'Brien [12]), an intelligent front-end to the statistical package GLIM.

The BEM architecture proposed here offers several advantages in KBS design over these systems. First, it allows a *logical treatment of data* from back-end applications. The back-end is treated as an external database. All knowledge of the operation of the back-end — command syntax, calling procedure, output structure, etc. — is kept local to the the BEM. Back-end activities are represented in the domain knowledge base as ordinary logical predicates, and are only treated differently at the meta-level.

Second, it provides for the *modular construction* of systems. Because back-end applications are treated as databases, they are not intrinsic to the operation of the KBS. Back-end applications may be added or removed, with minimal changes to the structure of the system. The result of this is a sharp conceptual division between problem solving, and controlling back-end applications.

Finally, no modifications to existing back-end applications are required. Very often users of software packages do not have access to the source code, and cannot customise applications to work with a KBS. The framework described allows communication with applications using the standard I/O channels.

2   Logical Treatment of External Data

It is rare for a knowledge base for a KBS to contain all the information necessary for problem solving. In many cases, information is missing because it cannot be known by a knowledge engineer at design time, or because the costs of entering and storing this data is prohibitive. Additionally, there are many tasks for which the implementation language of the KBS may be inappropriate. As a result, knowledge-based systems must be able to operate without having immediate access to all required information. The missing information may be obtained from sources external to the knowledge base. We shall treat back-end applications as such a source.

Logic-based problem solvers treat a user's query as a *goal* that is provable from the clauses that comprise the domain theory. This can be represented by the meta-level proof predicate

$$demo(P, G),$$

which states that for a program P and goal G, $P \vdash G$ (Bowen and Kowalski [2]).

To handle information from an external application, it is convenient to regard the application as an extension to the domain theory. For a back-end application B, the provability relation becomes

$$demo(P \cup B, G),$$

which states the addition of data producible by the back-end program allows us to conclude

$$P \cup B \vdash G$$

So a domain program need not be restricted to a single database, but can be made up of information from several sources. One of these consists of logical formulae, coded in a machine-understandable format. The other is the back-end application (BE). The BEM allows a back-end to be treated as an independent, external database, and the information supplied by the back-end via the BEM is in the form of ground assertions. This approach is the same as that taken by Query-the-User (Sergot [8]), which extends the proof procedure to handle data from a user, rather than a back-end program.

A problem solver using this approach can be implemented by a meta-interpreter that requests missing information from a back-end. Predicates are designated at the meta-level to be either explicitly defined (present in P), or supplied by the back-end (obtainable from B). This is done through a series of statements of the form *backend(Goal)*. When the meta-interpreter encounters a goal G for which *backend(G)* is true, the system issues a command to the back-end application. The result is taken as a solution to that goal. If the back-end is unable to provide a solution, the goal fails. Here, in a fragment from a meta-interpreter that recognises back-end goals, the call *bem(G)* sends the goal G to the back-end manager to be solved.

```
solve( Goal ) ←
        backend( Goal ),
        bem( Goal ).
solve( Goal ) ←
        not backend( Goal ),
        clause( Goal, Body ),
        solve( Body ).
```

Because data from the back-end application is in effect being added to the domain program, we encounter the standard problem of ensuring consistency during knowledge acquisition (Kowalski [7]). If we restrict ourselves to a definite Horn clause representation, this generally poses no problem, since a program consisting of definite Horn clauses cannot itself be inconsistent.

Finally, we must consider the effect of issuing commands to an external program. We have treated external data as having a declarative meaning, but must also recognise its procedural effect. Sending a command to an application may change the state of that application, requiring the maintenance of the consistency of the *application's* state. This issue is discussed in more detail in Section 5.4.

2.1   Negated Back-end Goals

Since back-end goals are represented as ordinary predicates, they may be negated, where negation is taken to mean 'failure to prove' in the usual sense of negation as failure. Consider the goal *not file(X)*, where *file(X)* is an back-end goal. For example, take the clause

```
newFile( File ) ←
        not file( File ),
        create( File ).
```

and the goal *newFile(foo)*. The BEM converts the back-end goal *file(foo)* to the UNIX command ls foo, and attempts to execute it.

If there is no such file, the back-end cannot accomplish the activity, and produces an error notification. The BEM must recognise this and fail the front-end goal. The goal *file(fred)* fails, so *not file(fred)* succeeds.

3   Classification of External Sources

In designing the interface between a KBS and back-end application, we require a classification of these applications. Such a classification is useful for providing guidelines on the design choices and implementation methods used in our systems. Our classification is based on analysing two main characteristics of an external application, its *operation mode* and its *internal state*.

According to the operation mode characteristic, applications can be categorised as *batch* or *interactive*. The batch mode of working can be typically described as *read-compute-output-stop*. Although this mode of operation has become less common with the development of new computing tools, batch applications are still used by a large community of users in a variety of domains. When front-ends are built for a batch application they tend to be fairly simple; interaction with the system contains few or no feedback loops. An interactive application, on the other hand, introduces more complex procedures that allow interaction in different stages where the output of one stage is being fed into the input of the next. In general, the batch mode of operation can be treated merely as a special case of the interactive.

External applications can also be divided into those that maintain an *internal state*, and those that do not. For example, many modelling packages keep an internal database for the creation of new instances of data structures and storing of intermediate computations. Applications that maintain their own state pose a difficulty for the KBS, which must model that state in some way. Stateless applications, on the other hand, are comparatively simple to deal with. An example of a stateless application is the set of UNIX utilities that perform processing but do not maintain an internal representation of their activity.

This classification provides us with the means for measuring the complexity of the systems that we attempt to build. The space of possible external applications can be divided along two axes: batch/interactive, and state/no state. The simplest are batch applications with no internal state, while the most complex are those interactive applications that keep an internal state. To build general KBS/back-end systems, we must solve the problems that arise in the more complex case — interactive systems having internal states — and it is these that we will concentrate on.

A final pragmatic restriction on the types of applications that we can handle concerns I/O. While systems that perform *text-based I/O* pose no problem, many applications accept input from non-textual sources (mice, etc), and produce graphical output. Applications of this type are outside the scope of this paper.

4   Design of the KBS

In this section, we discuss the architecture of the combined KBS/back-end, and explain how a knowledge base is constructed for use with the BEM.

4.1   Architecture of the System

The architecture of the complete KBS can be described as in Figure 1. A problem solver (PS) provides a means of performing inference in a problem domain. This domain is represented in a domain knowledge base (KB), consisting typically of rules about the domain. Additional information comes from one or more back-end applications (BE), which are under the control of the Back End Manager (BEM).

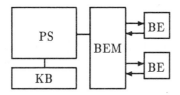

Figure 1: The Combined KBS–BEM Architecture

In our implementation of this architecture, the problem solver is a logic-based, backward reasoning shell written in Prolog, and based on a blending transformer that augments object-level programs with meta-level functionality (Cosmadopoulos and Southwick [3]). The blending transformer replaces the more standard approach of basing the shell on a Prolog meta-interpreter (e.g. APES, Hammond and Sergot [5]).

This problem solver provides some extra facilities necessary for expert system construction, such as rule-trace explanations, a Query-the-User model for user dialogue (Sergot [8]), and a reason maintenance system for maintaining a consistent set of beliefs and reducing redundant computation (Southwick [9]).

4.2   Primitive Actions

We have seen that predicates in our knowledge-base that are to be sent to the back-end are designated at the meta-level by a declaration of the form:

   backend(Goal).

Let us call these back-end goals *actions*. We define an action to be a primitive activity that can be accomplished by a back-end application. An action is primitive in the sense that it cannot be broken into subactions in the knowledge representation. Of course, a single action may be converted to a series of back-end commands, but this is not important to the front-end domain representation.

This approach allows the writing of domain rules containing subgoals that are back-end actions. The result is a clean representation of domain knowledge. Actions are predicate subgoals like any other; no special representation is required. The declarative nature of the domain rules is left intact.

As an example of a domain rule that involves back-end actions, suppose we want to use an application package that computes tax payments. Consider a knowledge base that contains the following rule:

   totalTax(Person, Tax) ←
      salary(Person, Salary),
      allowance(Person, Allowance),
      tax(Salary, Allowance, Tax).

If the the goal *tax* is specified as an action, it is solved by the back-end, under the control of the BEM.

Backend goals are expected to be fully and correctly specified so that the back-end is capable of executing them with no further need for communication with the front-end. To do this, we need to 'wrap up' these back-end goals with precondition statements that serve to constrain the input arguments to the back-end goal, and postconditions that check the results. Rules that invoke back-end goals, then, take the general form

$$domain\_rule \leftarrow$$
$$preconditions,$$
$$backend\_goal,$$
$$postconditions.$$

Preconditions ensure that required arguments are instantiated, or are of the correct type. Postconditions can be used to check the results from the back end, or to record the internal state of the back-end for use in future computation. In the *tax* example, the preconditions ensure that input arguments are numbers:

$$tax(\ S,\ A,\ T\ ) \leftarrow$$
$$numeric(S),$$
$$numeric(A),$$
$$be\_tax(S,A,T).$$

The goal *be_tax(S,A,T)* is a action handled by the BEM, and is specified as such by the statement

$$backend(\ be\_tax(S,A,T)\ ).$$

4.3   Building a Knowledge Base Using the BEM

The process of building a knowledge base that will interface with the BEM can be split into two parts. First, the system designer specifies the actions needed to complete the task, in a high-level way. The domain knowledge base is then written in the form of rules that use these actions. At this point, the designer needn't worry about the implementation of action definitions in the BEM — this is handled separately.

Once a set of required actions have been identified, the BEM specification of these actions may be written. This involves defining the process whereby front-end goals are translated into back-end commands, and output from the back-end is collected for use by the front-end.

This gives us a clean division between front-end and back-end definitions. Note especially that these two tasks need not be done by the same person: it may be that one person is expert in the domain, while another is conversant with the intricacies of the back-end.

5   The Back End Manager

In this section, we describe the function of the BEM, and discuss some of the particular issues that are involved in coupling KBSs and back-end applications. The most important of these concern control and communication with the back-end.

The operation of the BEM in managing communication can be summed up as follows: a front-end action is translated to a series of commands for execution by the back-end. The output containing the result of this execution is examined by the BEM, and information relevant to the front-end is extracted. This information is represented in a form that is intelligible to the front-end before being passed back.

5.1   Control of the Back End

To interface to an interactive application, the implementation platform must be capable of multitasking. At least two processes must be run concurrently; the KBS and the back-end. In addition communication channels are required for data transfer to and from the back-end.

The BEM must initiate the back-end processes, establish communication channels, control dialogue with the back-end, and ensure its graceful termination. In addition the BEM must be able to cope with conditions such as abnormal termination, error messages, or 'unreasonable' output.

In a UNIX environment, (the implementation platform for the BEM) the back-end is started by the BEM as a subprocess, and communication channels are implemented by means of *pipes*. More specifically, in our implementation of the BEM, the back-end's standard input channel is set as the end of one communication pipe, and its standard output channel as the end of the other. As a result, no alteration of the back-end program is required, as long as it communicates via standard input and output.

Communication between the problem solver and BEM can be done by direct subroutine call. Alternatively, greater modularity can be gained (at the expense of greater overhead costs) by establishing a *message passing* protocol for communication (Edmonds et al [4]). If all communication between KBS modules is done via messages, then individual components can be implemented as separate processes. They need not be on the same physical machine, and can communicate over a network if necessary. In fact, the different components need not be written in the same language. The implementation language for each component may be selected to reflect the requirements of that module.

5.2　Translating Back End Commands

One of the main tasks of the BEM involves the translation of a front-end goal, in the KBS language, to a corresponding sequence of commands in the syntax of the back-end. These are then issued to the back-end to produce the desired behaviour. The degree of complexity of this translation will determine the method chosen. We shall identify the characteristics of different back-end translation tasks, and outline two possible approaches to these tasks.

5.2.1　Templates

For back-end applications that have a simple and well-defined input, it may be possible to map input to output in a straightforward fashion. In such a situation a *template* approach is sufficient, mapping a command in the syntax of the front-end to a command or sequence of commands in that of the back-end. The BEM could use templates in constructing back-end commands as follows:

```
bem(Goal) :-
    template(Goal, BE_Command),
    dispatch(BE_Command),
    extract(BE_Command, Result),
    apply(Result, Goal).
```

A template is found for a back-end goal, giving a command that is dispatched to the back-end. A result to the command is extracted from the back-end, using contextual information provided by the back-end command. Finally, the result is applied to the goal, providing any variable bindings required for a solution.

In the following, let us take the operating system itself as a back-end, for explanatory purposes. A simple template for a command that lists the contents of a UNIX directory is

```
template(directory, ls).
```

Even simple, one-to-one correspondence between the front-end and back-end commands may require some additional processing to yield a command suitable for the back-end. As an example, consider a front-end goal *file_name(File)*, which succeeds if *File* is the name of a file on disk. The BEM translates this command using a template that performs variable substitution and insertion:

```
template(file_name(File), Command) :-
    concatenate('ls ', File, Command).
```

Additionally, problems of this sort often require some *control* over the translation. This control may be as simple as logical tests (if-then-else), or may require more sophisticated control structures (loops, etc). We may want to write something like:

```
IF input = "directory" AND num_args > 3 THEN
    {
    OUTPUT "ls ";
    FOR i=1 to num_args
        OUTPUT arg(i)
    }
```

This kind of control is needed if input actions may have arguments of varying number and type, resulting in possibly many different forms of output. This gives a one-to-many translation. Alternatively, we may allow certain arguments, if not present, to be taken as defaults, giving a many-to-one translation. These last modifications blur the distinction between filling a template and dispatching a command, since output to the back-end is done during processing.

5.2.2   Grammar-based Translation

In many situations, where the back-end has a command grammar significantly different to that of the front-end, the technique described above will not suffice. These cases are identified by the complexity of the input to be translated. An example is an arbitrary Prolog term, which may be made up of subterms of any form or depth. In these cases, some *interpretation* of the input must be done in order to understand how it is to be translated. The most appropriate way to do this interpretation is by implementing a translator that can parse the input into its components, and deal with these components in the right way.

As an example of input that requires interpretation, consider the interface of a Prolog-based problem solver to a package performing arithmetic using reverse polish notation.

```
(1+2*3(4-5))   --->   +(1,*(2,*(3,-(4,5))))
```

To construct the appropriate output, the input structure must be interpreted. Of course, it is possible to use a template approach to deal with any specific instance of input, but a new template would need to be written for *each* possible input form. This is clearly unreasonable for applications with varied input. Alternatively, one could write special-purpose code to extract certain kinds of structure from an input term. A better solution is to write a *compiler* from the input to the output language. This consists of a parser for the input language, and an interpreter which transforms the parse tree to the required output syntax. The use of grammar rules that direct a parser offers a solution that is general and complete.

If both the BEM and the front-end are written in the same language and the input is a structured term in that language, then the parsing stage may be redundant. In addition, if the input is in some form that is understood by the back-end, then this list can be treated as though it has *no internal structure*, and passed directly through the translator to the back-end. In the above example, if the arithmetic expression can be passed directly to the back-end, no parsing is required. If the expression must be 'understood' to be translated, then a parser should be used.

In order to build a parser, the first step is to define a grammar that will recognise correct forms of input, and then attach translation instructions to the rules of this grammar. This could be done in Prolog, since it is naturally suited to parse Prolog expressions. Alternatively, if a C-language based approach is desired (for reasons of speed or modularity), the best tool to use is the parser-generator yacc (Johnson [6]).

5.3   Output Extraction

Once a command has been issued to the back-end, the BEM must extract the pertinent information from the output of the back-end for use by the problem solver. Back-end applications have varied means of presenting results.

Output from a command may include a preamble, which serves to aid the user, provide header information for column output, etc. This is generally of no interest to the front-end, but may be useful to the extraction process. The components of interest in the output are often record-like; a collection of fields and separators. It should be noted that most applications do not have a well-structured form of output that would allow for a grammar-based extraction process.

The task of extraction is to filter out 'noise' such as the headers and field separators, and to recognise the required data. This is then used by the BEM to produce an *answer* to the original back-end query of a form suitable for the problem solver.

As an example consider the output of the unix command ls -l

```
-rwxr-xr-x  1 root      wheel        98304 Sep  7  1989 xdvi
drwxrwxrwx  1 root      wheel          512 Oct  6  1989 lib
```

A suitable Prolog representation of this is terms of the form *entry(Name,Type,Size)*:

```
entry(xdvi, exec, 98304).
entry(lib, dir, 512).
```

To construct a response of this form, the BEM requires knowledge of the form of the output, as well as what constitutes a meaningful answer for the problem solver.

Often, knowledge of the back-end application together with its current state and command history determines how a section of output is to be interpreted. This state knowledge may be used to provide a context sensitive extraction engine. As an example of the way contextual information may be required to interpret output, consider output containing the string bad, which may correspond to a (possibly uninteresting) component of a textual message in one situation, while signifying the hexadecimal representation of the number 2989 in another.

The extraction component of the BEM needs the following capabilities:

- It should recognise textual labels in the output of the back-end which serve as locators for data. Examples are column headers or terms of the form
  "The Answer is X = 5''.

- It must understand the syntax of the output — in the above UNIX example it must be aware of the significance of each column and be able to determine that the entry for lib is a directory.

- It may use knowledge of the commands issued to the back-end to interpret the meaning of the output, giving expectation driven extraction.

- A back-end application may produce a stream of output, from which several pieces are to be extracted to produce an answer. The BEM must have some means of storing and manipulating these answer components.

- It must return results to the front-end in a suitable form.

In our implementation of the BEM, no contextual information is required to disambiguate output. Extraction was implemented using the UNIX pattern scanning and processing language awk (Aho et al [1]) to filter the application's output, producing Prolog readable terms as a result.

5.4   Maintaining Back End Consistency

The interface to back-end applications is done not only to get information from the back-end, but also to control the back-end application. This distinction becomes important when we consider the effect that commands may have on the back-end. Many back-end programs have their own internal state, which may be changed by commands issued by the front-end. A numerical analysis package, for example, may keep an internal representation of the state of the analysis. In normal interactive use, this state is modified by commands issued by the user.

If the back-end state can be changed, the state of the back-end must be modelled in the front-end in order to ensure the consistency of the back-end state and to prevent redundant re-computation. If the back-end state changes, and the front-end does not realise this, for example, it will no longer be able to accept back-end activity as valid.

One easy way to ensure the consistency of the back-end state is to prohibit backtracking over back-end goals. Calls to the back-end are treated deterministically — once a command has been issued and executed, it cannot be undone.

While this solves the problem, it does so in an inflexible fashion. There are cases when it is desirable to be able to redo back-end actions, as part of the normal search strategy of the problem solver. One way of implementing this ability is by storing a *snapshot* of the state of the back-end. If, on backtracking, a back-end action is to be redone, the back-end may be restored to its previous state. Some application packages have this functionality built-in. The GLIM system, for example, allows the current state of the system to be dumped and restored, which was used in the implementation of the state restoration facility in GLIMPSE (Wolstenholme [12]).

If such a facility is not available, and backtracking is required, then a model of back-end state must be maintained by the front-end. In the extreme case, restoration of state could involve having to kill the back-end process, and restart it, rebuilding the back-end state from the the front-end model of that state.

In some cases, it is possible to 'simulate' backtracking in the BEM. This can be done where the back-end returns multiple solutions for a goal. When such a back-end goal is evaluated, the BEM finds *all* possible solutions for the goal, and records them. On backtracking, successive solutions may be used. To the front-end, there is no difference in behaviour. This adds a measure of complexity to the BEM, however, which must handle all solutions correctly.

6   An Example Application

In this section we provide an example of the working of the back-end manager, by showing how some front-end actions are handled by the BEM. The back-end application used is the statistical system GLIM. We will define two actions for use in the front-end knowledge base. One defines a vector, and the other performs an arithmetic calculation on that vector. Let us call these actions *vector* and *calculate* respectively.

These actions are used in rules in the knowledge base as ordinary goals, for example:

> compute_vector(Name, Len, Vector, NewName, NewVector) ←
> vector(Name, Len, Vector),
> calculate(NewName, (Name+2)*2, NewVectorValue).

Suppose this rule is invoked with

> compute_vector(vectorA, 5, [1,2,3,4,5], vectorB, NewVector).

When the back-end goals in the body of the rule are encountered by the problem solver, they are sent to the back-end manager for evaluation. The BEM then constructs a series of commands to be dispatched to the GLIM process. The GLIM command that corresponds to *vector(vectorA, 5, [1,2,3,4,5])* is

```
$DATA 5 vector_name $READ 1 2 3 4 5 $
```

For *calculate(vectorB, (vectorA+2)*2, Value)* the GLIM commands are

```
$CALC vectorB = (vectorA+2)*2 $
$PRINT vectorB $
```

where the PRINT command is used to output the value of the calculated vector.

GLIM produces a stream of text as output. For the `$PRINT vectorB $` command above this has the following form:

```
??    6.000    8.000    10.000    12.000    14.000
```

The BEM extracts from this output the Prolog representation of the value of vectorB:

[6.0, 8.0, 10.0, 12.0, 14.0]

This example, though simple, illustrates a number of interesting points. GLIM is an application that has an internal state; the effect of the *vector* command is to set the value of an internal vector. Subsequent commands (such as *calculate*) referring to this vector will use the value corresponding to the current state. One ramification of this is that large vectors do not have to be explicitly represented in the front-end; they may be stored in the back-end database and simply referred to in the front-end.

The *compute_vector* predicate is written using explicit vector names, which are required by the back-end. This formulation is dictated by the needs of the backend, producing a specification that is not back-end independent. Alternatively, the above example could have been encoded as

alternative_compute_vector(([1,2,3,4,5]+2)*2, VectorValue) ←

Where the GLIM commands for *alternate_compute_vector* are

```
$DATA 5 tmp_vector $READ 1 2 3 4 5 $
$CALC tmp_vector = (tmp_vector+2)*2 $
$PRINT tmp_vector $
```

This implementation would require additional processing. The term $[1, 2, 3, 4, 5] + 2) * 2$ needs to be decomposed and the vector it contains must be recognised. A name must be generated for a temporary back-end variable corresponding to the vector. In general such terms can be of arbitrary complexity and would necessitate the use of a grammar-based translation method. This contrasts with the first solution, which could easily be handled by a template approach.

7 Summary and Conclusions

We have presented a method for accessing external data for use by knowledge based systems, and have discussed some of the important issues involved in this activity. Key contributions include:

- A back-end manager that controls back-end application operation and communication.
- Modular construction of KBSs.
- All knowledge of the operation of the back-end is kept local to the the BEM.
- Back-end applications are treated as external databases, allowing the construction of declarative front-end knowledge bases.
- Techniques for translating front-end goals to back-end commands.
- Methods for extracting results from back-end output.

The back-end manager presented in this paper has been implemented, and the methodology described has been tested in a KBS that provides a front-end to GLIM. Our implementation of the BEM is written in Prolog, and is called directly by the problem solver. The extraction component of the BEM, however, is an awk process, connected between the BEM and the back-end via UNIX pipes. During the course of developing the ideas in the paper, we have experimented with implementations using yacc for grammar-based translation, and a 'C' based BEM.

8   Acknowledgements

Thanks are due to Chris Evans and Damian Chu, who read and commented on earlier drafts of this paper. The authors would also like to thank their colleagues from the Universitat Politecnica de Catalunya (Jesus Lores, Jose Catot and Paul Fletcher) for their many helpful discussions. The work described in this paper was funded by ESPRIT project 2620: FOCUS.

References

[1] A. V. Aho, B. W. Kernighan, and P. J. Weinberger. Awk — a pattern scanning and processing language. Technical report, Bell Laboratories, Murray Hill, New Jersey, 1977.

[2] K. A. Bowen and R. A. Kowalski. Amalgamating language and metalanguage in logic programming. In K. Clark and S. Tarnlund, editors, *Logic Programming*, pages 153–172. Academic Press, 1982.

[3] Y. Cosmadopoulos and R. W. Southwick. Using meta-level information for expert system control: A 'blending' transformer approach. In N. Shadbolt, editor, *Research and Development in Expert Systems VI*, pages 54–65. Cambridge University Press, 1989.

[4] E. Edmonds, E. McDaid, A. Prat, P. Fletcher, and J. Lores. System architecture and KBFE/back-end interface specifications. Technical Report FOCUS/LUTCHI/UPC/5/1.3-C, Numerical Algorithms Group, Oxford, 1989.

[5] P. Hammond and M. J. Sergot. A PROLOG shell for logic based expert systems. In *Proceedings of the Third BCS Expert Systems Conference*, Cambridge, 1983.

[6] S. C. Johnson. Yacc: Yet another compiler-compiler. In B. W. Kernighan, editor, *UNIX Programmer's Manual*. Bell Laboratories, 1978.

[7] R. A. Kowalski. *Logic for Problem Solving*. North Holland, Amsterdam, 1979.

[8] M. J. Sergot. A query-the user facility for logic programming. In P. Degano and E. Sandewall, editors, *Integrated Interactive Computer Systems*, pages 27–41. North Holland, 1983.

[9] R. W. Southwick. A reason maintenance system for backward reasoning systems. In *Proc. 5th International Symposium on Methodologies for Intelligent Systems*, 1990.

[10] I. S. Torsun and Y. M. Ng. Tightly coupled expert database systems interface. In B. Kelly and A. Rector, editors, *Research and Development in Expert Systems V*, pages 210–223. Cambridge University Press, 1988.

[11] Y. Vassiliou, J. Clifford, and M. Jarke. How does an expert system get its data? Technical Report CAIS Working Paper 50, New York University, 1983.

[12] D. E. Wolstenholme and C. M. O'Brien. GLIMPSE: A statistical adventure. In *Proceedings of the 10th International Joint Conference on Artificial Intelligence*, pages 596–599, 1987.

A GENERIC MODEL OF KNOWLEDGE-BASED SYSTEM TOOLS

Lewis Peake
CCTA, HM Treasury
Gildengate House, Upper Green Lane
Norwich NR3 1DW

Abstract

The Central Computer and Telecommunications Agency (CCTA) of HM Treasury has developed a Generic Model of KBS tools. The Model is intended to facilitate an understanding of KBS technology by representing the processing capabilities embodied within KBS development tools. In this way the Model provides a major input to the GEMINI project (to develop a method for KBS analysis and design) and contribute to other KBS-related objectives. The Model will, for example, be of central importance in documenting a procedure for evaluation and selection of KBS tools and also defines what needs to be specified in detailed design.

The approach adopted was to use entity-relationship-attribute (ERA) modelling, a technique which has been used successfully in previous studies, to document the principle concepts of methods and tools. Initially, a selection of powerful, well-established KBS tools was modelled. The Generic Model is an abstraction of the significant attributes of these products. A powerful feature of the Model is that it represents conceptual aspects of KBS functionality at different levels of detail. A subset of the Model is presented.

Product vendors have been involved with the development of the Generic Model and others will be helping to validate it by reference to their own products. The project represents approximately three man years effort and has resulted in several benefits, including the acquisition of in-house modelling expertise and an enhanced understanding of the concepts underlying KBS tools. It has been assumed that the Generic Model will remain valid in the short term, but it is subject to revision, particularly in the light of new developments in KBS technology and its changing relationship with conventional technology.

1. Introduction

The Central Computer and Telecommunications Agency (CCTA) of HM Treasury has an overall aim to add value to the development and application of IT in central government. Within CCTA the Information Systems Engineering (ISE) Division has a prime focus on 'common good' activities which determine the efficiency, effectiveness and economy of the management of IT projects and the development and maintenance of those systems. The Division's role is to influence and assist government departments to improve productivity, improve quality and protect investment in the management and implementation of their information systems.

CCTA strategy concentrates on ensuring that better and more appropriate methods and tools are available at the departmental work place. In recognition of the increasing relevance of knowledge-based systems (KBS), ISE Division is actively engaged in a programme of work being carried out to increase the prospects for success where KBS solutions are implemented for administrative IS requirements. The Division is also committed to promoting the uptake of KBS for achieving business benefits.

The Generic Model of KBS tools has been developed by CCTA's ISE Division to provide a major input to the GEMINI project (to develop a method for KBS analysis and design) and to contribute to other Divisional KBS-related objectives. The Model facilitates an understanding of KBS technology by providing an explicit description and definition of the inference-based processing capabilities embodied within KBS development tools. As such it provides an implementation-independent definition of the object types which need to be specified in a KBS physical design.

The Generic Model is an example of an entity-relationship-attribute (ERA) model based upon a logical interpretation of the subject under consideration. ERA modelling is a technique which has been used successfully in previous studies, both by CCTA and commercial industry. The Generic Model is an abstraction of the significant attributes of KBS technology to provide a generalised view of the functionality currently available in KBS tools. A powerful feature of the Generic Model is that it represents conceptual aspects of KBS functionality, such as backward chaining, at different levels of detail.

2. Aims and objectives of the Generic Model project

To make the most effective use of resources, it is necessary to understand the underlying concepts of the available technology. KBS is a comparatively recent technology which is gradually becoming established and integrated with existing systems; an understanding of the basic mechanisms used within KBS will assist in its full exploitation. The Generic Model facilitates this aim by providing an explicit description and definition of the inference-based processing capabilities embodied within KBS development tools. In this context the project constitutes an important component of the GEMINI work programme.

The overall aim of the Generic Model project can be broken down into the following specific objectives:

- to highlight the functionality available within KBS tools, so as to identify their appropriateness for particular applications;

- to provide the GEMINI project with a detailed analysis of the processing capabilities, and thereby a basis for classification, of currently available KBS tools;

- to reduce the risk of failure of projects incorporating KBS elements, largely by providing important reference material for a KBS Appraisal and Evaluation Volume which will assist organisations in KBS tool selection;

- to improve the KBS design process by providing a means of targeting strengths and circumventing constraints;

- to assist in translating a system requirement (expressed in an intermediate representation such as the GEMINI standard notation) into a physical design, by defining the major components of a target tool;

- to help to establish standard terminology for KBS;

- to encourage future development and research of KBS tools with a view to standardisation of functionality across products;

- to provide the basis for a comprehensive KBS tool specification.

3. What is the KBS Generic Model?

3.1 The ERA modelling technique

The Generic Model is an example of an entity-relationship-attribute (ERA) model based upon a logical interpretation of the subject under consideration. Each ERA model consists of a diagram, extensively documented using 'entity definitions'. These statements identify the logical concepts (entities), their attributes and the relationships between them, and explain their global role within the model. In the case of the Generic Model, this is supported by a set of 'walk through' documents which are intended to guide the reader through the complexities of the Model, breaking it down into logical subsets.

ERA modelling is a technique which has been used successfully in previous studies, both by CCTA and commercial industry, to document the principle concepts of methods and tools. The models have been compiled by a small group of specialists and experienced consultants which eases the problems of imposing consistent usage of terminology and concepts. ERA models follow a formal notation; this and the comprehensive documentation assists in validation and quality assurance. A paper to provide more detail on the terms and syntax of the modelling notation used within this project may become available.

Limitations of the technique

To determine which concepts are included within, or excluded from, an ERA model or how to portray the concepts is rarely straightforward. For example, it is necessary to consider the appropriate level of abstraction. Justifying such decisions brings its own problems and the modeller must be prepared, on occasions, to completely revise what was thought to an acceptable model. Much of the process is based on the experience of the staff involved, which includes ERA modelling expertise and, in this case, experience of KBS tools.

It is almost impossible to ensure the completeness of an ERA model. It could even be argued that certain concepts are mutually exclusive. Some concepts which are not explicitly represented as entities, may be indirectly portrayed, for example by the relationships between entities. It may be necessary to follow a particular path through the model to see this. If it can be collectively agreed that the model comprehensively conveys those concepts needed to fully describe and define its subject, then it may be considered to be complete. Subsequent attempts to use the model to explain the subject should highlight any omissions or superfluities.

3.2 The Generic Model

The objective in drawing up an ERA model of a software development tool is to impart an understanding of what the product delivers, considered at a logical or abstract level, rather than the physical level of implementation, in terms of features, facilities and mechanisms and how these may be logically combined. The approach adopted was initially to model a selection of powerful, well-established KBS tools. The Generic Model is an abstraction of the significant attributes of these products to provide a generalised view of the functionality currently available in this class of software. Only concepts that are supported by existing tools have been included within the Model.

The Model is an attempt to encapsulate the underlying principles of the processing capabilities of KBS tools, but it is not intended to embrace all concepts within all types of KBS products: languages, shells and toolkits. Ideally, one model would show all the possible features and each product vendor could identify the concepts which they have incorporated within their product. In practice, this does not appear to be feasible. However, the Model does largely fill this role for shell-based tools and also represents some of the features found within languages and toolkits.

The Generic Model is a large and complex structure of almost 300 entities with many relationships identified between them. This can lead to problems as to who is in a position to understand what is portrayed and who can validate such detail. However, the Model has been compiled by the close collaboration of several people, some developing it, others reviewing. This approach provides the opportunity to cross-validate the finished product and also enhances quality assurance.

Limitations of the Model

The Generic Model has been compiled to emphasise the processing capabilities that can be delivered to an end user rather than concentrating on the facilities available to the applications developer. This is intentional; some consideration has been given to the development environment, but the major consideration is on application functionality and not on building that application.

Another potential shortcoming of the Generic Model is that it does not intrinsically address implementation issues such as usability, performance, reliability and portability.

These attributes are clearly important when it comes to product differentiation, but are likely to be subjective or dependent upon the hardware which is supporting the particular tool; essentially they vary in degree rather than kind.

Within the study there has been a limited amount of resource available to undertake the modelling work. This means that it was impossible to look in detail at all, 200 or so, KBS products that are currently on the international market. This study is based on a range of products which are believed to be representative of deductive KBS tools currently available. It is unlikely that a single product will offer all the features of the Generic Model, though some of the most extensive may come close.

Part of the way into the project a conscious decision was made to exclude certain advanced concepts, such as blackboard architecture and object orientation, to prevent the Model becoming too complex and unmanageable. These concepts were considered to be either poorly defined, peripheral to KBS or of little additional value in meeting the objectives. For similar reasons, induction was excluded from the Model, but one inductive tool was partly modelled.

4. A subset of the Model

Because of the size and complexity of the Generic Model it would not be feasible to discuss its entire content in a paper of this kind. Fortunately the Model documentation included so-called "walkthrough" guidelines which broke the content down into 19 logical subsets. Hence a more manageable subset of the Model is presented, but one that is highly significant. These subsets facilitate greater in-depth analysis of groups of entities which are closely related, but not necessarily clustered together on the complete diagram. This approach enhances the reader's understanding of the entire Model.

One of the most important aspects of KBS development tools, for the end user as well as the knowledge engineer, is the dynamic ability to retrace paths of inferencing and to re-enter values. This allows the user to identify the source(s) of instantiation values and the reasons for conclusions drawn by the inference engine; it can provide explanations for unexpected results and the possibility of changing them. The Tracking Subset of the Generic Model (Figure 1) represents the realisation of these features within KBS tools.

A brief summary of how to interpret the modelling notation and documentation is given in Annexes 1 and 2. An additional feature of the subset diagram is that entities with boxes in bold outline are key entities within the subset and all of their relationships are shown. Other entities, some of which are peripheral to this particular subset, have other relationships which have not been shown here. Zigzagging.links indicate relationships which have been simplified within the subset. Some entity names are followed by a synonym which may correspond to more familiar usage. A list of the key entity definitions can be found in Annex 3.

To some KBS practitioners, it may appear that there is too great an emphasis on rule-based inferencing in this subset. The content is based on a wide range of current products, most of which offer rule constructs of various kinds. In the Model, the global supertype of a rule is any named group of actions which may be effected during a knowledge-based consultation - with or without a premise. This broad concept can therefore be applied to any representational paradigm such as frames, objects or Prolog predicates.

A powerful feature of the Generic Model is that it represents important KBS concepts, such as backward chaining, at different levels of detail. In the Tracking Subset backward chaining is conveyed by the interaction between the entities Rule Execution and Fired Rule Justification (Figure 2). Roughly speaking, either entity may be the cause or the effect of the other.

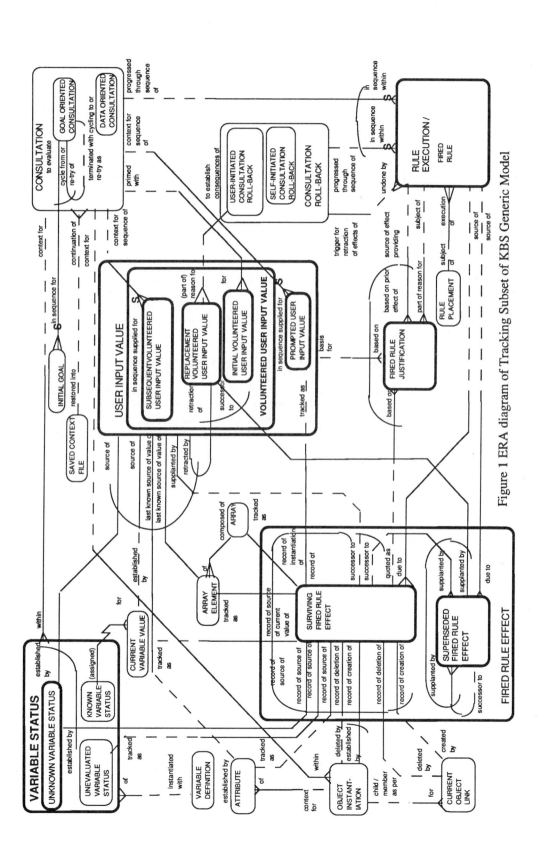

Figure 1 ERA diagram of Tracking Subset of KBS Generic Model

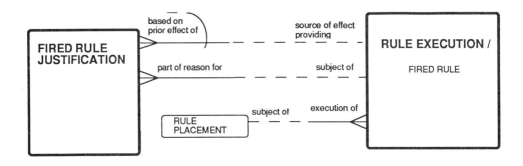

Figure 2   Detail of Tracking Subset showing backward chaining

It is important to remember that these entities are at a lower level than Rule Specification - they represent the results of instantiations of rules; but they are still generic representations of a single event. If this was not the case then these relationships would be mutually exclusive because, even though a rule may be called recursively, each execution of that rule is unique and hence, by definition, cannot effect itself! This may sound like common sense, but it is a typical source of confusion when dealing with different levels of abstraction in conceptual modelling.

Lower level aspects and components of backward chaining are also represented elsewhere in the Model, in the form of condition expressions, inference rule consequents, and so on. However, although the process of backward chaining is repeatedly referred to within entity definitions, the chaining mechanism is not directly traceable via the relationships. This reflects the intention to portray a user's view of functionality - the 'what' as opposed to the 'how'. But the distinction is a fine one and represents one of the areas that may need to be addressed in future revisions of the Model.

Another concept represented within the Tracking Subset, and characteristic of KBS, is the facility for the user to interrupt and revise consultations (this is sometimes referred to as "What if?", but this term is also applied to the more sophisticated concept of exploring alternative scenarios within a single consultation). This is illustrated in Figure 3.

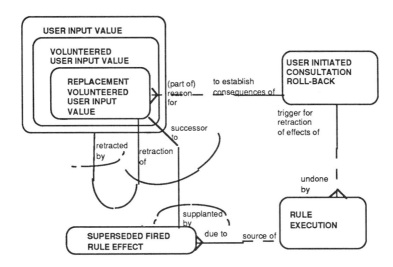

Figure 3 Detail of Tracking Subset showing user-revised consultation

5. Project summary and current status

5.1 Resources, timescales and deliverables

Four CCTA staff and two specialist consultants have been involved since the ISE Division started work on this project in October 1988. The first stage of the project involved the modelling of a number of proprietary products; some of these models have been reviewed by the product vendors. Other tools have been partially modelled by the CCTA team. These exercises were not completed mainly because of the time constraint, but any important, resultant information was fed into the study. The final stage of the project produced the Generic Model which was completed in April 1990. This represents approximately three man years effort.

5.2 Circulation

The Generic Model will be available to a limited number of people, mainly on a 'need-to-see' basis along the lines of the distribution of the SSADM Generic Model, for the SSADM tools' conformance scheme. The Model content is of a highly specialised nature which will be relevant, in varying degrees, to standards makers and to architects and developers of system engineering methods and tools. Clearly, the Model is expected to be of most relevance to those developing the GEMINI Method. It is also intended that anyone who has substantially assisted in the exercise receive a copy in appreciation of their efforts.

The specific groups intended to have access to the documentation for the KBS Generic Model are:

- CCTA staff involved in the follow-up studies as detailed in the objectives and in the plan;

- GEMINI study teams;

- Product vendors/ suppliers who will validate the Generic Model.

5.3 Validation by product vendors

During the Model development it was possible to analyse and model only a small selection of KBS development tools on the market. Because of the pace of development in this specialist field, and because of limited resources available to the CCTA team, the list of tools modelled is not exhaustive. A great deal of indirect knowledge and background reference material was also fed into the project but nevertheless certain important aspects of inference-based processing which are present in some of the latest and most powerful tools might have been excluded, where their inclusion would have been valuable.

In view of this, and because of the positive response shown by vendors of products which have been modelled in the project, it is seen as imperative that vendors of other leading KBS tools validate the Generic Model by reference to their own products. Several vendor organisations have expressed an interest in validating the Model and such collaboration has already been initiated by CCTA.

5.4 Benefits accrued to date

CCTA staff have been involved in the modelling exercise at an extremely detailed level. This has resulted in several benefits, including:

- high quality ERA models of several proprietary KBS products which are a basis for assessment and informed opinion;

- the acquisition and spread of in-house modelling expertise for use on other projects;

- an enhanced understanding of the concepts underlying KBS tools which has been, and continues to be, of value to CCTA's KBS-related objectives - notably the GEMINI Project and the production of the KBS Appraisal and Evaluation report.

5.5 Maintenance of the Model

The Generic Model is complete but subject to revision, particularly in the light of new developments in KBS technology. Products are being continually developed, new products are being marketed and the technology is generally advancing. This implies that the future maintenance and development of the Generic Model needs to be considered. A constraint on undertaking a continuous update program is that revising the Generic Model will not be a minor task, and modelling expertise is scarce and thus expensive.

It has been assumed that the Generic Model will remain valid in the short term, say two to five years. This is because it has been based on a broad set of products currently available, some of which are innovative in their approach to processing. In the longer term, it may be necessary to re-investigate the available technology which may become radically transformed. It is also probable that the distinction between KBS and conventional technology will become increasingly blurred. The strategy of a future study would have to take account of the prevailing circumstances.

6. How will the Generic Model be used?

6.1 GEMINI

An ERA model of the GEMINI Extended Method Definition has been produced as part of the recent Development Study. This exercise drew upon the formal notation of the technique adopted by CCTA in developing the Generic Model. The modelling expertise acquired by CCTA has already proved valuable in reviewing this work package and should be of further value in subsequent phases of the development of the Method.

The Generic Model will provide the main phase of the GEMINI development work with a detailed, formal representation of the processing capabilities of currently available KBS tools. It should then be possible to identify the interface between the Generic Model and the GEMINI standard notation and to use both in conjunction to assist in the move from a logical system requirement to a physical design. One way in which this should be achieved is by helping to identify the major components required within the specification of the GEMINI intermediate representation or standard notation. On a more general level it is also intended that the harmonisation of both Models will help to establish standard terminology for KBS analysis and design.

6.2 Appraisal and Evaluation Volume

The Generic Model will underpin the documentation of criteria for evaluation and selection of KBS development tools. This will be done by analysing the concepts incorporated within the Generic Model and interpreting these in terms of criteria aimed at the production of a list of attributes or facilities that need to be considered during the procurement of a KBS product. The resulting report will constitute the Knowledge-Based Systems Volume of the CCTA Appraisal and Evaluation Library. The Generic Model should assist in the process of determining a logical structure (i.e. grouping of features) for the report.

While the list of attributes to be considered during a procurement exercise should be complete, it needs to be based on currently available technology and not a theoretical concept which may not be achievable. At some point in the future, the Appraisal and Evaluation Volume is likely to be revised for the following reasons:

•   in response to user feedback to ensure that it relates to practical issues involved in software selection, reflecting changes in the management and development methods;

•   to reflect major changes in the technology.

The proposed KBS Appraisal and Evaluation Volume will be published by HMSO and distributed in accordance with the other reports in that series. It is intended that this report will increase awareness of the technology and allow soundly based procurement of KBS tools within government departments.

6.3 Other possible future uses of the KBS Generic Model

KBS Applications

CCTA may undertake a study to categorise application problems into types (in terms of processing requirements) and produce a model for each type. These models could be used to produce a Generic Model for applications. This Applications Generic Model could be used in conjunction with the KBS Tools Generic Model to identify types of application problem and features of applications suitable for development using KBS products.

Choosing an appropriate class of development tool

The Generic Model offers potential for use in one or more studies to assess the similarity and disparity between software product sets. For example, a study could be undertaken to differentiate the processing capabilities of application generators (AGs) and KBS tools by comparing the KBS Generic Model with an earlier generic model produced for AGs. The objective of the comparison would be to identify heuristics indicating which of these two classes of development tool appear to be appropriate for particular types of application. This exercise could be expanded to cover other classes of processing tool.

Strengths related to standards and methods

The Generic Model may highlight logical links to areas of processing which the technology is not currently able to provide. One topic likely to come into this category is product integration, the aim being for standards to enable IS tools to interwork in such a way that the user is unaware of the technological differences in the tools supporting the application. To assist in this aim a major area of investigation, within the ISE Division, has been into how KBS and DBMS tools can be used, within a single application, in a coherent and integrated way.

7. Summary

Development of the KBS Generic Model by CCTA has already proved to be a worthwhile exercise in terms of providing input to GEMINI and in helping to achieve other KBS-related objectives. By providing a formal representation of the processing capabilities of currently available KBS tools, the Model should facilitate the specification of the GEMINI standard notation for translation from a logical system design to a physical implementation. It is also intended that the Model will help to establish standard terminology for KBS analysis and design.

In more general terms, the indirect and related benefits of the Model are seen as increased awareness of the advantages of using KBS technology, reduced risk for projects implemented using KBS and more accurate identification of KBS applications. One specific way in which these benefits should be realised is via the documentation of a procedure for evaluation and selection of KBS development tools - the KBS Appraisal and Evaluation Volume, which will be partly based on the Generic Model. Other uses for the Model are also envisaged, for example in comparing KBS tools with other classes of tools.

Product vendors have been involved with the development of the Generic Model and others will be helping to validate it by reference to their own products. CCTA have been encouraged by this positive response from industry and look forward to a continuing collaboration to the mutual benefit of all involved. This has direct bearing on future maintenance of the Model in response to developments in KBS technology and on the possible future response of vendors in terms of the provision of functionality within their products. It is intended that the Generic Model should therefore serve as an exemplary approach to understanding advanced technology and responding to it.

A Generic Model of Knowledge-Based Tools: Annexes

A1 ERA Documentation

The documentation within the report for each ERA model consists of two parts; these are:
- a diagram;
- a list of entities and entity descriptions.

The diagram and entity details are to be used together to explain fully the model and what concepts have been incorporated.

Diagram
The diagram is to be based on the diagramming techniques detailed in annex A2.

List of entities
An index lists all entries alphabetically. This is followed by the individual entity descriptions each of which consists of four part which are:
- an entity definition;
- a list of relationships;
- a list of attributes;

Entity Name
An entity name is a label for something which is precisely defined in the model as having a given set of ATTRIBUTES and RELATIONSHIPS. For this reason an entity name is distinguished by use of BLOCK CAPITALS, a convention which is reserved exclusively for this purpose.

Entity Definition
The entity definition is used to explain why the concept is included within the model. The narrative identifies the logical concepts and how they are incorporated within the diagram. The relationship and attribute details provide the description of the entity. If an entity is a subtype, the entity definition highlights the entity of which it is a subtype (though the naming convention should also help identify these links).

Relationships
The list of relationships is taken directly from the diagram to show how the entities interact with each other. The narrative for mandatory relationships is preceded by "must be" while that for optional relationships is preceded by "may be". An *exclusion arc* is used to show that only one of the relationships covered by the arc can be valid at any one time.

Attributes
A list of attributes indicates which characteristics of the entity have significance to the way in which the model has been drawn. Items in these lists help to put the concept into overall context. The concept may not be described listing all the possible attributes, but all attributes which were significant in deciding the structure of the model will be mentions, and there will be an indication as to other factors which may also be relevant. Attributes can be applied to the entity in four ways by being:
- mandatory;
- optional;
- conditional;
- derived.

A2 ERA Diagram notation

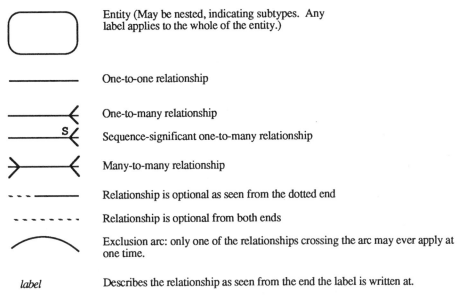

Entity (May be nested, indicating subtypes. Any label applies to the whole of the entity.)

One-to-one relationship

One-to-many relationship

Sequence-significant one-to-many relationship

Many-to-many relationship

Relationship is optional as seen from the dotted end

Relationship is optional from both ends

Exclusion arc: only one of the relationships crossing the arc may ever apply at one time.

label   Describes the relationship as seen from the end the label is written at.

Examples:

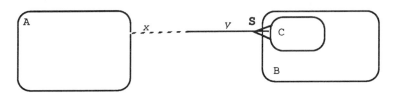

A bears an optional relationship x with a sequence of one or more C. C is a subtype of B. C always bears relationship y with one A. .

A3 Tracking Subset: Entity Definitions

Each CURRENT VARIABLE VALUE
has significance as a currently assigned value for a given VARIABLE within a given CONSULTATION.

> Each SINGULAR CURRENT VARIABLE VALUE
> has significance as a sub-type of CURRENT VARIABLE VALUE which is for a VARIABLE which is allowed only one value at a time.
> Each FUZZY CURRENT VARIABLE VALUE
> has significance as a sub-type of CURRENT VARIABLE VALUE which is one of a set of values 'known' to the associated CONSULTATION which is for a VARIABLE which is allowed more than one value at a time.

Each FIRED RULE JUSTIFICATION
has significance as one of possibly several factors which caused/enabled the associated FIRED RULE to be achieved. Note: PROCEDURAL RULES would not have/need justifications.

Each FIRED RULE EFFECT
has significance as a record of one of the changes made to data within the CONSULTATION during the execution of a rule.

Each SURVIVING FIRED RULE EFFECT

has significance as a sub-type of FIRED RULE EFFECT which is a record of a change made to data within the CONSULTATION where that change has not subsequently been superseded. By quoting the source of the change, ie the RULE responsible, this record enables the user to interrogate the inference engine as to where any derived data value came from. Note: any value not attributed to the user or a fired rule is due to consultation initialisation or 'cycled' from previous consultation.

Each SUPERSEDED FIRED RULE EFFECT

has significance as a sub-type of FIRED RULE EFFECT which is the record of an effect which has subsequently been supplanted by another effect or user input.

Each RULE EXECUTION

has significance as a record of the fact that the specified RULE has been 'fired', ie its CONSEQUENTS, if any, applied and its ACTIONS, if any, executed.

Each USER INPUT VALUE

has significance as a user-supplied value for a given data item.

Each VOLUNTEERED USER INPUT VALUE

has significance as a sub-type of USER INPUT VALUE which the user elected to supply rather than being prompted. (Compare with PROMPTED USER INPUT VALUE).

Each INITIAL VOLUNTEERED USER INPUT VALUE

has significance as a sub-type of VOLUNTEERED USER INPUT VALUE which the user can supply prior to any inferencing occuring within the consultation concerned. Note: such 'priming' of a consultation is only possible when the consultation concerned is in 'interactive' mode and is not a 'cycled' or 're-tried' consultation.

Each SUBSEQUENT VOLUNTEERED USER INPUT VALUE

has significance as a sub-type of VOLUNTEERED USER INPUT VALUE which occurs after inferencing has started. Such values could trigger DEMON RULES (Compare.with INITIAL VOLUNTEERED USER INPUT VALUE).

Each REPLACEMENT VOLUNTEERED USER INPUT VALUE

has significance as a sub-type of VOLUNTEERED USER INPUT VALUE which, because it is changing a previously 'known' value, may cause a USER INITIATED CONSULTATION ROLL-BACK. It does this only if the previous value had been used as a justification for 'firing' one or more rules.

Each PROMPTED USER INPUT VALUE

has significance as a sub-type of USER INPUT VALUE where the user was 'asked' to supply a value as a result of an action within a FIRED RULE.

Each VARIABLE STATUS

has significance as a record of whether a given VARIABLE, within the context of a given CONSULTATION, currently has a value or not.

Each KNOWN VARIABLE STATUS

has significance as a sub-type of VARIABLE STATUS where at least one value exists for the VARIABLE concerned. (Note: for values with certainty factors, only those where the factor is currently greater than a specified threshold are deemed to be 'known'.)

Each UNKNOWN VARIABLE STATUS

has significance as a sub-type of VARIABLE STATUS where no value with a certainty factor above the specified threshold currently exists for the VARIABLE concerned.

Each UNEVALUATED VARIABLE STATUS

has significance as a sub-type of VARIABLE STATUS which signifies that, as yet, no value has been assigned to the VARIABLE concerned. In addition, during backward reasoning, this status signifies that no attempt has been made to establish a value for the variable. A variable which the inference engine has tried and failed to evaluate would have an UNKNOWN VARIABLE STATUS. Thus the inference engine 'knows' not to try, again, to evaluate it.

CYBERNETICS: AN EXPLANATION

Professor Kevin Warwick
Department of Cybernetics, University of Reading,
Whiteknights, Berkshire.

Abstract

Cybernetics is a modern discipline which offers great
potential in the realisation of realisable applied Expert Systems. In
this paper, the subject area of Cybernetics is considered in a broad
sense, particular emphasis being placed on practical and application
issues.   It is also shown how fields such as neural networks, expert
systems, intelligent control and multi-sensor fusion fit readily into
the overall topic.

1. Introduction

Cybernetics is a science for today, and has an important
role to play in an increasingly more technological world. Cybernetics
is concerned with systems and their control, information and feedback
being key features. In fact it was Norbert Wiener (Wiener, 1948) who
first coined the term Cybernetics in 1948, defining it as 'control and
communication in mechanisms, organisms and society'; thereby pointing
very much to a generalising discipline. Since that time, technical
advancement has been rapid, and it is difficult to conceive Wiener
envisaging the critical role that systems, information and communications would play. A central aspect of this advancement is the
development of computer systems, and indeed these now play an important
part in much technical Cybernetics work.   A key overall factor is the
requirement for a group of elements to operate as an interconnected
whole system, rather than as individual entities, the study of such
systems is called Cybernetics.
Many present-day technological devices, particularly those
of a domestic or personal nature are designed to function only as an
overall system. Hence, when things go wrong, the whole system is
replaced or, as a minimum, a major part is modified.   Watches, washing
machines and coffee machines are all good examples of this. Modern production and manufacturing is also now much more based on a systems
approach (Warwick,1990), with the overall production or manufacturing
process being the key feature, rather than the performance of individual
workstations.   The trend towards a more important role for overall
system design is continuing, with a general move away from individual
component roles and maintenance.   Going hand in hand with this trend is
the increasingly important role which is being taken on by Cybernetics.

2. Cybernetics in General

As a discipline Cybernetics is not interested in elements
in isolation, but rather is concerned with groups of elements which form
a system.   Such systems can range from minute biological systems to
planetary bodies, including a view of the Earth as a living system

(Lovelock, 1987). Interest lies in the multitude of interconnections which occur between individual parts of a complex system, in particular the way in which their properties interlink and their characteristics vary due to the interactions.

The relative study position is worth emphasising, in that a particular group of elements can, when required, be thought of as a system in entirety, whilst at other times this grouping can be thought of merely as part of a much larger system. As an example, a car engine can be regarded as a dynamic system in itself, however it may well be that the overall system under consideration includes the car and driver as a working whole. Indeed this example can be taken a stage further if the car and driver are merely considered as part of a large transport system; the car engine is then only a small element or sub-system. The features and properties of any particular object cannot therefore be correctly evaluated and studied until one considers the nature and role of the overall system being studied, and the part which the object in question plays. This necessarily means that the multitude of connections and interactions which exist between individual objects and their surroundings, must be taken into account.

In any study that is carried out as to a system's behaviour, no matter how comprehensive this study may be, it is almost certain that all influential factors cannot be taken into account, whether they are acting directly or indirectly. Some random factors will therefore necessarily exist, which have not been taken into consideration. Such factors are particularly important when systems are considered in which prediction or forecasting are involved.

Cybernetics' ideas are aimed at achieving the following goals:

(i)   Establishment of important facts, which are general for all or for some classes of systems.
(ii)   Reveal limitations which are characteristic of certain systems and to establish their origin.
(iii)   Find general relationships to which the systems comply; based on factual collected data.
(iv)   Indicate ways of utilizing relationships and facts for practical use and profit.

It can be seen from this list that Cybernetics is a broad discipline which has links with many other areas in which some form of systems is involved. A few examples are Economic Systems, Biological and Chemical Systems, Ecological Systems as well as Applied Science, Engineering and Mathematics.

3. Cybernetics in Industry

As a discipline, Cybernetics is very relevant to industrial problems, this being especially true on today's production lines with high throughput rates and interactive processes. By viewing an overall system from a general stance, the cybernetic result is that 'what is obtain from the system as a whole is greater than the sum of its parts'.

Overall profit, through productivity and output, is in most cases the main operating directive within an industrial framework. Cybernetics is therefore directly relevant in that individual elements

in the form of production workstations or human operators are viewed as
to their role in the system as a whole, and their interactive performance in terms of overall profit.   The individual components or
stations of a production process are thus governed by the requirements
of the overall system.
          In a production environment the move towards Just-In-Time
manufacture pushes processes much more into the Cybernetics domain. In
order for the system to operate efficiently and effectively, each of the
production elements must operate in terms of both state and time, under
the constraints of the requirements handed on from the overall system.
J-I-T manufacture also increases the need for more on-line sensors and
monitoring points, in order to check on correct operation, quality and
reliability.
          Human operators are still employed for many industrial
tasks, and it must be remembered under these circumstances that the
overall industrial system is the main area of study, with human, machine
and their inter-communication, being elements of the whole system.
From a cybernetic viewpoint, the system in its entirety is the major
critical issue, which means that questions regarding whether a particular human operator should be replaced by a piece of high technology,
or indeed vice versa, are of lesser significance – as long as one is
explicitly clear which system is of primary concern.

4. Technical Research

          In order to further discuss how Cybernetics has an influence
on present-day thinking a number of important research areas are outlined here.   In general these call on fundamental aspects of physical
measurement and instrumentation, control and systems theory, automation
and production design and electronic/computer systems.   To this end, IT,
Manufacturing Processes and Electronic Systems are seen to be disciplines which fall within the overall Cybernetics framework.   More
detailed examples are:

(i)   Neural Networks: Neural nets are now of great interest,
          both from a fundamental viewpoint, looking at new structures
          and learning algorithms, but also from an applications
          viewpoint with many successful implementations (Wu and
          Warwick, 1990; Bushnell, Bishop and Westland, 1990).
(ii)   Just-in-time Manufacture: this is of interest for many
          present-day production processes, where the overall
          production design is of main concern. The sub-systems and
          individual production elements are considered in terms of
          their role within the complete system.
(iii)   Intelligent Controllers: flexibility offered by computer
          control systems is in direct contrast to that provided by
          fixed gain analog controllers. This allows for the possi-
          bility of Expert Systems (Kuan and Warwick, 1990) and AI
          Coordinating Systems to provide a decision making hier-
          achical controller.
(iv)   Sensor Integration: this is concerned with the integration
          of information from several different, possibly diverse,
          sensors. Self-checking and fault conditioning modes are of

interest with the aim of obtaining information on particular
sensory targets.

5. Conclusions

An attempt has been made here to show how Cybernetics
relates to today's requirements, particularly within an applications
environment and especially where computer systems are employed in
design, development and production processes.   Pattern recognition,
robotics, computer graphics and sensor integration are all of immediate
interest in the field of Cybernetics, particularly where they form
elements in an overall system which involves the control of and communication between those elements.
By considering cybernetic systems in an integrated way,
aspects of measurement, control and feedback can be seen to be of great
relevance in automation, production and indeed industrial processes in
general.
There have been numerous considerable technical advances
over the last forty years, and equally Cybernetics·has progressed to
provide a powerful tool for the study of complex systems.   Often viewing
an overall system from a more general framework can make objectives
clear and decisions simple to deduce and easy to make.

6. References

Wiener, N. (1948 and 1961). Cybernetics: or control and communication in
the animal and the machine. MIT Press and Wiley.
Warwick, K.(1990).   Automatic control in manufacturing – current status.
Advanced Manufacturing Engineering, 1, no. 3, 17–20.
Lovelock, J.E. (1987).   Gaia. Oxford University Press.
Wu, P. and Warwick, K. (1990).   A new coupling algorithm for speech
processing. Proc. Expert Systems 90, London.
Bushnell, M., Bishop, J.M. and Westland S. (1990). Computer recipe
prediction using neural networks. Proc. Expert Systems 90, London.
Kuan, K.K. and Warwick, K. (1990). 'Expert system techniques in power
distribution design', Proc. Expert Systems 90, London.

A NEW NEURAL COUPLING ALGORITHM FOR SPEECH PROCESSING

P. WU, and K. WARWICK

DEPARTMENT OF CYBERNETICS, UNIVERSITY OF READING, UK

Abstract

In recent years neural networks have been successfully developed to process speech signals. The neural network feature maps show great advantages when compared to a phonetic typewriter or to phoneme recognition. In Kohonen's work (1988) the coupling feedbacks between neurons follow the shape of a "Mexican hat". In this paper an improvement is made such that information from the relationship of phonemes is considered to guide the heading direction forward to the correct phoneme. The logic relation can be completely represented by the coupling feedback parameters. This means that the possiblity exists to set the rules of language into a neural network system. Several simple experiments are made and results are discussed.

1. Introduction

It has been shown through a number of experiments that neural networks can be used for a phonetic typewriter. Algorithms can be looked at as producing self-organising Feature Maps in which each fixed position corresponds to a selected phoneme. It has also been shown that if an utterance of an isolated word or perhaps even a sentence is input to the neural network system, a route of changing phonemes in the phonetic feature map can be seen.

A neural network system for Chinese phonemes has been built up by software simulation in a Sun computer. Methods of connection between different neurons have been improved from "Mexican hat" to a completely different shape as is explained shortly. Feedback from one neuron to help fire a number of special grouped neurons has been designed. It has great benefit with regard to the Chinese language in which the phonemes can be divided into several groups, and further it is apparent that an utterance of a Chinese square character is formed by simple rules.

2. Basic structure of the Neural Network System

After storing natural speech data as phonemes in memory, the signal is converted into a spectral representation and 17 narrow-band channels are employed as sharp cut-off filters. A neural network with size 20 by 20 neurons is considered, where the energy inside each of the 17 channels is calculated as an input component to the neural network system. Two adjusting feedback systems have been designed and a criterion is set for spectrum energy normalization.

A neural network with 400 neurons (20 by 20) has been formed by computer simulation and the states of the two

dimensional neural network system appear on the screen with 127
grey-scale levels. Kohonen's algorithm of network activity output
is used in the structure, and a monotonic function is introduced
to the system to set the output value of each neuron. Kohonen's
shortcut learning algorithm has also been chosen to update the
weighting vectors. A new coupling algorithms between different
neurons will be introduced later in this paper.

3. The characteristics of Chinese phonemes

The Chinese phoneme groups in our system are as follows:
Group 1 { b, p, m, f, d, t, n, l, g, k, h, j, q, x }
Group 2 { zh, ch, sh, r, z, c, s }
Group 3 { i, u, u" }
Group 4 { a, o, e, ai, ei, ao, ou, an, en, ang, eng, ong }
Group 1 and group 2 are initial consonant groups, whereas group 3
and group 4 are vowel groups. There are three rules to note in the
pronunciation of Chinese characters. First is the utterance of a
single expression by choosing one single phoneme from group 2,
group 3 or group 4. Second is combining an expression by choosing
first one phoneme from group 3 and a second phoneme from group 4
to form a diphthong pronunciation. The third is to choose a first
phoneme from group 1 or 2 and then a second from group 3 or group
4, otherwise the second phoneme is replaced by a combination of
first one phoneme from group 3 and secondly one phoneme from group
4. All the Chinese characters obey these simple rules. This means
that no more than 3 basic phonemes in the 36-element-list make up
a Chinese character pronunciation.

4. Improvement of activity function

In Kohonen's paper the network activity function $\eta(i)$ is
written

$$d\eta(i)/dt = \sum_{j=1}^{n} \mu(i,j)\xi(i,j) + \sum_{K \in S(i)} \omega(k,i)\eta(k) - \gamma(\eta(i)) \qquad (1)$$

where the first term on the right hand side corresponds to the
coupling of input signals to the neuron throught the different
transmittances; note a linear, superposition effect was assumed
for simplicity. The $\mu(i,j)$ term indicates the strengths of the
neural junctions, whereas $\xi(i,j)$ is the signal value at the jth
input of the ith neuron. The feedback coupling from neuron k to
neuron i is denoted by $\omega(k,i)$, where k runs over the subset s(i)
of those neurons that have connections with neuron i. The last
term, $-\gamma(\eta(i))$, represents a nonlinear leakage effect. A "Mexican
hat" shape is provided for the $\omega(k,i)$ and the distance between
neuron k and neuron i measured by (i-k) can uniquely decide the
value of $\omega(k,i)$, because a two dimensional neural network system
is chosen so the distance is measured in a two dimensional way.
In the neural network system described in this paper the
"Mexican hat" has been improved into a shape. The $\omega(k,i)$ is not
only decided by the distance between neurons, but also by the
special grouped phoneme feedback coupling. In Chinese language

there are different group phonemes, and according to the rules of
Chinese square character utterance, positive feedback or negative
feedback from one neuron to another can be easily set. This means
that it is easy to fire the next correct neuron by introducing
positive and negative feedback if at a particular moment one
neuron has already fired.

In order to explain the principle of operation consider
that pixel (a,b) belongs to phoneme A and pixel (c,d) belongs to
phoneme B in a two dimensional phonetic feature map. We can say
that the order of neuron at (a,b) is N_a and the order of the
neuron at (c,d) is N_b; if neuron N_a is firing, according to the
rule of combination a group of phonemes in the set $S(i)$ are found
which are possibly firing; if N_b neuron is in the group, $\omega(N_a, N_b)$
can be set a little bit higher to give a slightly more positive
feedback; otherwise $\omega(N_a, N_b)$ needs to be reduced for a slightly
more negative feedback.

If all the ω values have been changed like this, the
symmetric relationship of ω which is $\omega(i,j) = \omega(j,i)$ can be
broken. This means possibly that N_a neuron's firing will cause N_b
neuron's firing, although N_b neuron's firing doesn't fire neuron
N_a according to the rule mentioned before. A new rule is created
that the original negative feedback or positive feedback is set to
zero if this happens. If ω is kept in symmetric form we can be
sure that a stable bubble will be formed, otherwise the stability
of the states of neural network is not guaranteed.

Network activities now can be written

$$d\eta(i)/dt = \sum_{j=1}^{n} \mu(i,j)\xi(i,j) + \sum_{K \in S(i)} \omega'(k,i)\eta(k) - \gamma(\eta(i)) \qquad (2)$$

where

$$\omega'(k,i) = \omega(k,i) + \omega''(k,i) \qquad (3)$$

and $\omega(k,i)$ is still of "Mexican hat" form which makes a
contribution to form a bubble, although the coupling feedback
value is modified by the new term $\omega''(k,i)$.

5. Process of changing w(k,i)

Firstly Kohonen's algorithms are required in order to
produce a self-organised feature map for Chinese language
phonemes, in which the whole learning process just involves
individual phonemes. No information from the relationship between
different phonemes is considered, although feedback is introduced
in the trained neural networks. An appropriate positive value α is
chosen such that all neurons are queued and treated one after
another. The algorithm is shown in Figure 1.

6. Conclusion

Several simple experiments have been carried out for
testing the idea presented. After changing the shape from that of
"Mexican hat", a stable bubble can be well formed. The effect can
be caused in two ways, firstly, from formula (2), if a certain net
area is firing, the feedbacks contribute to fire another neuron;
second, if the bubble has gone from the original area the effect

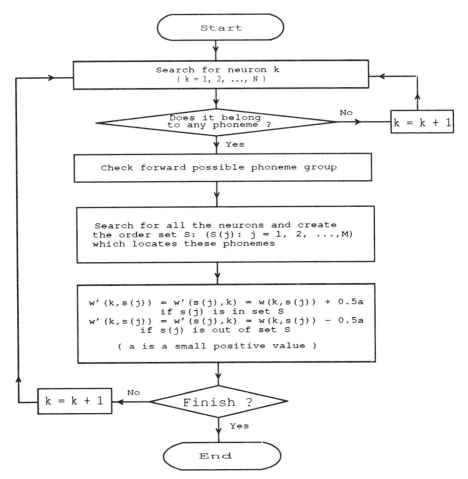

Figure 1. Algorithm for modyfying coupling feedback w(k,i)

of feedbacks has gone as well because the state value of an
unfiring neuron is zero.

It is well known that speech is a very changable signal.
After the learning process, each phoneme occupies a certain
position in our feature map, such that the feature parameters
corresponding to each phoneme are relatively stable, although the
utterance of a word causes phonemes to be affected by the last or
next phoneme. Our new structure gives an emphasis which guides the
changing bubble route in the feature map in a good direction,
which can also be looked on as re-arranging the parameter
distribution space. This calculation is nonlinear so that a very
complicated transform in parameter space occurs, and the feature
parameters belonging to different phonemes can be split to achieve
better recognition. In other words, by introducing much more
information on phoneme relationships the recognition result can be
improved.

References

1. Kohonen, T. (1988). "The 'neural' phonetic typewriter". IEEE computing Magazine, Vol. 21, No. 3, March , pp. 11-22.
2. Hopfield, J. J. (1984). "Neurons with graded response have collective computational properties like those of two-state neurons". Proc. Natl. Acad. Sci. USA, Vol. 81, pp. 3088-3092, May.
3. Hopfield, J. J. and Tank, D. W. (1986). "Computing with neural circuits: A Model". Science, Vol. 233, pp. 625-633, August.
4. Wu, P., Warwick, K. and Koska, M. (1990). "Neural network feature maps for Ch i nese phonemes". Proc. International Conference, Neuronet 90, Prague.
5. Pao, Y-H. (1989). "Adaptive pattern recognition and Neural Networks". Addison-Wesley.

COMPUTER RECIPE PREDICTION USING NEURAL NETWORKS

Dr. J.M.Bishop, Mr. M.J.Bushnell & Dr. S.Westland*.
Neural Network Research Group, Cybernetics Department, University of
Reading, Whiteknights, Berkshire.
*Vision Research Group, Department Communication & Neuroscience,
Keele University.

Abstract

Conventional computer colour recipe prediction systems employ optical models (commonly the Kubelka-Munk theory) to relate measured reflectance values to colorant concentration. However, these systems provide only an approximate model and hence situations exist where this approach is not applicable. An alternative method is to utilise Artificial Intelligence techniques to mimic the behaviour of the professional colorist. The purpose of this paper is to describe recent research being carried out at Reading University, sponsored by Courtaulds Research, to investigate the use of neural networks which learn how to predict recipes based on the acquisition of knowledge from previously formulated recipes.

1. Introduction

Traditionally, recipe prediction has been carried out by professional colorists who have learned through experience how dyes behave in mixture. The process would generally involve the colorist creating a recipe, testing it by carrying out a dying, then modifying it to obtain a good visual colour match. This process could involve several dyings before a satisfactory match was produced, leading to high laboratory costs and large time delays for the customer.

Since the development of low-cost digital computers, instrumental colour measurement systems have become widely used in the coloration industry. One of the most important applications of computer colour systems is the prediction of dye recipes. Computer systems have several advantages over the traditional method;

1: Accurate recipes can be produced in fewer dyings thus reducing costs and time.

2: The computer system can find many recipes to produce the required colour, enabling the dye house to choose the cheapest recipe, whereas a colorist would generally find only one recipe.

3: Recipes can be chosen which minimise metamerism. Metamerism describes the phenomena in which perceived colour is light source dependant. A colour that appears to be a good match under one light source may be a poor match under a different light source.

Most commercial systems use the Kubelka-Munk theory which relates the measured reflectance values of a sample to colorant concentrations via scattering and absorption coefficients. This theory is only an approximation of an exact radiative transfer theory. Exact theories are well documented in the literature (Chandrasekhar, 1950) but have rarely been used in the coloration industry.

In order for the Kubelka-Munk approximation to be valid the following restrictions are assumed;

1:      The scattering medium is bounded by parallel planes and extends over a region very large compared to its thickness;

2:      The boundary conditions, which include the illumination, do not depend upon time or the position of the boundary planes;

3:      The medium is homogenous for the purposes of the calculation;

4:      The radiation is confined to a narrow wavelength band so that the absorption and scattering coefficients are constant;

5:      The medium does not emit radiation (e.g. fluoresce);

6:      The medium is isotropic.

There are many applications of the Kubelka-Munk approximation in the coloration industry where these assumptions are know to be false. In particular, the applications to thin layers of colorants (e.g. printing inks (Westland 1988)), and in the case of fluorescent dyestuffs (Ganz, 1977 & McKay,1976), have generally yielded poor results.

The professional colorist makes predictions without the use of Kubelka-Munk theory, based upon accumulated experience of the behaviour of colorants, and is able to predict recipes for new shades to a high standard. Initial results suggest that neural networks mimic this ability to acquire knowledge as a function of experience and hence learn the mapping between colour and colorant formulation without using approximations such as Kubelka-Munk theory. An advantage of this approach is that it could be applied, not only to textile dying, but to any coloration problem for which a suitable database exists, *even where there is no well defined theoretical model*. Such problems can occur when using inks, fluorescent dyes and metallic paints, which are all difficult to predict using conventional techniques.

2. What Are Neural Networks ?

The human brain consists of many millions of neurons interconnected with each other. These neurons are considered to be very simple processing units which operate in parallel. The output of each neuron is some function of its input, which is cascaded in parallel to all the other neurons to which it is connected. Although individual neurons operate slowly in comparison to electronic systems, the brain is still capable of performing certain types of processing (such as scene analysis in vision) much faster than conventional computational techniques. Neural networks are an attempt to obtain similar results in electronic systems by modelling this structure.

2.1 Parallel Distributed Processing (PDP)

Initial research in neural networks was performed by Cybernetists, Psychologists and Neurologists, and represented an attempt to understand the workings of the brain by modelling the way it was thought to function. The elements of a PDP network are simplified models of actual neurons (see Figure 1). The networks consists of a set of such elements linked together and suitably weighted. These weights define the strength of the connections between each unit.

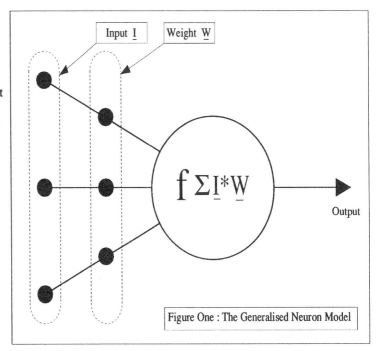

Figure One : The Generalised Neuron Model

Neural networks differ from conventional computer architectures in several important ways. The main difference is that in conventional systems, memory is separated from processing whereas in neural networks, information is distributed throughout the network in the form of interconnection strengths between processing units. Instead of programming a solution to a specific problem, the neural network learns by adapting these interconnection strengths as it acquires knowledge over time.

3. Learning in Neural Networks

Although the interconnection weights in a neural network can be defined by hand, this approach is only practical for very simple problems. In a network of any complexity the number of interconnections is large and there is no way of knowing the set of weights which give the desired mapping between the input and output of the network. What is required (and what makes the neural network approach so powerful) is a method by which the network can set up its own weights to give the correct output.

Many different learning paradigms have been developed for neural networks. One learning rule which has been developed for multi-layered systems is a generalisation of the Widrow-Hoff or Delta Rule (Widrow & Hoff, 1960). This rule, known as the Generalised Delta Rule (Rumelhart, Hinton & Williams, 1986), works by propagating an error term backwards through the network and making weight changes such that overall error in the net is minimised.

3.1 The Generalised Delta Rule

In one learning sweep with the generalised delta rule, the following sequence of events occur;

1: The network is presented with an input pattern (all the input units of the network are set to the required values).

2: This input vector is used to compute the output values by feeding forward through the net and computing activation values for all the other units according to the weight values.

3: The output vector for this pattern is compared to the required, or target, pattern and the error is calculated for every output unit.

4: Error terms are recursively propagated backward through the net to the other units in proportion to the connection strengths between the units.

5: The weights are then adjusted in such a way as to reduce the error terms, in a similar manner to the simple delta rule.

6: Repeat the process for all the input/target pattern pairs in the training set.

This process of presenting to the network all the patterns for which it is to be trained is defined as an epoch. Training continues for as many epochs as necessary to reduce the overall error to an acceptably low value.

4. The Application To Recipe Prediction

In devising a suitable network for use in the problem of recipe prediction several problems arise. The network must take information on a colour and map this to a dye recipe. To do this it is necessary to have some method of representing colours numerically. The international standard for colorimetry is the CIE system which takes measured relative reflectance values and converts them into three coordinates in a three dimensional colour space. There are two common ways of representing these numbers, known as CIELab and CIELCH. In both methods, the "vertical" axis is the lightness axis, L. The other two numbers are either taken as two orthogonal axes in the horizontal plane, a and b, or polar co-ordinates C and H. The a and b co-ordinates of the CIELab system represent the "redness/greeness" or the "yellowness/blueness" of the colour whereas the C and H of the CIELCH system represent the chroma (or saturation) of the colour and the hue. Chroma is measured radially in colour-space and corresponds to the intensity of the colour. Hue is an angular measurement where 0 degrees is pure red, 90 is yellow, 180 is green and 270 is blue.

A second problem is to decide how the network should be structured. The number of input and output units to use depends directly on the data being used, but the architecture of the hidden layers is not obvious. At present there is no well defined method of determining optimal network structure, but some rules of thumb have emerged. Theoretically, one hidden layer should be sufficient to learn a solution (Funahashi, 1989), but more layers may help to obtain quicker solutions or provide better generalisation. To obtain good generalisation to unlearned patterns the number of hidden units needs to be less than the number of training patterns used. However the more hidden units that are used, the faster the network will learn.

5. Experimental Results

The dye system used in these initial tests consisted of three dyes on a nylon substrate. Because the aim of these experiments was to investigate the feasibility of using neural networks to perform recipe prediction it was not necessary to use actual production data in the tests. Test data used was obtained by synthesising dye recipes using the ICS-TEXICON colour system which gave colour data for a number of test recipes. The data was given in both CIELab and CIELCH format. To investigate the effect of data format on the ability of the network to learn, two tests were performed on the test data, one using the LCH colour co-ordinates and one using the Lab system.

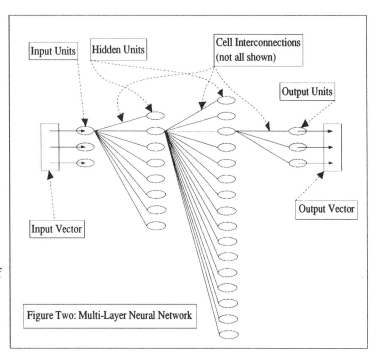

Figure Two: Multi-Layer Neural Network

The three dyes used in these tests were Nylosan Blue EGL, Nylosan Yellow ERPL and Nylosan Scarlet F-3GL. Recipes were synthesised using varying concentrations of single, two and three dye mixtures from this group.

5.1. Network Architecture

The neural network used consisted of three input units (one for each colour co-ordinate), 24 hidden units, arranged in two layers of 8 and 16 units respectively, and three output units, corresponding to the concentrations of the three dyes (see Figure 2). The input and target data had to be scaled to fit the activation range of the neurons as these can only take values between zero and one due to the nature of the activation function. In some cases, using the Lab data, a linear offset of 0.5 had to be added to the scaled values of the a and b co-ordinates as these can take negative values, which the network cannot generate.

A modified back propagation learning rule was used to train the network, using an extra momentum term. The learning rate was set low, as empirical evidence showed the the network quickly became unstable if high rates were used. The system was trained on approximately half of the synthesised dye recipes, with the other half being retained to test the network. The results were analysed using the ICS-TEXICON system mentioned above (using the 1983 CMC equation to evaluate colour difference, ΔE).

5.2 Experiments using data in LCH format

The first tests performed used data in LCH format and was trained over 3000 training epochs. Observation of the network during training showed that after some initial progress the network ceased learning and so training was aborted. Examination of the results illustrates particularly poor performance for the blue and scarlet mixture recipes. This is caused by the discontinuity in hue angle: values close to 360 degrees are similar in hue to angles close to 0 degrees. Thus colours that are almost identical can have a disproportionately large variation in the hue angle input to the net.

5.3 Experiments using data in CIELab format

CIELab tests used the same data set and conditions as the LCH tests, but with the input in Lab format instead of LCH. Observation of the network during training showed a consistent decrease in error over time. Training was continued for 55000 epochs in order to achieve a low overall error before testing the network on unseen data.

From analysis of the above results it was clear that the LCH format is not suitable for use with this type of network and all further experimentation has used the Lab format for colour measurement.

5.4 Data compression to achieve zero dye concentrations

Although the Lab results show a considerable improvement over the LCH data, the networks performance on the single dye recipes remains poor, with only 24% of predictions resulting in a ΔE value of less than one. This high failure rate was caused by the inclusion of incorrect dyes in the recipies. This occurred because of the nature of the sigmoid logistic activation function (Rumelhart, Hinton and Williams. 1986). Due to the exponential behaviour of this curve at its extremities, it is difficult for the units in the network to achieve activation values close to 0 or 1, as these values require theoretically infinite inputs. Even to approximate to this behaviour requires the network to develop extremely large interconnection weights. To alleviate this problem the dye concentration data was compressed still further and a linear offset added such that the data fitted the range 0.1 to 0.9, where the logistic curve has a gradient not close to zero. This led to a marked improvement in single-dye performance, with only 14.3% of predictions failing (CMC colour difference greater than 0.8). Overall results show that over 77% of the network predictions would give a good colour match (see Figure 3).

Figure 3a: Test [5.4]

Error distribution of predictions

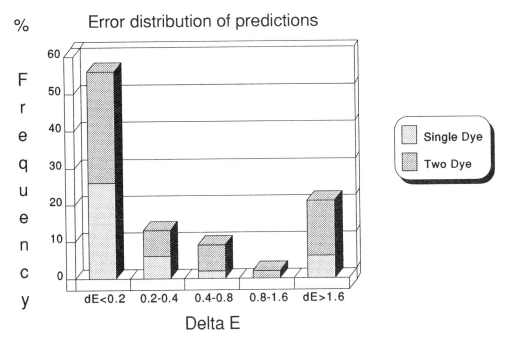

Figure 3b: Test [5.4]

Error distribution of predictions

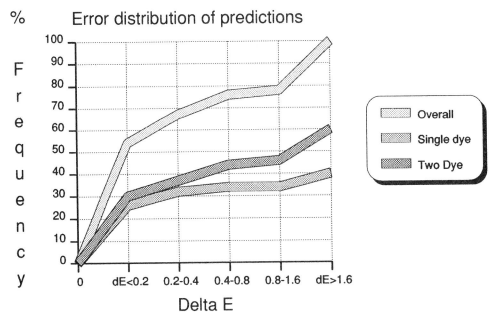

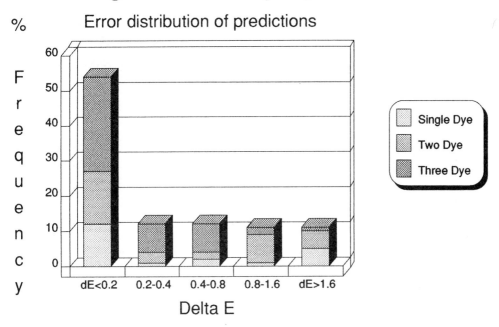

Figure 4a : Test [5.5]

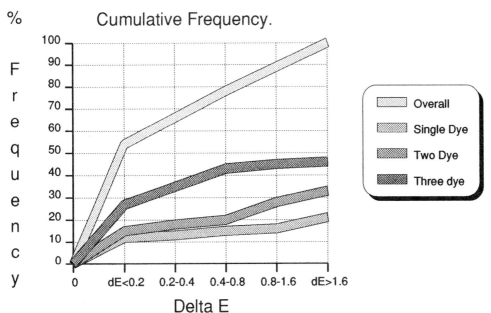

Figure 4b: Test [5.5]

5.5 The inclusion of three-dye mixtures

Using the same techniques describe above, the effect of using a larger training set which included a number of three dye mixtures was investigated. The results for the three dye mixtures were excellent, with only 6.5% of predicted recipes resulting in a poor colour match. However, the two-dye and single-dye performance suffered some degradation (see Figure 4).

6. Conclusion

Initial results using a multi-layer network trained using the generalised delta rule have demonstrated the feasibility of using neural networks for computer recipe prediction and indicate that the technique is worth investigating further. Although the results from the LCH data were poor due to the hue angle problem discussed earlier, the network is capable of successfully learning recipes using Lab format data.

The results from tests [5.4 & 5.5] are very promising, particularly when predicting three-dye recipes. There are still some problems to be overcome when formulating recipes that do not use all the available dyes, as spurious dye concentrations still sometimes occur. However, compressed data gave significantly better predictions in these cases than were obtained in test [5.3]. In commercial systems, not all the dyes available are used in all recipes. Usually a recipe would be formulated using no more than five dyes from a possible group of 20 or more, therefore it is extremely important that a neural network system should produce good recipes when some of the available dyes are not used.

Initial results are promising, resulting in an overall pass rate of over 75%, with most of the failures in the recipes involving fewer than three dyes. If this performance can be obtained with larger scale experiments it would match that of commercial production systems.

7. References

Chandrasekhar, S. (1950). "Radiative Transfer", Clarendon Press, Oxford.

Funahashi, K. (1989). "On the Approximate Realization of Continuous Mappings by Neural Networks", Neural Networks, Vol.2. pp. 183-192.

Ganz, E. (1977). "Problems of Fluorescence in Colorant Formulation", Colour Research and Application, Volume 2, pp. 81.

McKay, D.B. (1976). "Practical Recipe Prediction Procedures including the use of fluorescent dyes", PhD Thesis, University of Bradford (UK).

Rhumelhart, D.E., Hinton, G.E., & Williams, R.J. (1986). "Learning Internal Representations by Error Propagation", in Rhumelhart & McLelland, "PDP: Explorations in the Micro-Structure of Cognition", Vol.1, MIT Press.

Westland, S. (1988). "The Optical Properties of Printing Inks", PhD Thesis, Leeds University (UK).

Widrow, G & Hoff, M.E. (1960). "Adaptive Switching Circuits", Inst. Radio Eng. Western Electronics Show & Convention, Convention Record Part 4. pp. 96-104.

EXPERT SYSTEM TECHNIQUES IN POWER DISTRIBUTION DESIGN

K. K. Kuan
Department of Engineering
University of Warwick
Tel : 0203-523523

Professor K. Warwick
Department of Cybernetics
University of Reading
Tel : 0734-318210

ABSTRACT :

This paper examines the use of expert system techniques in power systems design. The UK 11 kV ring main distribution network is selected as the application because there is a need to replace life expired switchgear within the next few years. With recent advances in technology, many alternative switchgear compete for consideration. The designer is faced with the difficult task of selecting a configuration to meet conflicting objectives of reducing costs and improving/maintaining supply availability. The choice depends on the perceived judgment of the designer on the relative importance of the various factors as cost, reliability, etc. that affects the choice. The design is also dependent on rules of thumb gained from past experience in operation and maintenance of a well developed network. To validate the design, reliability and cost calculations need be performed to ensure the relevant constraints are met. Hence, the design involves making of unstructured (heuristics) and structured decisions. In real world problems, it is not likely that the use of AI techniques (e.g. expert systems) alone would offer a solution. An integration of conventional algorithms for structured type decisions and expert system techniques for unstructured type decisions is thus pursued. A prototype application for a simplified ring network has been developed and results indicate that expert system techniques, when combined with traditional approaches, improve the design process by making the coverage of the design space more comprehensive.

1.0 INTRODUCTION

Design may be defined as the activity where various techniques and scientific principles are used to make decisions regarding the selection and placement of materials/ equipment to form a system or device which satisfies a set of specified and implied requirements. The main requirement of a design would normally be the performance of the task(s) for which the design is intended, irrespective of the many constraints that tend to reduce the size of the satisfactory solution set. These constraints have to be observed and may vary in nature such as economic (e.g. cost), operational (e.g. response time) and physical (e.g. size).

The design of any engineering system is performed by individuals who have acquired through years of experience the necessary technical skills and acumen to innovate competently in their given field of expertise. Many decisions affecting the design are often made intuitively whereas others are based on hard facts, such as results of mathematical formulae. In any decision making, the designer will, often subconsciously, attempt to minimise the amount of computational effort required. This quest for efficiency results in reliable "rules of thumb" being developed. In a metaphorical sense, these are "short cuts" employed in the mental reasoning process. Due to this abstraction, a veteran in the field of design may feel the tasks he performs are mundane, and even trivial. It remains, however, that executing the series of decisions that constitutes engineering design still requires a vast amount of knowledge and computational capacity. This wealth of knowledge is so efficiently stored in human memory that when recalled, the information is often of no obvious formal format or predefined order. Hence, intuitive reasoning, "gut feelings" and "rules of thumb" rather than concrete facts and mathematical formulae, dominate the cortex of a human expert. Indeed, researchers are becoming increasingly convinced that this ill-defined knowledge and its interpretation is what constitutes true intelligence. It is this form of "data" that expert systems use so well.

The electricity supply industry in UK today is faced with a variety of problems related to availability of expertise which could be alleviated by using an expert system approach. There is a concern of the retirement of employees and subsequent loss of expertise, much of which is not found in literature or textbooks. Operation and maintenance of complex and costly equipment often require the availability of an expert. Thus, disessimination of rare expertise, more effective and efficient use of the human expert, and the formalisation and clarification of knowledge are motivations for using expert system techniques.

It need be recognised, however, that expert systems development is not a panacea for all problems. Such an approach is only viable for ill-structured problems where the available knowledge is often sparse, fragmented and of experimental or heuristic origin. The process of gathering human expertise and encoding it is time consuming and expensive. But where returns on investment is high, where human expertise is scarce or being lost, or when the expert is needed simultaneously in different places; expert systems development is justified.

2.0 ELECTRICITY DISTRIBUTION SYSTEM DESIGN

The UK 11kV electricity distribution network has evolved over the last few decades to one of the most complex power systems in the world. Typically, the distribution system comprises a 415/240 V network supplied from 11kV/415V substations. 11kV distribution feeders, each supplying about ten or twelve such substations, emanate from primary substations which are supplied at 33kV, 66kV or 132kV. To afford supply security, especially in areas of high load density, looped or ring networks are used. These ring networks are operated as radial systems by leaving one isolating switchgear near the centre of the ring open (Figure 1) . The most common switching and isolating switchgear used at the substations is the ring main unit (RMU). The incoming 11kV feeders are provided with load-breaking disconnectors, with the transformer connected to the ring system through a load-break switch in series with a current-limiting fuse. The switch-fuse arrangement protects against a transformer fault and can disconnect a faulted transformer without breaking the 11kV ring-main cable interconnection. (Figure 2).

A large percentage of these ring main units will need to be replaced within the next few years. The replacement of life-expired switchgear presents the opportunity to re-appraise old concepts of network design and operation in the light of latest technological advances in both techniques and equipment. Replacement of 'like' for 'like' units is questionable and discussion as to the future form of the 11kV distribution network [1-6] is considerable. Proposals vary from more use of 'teed' connection to the ring main feeder to utilising various degrees of 'alternative' switchgear types [1-6] which resemble the RMU in basic operational facilities. A new form of radial feeder protection [22] at the primary substations permits the discarding of fuse protection at the transformer, hence enabling simpler forms of switchgear to be used. In this paper two alternatives to the RMU are considered, the ring disconnect unit (RDU) and the switch disconnector (Sw Dis) (Figures 3 & 4). The RDU replaces the traditional isolating switch by a plug type connection. The ring network need to be rendered 'dead' for the plugs to be removed or plugged-in. The switch disconnector provides only one isolating switch to the ring main feeder, hence reducing the number of switches. However, again this requires the entire ring to be 'dead' for any isolating operation.

The aims of design change considerations are the minimisation of capital investments and operating costs whilst improving or maintaining current standards of supply reliability. Obvious financial benefits could be realised be employing new, improved, simplified, maintenance-free, less costly switchgear (e.g. RDU) and/or reducing the numbers and duty of such switchgear in the network. Considerations of remote fault location and automatic switching used in conjunction with new and simpler switchgear for better network operations are also attractive propositions.

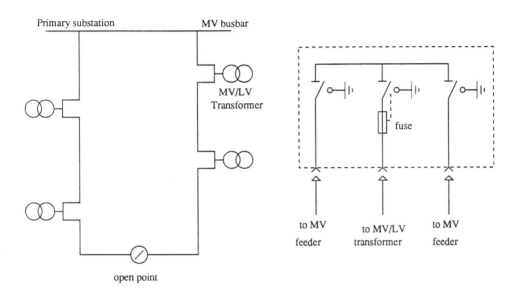

Fig. 1 Looped Network Arrangement

Fig. 2 Ring-Main Unit

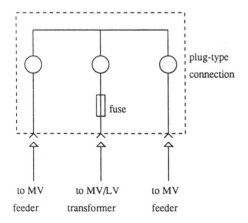

Fig. 3 Ring-Disconnect Unit

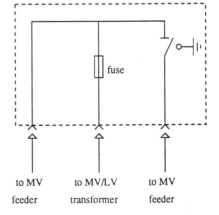

Fig. 4 Switch-Disconnector

Hence, with the many options available, the designer is faced with the complex task of selecting switchgear to meet the above, often conflicting, objectives. The design of distribution networks depends on data of the various types of consumers, on measurements and experience from existing systems with similar mixes of consumers, as well as the designer's local knowledge and experience. The selection of switchgear therefore depends on the designer's judgement of the relative importance of the various factors such as cost, reliability, maintenance, etc., that affects the choice for a particular substation supplying a type of load (e.g. industrial or domestic). Certain "rules of thumb" developed from years of experience with network operations also affect the decision. If the design was to be thought of in terms of a particular consumer, or group of consumers, at a particular time, there would be a specific switchgear (and cables and size of transformer, etc.) which would minimise the cost of the network. However, this would result in a great variety of different equipment being used within the power distribution network. Two main factors act against this approach : the necessity for carrying replacement stock and the commercial advantage of buying in bulk. This provides an incentive towards working in terms of certain adopted 'standard' equipment within each supply authority, nationally and, to some extent, internationally. The goal of network design being optimisation of overall network cost and performance, the choice of switchgear for any substation must be reviewed against those for other substations in the ring network. This implies the decision making process to be an iterative one.

Hence, the design or re-design (or design improvement) problem in our case, begins with a process of synthesis; of generating initial concepts from which the design will evolve. Rules formulated by experienced designers/system planners can be used to produce the preliminary design(s) for more detailed synthesis and evaluation. Knowledge for further synthesis and evaluation are often rule-driven and can be captured in expert systems.

3.0 ADOPTION OF EXPERT SYSTEM APPROACH

The heuristic nature of the design decision process lends itself favourably to a solution using expert systems. Many applications of expert systems to various power systems problems have been reported [7-13]. However, unlike most of these systems where an expert system is used to solve much of the entire problem, we believe that the utility of expert systems lies in the augmentation of "unstructured" decisions within a problem [27]. The more "structured" part of the problem should be solved, whenever possible, by conventional algorithmic techniques. The reason for this, as noted by other expert systems practitioners, is that for most real world problems, the application of artificial intelligence techniques (e.g. expert systems) alone is insufficient to solve the problem. Typically, they need to be augmented by well established techniques in the problem's particular field (e.g. signal processing, pattern recognition, etc. [28]). This is exemplified by the power distribution system design problem. The process may be represented in Figure 5.

The initial step involves deciding how each substation is to be connected to the ring main feeder. Each substation may be "teed-off" from the ring main feeder or "looped-in" with the ring main feeder. This unstructured decision is made using rules formulated by experts in the fields of planning, operation and construction of the distribution network. These rules takes into consideration the various aspects of costs, operation and reliability of supply of the system. For example,

rule 1 (operational consideration)

IF station_load is greater than 1000 kVA
THEN type of connection is teed

rule 3 (supply reliability and cost consideration)

> IF low voltage feedback is adequate
> AND route length is less than 50 m
> THEN type of connection is looped

The result of this inference process would be a "skeleton" design of the ring main network. This design can then be further synthesised by examining the rules to decide the best choice of switchgear for each substation.

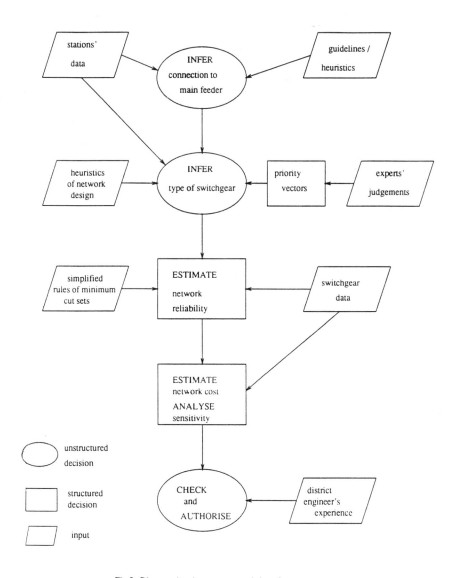

Fig 5   Diagram showing process consisting of
structured and unstructured decisions

To select the best choice of switchgear, it is necessary first to translate the designer's judgement on the relative importance of the factors affecting the choice of the switchgear into a prioritised set of 'alternative' switchgear types. To do this, the analytical hierarchy process [14] is used. This method is useful to model problems incorporating knowledge and judgements in such a way that issues are clearly evaluated and prioritised. The process reflects an apparently innate mental process. When presented with many elements comprising a complex situation, the human mind collates them into groups according to whether they share certain properties. This model of the mind allows a repetition of this process in that the identifying common properties are considered as the factors of a new level in the system. These factors may, in turn, be grouped according to another set of properties, generating the factors of yet another level, until a single 'top' factor which is identified as the goal of the decision process, is reached. This system of stratified levels is termed a hierarchy (Figure 6). The essential issue is the strength with which the individual factors of the lowest level influence its top factor, the overall goal. Since this influence will not be uniform over the factors, there is a need to identify their priorities. This determination of priorities of the lowest factors relative to the goal can be reduced to a sequence of priority problems, one for each level. Each priority problem can then be reduced to a sequence of pairwise comparisons.

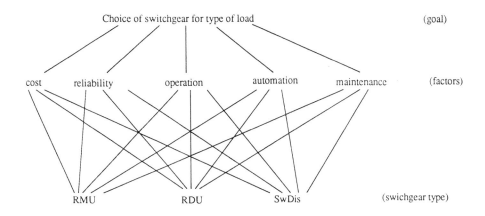

Fig. 6 Example of a hierarchy

In its most elementary form, the process determine priorities by setting the factors of one level of the hierarchy in matrix form. These factors are then compared pairwise in their strength of influence on one factor in the next higher level. A scale of 1 - 9 is used for comparisons, with 1 being representative of equal importance and 9 representative of one factor being of absolutely more important in influence than the other. The number reflecting the comparison is inserted in the appropriate row/column of the matrix. The computation of the normalised principal eigenvector of the matrix results in the vector of priority ordering. For example, for the bottom level of the hierarchy shown :

Cost	RMU	RDU	Sw Dis	E-vector
RMU	1	1/5	1/7	0.067
RDU	5	1	1/5	0.219
Sw Dis	7	5	1	0.714

Hence, with cost as the factor of choice consideration for switchgear selection, the switch disconnect (Sw Dis) type of switchgear commands the highest priority. To arrive at the overall priority vector which takes into account all the various factors, the normalised product of the prioritised vectors for the bottom level and that of the higher level is obtained :

	C	R	O	A	M	choice	E-vector
RMU	0.10	0.11	0.93	0.70	0.09	0.84	0.49
RDU	0.39	0.94	0.10	0.10	0.94	0.40	0.93
SwDis	0.91	0.33	0.35	0.70	0.33	0.24	1.17
						0.18	
						0.20	

The normalised overall priority vector is then :

$$
\begin{array}{ll}
\text{RMU} & 0.19 \\
\text{RDU} & 0.36 \\
\text{SwDis} & 0.45
\end{array}
$$

In essence, the analytical hierachy process is similar to Kelly's personal constructs theory [29] which is widely used in knowledge acquisition of expert systems. However, the computation of priority vectors in the analytical hierachy process enables a mathematical approach to the problem of choosing an alternative which most strongly fulfills the entire set of goals. The method thus enables the coding of unstructured judgements of the expert(s) as knowledge in the expert system.

The vectors thus arrived at for the different types of load (e.g. industrial, domestic, commercial, etc.) are encoded into the knowledge base and used together with the rules of network design and operation to infer the best choice of switchgear type for each substation. For example,

rule 6
　　　　IF type_of_connection is teed
　　　　THEN switch_selected is not RDU

rule 9

　　　　IF consumer_type is industrial OR commercial
　　　　THEN switch_selected is not RDU

Having thus inferred the network configuration, the design need be evaluated for its reliability to ensure that the required supply availability is met. Many different ways are used to judge the reliability of a given distribution network. One is to state certain specific engineering requirements, e.g. a failure at any primary substation may not cause a fatal outage for any consumer or that each substation must have an alternative feeding path. Another is to locate the critical consumers and determine the maximum expected annual outage time for each. Yet another would be to compute the estimates of outage periods for each consumer and assess these from either the utility's or consumer's point of view.

The last approach was adopted and the value for the customer costs associated with outages is considered as a cost component. Hence, the most important factors to be considered are the expected annual outage rate and outage time for individual substations, and their total value in the inferred network configuration, and combination of network components. The solution seeks to estimate the influence of each selected switchgear on the outages at each substation. Both the reliability parameters for the switchgear selected/used and their location in relation to the paths from the feeding points to the substation must be taken into account.

A suitable method for this estimation is based on the determination of minimal cut-sets [17]. This method is valid for partially meshed but radially operated distribution networks. Only active failures are considered as most component failures are of this type (e.g. short circuits). The first-order minimal cut-sets of both the normal and backup feeding routes are determined for each substation. This is a minor approximation as simultaneous independent failures are rather rare. Using simple rules, the influence of each switchgear on the unavailability at the load point is determined. For example,

> rule 25
>> IF component is a normal_min_cut_set
>> AND component is a backup_min_cut_set
>> THEN component_outage_time is component_repair_time

From the database of switchgear failure rates, repair and switching times, the estimated number of outages per year and the mean outage duration for each load point can be computed using :

$$\lambda_o = \sum_{i \in I} \lambda_i + \sum_{j \in J} \lambda_j \qquad (1)$$

$$\overline{A} = \sum_{i \in I} \lambda_i t_{ri} + \sum_{j \in J} \lambda_j t_{sj} \qquad (2)$$

$$r_m = \frac{\overline{A}}{\lambda_o} \qquad (3)$$

where

λ_o	: the estimated number of outages per year
λ_i, λ_j	: active failure rate of component
$\overline{A}$	: the unavailability at the load point
t_{ri}	: repair time of component
t_{si}	: switching time of component
r_m	: the mean outage duration
I	: set of components whose failure results in outage time equal to repair time
J	: set of components whose failure results in outage time equal to switching time

Costing of the inferred network design is easily obtained from the data of costs of the various switchgear types. Since the switchgear choice is expressed as a priority vector, a sensitivity analysis of supply reliability of different possible network configurations against cost of each network configuration can also be easily done. Fig. 7 shows typical outputs from the system.

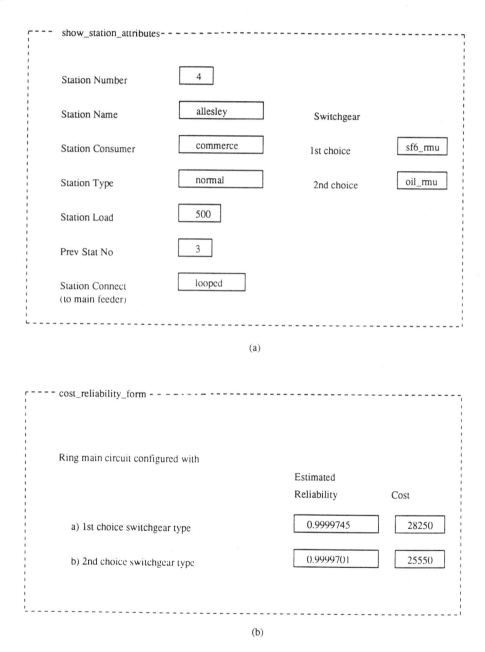

(a)

(b)

Fig 7 Typical Output from system

Hence, it is seen that the embedded expert system components provide the necessary heuristic processes for unstructured decisions, in the absence of human experts, to generate possible solutions which will enable other algorithmic processes to continue in the global problem. It is worthwhile to note that the final "unstructured" decision of checking and authorisation is not automated. The ultimate onus in ensuring the design is adequate lies with the human expert.

4.0 IMPLEMENTATION

An expert system can be constructed with a variety of AI languages such as LISP, PROLOG or by the use of general purpose expert system tools, many of which are available on the market. In developing an application, it is advantageous to use an expert system tool or shell as it allows effort to be centred on knowledge acquisition and encodement, rather than the learning of a new computing language. An expert system shell is basically an expert system with the knowledge base removed. The person developing the system adds the rules, thus providing the knowledge base. The end user of the resulting expert system provides the information that goes into the database or allows information from the knowledge base to be placed into the database. The support facilities of popular commercially available shells often include an editor for this purpose.

In this application, the XIPlus shelltool (Expertech) has been chosen for the following reasons :

- a PC based shell and hence applications developed are easily transportable for
    use in industry
- supports both backward and forward chaining of inference
- comprehensive menu-driven system (user friendly)
- good set of building tools for developing applications
- interface facilities for external programming languages (C, BASIC)
- interface facilities for external packages (graphics, spreadsheets)

Knowledge representation in XIPlus is by production rules and expressed in a form similar to simple natural language. A typical example :

rule 7 :

    IF switch_of_prev_stn *is*   RDU
    THEN switch_selected *is not*   RDU

where the identifier, switch_of_prev_stn   *is* (a relation) given the value, RDU. A negative value can also be declared using the relation   *is not*   as in the consequent part of this rule.

Knowledge can be entered directly in the form of *If-then*   rules using the editor provided by XIPlus. This has the benefit that syntactic errors are being checked as the knowledge base develops and any particular rule may be tested as it is entered into the knowledge base.

XIPlus allows both backward and forward chaining forms of inference and provides a smooth interface between the two. When XIPlus needs to find a certain value to fire a particular rule, it will invoke backward chaining to find the appropriate value by either inferring further data or by asking predefined questions or generate questions in an attempt to obtain the value from the user. Control of the inference by the user can be effected by using facilities such as *if* **done** *then* **check** rules within the knowledge base, or by using direct commands as **force**, etc., or by use of forward chaining rules (demons). Backward chaining is also used by the system to provide explanations to the user during the consultation.

As expert system shells are essentially expert systems developed for particular applications and then made commercially available as a tool without the knowledge base, one is often faced with the need to structure the knowledge and problem to suit the shell being used. This also imposes limitations to the control of the system as has been encountered in the development of the prototype. Primary disadvantages of the XIPlus shell are the absence of an iteration primitive and lack of complex knowledge structures (e.g. arrays). However, these are seen as minor irritations that can be circumvented by careful structuring of demons and rules in the knowledge base. As the system evolves, it may well prove necessary to write a shell dedicated to the application.

5.0 CONCLUSION

Design is a complex process and hence not easy to translate into explicit rules. The challenge lies in successfully decoupling the problem into its knowledge-based and procedural-based components. The knowledge-based component enables heuristics or rules of thumb to be used when a straight-forward analytical approach is not easily available. The procedure-based component allows conventional optimization algorithms and other programming techniques to be used. The difficulty lies in developing rules to include design constraints without compromising design objectives.

Initial trials have revealed the current prototype system output to be inadequate. Studies are underway in the explanation of design constraints and justification of design decisions to the expert for validation. Work is also pursued in the presentation of the results in a more "usable" form such as graphics and tables. All these have fundamental implications on the design of the system architecture, particularly in the area of knowledge representation. However, this paper has demonstrated that the approach of integrating artificial intelligence/expert system and other conventional techniques is useful and has applications to the areas of power systems design.

It is hoped that results and experience gained from the prototype will help to improve and extend the application to include load flow studies, faults analysis, etc. and hence cater for design of the entire power distribution network.

ACKNOWLEDGEMENT

The support of East Midlands Electricity plc (UK) for this work is gratefully acknowledged.

REFERENCES
[1]   Fisher,A.G. & Harpley,R.M.,"HV Urban Network Design - where next ?", Distribution Developments, pp 24-29, June 1985.

[2]   Blower,R.W.,"New Technology for Secondary Distribution Systems", Electronics & Power, pp 329-332, May 1987.

[3]   Michel,A. & Hollingworth,G.,"Ring-main Distribution - witnessing the evolutionary process", Electronics & Power, pp 608-609, August 1986.

[4]   Seed,J.J.,"Developments in Distribution Switchgear", Electronics & Power, pp 600-601, August 1986.

[5]   Wilson,R.G.,"Automation of 11kV Urban Systems", Distribution Developments, pp 15-17, June 1985.

[6]   Wilson,R.G. & McMillan,R., "Automatic Operation of 11kV Distribution Switchgear", IEE Conference Publ. No. 261, pp 74-76, May 1986.

[7]   Lui,C.C. & Venkata,S.S., "An Expert System Operational Aid for Restoration and Loss Reduction of Distribution Systems", Proc. IEEE Power Industry Computer Applications Conference, pp 79-85, 1985.

[8]   Sakaguchi,T. & Matsumoto,K., "Development of a Knowledge Based System for Power System Restoration", IEEE Trans. PAS, Vol. 102, No. 2, pp 320-326, February 1983.

[9]   Russell,B.D. & Watson,K., "Power Substation Automation Using a Knowledge Based System", IEEE Trans. PWRD, Vol. 2, No. 4, pp 1090-1095, October 1987.

[10]   Pao,Y.H. & Liacco,T.E.D., "Artrificial Intelligence and the Control of Electric Power Systems", Proc. IFAC System Security Analysis & Control Conference, pp 2059-2064, 1984.

[11]   Fukuti,C. & Kawakami,J.,"An Expert System for Fault Section Estimation", IEEE Trans. PWRD, Vol. 1, No. 4, pp 83-90, October 1986.

[12]   Taylor,T.,Wall,J. & Lubkemam,D., "Knowledge Based Expert System for Power Engineering Problems", Proc. IASTED, Bozeman, pp 357-361, 20-22 August 1986.

[13]   Sakaguchi,T. et al, "Prospects of Expert Systems in Power System Operations", International Journal of Electrical Power & Energy Systems, Vol. 10, No. 2, pp 71-82, April 1988.

[14]   Saaty,T.L., "Modelling Unstructured Decision Problems : Theory of Analytical Hierachies", Mathematics & Computers in Simulation, Vol. 20, No. 3, pp 147-158, 1978.

[15]   Cory,B.J., "Expert Systems for Power Applications", IEE Review, pp147-149, April 1988.

[16]   Jackson,P., "Introduction to Expert Systems", Addison Wesley, 1986.

[17]   Billington,R. & Allan,R.N. "Reliability Evaluation of Engineering Systems", Pitman, 1983.

[18]   Gower,J.C. & Eason,K.D., "Defining Information Technology Systems for Electricity Supply Distribution", Proc. INTERACT 84, pp 563-569, 1984.

[19]   Hayes-Roth,F., Waterman,D.A. & Lenat,D.B., "Building Expert Systems", Addison-Wesley, 1983.

[20]   Barr,A. & Fiegenbaum,E.A., "The Handbook of Artificial Intelligence", Pitman, 1982.

[21]   Taylor,T. & Lubkeman,D., "Applications of Knowledge Based Programming to Power Engineering Problems", IEEE Trans. Power Systems, Vol.4, No. 1, pp 345-352, February 1989.

[22]   Sanderson,J.V.H. et al, "Remote Detection of Distribution Transformer Faults on 11kV Radial Distributors", IEE Conference Publ. No. 273, Feb 1987.

[23]   Forsyth,R., "Expert Systems", Chapman and Hall, 1984.

[24] Kidd,A.L., "Knowledge Acquisition for Expert Systems", Plenum Press, NY, 1987.

[25] Wollenberg,B.F. & Sakaguchi, T., "Artificial Intelligence in Power Systems Operations", Proceedings IEEE, Vol. 75, No. 2, pp 1678-1685, Dec 1987.

[26] K.K. Kuan & K. Warwick, "An Expert System Aid for Distribution System Design", IEE Colloquium on Heavy Current CAD Applications, London, 30 January 1989. Digest 1989/14, pp 3/1-3/4.

[27] Simon H.A., "The new science of management decisions", Prentice Hall, 1977.

[28] Smith, R.G., "On the development of commercial expert systems", AI Magazine, pp 61-72, Fall 1984.

[29] Kelly, G.A., "The psychology of personal constructs", W W Norton, NY, 1955.

A REAL TIME KBS IN MARINE NAVIGATION

F.P. Coenen
Liverpool University,
Department of Computer Science.
G. P. Smeaton
Liverpool Polytechnic,
Department of Maritime Studies.

Abstract

In this paper the development of a real time KBS to assist
in avoiding marine collisions is described. The system is
designed to produce collision avoidance advice in real time
taking into consideration the location and movement of all
vessels in the vicinity and land constraints.

The system is founded upon a number of knowledge bases
representing knowledge about the collision avoidance problem
domain obtained from international regulations and expert
mariners. Information concerning the current situation is
passed to the system via a number of sensors. This
information is then analysed and appropriate navigation
advice produced. The advice is monitored and if necessary
updated on the basis of a 20 second loop.

The current status of the system is in the form of a
proto-type. Initial testing, in a simulated environment,
using experienced master mariners has produced encouraging
results indicating that, after further development, a
commercially viable system may be produced.

Work is continuing at present to extend the rule base and
to take into account further chart constraints. It is
considered that at present the proto-type system is the first
in its field and that a promising basis has been laid for a
potentially valuable and effective information system for
marine navigation.

1. The Domain

The principal aim of any commercial marine navigation
exercise is to proceed from A to B as efficiently and as
safely as possible. Primarily this involves not colliding
with other vessels or land masses, but it also involves not
causing other vessels to collide or run aground.

The navigation process can be broken down into two stages
(a) planning and (b) execution. The first is carried out
prior to the commencement of the voyage and results in a
passage plan drawn up by members of the ship's staff. During
the execution stage the plan is implemented. This involves a
number of "watch keeping officers" working round the clock in
shifts, sometimes for more than ten days in succession,
ensuring that the plan is executed without colliding with
other vessels.

Collision avoidance is carried out according to a set of
regulations called the Collision Avoidance Regulations
(I.M.O. 1983). However almost daily we hear of collisions and

groundings. This prompted a research team at Liverpool
Polytechnic to investigate the possibility of computerised
decision support for the watch keeping officers, using
current KBS technology. A number of earlier systems, based on
algorithmic techniques had been proposed (Hollingdale 1979).
However these were only partially successful in solving the
collision avoidance problem and hence failed to gain any
acceptance within the industry.

The existence of a set of regulations lent itself to a KBS
application immediately. However the nature of the watch
keepers task, which involved keeping a constant lookout,
meant that a traditional consultative KBS, where the user
answers questions or fills in forms when prompted by the host
machine, would be unsuitable. The system had thus to gather
all the necessary information concerning its domain from
external sensors and relate this to a chart database without
the assistance of the user. Further more the time constraints
involved, a collision can occur in a matter of minutes, meant
that the system had to operate in real time. A user
independent, real time KBS to provide decision support for
the watch keeper when executing a passage plan was therefore
envisaged.

The investigation has now been completed and has resulted
in a prototype advisory system which has been well received
by the commercial navigators on which it has been tested. The
prototype produces navigational advice to avoid collision and
to maintain the desired passage plan or regain the passage
where a departure from the plan has taken place, without the
need for any user interaction. The advice is generated in
such a manner that land constraints and the location of other
vessels in the vicinity and their intended manoeuvres are
taken into consideration.

An interface is provided to allow the user to interrogate
the system or to input further data which can only be
obtained "visually". This input is in the form of a natural
language sub-set which is interpreted by the system through a
simple parser.

The system operates on a 20 second loop and hence the
advice is updated at 20 second intervals. Currently it is
mounted an IBM AT but it is envisaged that it will eventually
be integrated with the hardware that forms an essential part
of many marine radars in use today. The software was written
using Prolog with supporting mathematical routines written in
C and the necessary interfaces in Assembler code.

This paper describes the approach to domain modelling,
knowledge analysis and system development adopted by the
research team to develop a real time, user independent KBS.
Although there are other research teams working in this field
(Blackwell et. al. 1988; Sugisaki et. al. 1988), it is
believed that the system described here is the first in the
field.

2. Domain Analysis and Modelling

The system's domain consists of the ship on which the
system is fitted (ownship), a theoretically unlimited number

of other vessels referred to, for historical reasons but
perhaps unfortunately, as targets and the surrounding land
masses. Information relating to ownship is delivered to the
system via sensors from ownship's gyroscope and log
(speedometer) and its position fixing system.

Knowledge of the movement of other vessels in the vicinity
is made available from radar information in the form of
relative positions, and course and speeds in relation to
ownship. This information is then processed and a unique
description of the movement of all other vessels in the
vicinity made available by allocating two descriptors to each
target and storing them in a database. The two descriptors
are referred to as the Primary and Secondary Status
Descriptors (PSD and SSD). An analysis of the Collision
Avoidance Regulations indicates that the movement of vessels
within the context of the regulations can be uniquely
described using only 10 PSD and 10 SSD combined in 100
geometrically realisable couplings. The possible PSDs and
SSDs available are given in Table 1.

Primary Status Descriptors (PSD)	Secondary Status Descriptors (SSD)
target_overtaking_ownship	clear
ownship_overtaking_target	head_on
ownship_overtaken_by_target	on_collision_course
target_overtaken_by_ownship	crossing_stbd_port
stopped	crossing_port_stbd
target_head_on	passing_to_stbd
target_crossing_stbd_port	passing_to_port
target_crossing_port_stbd	passing_ahead
target_crossed_stbd_port	passing_astern
target_crossed_port_stbd	passing_clear

Table 1: Primary and Secondary Status Descriptors

The use of descriptors provides a simple and concise way
of encapsulating the movement of objects otherwise defined by
a set of numeric values, namely range, bearing, true course
and speed, relative course and speed, closest point of
approach, time of closest point of approach etc. A similar
approach using descriptors was used to describe other aspects
of detected targets, for example the degree of risk
associated with each and whether the target can be expected
to implement a manoeuvre of its own or not.

The degree of risk associated with a target is ascertained
with heuristic guidance based on well documented marine
domain theory (Goodwin 1975) and is described by a pair of
Risk Status Descriptors. Domain theory in this context is
essentially concerned with the theoretical area about ownship
which the navigator wishes to keep clear. The Primary and
Secondary Risk Status Descriptors (PRSD and SRSD) available
are given in Table 2.

Primary Risk Status Descriptors (PRSD)	Secondary Risk Status Descriptors (SRSD)
emergency risk_of_collision_situation close_quarters_situation collision_situation_developing no_collision_situation_exists clear_pass	unsafe safe

Table 2: Primary and Secondary Risk Status Descriptors

The expectancy of a target manoeuvre is described by an Expected Target Manoeuvre Status Descriptor (ETMSD). This is arrived at by considering the view of the current situation from each detected target in turn.

Ownship's location in relation to surrounding land masses is made available using standard Geographic Information System (GIS) techniques (Samet 1984). A chart test area measuring 128 by 128 nautical miles was tessellated down to a resolution of 2 nautical miles, and stored in a quadtree data structure. A square section of this chart area surrounding ownship, measuring 24 x 24 nautical miles, is maintained in a database where the system can interact with it on each cycle. This interaction is achieved using a number of algorithms developed by the research team. The system is therefore always "aware" of the location of near by land masses, if any.

The use of descriptors and GIS methods to model the system domain thus provides the system with an accurate description of the current situation. The design of the descriptors is such that they can be easily utilised by the system's knowledge base when generating solutions to collision situations.

3. Knowledge Analysis

The Collision Avoidance Regulations are the primary source of information from which the KB was constructed. However these regulations are subject to a substantial amount of interpretation. There are several reasons for this:-

a)   The regulations concern themselves primarily with two ship encounters only.
b)   The definitions within the regulations are often ambiguous.
c)   Open textured terms such as "in good time", "substantial" and "safe distance" are often used.
d)   The possibility of land constraints are not specifically considered.

The interpretation of the regulations, a process described in the maritime industry by the term "good seamanship", could

therefore only be obtained by interviews with expert
mariners. These were freely available to the research team
from two sources. Firstly in the form of professional
navigators following Department of Transport (D.Tp.)
professional courses within the Department of Maritime
Studies at Liverpool Polytechnic. Secondly in the form of
those staff members of the Department considered qualified by
the D.Tp. to teach on these courses.

   Further sources of information included a large amount of
data obtained from the Polytechnic's marine radar simulator
and existing well documented legal cases involving marine
collision. The simulator data had been collected over a 10
year period and consisted of hard copies describing some 60
diverse scenarios each of which had been run on as many as
100 different occasions. An analysis of these print-outs
provided the research team with a ready set of test
scenarios. These were then augmented by further scenarios
obtained from information contained in the documented
collision cases.

4. System Development

   The system was developed following the standard KBS or
experimental software life cycle paradigm (Figure 1).
Initially a sub-set of the problem domain was considered,
namely two-ship encounters, and a solution generated. The
result was then analysed and subjected to the critical
appraisal of experienced mariners. Development then continued
by expanding the domain in stages to include multi-ship
encounters, restricted visibility and chart constraints.

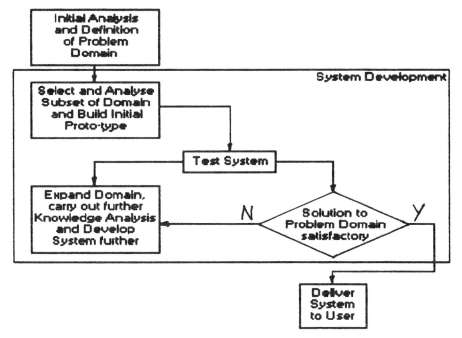

Figure 1: The KBS or Experimental Software Life Cycle

4.1 Two Ship Encounters

The first step was thus to consider the analysis and description of individual two-ship open water encounters, in clear visibility. In previous systems which attempted to provide a computer solution to the marine collision avoidance problem this had been carried out mathematically, a method that did not lend itself readily to incorporation in a rule based formalism. An alternative method was thus required. Mariners themselves use a nautical jargon based on natural language to describe individual situations. As the intention of the system was to emulate these experts a similar approach was adopted. This gave rise to the domain modelling techniques using the descriptors described above.

All possible two-ship encounter descriptions were then analysed and matched with appropriate broad Collision Avoidance Base Actions, assuming that the targets themselves were non-malevolent and that they would abide by the Collision Avoidance Regulations. The result of this analysis was the production of a Two-Ship Encounter Knowledge Base.

The possibility that a target might not behave as required by the Collision Avoidance Regulations was also considered and a second Encounter Knowledge Base constructed for use in these "emergency" situations. To guide the selection of the appropriate rule base a top level Preliminary Advice Knowledge Base was included.

The system also had to advise the user on how best to resume the passage plan once a collision avoidance action had been successfully completed. Another Knowledge Base was thus produced, reference to which resulted in a Return Action designed to cause ownship to resume her passage plan. It was

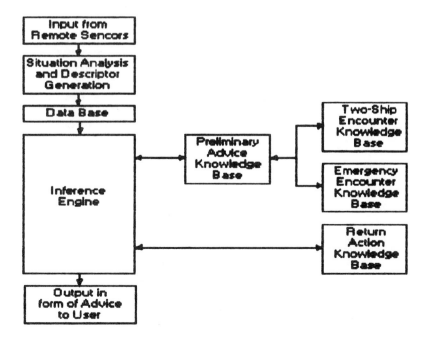

Figure 2: Architecture for Two Ship Encounter System

observed that this action would also be appropriate where
ownship had "wandered" off course and thus a course
monitoring ability was included in the system.
     A series of tests carried out at this stage showed that
the system could successfully resolve every two ship
encounter put to it. Although this level of success was also
achieved by earlier systems using algorithmic methods, it was
encouraging that a knowledge based approach resolved the two
ship problem successfully so early in the study. The
architecture of the system at this stage is given in Figure
2.

4.2 Multi-Ship Encounters

     A system that can resolve clear visibility, open water,
two ship encounter situations however is of little practical
value. Multi-ship encounters were thus considered next.
Initially it was assumed that in a multi-ship encounter none
of the targets would themselves manoeuvre. The aim of the
advice produced at this stage was thus to avoid simultaneous
and/or sequential encounters and not to impede the passage of
any other targets. This was produced using a generate and
test technique. A Collision Avoidance Base Action was
generated for the most hazardous target as if it were a two
ship encounter. The efficacy of this action was then tested
on each additional target. If successful the solution was
accepted and output to the user in the form of advice.
Otherwise a new solution was generated and the test procedure
repeated. This sequence continued until an appropriate
solution was arrived at. If necessary a default emergency
action, which could not be rejected, was selected.
     The identification of the most hazardous target was
carried out using a set of heuristics based on a number of
numeric factors such as the relative speed of targets, angle
of approach and location. The establishment of risk levels is
of course very subjective. However the identification of a
most hazardous target in this case served only to provide the
system with a suitable starting point for the generate and
test sequence and to reduce the solution generation time
required. An alternative target could just as well be used
for this purpose, but the generation time may be
substantially extended.
     To accommodate the need for alternative actions the
Standard and Emergency Encounter Rule Bases were extended so
that as many as eight alternative Base Actions, culminating
in a Default Action, were available for each individual
situation type. It also became apparent that some Collision
Avoidance Base Actions selected for the most hazardous target
would obviously be unsuitable when tested on additional
targets. These situations were identified and formulated into
a set of Collision Avoidance Heuristics to guide the
selection of an appropriate Base Action and so avoid
unnecessary processing.
     It was also discovered that the most direct return actions
initially designed to return ownship onto passage after a two
ship encounter were not always suitable in a multi-ship

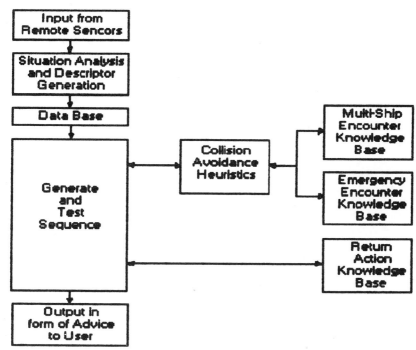

Figure 3: Architecture For Multi-Ship Encounter System

encounter. Hence the Return Action Rule Base was also expanded so that alternative actions were available for each of the most direct actions.

Further tests, including the simulation of a number of reported collision cases, showed that the system at this stage could cope successfully with simple multi-ship encounters (Smeaton, Bole & Coenen 1988; Coenen, Smeaton & Bole 1989). Thus the extension of the rule based approach indicated a level of success surpassing previous work in the area.

However the tests also showed that in most multi-ship encounters the Collision Avoidance Regulations would require that at least one of the targets also take avoiding action. This led to consideration of an alternative view of the situation to determine likely manoeuvres on behalf of detected targets. These were described using the ETMSD described previously. This was the second major departure from all previous work. Information concerning the likely manoeuvres of neighbouring targets allowed for further expansion of the Encounter Rule Bases, the Collision Avoidance Heuristics and the Return Action Rule Base, and for the introduction of further Collision Avoidance Base Actions.

Consideration of the alternative view also led to a further concept, that of courtesy manoeuvres. These were manoeuvres to be implemented when ownship was not in an encounter situation but a neighbouring target was and hence could be expected to manoeuvre. This was a consideration that would also be taken into account by expert mariners. The courtesy manoeuvre concept was thus applied to the Standard Encounter Rule Base and Collision Avoidance Heuristics by

including an option to implement early Collision Avoidance
Base Actions designed to create more sea room for
neighbouring targets where applicable.

The system's architecture expanded to include multi-ship
encounter requirements, is given in Figure 3.

4.3 Restricted Visibility

The next stage was to consider the special requirements
contained in the Collision Avoidance Regulations concerning
encounter situations in restricted visibility. In a two-ship
encounter in clear visibility, depending on the geometry of
the situation, the Regulations require either both ships to
give-way or one to give-way while the other stands-on, i.e.
maintains course and speed. In restricted visibility the
obligation to stand-on is removed. Thus a further knowledge
base was required. This resulted in the creation of a
Restricted Visibility Standard Encounter Knowledge Base and a
set of associated Restricted Visibility Collision Avoidance
Heuristics to be used in conjunction with this rule base.

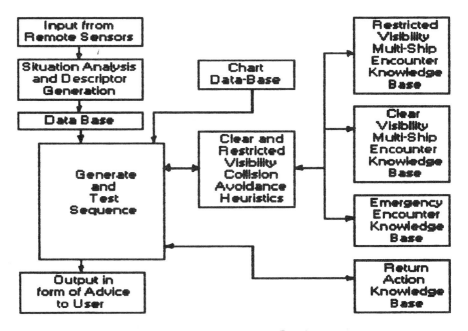

Figure 4: Architecture For Proto-Type System

4.4 Chart constraints

The third major improvement on previous work was the
inclusion of geographic constraints. Due to the limited
amount of research time available at this stage the method of
taking these constraints into account was only considered in
outline. The limited amount of testing carried out however
showed that the system could interact intelligently with
chart information and produce navigation advice that took

into consideration the presence of chart features such as
land masses and shallow water areas.
    The final architecture for the proto-type system at its
current state of development is given in Figure 4.

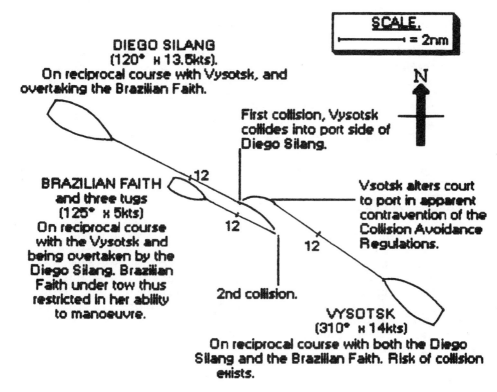

Figure 5: The Vysotsk (1981)

5. Operation

    The operation of the system described here can best be
described using an example. Figure 5 shows a typical multi-
ship encounter involving three vessels (the numbers on the
target track lines indicate time in minutes). The scenario is
actually based on the well documented case of The Vysotsk
(1981). In this case the cargo liner Vysotsk was meeting
another vessel, the Diego Silang, which in turn was
overtaking a third vessel, the tanker Brazilian Faith which
was under tow and therefore unable to manoeuvre. Any
starboard alteration on behalf of the Diego Silang was thus
limited by the presence of the Brazilian Faith. No
satisfactory explanation of the movements of the Vysotsk was
provided at the enquiry; however the evidence showed that she
eventually altered course to port in apparent contravention
of the Collision Avoidance Regulations and collided with the
Diego Silang. The latter vessel, disabled, then veered round
to starboard and was involved in a second collision with the
Brazilian Faith (Holdert & Buzek 1984).

Testing has shown that the resulting three-way collision could have been avoided if either the Vysotsk or the Diego Silang, or both were fitted with the system. If we consider the scenario from the point of view of the Vysotsk first the system will describe the other two vessels using the PSD and SSD pair:-

reciprocal_course head_on.

The Brazilian Faith would be considered the most hazardous and reference to the Base Strategy Rule Base will result in a starboard course alteration. This strategy will then be passed to the generate and test sequence where it will be accepted on the first iteration and thus output to the user.

If we now look at the scenario from the point of view of the Diego Silang the Vysotsk will be described by the PSD and SSD pair:-

reciprocal_course head_on

and the Brazilian Faith by the pair:-

ownship_overtaking passing_to_starboard

In this case the Vysotsk is considered to be the most hazardous and reference to the Base Strategy rule Base will result in a starboard course alteration. This will then be adjusted during the generate and test sequence so that it is implemented earlier than initially envisaged to take into consideration the presence of the Brazilian Faith. The resulting advise to the Diego Silang then consists of an early course alteration to starboard to avoid collision with the Vysotsk and designed to pass round the stern of the Brazilian Faith.

The out come if both the Vysotsk and the Diego Silang were fitted with the system is indicated in Figure 6.

6. Conclusions

During testing the system described here has produced encouraging results demonstrating its potential to become, in the fullness of time, a major aid to navigation. The system's success can be attributed primarily to the KBS techniques used to represent knowledge about the Collision Avoidance Regulations and the use of GIS methods to represent chart data. This gives the system access to a substantial amount of information concerning the solution of collision situations much of which could not be considered by previous systems. The result is that the system can produce practical navigation advice where necessary that takes into consideration the constraints imposed by the situation at hand.

Further development is currently being carried out in the form of further testing and expansion of the knowledge bases. Work is also progressing on the chart database and the intelligent interaction with this databases.

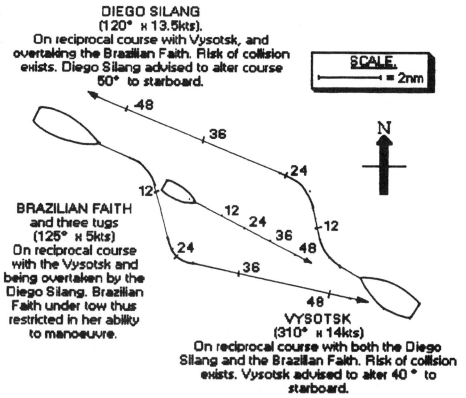

Figure 6: The Vysotsk   (1981), System fitted to   both Vysotsk and Diego Silang

REFERENCES.
1.   Blackwell, G.K., Colley, B.A. & Stockel, C.T. (1988). An
     intelligent Knowledge Based System for Marine Collision
     Avoidance. Maritime Communications and Control Conference,
     Inst. Mar. Eng., London.
2.   Coenen, F.P., Smeaton, G.P. & Bole, A.G. (1989).
     Knowledge-Based Collision Avoidance. J. of Nav, Vol 42.
3.   Goodwin, E. (1975). A Statistical Study of Ship Domains.
     Unpublished CNAA Ph.D. Thesis, City of London Polytechnic.
4.   Holdert, H.M.C. & Buzek, F.J. (1984). Collision Cases,
     Judgements and Diagrams. Lloyd's of london Press.
5.   Hollingdale, S.H. (ed) (1979). Mathematical aspects of
     Marine Traffic. Academic Press.
6.   I.M.O. (1983). The International Regulations for
     Preventing Collisions at sea.
7.   Smeaton, G.P., Bole, A.G. & Coenen, F.P. (1988). A Rule
     Based System for Collision Avoidance. International
     Conference on Maritime Communications and Control, Inst.
     Mar. Eng., London.
8.   Sugisaki, A.M., Imazu, H., Tsuruta, S., Inaishi, M. &
     Matsumura, H. (1988). Expert Systems for Coping with
     Collision Avoidance and the "Ex Post Facto" at Sea.
     Conference papers of the International Navigation
     Congress, Sydney, February 1988.

REAL TIME EXPERT SYSTEMS IN THE COGSYS ENVIRONMENT

Tony Morgan
SD-Scicon
Pembroke House
Pembroke Broadway
Camberley
Surrey GU15 3XD

Abstract

COGSYS is a comprehensive real time expert system tool, developed over a period of three years for a consortium of 35 major international organisations. This paper discusses the methods available for the construction of application systems within the COGSYS development environment.

Knowledge is represented through a specialised Knowledge Representation Language (KRL). This has a syntax which is slightly unusual for an AI language. It deliberately sets out to provide a modern block-structured style. Processing is organised in units which can be scheduled under control of the knowledge base itself. A particularly important and innovative feature is the use of temporal windows to represent quantities whose values vary during system operation. This supports reasoning with time-varying quantities and the maintenance of dynamic justification links.

External input and output is handled through a General Purpose Interface (GPI), which can be configured by the developer to match the needs of the application. Considerable structuring facilities are provided, both for the knowledge base and for dynamic data. This encourages a modular and easily-maintained design, as well as providing the basis for the real time operation.

1. Introduction

This paper introduces an approach to the development of knowledge based systems for real time applications. Real time processing has been accepted as an important but difficult area for expert systems. Experimental systems have often failed to scale up to realistic applications. The absence of what could be termed 'industrial grade' expert system tools has prevented exploitation of the technology, in spite of its obvious attractions. To address this problem, a group of major organisations formed an alliance to support the development of a suitable technology. The result was a collaborative 'club', of the type pioneered under the UK's Alvey program, under the name COGSYS (for COGnitive SYStem). COGSYS followed an earlier Alvey club called RESCU, which had already demonstrated a practical approach to the problem (Leitch & Dulieu, 1987).

Unlike RESCU, funding for the COGSYS club has been provided totally by the 35 or so member organisations. A sample of the sectors represented includes computer manufacture (*e.g.* IBM, DEC), process automation (*e.g.* Kent, Turnbull), energy (*e.g.* British Coal, British Nuclear Fuels), food (*e.g.* Whitbread, Heinz), chemical (*e.g.* ICI, Kodak), and petroleum (*e.g.* BP, Shell). The members share a common concern over the availability of the technology, and their possible competition in other areas has not proved to be an obstacle to collaboration within the club framework.

The result of the club venture has been the development of the COGSYS product, which is an expert system environment designed specifically for real time applications. This product is currently installed on two club test sites. These are a plant manufacturing laminated plastic bottles at CMB Technology, Wantage, and a synthetic gas production plant at the British Gas Midlands Research Station. The club is initiating a commercial venture to market, sell and support the product from the third Quarter 1990.

For real time use we need to think in terms of an application system: the expert system configured to deal with its external domain. In an industrial situation the external domain is commonly some kind of processing plant which is to be monitored or controlled. A common error is to assume that the main difficulty for real time expert systems is the need to produce results rapidly. While this is true in part, it is not the whole story. The crucial problem in real time systems is the need to respond to external events on an *appropriate* timescale. This is difficult because external events are generally not synchronised to the internal state of the computing system (expert or otherwise), and may occur at any point.

Expert systems generally rely on chains (possibly long chains) of rules to reach their conclusions. It is difficult to reconcile the needs of a systematic inference procedure with the need to redirect attention at random points. Past approaches to building such systems have often relied on fast hardware to remove the problem. If an inference cycle can be completed rapidly, the system can be re-started with new external conditions as part of its initial data. In effect this is fast batch processing, rather than continuous on-line operation, since the plant signals do not affect conclusions during individual inference sequences. Such an approach is perfectly feasible, and real time systems of this type have been built using high powered AI workstations (*e.g.* Knickerbocker *et al*, 1985).

For many industrial applications this approach is unsatisfactory. The high cost of specialised computer hardware, coupled with caution over its long term maintainability and the availability of the specialist staff required, have inhibited many organisations from proceeding beyond relatively small-scale experiments.

A secondary difference between real time expert systems and the more common consultative systems is the continuous nature of the processing; see, for example, Bennett (1987). There is often no final 'conclusion' from the system, since it is interacting with a continuous external process. Most expert systems generate significant amounts of data as part of their inference procedures, in addition to input data from the user. Consultative systems often have relatively primitive memory management mechanisms, which rely on a conclusion being reached before the available storage is exhausted. Such systems are clearly unsuitable for the continuous processing which is so characteristic of real time applications.

In the past, the specialised nature of real time expert system applications presented organisations with a compromise between performance and standards. Generally speaking, most of the development work to date has concentrated on exploring the real time capabilities of expert system technology on fairly small, well contained, problems. A review article by Laffey *et al* (1988) describes many of these experimental systems. The major difficulty faced by developers has been the unsuitability of the available development tools to match the requirements.

The aim of COGSYS is to resolve this problem by producing a comprehensive expert system toolkit designed specifically for real time applications. COGSYS provides a development and operational environment based on conventional hardware and familiar representational styles. This paper provides an overview of the facilities available to support development staff in producing an application system.

2. The COGSYS environment

As Figure 1 shows, COGSYS actually consists of two linked sub-systems.

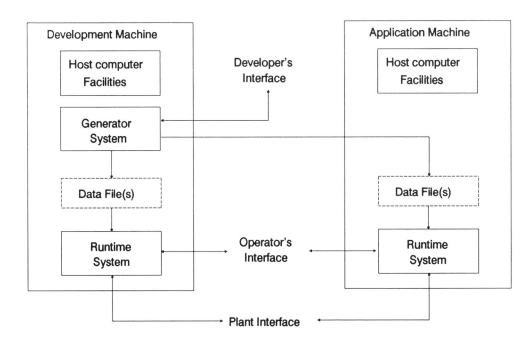

Figure 1. Generator and Runtime systems

The Generator system is used by the application developer to create and refine the application. The Runtime system contains the plant and operator interfaces and the mechanisms for on-line operation. There is considerable flexibility over the way in which these sub-systems can be configured. Both require only industry-standard hardware, rather than the more exotic workstations. The DEC VAX range has been chosen by the club as the initial host system, but COGSYS has been designed to be portable to other machines as required. The current version of the Generator system is written mainly in POP-11, using a heavily modified version of the POPLOG environment (Sloman 1983). The Runtime system is written in C, for efficiency.

The requirements for COGSYS were specified by a large number of organisations. The range of application types envisaged, and the different design philosophies across these organisations, have led to an open approach to development.

- The Runtime and Generator systems can be mounted on the same or on different machines.

- One Runtime application can occupy a dedicated machine, several applications can share one machine, or one application can be spread over several networked machines.

- Development staff can share a single multi-user machine, or can be distributed over several machines.

- The size, structure, and composition of development teams can be varied to suit the type of application and the internal policies of the organisation concerned.

Although applications will differ in detail, their development will follow the same general pattern. Two main tasks are involved in development. One is to define the knowledge base. The other is to define the interfaces used by the Runtime system. Knowledge is coded in a Knowledge Representation Language (KRL). Runtime connections to the outside world are defined in the General Purpose Interface (GPI) specifications. Both of these elements are discussed in more detail below. The end result of the development process is a compiled application system which can be loaded onto the Runtime machine. There is a deliberate 'fire-wall' between the two sub-systems. It is not possible for the Runtime knowledge base to be modified without using the Generator system. This ensures that updates can always be released in a controlled manner.

A number of other facilities are provided to support the developer in more advanced applications. One example is the provision for extending the KRL itself. This requires the creation of external routines which are then bound to a copy of the COGSYS environment. Users can access the new facilities on an equal footing with the normal built-in functions. Another example is the capability for incorporating special handlers, to interface to unusual devices or to provide varying degrees of pre-processing to data from the plant. The relationships between these activities are illustrated in Figure 2.

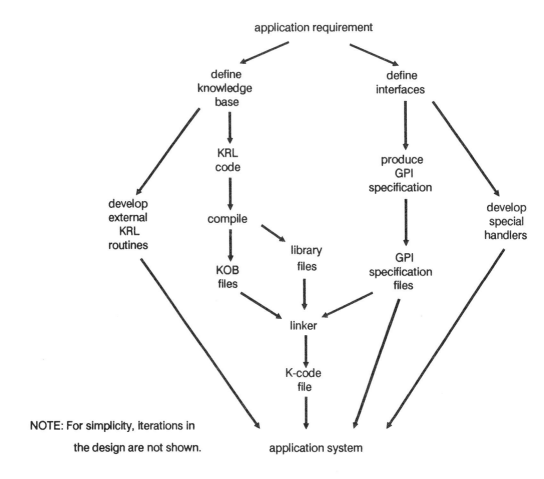

Figure 2. The development process

3. Knowledge Representation

The knowledge base is defined using a Knowledge Representation Language (KRL). The KRL has a block-structured form, superficially looking like modern high-level languages such as Pascal, Modula-2 and Ada. However, its semantic content addresses issues which are specific to real time knowledge based systems. The KRL syntax was deliberately chosen to resemble the languages likely to be familiar to plant and process engineers, who will generally be the application developers. This will ease the recruitment and training of suitable staff. It should also simplify the introduction of COGSYS into most organisations, since the developers can concentrate more on expressing the domain problems and less on adapting to a 'foreign' computer language.

In the design of the language a conscious effort was made to avoid placing unnecessary constraints on the developer, consistent with the need for automatic checking of the final KRL. The language therefore provides a large number of options which can be used to adapt the style of the system to the problem at hand. To prevent these options from becoming confusing to the developer, they are generally provided with default values. This allows them to be ignored unless specifically required for an application. This section provides only a brief overview of the KRL. For further details refer to Morgan (1990).

The basic data units in COGSYS are Cognitive Entities; for brevity, referred to here as 'entities'. Entities are the objects about which COGSYS reasons. They may relate to external data (such as a plant measurements) or may be formed as conclusions from inference procedures. They are defined in the KRL from a number of pre-specified types, which can be extended by the application developer if required. Structures can be defined as aggregates of other types (including other structures). Entities may also be arranged in arrays, each array element being of the same type but individually accessible through its index.

COGSYS provides an important additional feature: temporal windowing. Rather than an entity being associated with a single value (the default case), an entity can maintain a series of values, each relating to a different point in time. These can be defined by the number of past values to be held (*e.g.* hold five consecutive values), or by an expiry age (*e.g.* forget values older than 30 seconds). As entities are updated, the system maintains the values in the correct relationship, 'forgetting' older values which lie outside the temporal window. The values are stamped with a real time and date.

The structures defined by the developer are not constrained to any particular pattern, but it is likely that many applications will adopt a hierarchical structure, mirroring a perceived relationship between the most abstract and the most concrete concepts in the domain. This closely resembles the Blackboard approach (Engelmore & Morgan, 1988), with the structures for different classes of entity corresponding to the levels of the blackboard.

The COGSYS KRL emphasises a structured approach to design. An application system is composed from a number of modules,. In practice, modules are arranged as files in the host operating system. Each module contains a number of blocks. One module contains a special (mandatory) block defining some general knowledge base parameters for general attributes such as the inheritance links to be used. Four other kinds of block are used:

- Demons, which are triggered by the existence of a specified data pattern or event, or at regular intervals;

- Activity blocks, which contain sequences of actions to be performed;

- Rule sets, a package of rules used to infer entity values;

- KRL functions, which are called with arguments and which return values.

The activity blocks correspond roughly to the Knowledge Sources (KSs) of classical Blackboard systems. They form a particularly important structuring device in COGSYS, since they correspond to units of machine scheduling. Activities are allocated priority levels and 'zone' identifiers indicating the range of entities used for input or output.

The zone and priority specifications interact in the following way. If one activity is running, and a second activity sharing one or more of its zones becomes activated, then the system will examine the relative priorities of the two activities. If the new activity is of a higher priority, it will generally force the previous activity to abort. This will present a 'clean' set of data for the new activity. If the new activity is of a lower priority, it is simply detained until the first activity has completed. This default behaviour can be inhibited by the developer, so that an interrupted activity is suspended rather than aborted.

A lower level of system scheduling protects against simultaneous access to the same data item by different activities. Entities are 'claimed' by activities as they are required, and only released on termination of the activity. An activity wishing to use an entity already claimed by another activity must wait until it is released. If the system detects a closed chain of waiting activities, it resolves the deadlock by aborting the lowest-priority activity. More detail on the activities within the Runtime system are given by Morgan (1990).

Both backward- and forward-chaining mechanisms are provided. Backward- chaining ('Infer') is used for a lazy style of inference of entity values. This can be invoked simply by reference to an entity in the KRL. When the value of the entity becomes required, the existing value is used. If the value is not known, the entity becomes the current goal for the backward-chaining mechanism. Forward-chaining is invoked by a built-in function ('Consequences'), with defined bounds to limit the length of chaining (for example, a specific number of rule firings).

The application KRL is developed using a context-sensitive editor, which allows the knowledge engineer to concentrate on the design of the knowledge base rather than details such as the layout of the program text.

The following code fragment gives some idea of the general form of the KRL (but should not be taken as representing a serious fault diagnosis mechanism). Firstly, a new structure ("Pipe"), is defined, with appropriate fields. Three pipes of this type are next identified as cognitive entities and their order defined in terms of a "Predecessor" relationship. The exclamation mark ("!") is used to indicate a reference to a cognitive entity rather than the value of the entity. Finally a generic rule is defined to express the relationship between flow in successive pipes. The intention of the rule is to mark as suspect any pipe with a flow differing from its predecessor. The wild card indicator ("#") is used to bind local values within the rule, *i.e.*, the entities #PipeA and #PipeB will be bound to one of the entities Pipe1 to Pipe3 within the scope of the rule.

```
...
TYPE Pipe :     STRUCTURE
                Predecessor     : DESCR,
                Suspect         : TRUTH,
                Flow            : NUMBER
                ENDSTRUCTURE;
COG Pipe1 : Pipe,  Pipe2 : Pipe,  Pipe3 : Pipe;
/* definition of configuration as Pipe1 > Pipe2 > Pipe3 */
Pipe2.Predecessor  IS  ! Pipe1
Pipe3.Predecessor  IS  ! Pipe2
/* the generic connection rule defines a simple fault detection test */
RULE Generic_Connection
' An entity is suspect if the flow within it differs from its upstream item's flow '
        IF ! #PipeB.Predecessor = #PipeA THEN
            IF ! #PipeA.Flow = #PipeB.Flow THEN
                    #PipeB.Suspect IS FALSE;
        ELSE
                    #PipeB.Suspect IS  TRUE;
            ENDIF
        ENDIF
ENDRULE
... etc.
```

The KRL is checked for syntax (and, to some extent, for semantics) before being compiled into KOB (Knowledge OBject) files, as shown in Figure 2. An intelligent linker produces a loadable knowledge file for the Runtime system by combining KOB files in the appropriate manner. This includes a facility to insert new versions of KOB files into existing applications without requiring the complete re-compilation of the entire application. The lack of this feature limited MXA, a previous real time system (and a remote ancestor of COGSYS) to small experimental applications, in spite of its many other good points. (A description of MXA is given by Tailor, 1988.) The linker also uses definitions from the GPI specification to allow reference to I/O entities from within the KRL.

4. The General Purpose Interface (GPI)

In a realistic environment, any real time application will need to receive input from, and provide output to, the outside world. The problems associated with integrating I/O in a blackboard architecture are described by Hewett & Hayes-Roth (1989). COGSYS deviates from this model by providing a separate General Purpose Interface (GPI).

External data sources and sinks are collectively termed 'devices' in COGSYS. Each device has a custom interface or device handler associated with it. Although devices are external to the COGSYS application, they may reside on the same host machine. Examples would be a process simulator, a database interface, or even another COGSYS application.

Individual data values are termed Points. These cover dynamic data read from a device (or derived from it), data to be output to a device, or static configuration data. Points can be thought of as record structures. Each point can have a number of fields, defined by the developer. The format for each point is held as a 'template', which defines the name of the point (used by the KRL), a textual description, the data format, the number of trended values (see below), permitted ranges or enumerated values for use in validation, and internal data for use by the Runtime system and by the GPI editor. Points are also allocated an access level to control on-line access to the data in the Runtime system through the standard Human-Computer Interface (HCI) provided with the system. For example, a Supervisor may have different access rights to an Operator in a plant environment.

If required, the value of any GPI point can be held as a time series, referred to as 'trending'. This feature in the GPI is used to support temporal windowing in the KRL. The developer can specify the depth of trending (the number of values to be held for each point). The default is simply to hold a single value, which is over-written by each update as it arrives. The specification of trended values creates an appropriate set of buffers in the Runtime system and allows reference to past values from within the KRL. Each value is time-stamped, and it is possible to access values through the KRL either by time or by relative displacement from the current value.

It is often convenient to treat a set of values together; for example, a collection of values which arrive packaged into the same message from a remote sensor unit. A Scan Group is a set of points which are treated as a single unit for input or output. Normally this will be on a periodic basis; for example, polling a particular set of sensors at regular intervals. Groups may also be defined to collect together a related set of points which are to be scanned 'on demand'; for example, through the use of an external function call from the KRL.

The decoupling of I/O processing from KBS operations through the GPI allows asynchronous operation of reasoning and any data input or output. This particularly important since some I/O tasks may require a significant amount of processing. The general scheme for I/O is shown in Figure 3. Each device has its own specialised driver. A typical device in a process plant environment might be a remote Programmable Logic Controller (PLC). Data acquisition is usually triggered under clock control by a scanner, which uses sampling rate information defined in the GPI specification. Input values are held in a double-buffered arrangement, in case the current value is locked by the KBS.

The new values can be pre-processed before storage in the GPI datastore. Examples of pre-processing are filtering of noisy data, derivation of secondary data (such as rate of change from successive differences) and scaling from binary to engineering units. The method of storage of the data (raw and/or processed) is defined in the GPI specification. If a related demon has been specified in the KRL the demon condition is tested, and, if appropriate, a soft interrupt is issued. The locations of the GPI values are available to the KBS, and can be accessed directly

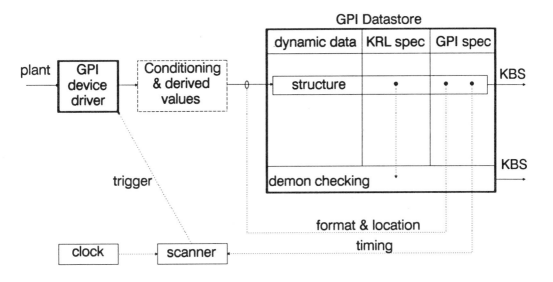

Figure 3. Real time I/O

without any need to copy into the KBS datastore. This, coupled with the dynamic memory management procedures, provides efficient I/O handling. A buffered form of interrupt is also provided, so that the KBS can be alerted to important external events without polling, and without unnecessary disruptions to sensitive chains of reasoning.

Each COGSYS application will have a GPI configuration defined as part of the development process. The Generator system provides tools to support this activity. GPI configuration data is held in a set of files referenced by the application name. The files define the GPI points, GPI devices, and their associated templates. The development can be carried out in a multi-user environment, since COGSYS provides record locking during editing. This encourages the use of development teams, rather than individual developers working in isolation.

Several GPI editors are provided. These are context-sensitive, and adapt themselves to the data being edited. All editors provide a 'form-filling' type of interface, as a way of prompting the user for the data required, and follow a similar screen layout and key usage. Where several similar elements are required, the editors allow existing elements to be read in and used as a basis for creating variants.

In the case of points and devices, the editing is guided by the use of the appropriate template. Templates have their own special editor, which is invoked automatically if the user needs to specify a point or device which does not already have a template. A specialised Scan Group editor is also provided. This is not template driven since the format is fixed by the system.

The preparation of the GPI specification will typically involve the following steps. The order of these may vary between applications.

- Identify all I/O requirements. This should include access to other local automation facilities (such as co-resident databases) as well as plant I/O.

- Decide on the treatment of data from each point. This may be trivial if the treatment is straightforward, but COGSYS allows considerable flexibility in the way in which points are grouped and processed.

- Identify the device handlers required. These may be available as a standard provision in COGSYS, developed by the user for some unique device, or provided by a third party (such as a supplier of process equipment).

- Plan the timing of the I/O, including the periodicity of regular scans and the need for 'on demand' I/O.

- Use the GPI editors to prepare the GPI specification.

Depending on the scale and the nature of the application, these activities may be carried out concurrently with the development of the KBS. This is helped by shared use of a common development resource. For example, GPI specifications prepared by process engineers can be read (but not edited) by knowledge engineers. GPI specification preparation is shown as part of Figure 2.

5. Conclusions

COGSYS has been developed over a period of three years. During that time around a dozen people have been involved in the development, and over 10 man-years of effort expended (not including the time spent by the club members). The development was substantially completed early in 1990, with some tuning work remaining for completion before general release. Early versions of both the Generator and the Runtime systems are now installed on two club test sites. These are a plant manufacturing laminated plastic bottles at CMB Technology, Wantage, and a synthetic gas production plant at the British Gas Midlands Research Station. Limitations of space precludes discussion of the test site implementations; for further details see Williams & Kraft (1989) and Davison & Kraft (1990). Experience from these test sites is being used to refine the system before public release. The club is initiating a commercial venture to market, sell and support the product from the third Quarter 1990.

The main development objective has been the use of COGSYS in operational situations: in factories, power stations, refineries, and other applications requiring time-dependent reasoning. The basic technology of expert systems is well known, and examples can be constructed with a trivial amount of effort using one of the many development tools available. However, hard-won experience has shown the inadequacy of much existing technology in practical industrial use. The aim of COGSYS is to turn the promise of expert systems into operational fact.

Acknowledgements

The results described in this paper are the outcome of a considerable amount of work by the SD-Scicon development team, led by Ryllan Kraft. The COGSYS club has been ably guided by its chairman Dick Peebles over the whole of the three year development period. The evolution of the KRL has been shaped through the efforts of the Technical Sub-Committee of the COGSYS club, headed by Derek Irving, whose efforts are gladly acknowledged. Thanks are also due to Digital Equipment Corporation (in particular Tim Barber) for the generous provision of resources during the development of COGSYS.

References

Bennett, M.E. (1987). Real-time continuous AI systems. Proc. IEE, Vol 134, Pt D No. 4, July 1987.

Davison, S.J. & Kraft, R. (1990). COGSYS: Real-Time decision support for process control. Proceedings of the Tenth International Workshop on Expert Systems and their Applications, Avignon, France.

Engelmore, R. & Morgan, T. (eds.) (1988). Blackboard Systems. Addison-Wesley Publishers Limited

Hewett, M. & Hayes-Roth, B. (1989). Real-Time I/O in Knowledge-Based systems. In Blackboard Architectures and Applications, V. Jagannathan, R. Dodhiawala & L.S. Baum (eds.), Academic Press.

Knickerbocker, C.G., Moore, R.L., Hawkinson, L.B., & Levin, M.E. (1985). The PICON expert system for process control. Proceedings of the Fifth International Workshop on Expert Systems and their Applications, Avignon.

Laffey, T.J., Cox, P.A., Schmidt, J.L., Kao, S.M. & Read, J.Y. (1988). Real-Time Knowledge-Based Systems. AI Magazine, Spring 1988

Leitch, R.R. & Dulieu M.R. (1987). RESCU Revisited: A review of a Practical Expert System. Proceedings of Expert Systems '87, Brighton, UK.

Morgan, T. (1990). Controlling Processing in Real Time Knowledge-based Systems. Submitted for publication.

Sloman, A. (1983). POPLOG - a Multi-purpose, Multi-language Development Environment. Cognitive Studies Programme, University of Sussex, UK, 1983

Tailor, A. (1988). MXA - A Blackboard Expert System Shell. In Blackboard Systems, Engelmore, R. & Morgan, T. (eds.), Addison-Wesley Publishers.

Williams, T.P. & Kraft, R. (1989). COGSYS: An Expert System for Process Control. Proceedings of the Fifth International Expert Systems Conference, London, UK.

ALDACS - A KNOWLEDGE-BASED SYSTEM TO
ASSIST POWER PLANT OPERATION

D BROWN, BSc and T F MAYFIELD MINucE, FErgS
Rolls Royce and Associates Limited
PO Box 31
Derby
DE2 8BJ

Abstract

ALDACS (Automated Leak Detection and Classification System) is a Knowledge-Based System designed to assist nuclear power plant operators in the event of a primary coolant leak. The system has been built as a pilot project, to assess the usefulness of Knowledge-Based Systems in the reactor control room. This paper describes the motivation for building the system, the program structure, and the process of knowledge elicitation. The importance of human factors is highlighted, and the paper brings out the practical measures taken to ensure success in human factors.

1. Introduction

Rolls-Royce and Associates Limited (RRA) is a nuclear/high technology design and consult--ancy company. In 1986 RRA set up a small section to develop Knowledge Based Systems (KBSs). The team has completed several successful projects, including MEEPLES (a system to schedule Company meetings) and friendly front ends for conventional programs. The subject of this paper is ALDACS - an experimental system designed to assist the operators of nuclear power plant.

ALDACS acts as a bridge between the operator and the reactor control and surveillance system, and consists of a data acquisition module, knowledge base, customised 'inference engine', and operator interface.

The objective of using the system is to reduce the work load on the operator under abnormal conditions. Current control and surveillance systems rely on single-sensor alarms: when there is an abnormal reactor transient, many alarms may be tripped, leaving the operators to try and deduce the cause. ALDACS will bring together data from diverse sources, perform deductions, and present information to the operator in a form which can be absorbed rapidly.

Human factors should play an important part in the design of any computerised operator aid, whether built as a knowledge-based system or not. A series of trials has been planned to test and gain user acceptance, and to measure the effect of using the system on operator performance. The trials programme, which is partially complete, includes:

Subjective assessment of human-computer interface by plant operators, amongst others.

Assessment of the performance of the system when connected to a plant simulation. The main purpose of this set of trials is functional testing of the system, but users will be able to comment on 'live' screens, and test the system against their own ideas.

Integrated testing of the system in a full-scale simulator of the reactor control room. This will allow objective measurement of the effectiveness of using the system.

It is hoped that the trials will show that ALDACS improves the speed and accuracy of operator response to (simulated) loss of coolant transients.

2. Motivation

2.1 The problem

Diagnosis of Nuclear Power Plant malfunctions is a very complex task. Much reliance is placed on the operators' knowledge, training and experience. The task is complicated by several factors:

Interaction between plant components, together with the feedback loops present, make it difficult to localise a fault.

Information sometimes has to be inferred from plant instrumentation, rather than being directly available.

An unexpected transient can trigger a large number of alarms, and with modern computerised systems, the trend is to provide an alarm for every parameter. There is a danger that the operators might be overwhelmed by the sheer volume of incoming data.

Stress is a factor which can lead to operational errors.

A good deal of work has been done in recent years to improve the operator-machine interface. Techniques such as grouping of instruments, mimics, and prioritisation of alarms aid the operators' task. However, there is still a basic problem with many control systems. The plant alarms,by and large, are based on single parameters. Information is presented to the operator at a cognitive level which is too low.

2.2 Knowledge-Based Systems

It has been suggested that KBSs might offer a solution to this problem. The general idea is that the KBS should take the stream of plant data as input, and reason on the data to a produce a higher-level interpretation of the plant state.

For example, instead of the operators seeing a profusion of alarms, such as:

Loop - no flow
SG - low pressure
Reactor - low flow
Pump - high bearing temperature
etc.,

they would see the cause of these symptoms:

Pump - unexpected stop

and perhaps a list of recommended actions, such as:

Reduce reactor power
Isolate Loop
Isolate SG

2.3 Project aims

In general terms, the aim of building ALDACS was to test the potential benefits of using a KBS in the reactor control room. In addition, there was a desire to demonstrate the technology, gain experience in specification and project control, and find the problems involved in building a real-time KBS.

2.4 Project goals

In order to achieve these aims, we were set the goal of building a small real-time diagnostic KBS. The system would be connected to a plant simulator, so that we could assess the effect of using the system on operator performance. The KBS was required to cover only a very limited range of the potential plant transients, however.

This 'deep thrust' was preferred to advancing on a broad front for two reasons:

A survey of the literature indicate limited success for systems which tried to do everything. Computer power is too limited to deal with the complexities of power plant, and theory is not able to cut down on the complexity.
The second reason was that given limited resources, more could be achieved. We would run into more problems, and certainly test our ideas harder, by building a specific system, rather than attempting to develop general theories which could not be fully tested.

This section has covered the motivation behind the project. The next section goes on to discuss what has been built.

3. ALDACS Structure

This section outlines the structure and working methods of ALDACS. Hardware and software are very briefly covered, and the simulator connection is mentioned. Programming details and coding are omitted so that the discussion can concentrate on the concepts.

3.1 System hardware and software

ALDACS was prototyped in KEE (Knowledge Engineering Environment - produced by Intellicorp Inc). KEE is a software package which is constructed using the programming language LISP, and has excellent development facilities. The system runs on a Sun 3/60 workstation, which provides a high-resolution screen and WIMP (Window Icon Menu Pointer) interface.

Although it was recognised that KEE was not really suitable for highly demanding real-time applications, it was considered much the best platform for the initial development of ideas. Now that the algorithms have been developed and tested, the system will be rewritten using a software package more oriented towards real time work. At the time of writing, we have not yet selected the package.

3.2 Data acquisition

ALDACS needs data on which to perform diagnosis, and this is provided by a whole-plant simulator via a serial line. A mixture of discrete data (e.g. alarm states) and continuous data (e.g. plant pressure) is fed across. The interesting features of the continuous variables are extracted using a conventional 'C' program. This uses statistical techniques to determine if the parameter is rising, falling or stable, and whether the parameter has stepped up or down in the recent past. The preprocessed data are passed to ALDACS, which uses a customised inference engine to diagnose the plant state.

3.3 Inference engine

The goal of the inference engine is to reason on plant data to form a conclusion about the plant state. What were the problems encountered in achieving this goal, and how were they overcome?

The first point to make is that diagnosis is always a process of abduction. That is, an initiating event will cause certain symptoms. If during plant operation we see the symptoms, can we infer a particular initiating event? The answer is no, not safely: it is always possible that an unforeseen combination of events has caused the symptoms.

A related problem is the possibility of multiple plant transients. For example, a power change imposes stresses on the plant which might cause a leak: the symptoms of the leak, however, are masked by the symptoms due to the power transient.

The third major area of concern is instrument failure. The KBS relies on a large number of different sensors. Even if each is individually very reliable, the odds are that one of the many instruments may be in a failed state.

Given these factors, it is clear that diagnosis involves a good deal of uncertainty. Simple black and white rules relating symptoms to causes are inadequate to the task. Some way of representing the uncertainty must be found.

The approach taken is based loosely on Bayesian logic. Put simply, Bayes' theorem implies that if a fault has a high probability of causing a symptom, and the symptom is rarely found in other circumstances, the presence of the symptom greatly increases our confidence that the fault is present. If the fault only sometimes causes the symptom, and the symptom is often seen elsewhere, the symptom is a weak indicator of the fault. Bayes puts these notions into numerical form.

This, then, is the system used by ALDACS. Each relevant symptom is given a 'weight' in the range -5 to 5, representing the extent to which the symptom helps to indicate or counter the belief that there might be a leak. For example, the symptom 'Pressuriser level falling' would be given a weight of 1 (the pressuriser level falls during a leak, but also falls during many other transients). A pressuriser low level alarm might be given a weight of 4. This alarm is seen during a leak, but is rarely seen at other times. Reactor scram due to abnmormal temperature scores -5, because although it can cause symptoms similar to a leak, it is highly unlikely to be associated with a leak.

In operation, ALDACS adds together the weight of each symptom. If the total score exceeds a threshold (50% of the potential score) the system reports that a leak might be present.

ALDACS makes use of one heuristic, which is that if there is a leak from the primary circuit it must go somewhere. The most likely leak sinks are all monitored, for example containment, the steam generator, and the primary circuit pressure relief valve. Monitoring the leak sinks not only provides independent evidence of a leak, it can also show the operator where the leak is and how to stop it.

4. Knowledge elicitation

Gathering the knowledge to put into a KBS is widely recognised as a difficult problem. This section examines the knowledge elicitation process. Some methods of gathering knowledge are outlined, the methods actually used are described. A summary of the lessons learnt concludes the section.

4.1 Elicitation methods

The 'traditional' method of building a KBS is via a series of intensive interviews with the domain expert. This can work well, but the interviewing process can become long, tedious and expensive. This method tends to be used when the aim is to replicate a specific person's expertise.

Questionnaires to be filled in and returned can be used when a number of people are to be consulted. The main advantages are that questionnaires are more structured and cheaper: the main problems involve misunderstanding of requirements and motivation.

Observation of the expert performing the task is a less direct method of acquiring the knowledge, and can work quite well when the expert finds it is difficult to articulate. This method could be applied by watching the operators handling a simulated leak.

Rule induction from plant behaviour is a possibility. However, leaks are very rare events, and it was not possible to run leak trials. Another option is to observe simulated leaks, but the simulation merely represents the compiled knowledge of plant experts.

4.2 Methods used

We decided to use a combination of questionnaires and round-table discussions. The main reason for this choice was that a number of different people with different areas of expertise had to be consulted. This meant that we had to impose some structure on the knowledge, so that the experts were talking a common language. Cost was also a factor. The following three stage process was used:

First questionnaire. This asked each expert to list all the indications which (s)he personally would use to detect a leak, or to eliminate the possibility of a leak. The expert was asked to consider the primary circuit and the leak sinks (containment, steam generator etc).

Second questionnaire. All of the indications mentioned by the experts were unified into a large questionnaire, together with their possible states. For example, the pressuriser level was listed, and could be rising, stable or falling, and abnormally high, normal or abnormally low. Each expert was asked to weight each symptom (eg pressuriser level falling - weight $+1$) in accordance with the quasi-bayesian scheme noted above.

Round-table discussions. The returned questionnaires showed areas where experts disagreed, mostly about the amount of weight to put on individual symptoms, but also about whether a symptom helped confirm or eliminate the possibility of there being a leak. The discussions were designed to achieve a consensus, by allowing individual experts to convince others that they were correct. Discussions were held with three separate groups of four experts each.

4.3 Results - lessons learnt

Having gone through the process described above, one might expect that the experts would be in broad agreement. Also, one might hope that the information supplied could be used to detect a simulated leak quickly and accurately. In fact a surprising number of disagreements remained, which had to be resolved by the knowledge engineer. The performance of the system in detecting leaks was patchy: some types of leak were detected much more easily than others, and several false alarms were raised. It can be seen that the quality of information supplied was deficient in some respects. What were the reasons for this?

The first point to note is that some leaks are genuinely difficult to classify. A leak to a steam generator, for example, has very little effect on the pressure or water level (the control system tends to compensate), and these small changes are easily masked by a power change.

A second factor is that the model of the knowledge required is very important. A basic assumption of ALDACS is that each parameter can be considered in isolation (at the time of writing). However, the difference between two plant pressures might be much more informative than the two pressures considered separately. Attempting to squash expert judgement into an inadequate model can produce poor results.

A related point is that the model must be expressed in terms familiar to the experts. If this is not done, problems of misunderstanding will become apparent very quickly. It may well be necessary to invent an intermediate model which both the experts and the knowledge engineer understand, and which is translated by the knowledge engineer into machine usable form.

With regard to the experts, it can be difficult to obtain staff with genuine expertise. They tend to be in demand! It is also impossible to obtain knowledge cheaply. Goodwill soon evaporates if one cannot pay for an expert's time.

Finally, it is very important to give people a full verbal briefing about the aims of the project and methods used. Posting a questionnaire does not lead to good motivation, and provides endless scope for unrecognised misunderstandings.

5. Human factors

5.1 Importance of human factors

As noted in the introduction, the acceptance of machine advice by the plant operators is a key issue. It was recognised at the outset that a human factors input was required. Many of the problems relating to operator error stem from an over-technological approach to the design of equipment and systems. Designers have not adequately identified the usability of their designs, and specifications have not recognised user requirements as being an important part of the overall design. Consequently, many software systems have been less efficient, more difficult to learn, and have poor interfaces as a result of a lack of structured human factors input. Martin (1973) was one of the first computer experts to draw attention to the problems faced by users when presented with poorly designed software displays. Since then HCI has become a major element in software system design, with human cognition being an underlying issue of research.

5.2 Human factors and knowledge-based systems

Many human factors guidelines now exist on display design and formatting, covering character size, formation, contrast, colour and so on. However, much of this information relates to office-type systems and is of a very general nature. There is a great shortage of guidelines related to specific applications, especially in the field of expert or knowledge-based systems. We conducted a search of the literature, but the results of the search were generally disappointing.

5.3 Human factors applied to ALDACS

The role of ALDACS, as mentioned above, is to interpret the plant instrumentation and present the operator with an assessment of the plant state. The question for the HCI designer is then how to present the information to the operator. From the available information it was not possible to make definite recommendations as to how this should be done. Therefore we decided to use the general advice available to create some trial screens. Guidelines for future work would follow from the trials. So, what type of interface to use?

At the simple end of the design spectrum, ALDACS could give a text message on screen, for example:

'Primary Coolant Leak to Containment'.

At the other end of the spectrum, the screen could show a full WIMP style interface, complete with mimic diagrams of systems, pushbuttons, highlighting and text.

We considered that the simple text message was not likely to be acceptable to the operators. They would in any case need to check the system's conclusions by referring to plant parameters. Therefore we decided to create a WIMP-style interface, and experiment with a variety of formats round this basic theme.

6. Interface trial design

6.1 Introduction - trial aims

The previous section examined the factors which led us to conduct trials of the Human-Computer Interface (HCI). This section describes how the interface trials were set up, and why. The aims of the trials were as follows:

To determine the optimum display design for ALDACS.

To provide data leading to guidelines for future systems.

Provide operators and contributors with an opportunity to interact with the system.

Standard experimental techniques were used to assess the displays, both quantitively and qualitatively.

6.2 Screen design

Several broad guidelines were adopted when designing the draft HCI screens. These were:

ALDACS should be essentially 'silent' until it is required to alert the operator.

Having diagnosed a leak, the system should provide an active mimic showing where the leak was on the plant, and state the degree of belief in the conclusion.

The system should show the operator, on demand, the evidence it used to diagnose a fault.

ALDACS should be accessible to the operator at all times, for browsing, inhibiting parameters, and checking the plant state.

The system should have a constantly updating display to show that it is operational.

6.3 Factors studied

Given the broad guidelines mentioned, several aspects emerged which required experiment. These were:

Text versus figure to express confidence in a conclusion. For example, is it better to report '80 % likelihood of a leak' or 'Probable leak'?

Is the plant mimic required? A text report too? Or are both required?

What is the best set of colours for the plant mimic, and highlighting? Is colour necessary, or will monochrome do?

Is it best to show a graphical display of parameter behaviour, or is text adequate?

Should the operator be given all the available evidence, positive and negative, or should there be some filtering?

How should the parameters be grouped?

Is it necessary to highlight parameters which help indicate a leak?

What is the best operator input device? Touch screen, mouse, or trackerball?

6.4 Equipment used

It was possible to use the Sun/KEE configuration for most of the experiments. However, there were some limitations, notably the fact that we only had a monochrome Sun. Therefore the trials were split into two. Some aspects of the HCI were tested interactively, using ALDACS as a base, while others were tested on a CAD system. The CAD screens were 'dead', but allowed us to build dummy displays quickly.

ALDACS screens - The basic screen consisted of two windows. The top one gave a text report, which either stated 'No (Primary Circuit) Leak' or gave the diagnosed leak path with its associated likelihood. This window also contained a flashing tile which indicated that the system was working. The lower window showed a primary circuit mimic together with the various possible leak sinks. If a leak was diagnosed, the leak path was highlighted. The user was able to click on a system mimic to obtain more evidence about the diagnosed fault.

CAD screens - The general format of the CAD screens was very similar to ALDACS. The main differences were that colour was used, and the evidence for a leak was presented in a variety of different formats.

7. Trial procedure

This section briefly outlines how the trials were conducted. The trials were organised in two parts, each taking around thirty minutes. Subjects saw the ALDACS screens first, followed by the CAD screens. A briefing note was provided prior to the trials, outlining the objectives and procedure. The experts who had provided the knowledge base were invited to the trials, to give a broad spread of knowledge and capabilities, and also to provide them with feedback.

7.1 ALDACS Screens

Subjects were given a brief introduction to ALDACS and shown how to use the mouse or trackerball. Then the trials were run as follows:

Subject response time - The screens were set up with only the mimic showing. A simulated leak was started. The time required for the operator to make a positive statement of the leak condition was measured.

Descriptive versus numerical likelihood - The text report window of ALDACS was switched on. Subjects were asked to state their preference for a descriptive version of the leak likelihood (possible, probable, very probable) against a numerical version (65%, 85%, 95%).

Mimic 'colours' - Subjects were asked to give marks out of 10 for four variations of component - background shades of grey. The mimic screen was then left in the subject's favourite choice.

Evidence presentation - Various methods of showing the detailed evidence for a leak were presented in pairs for selection. The user saw:

All parameters, or just those which were indicating a leak.
Parameters justified left or right.
Evidence chunked into groups of five or as one long list.
A large window showing all evidence at once but hiding the mimic, versus a small window which had to be scrolled but was clear of the mimic.
Abnormal parameters highlighted by asterisks, versus no highlighting.

User acceptance - The screens were set up according to the subject's preference, and a leak was started. The subject was asked to rate the acceptability of ALDACS, and how confident they would be about using the system. The subject was asked to rate the display in comparison with any other systems they might have seen.

Input device - The input device was changed from mouse to trackerball (or vice versa) during the trials. The subjects were asked to state their preference.

7.2 CAD screens

On completion of the ALDACS trials subjects were introduced to the CAD system. No interaction was required during the CAD session. The trials were as follows:

Default screen - Subjects were asked whether they preferred a mimic, or a simple menu giving access to all parts of the system.

Comprehensibility - The subjects were asked if the mimic page was easy to comprehend.

They were asked to say whether there was too much or too little information, and whether the text was easy to read.

Leak identification - The mimic was displayed in a highlighted state, but with no text display of the plant state. Subjects were asked to identify the status of the plant.

Parameter display - Subjects were shown a window overlaying the mimic, which displayed plant pressures. They were asked to rate in order of preference a graphical display, digital display, or both combined.

Evidence display style - Subjects were asked whether they preferred an ALDACS-style display (text format) or a colour-coded semi-graphical style.

Use of colour - The subjects were asked to compare the grey-scale ALDACS to the colour CAD system.

8. Trials results

8.1 ALDACS screens

There was no problem identifying a leak, with a spread in times from 18 seconds to 3 min 51 sec.

A small majority favoured text to percentage style of likelihood display.

There was a preference for a light grey background with grey components - leak paths being highlighted in white.

A small majority preferred showing all of the relevant parameters rather than just the abnormal ones. The subjects were equally divided on the merits of left-hand or right-hand justification. There were unanimous votes in favour of chunking lists of parameters and highlighting abnormal ones, and a large majority favoured the large display window.

No-one found the information unacceptable, with an almost equal division between acceptable and slight reservations. There was an almost equal split between subjects finding too little information and those thinking it about right. About a quarter said there was too much information. A large majority felt that the display was better than previous systems, with a fifth of subjects thinking the display was much better.

The majority preferred the trackerball input device.

8.2 CAD Screens

A large majority preferred the mimic display to the menu. The mimic was easily understood, with about the right information, and clear text.

None of the subjects had any difficulty identifying the plant state.

The combined digital/graphical display was easily the most popular form of showing parameters.

A full listing of the leak evidence was unanimously preferred, and almost all subjects preferred the colour coded display to the text version. A large majority wished to see a digital readout of the parameter as well as a verbal description.

9. Trials conclusions

The trials showed that none of the subjects found ALDACS unacceptable. Where reservations were expressed, they were more to do with the quantity and quality of the displayed information, rather than the fact that the computer was forming conclusions. No-one expressed any opposition to the idea that their activity could be guided by a knowledge-based system.

The bulk of the trials covered the usability of the system. We obtained a good consensus on most aspects of the HCI. More work is required where opinion was more evenly divided.

We did not perform exhaustive quantitative testing. However, the results we obtained were encouraging. Using the mimic and evidence page, subjects could come to a conclusion within 18 seconds of an alert. The maximum time of just under 4 minutes represented a single attempt to accurately assess the leak conditions from the evidence provided. All subjects could reach a preliminary assessment in less than a minute, with most requiring less than 30 seconds.

10. Conclusions

This section describes the general conclusions we have been able to reach from the project so far. The conclusions are a little tentative, as the project is not yet complete.

The first conclusion is that a KBS can be accepted by plant operators as a useful tool. They will use a KBS as long as it provides useful, understandable, and timely information, and as long as it is not imposed without consultation. Developers should also be aware of the working relationships which exist in the control room. In the field of human factors, it seems that a KBS is much like any other computerised system. The needs of the users must be accommodated if the system is to be a success: ignoring the user is a good guarantee of failure.

Knowledge elicitation can be difficult. The problem can be eased considerably by tailoring the knowledge representation to the experts' vocabulary. It may well be necessary to develop a 'paper' model of the field of interest, and translate the model into a machine-usable form.

The final conclusion is that real-time knowledge-based systems are feasible. A key to success is that the scope of the system must be clear and limited. A KBS which attempts to do everything will in all probability achieve nothing.

KNOWLEDGE BASED SYSTEMS AND SYSTEM ENGINEERING
INTEGRATION IN THE ESPRIT FRAMEWORK
Brice LEPAPE
CEC - DGXIII/A4 - Information Processing Systems
200 rue de la Loi - 1049 Bruxelles

Abstract

Information Technology (IT systems are increasingly penetrating all sectors of human activities: industry, services as well as day to day life of the citizens are more and more dependent on efficient and reliable IT systems, well adapted and integrated to the various needs of our society. Those systems can no longer be viewed as the result of a software development process but as a harmonised integration of the complex relationships between software, hardware and people, both developers and users. This is the system engineering approach where integration, complexity, openess/interoperability, quality and productivity are the challenging issues to be addressed.

Knowledge based systems (KBS) is an emerging generation of software components stemming from the AI discipline. They address applications where solutions cannot be expressed in a deterministic way focusing on the simulation of human expertise and behaviour. Being targeted to the knowledge level (as opposed to the procedural level in traditional software) such systems provide a promising step towards a better integration between IT systems and human activities. After their maturing period, carried out in a relative isolated way, KBS have proved their potential and the time has come to exploit, in an integrated framework, the complementarity of the two approaches. Such an integrated framework can be considered along the following dimensions:
-    From the holistic perspective of System Engineering, a KBS is one of the numerous potential components of a whole system. An evident integration path is therefore to provide the necessary means for such an embedding process.
-    System Engineering itself is a knowledge intensive activity which has been supported until now by traditional software tools with very limited possibilities to deal with this knowledge level. Providing knowledge based tools to support the development process of IT systems will improve the productivity of the developers and the quality of the resulting products.
-    The third line of integration is linked to the change of perspective introduced by knowledge engineering. The possibility to address the knowledge level of an application leads us to contemplate new design and development methodologies embracing a more complete view of the future IT systems, such as a closer integration of the user and a better understanding of the interactions within the system and with its environment.

ESPRIT is a precompetitive R & D Programme in Information Technology supported by the Commission of the European Community, where System Engineering and KBS are part of the Information Processing System Sector.

Numerous ESPRIT projects have tackled one or several of the integration paths described here above. It is anticipated that this step should be emphasised in the near future.

A COMPUTERIZED INTERACTIVE HOLE OPERATION PLANNING EXPERT('IHOPE')[1]

Hans G. Vogt and Per A. Zaring
Department of Production Technology and Department of Computer Science
Chalmers University of Technology, S-412 96 Gothenburg, SWEDEN

ABSTRACT

The report describes a computer supported method to choose tools and operational sequences for hole-machining. Beginning with the specification of the finished hole (diameter, grade of tolerance, surface roughness and workpiece-material) a suitable tool and method is chosen. The conditions for the finishing operation are evaluated (suitable cutting depths, suitable grade of tolerance of the pre-finishing and surface roughness). On the basis of these pre-finishing conditions one or more suitable pre-finishing tools and/or methods are chosen. These tools in turn may need certain pre-finishing conditions. The procedure is repeated until the proper tool has been found for machining the raw part. In this way the operational sequence has been determined according to the tools involved and their working conditions especially cutting depths. Equal to the choice by technical meaning an estimation of machining costs, available tools and machine tools is done. A prototype knowledge based system is presented that handles the issues mentioned above; IHOPE, The Interactive Hole Operation Planning Expert.

1. INTRODUCTION

The hole-machining process consists of a number of working steps and decisions that are to a great extent based on standardized default values referring to *normal conditions* [13] for tools, machines and workpiece materials. The evaluation of a finishing specification for a hole from drawing is a task which requires experience. The more experienced the engineer is the less there is a need for him to rely upon guidelines in the form of default values to make a decision and take an action, i.e. the greater his skill is in handling deviations from the norm. Thus the engineer often makes out his own standards and make decisions on a more *intuitive* basis to meet the situation at hand. He develops a type of *tacit knowledge* [5]. To succeed in formulating this knowledge explicitly and make it more generally available would mean qualitative as well as economic benefits in an operating environment.

---

1. This work is supported by the National Swedish Board for Techical Development(STU)

Our goal is to briefly describe the functioning and behaviour of a computer supported system for choosing tools and operational sequences for machining of holes. In the last section we outline some future research issues that have shown important in order to make the system operationally usable. Qualitative aspects of the application in the primary domain will not be discussed in this paper nor will the detailed architecture be described[2].

2. THE PLANNING SUPPORT SYSTEM

2.1 Basic Components and Characteristics

As a starting point we have used a report that describes a systematic way to manually choose tools and combine them into sequences [12]. In figure 1, the data in the table represent values corresponding to materialgroup **A** only. It shows a data sheet of technical data for manual planning of hole-making operations. In figure 2 there is a correspondent sheet for economical data i.e. relational costs for hole-making operations. Initially this process is rather mechanistic and we therefore have been able to easily translate it into a number of procedures. In addition to automatize these basic steps our intent is to add knowledge to the computer based system that the engineer for the time being does not possess. The quality of the decision process will be enhanced.

---

2. The technical principles for this prototype system are described earlier in a paper [3] The system is developed using an integrated software package (GURU) that supports data base management, spread sheets and forms management as well as a structured language and rule base management. This multi-environment itself will be discussed in more detail in forthcoming papers.

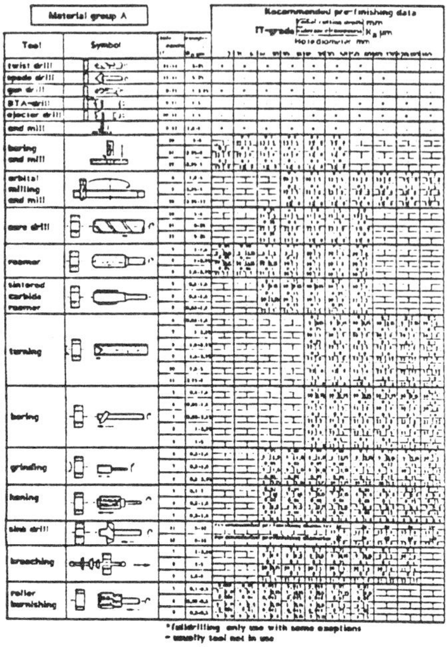

Material group A		Recommended pre-finishing data

fig.1: Technical data for choice of tool and operational sequence

Material group A	

fig. 2: Relative costs of tools for hole-making

This system should be regarded as a *decision support* system rather than a *decision making* system [11]. From the alternative solutions generated it can optionally make a choice or just rank them to facilitate a manual choice. The system permits manual modifying and adjustments of several intermediate results in the sequence-building process. Fig. 3 shows the overall structure.

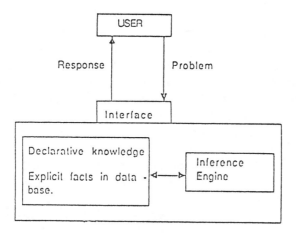

Figure 3: The overall structure

The ability to adjust the system behaviour and tune its performance to meet the situation at hand is one reason why we are mixing together various kinds of formalisms [9]. To the user the system is separated into three parts:

1. The update-system, that operates on the rawdata.

2. The sequence builder, that generates new solutions to unknown problems.

3. The reportgenerator with its report query management system(RQMS) and reportdatabase (RDS).

2.1.1 The update-system

This system is built up with a hierarchy of menus whose contents and appearance easily may be altered to fit specific needs from the user. The purpose is that not only data stored in the databases should reflect specific needs within an organization but also that the interfaces should be customized in an easy manner to permit different users to work with familiar concepts. The architecture of the underlying database is relational. The database contains the raw data and is split into 14 relations corresponding to grade of tolerance. This data is also available in two other, and larger, relations. This redundancy brings some advantages. Since we know what operations that has to take place in a query, and since we consider execution time to be of crucial importance, this structure enables faster access to data with less calculations performed each time. We here talk about strictly controlled redundancy meaning that the structure of the database implies rather complex operations to take place within a relatively small amount of time.

2.1.2 The sequence builder

Here information is produced from data stored in the database containing raw data. The static facts are retrieved from the database while the declarative, heuristic knowledge components are expressed as rules. Thus we recognize two major data-manipulation strategies: one that uses *procedural models* during the initial extraction and testing phase and one that is *rule based*. The rule based knowledge is classified as knowledge that is fragmentary, modular and often difficult, at a first sight, to place within a context.

During a session with IHOPE, approximately 3 minutes long, an operational sequence is created that fulfill a number of criteria. What criteria and to what extent they have influenced the solution is determined by the embedded rulebased system. The rules evaluate different kinds of situation-dependent parameters that might have influence on the operational sequence being created. The rulebased part of the system provides explanations of *why* and *how* certain actions are taken. This function, as well as many other functions described in this paper, is optional. To a well-trained eye the rulebased mechanism take too long a time to execute. In such a case the user can turn it off.

2.1.3 The reportgenerator

A complete and correct solution to a problem is given as a report. It is displayed optionally on screen and/or paper. In the report the initial starting parameters, input by using a form, as well as all other parameters given during the session as yes/no answers are shown. The solution might be accepted or rejected. If accepted, the complete record is stored on file. We call this file *the report database* or **RDS**. It is used in two ways by the system:

1. Through the **RQMS**.

2. In a hidden manner.

The second way it works has to be explained in a little more detail. When a consultation (or session) begins, the user is prompted for nominal diameter, surface roughness, grade of tolerance and materialgroup. After this, the system scans the **RDS** for possible solutions. If it does not find a complete solution the *sequence builder* starts its operations. Otherwise one or many reports is displayed. The user probably gets solutions that fit his needs but he still might consider building a new one because for example the tools in the solution sequences are not available. If he at this point invokes the sequence builder, the values of certain parameters are already known (once given) and there will be no need to reenter these values. The sequence builder instead get the values from the **RDS**. In this way the time taken to reach a new solution from partially known data is significantly reduced. Resource consuming activities like running the rulebases to generate certain facts about the hole or about the tools can be avoided and the user interaction is reduced.

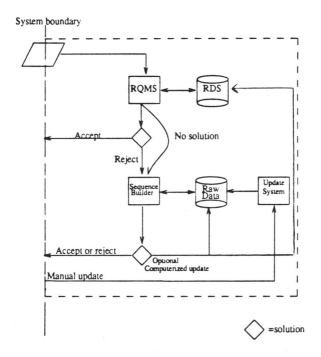

Figure 4: Above, a simple description of workingflow and dataflow within IHOPE.

2.2 The Planning Process and The System Behaviour

An operational sequence is created from a number of static objects (tools) grouped and stored as tables in a data base. The criteria for grouping tools are equivalent to those described earlier [12]. The main strategy during the extraction, grouping and testing phase is to prune the search tree as early and as much as possible in order to reduce execution time. Most of the procedures used in this phase produce output on both file and screen to enable access to partial results. The search tree is initially reduced with respect to grade of tolerance, hole-diameter and group of workpiece material. In the next phase the system tries to terminate with a sequence as short as possible, which means that it seeks a finishing tool with attributes corresponding to the initial request. If there is more than one tool found with the correct attributes then these are listed as candidates. The engineer will be free to choose one of these or to continue building larger sequences.

At this stage we have either found an appropriate tool that satisfies our needs or we have chosen to continue the process. Another possibility is that the system has not found an appropriate finishing tool. If no tool was found or accepted this causes our program to stop searching for finishing tools. The system has to build larger sequences with a pre-finishing tool as a starting point. Now it tries to combine every appropriate pre-finishing tool with other tools until the last one found is a finishing tool. The process begins with an examination of the cost attribute (the relation-number of machining costs) for each candidate pre-finishing tool in order to rank the objects and thus facilitate a selection. The system groups tools by grade of tolerance in descending order with relative costs displayed. The different groups are displayed one after another. At each level displayed the user must make a choice of tool to get to the next level. This cycle continues until a finishing tool is chosen. At this stage the creation of an operational sequence is completed. The chosen tools together constitute a chain. Every link in this chain represent a grade of tolerance, which can be regarded as the key attribute together with the tool name, and a number of other non ordered attributes such as radial cutting depth, minimum radial cutting depth, surface roughness, a flag indicating availability from stock and the diameter. The result is stored in a data base table

The data base contents can be accessed by using a query language similar to *SQL*. It may also be manipulated through a customized menu-guided system developed specially for the application described in this paper. The interface provides the user with all common functions for updating the data base. Ensuring the security of sensitive data is important. It is therefore possible to give different users different read and write access privileges.

The rule base is with a few exceptions invoked during the creation of the operational sequence. Some rule sets are used early in the session to check correctness of starting parameters and to check the type of machine that the engineer has intended to use. The latter may reduce the number of permissible tools considerably. This fact is of crucial importance since one of the great problems in many knowledge based applications is to avoid the *combinatorial explosion* [10]. In our case this means a reduction of execution time by a factor of 10 compared to other systems based on for example pure Lisp-routines. Since we do not use data structures such as *linked lists*, there is no need to communicate both valid, partially valid and invalid data between disk and RAM, i.e there is no need to read-in all elements of a list, before processing. Furthermore with our technique we avoid the resource consuming recursiveness of Lisp and similar languages. By using a **minimal set** of relations from a database, where each relation involved is designed to fit well defined purposes, IHOPE performs a relatively small amount of computations to keep the RAM organized and to provide the user with query results. The architecture of the database that we have developed is relational and it is clear that our way to represent data is suitable also for very moderate computer hardware. This is an important aspect when considering use and acceptance on a larger scale, beyond the laboratory. The analysis of the data structures we use, has shown that further improvements are possible. In practice this means that a session with IHOPE, in the near future, will take less than 2 minutes to perform. Below, we continue the discussion of the rule based part of this system with respect to gathering and formalization of knowledge.

3. PROBLEMS OF SPECIAL INTEREST

3.1 Knowledge Acquisition

According to Hart [8] domain experts can have three different roles. These are: as a provider of information, as a problem-solver and as an explainer. In the first role and the last one problems of communication occur because in these roles more than one person is involved. The task is either to *provide someone* with information or to *explain* something to *somebody*. Everyday language is in many respects insufficient for precise and nuanced communication of thoughts, knowledge and information. In some disciplines the need for exactness in communication has forced the development of new constructs. These are often based on everyday language but ranges wider with whole systems of new words and grammars. Here each formulation has a relatively well defined meaning and is in general equally interpreted among 'initiated' people. The process of *knowledge acquisition*[3] is the most time consuming of our activities. Having collected enough information to make a computer implementation, a running version very often becomes an important communication channel between the knowledge engineer and the domain expert because it yields a visible and easily understandable interpretation of the problem. As the knowledge in the program accumulates and the problem becomes clearer we often find better ways to represent and process the knowledge. To express some chunk of knowledge as a rule in a rule set one must be sure that this knowledge is suited for that kind of representation. Problems of choosing representations, refining programs, determining what knowledge that in some sense can be regarded as fuzzy and communicating with domain experts all belongs to the knowledge acquisition process [4]. The rule formalism permits us to store and process single facts that we do not yet know how to handle within a context. This possibility facilitates the problem of visualizing abstract courses of events. As a rule set grows larger we may distinguish some grouping criteria. That criteria may be so well defined and single rules may be so tightly coupled to other rules that the process as a whole finally can be considered as deterministic. In that case we have used the rule formalism to incrementally build a procedure, i.e. the ability to quickly and easily represent expertise for a program through usage of rules has sometimes helped us find a structure in a specific problem-solving process. As d'Agapeyeff mentions [2] the characteristics favoring implementation of expert systems include:

    (1) The sub-task can be readily identified.

    (2) There is no doubt as to the boundaries of the task.

    (3) A specialist performs the task very much better than the average

---

3. Buchanan *et al.* [1] define knowledge acquisition as 'the transfer and transformation of potential problem-solving expertise from some knowledge source to a program'.

practitioner.

(4) The task requires from 20 minutes to a few hours to perform.

(5) The specialist is confident that he can readily articulate the relevant expertise

Thus we have to combine suitable strategies to explore expert knowledge of different kinds as it emerges illustrated by Harmon&King [6] in figure 5.

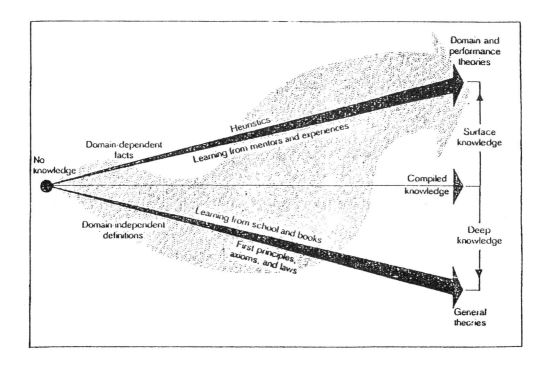

Figure 5: General pattern of proffessional development.

3.2 Learning systems

In a situation where the IHOPE system runs operationally, it presents better solutions the more problems that have been solved and stored in the **RDS**. With enough cases stored, IHOPE might be capable of emulating expert knowledge[4] in the area of hole machining. Thus the system will seldom generate **completely** new sequences from beginning. Instead it will modify previously stored cases utilizing certainty factors referring to correctness, adequacy and grade of fitness. The meaning of these concepts are subject to future research and will not be discussed here. So, we cansay that the system has the ability to learn from past experiences. The form used for representation of stored results makes it possible to handle thousands of solutions and yet keep the amount of stored data rather small. A solution is represented so that part of the physical record has to be interpreted via recalculation. Other parts of the record holds computed results explicitly. The former way of representation is used mainly when a value represent a result from a complex calculation, a select operation or a rulebase consultation. In this way it is possible to represent a whole solution with all its relevant aspects by splitting up the result in explicit ones and referenced ones. We thereby gain execution time but, above all, we can work with a very large number of previously stored solutions at the same time.

The solutions in the **RDS** are manipulated, ranked and weighted according to the wishes from a specific user in a specific moment through the **RQMS**. To this function we intend to add capabilities to provide the user with fast calculation power used in *whatif-analysis* where the value of one field in a stored record may be changed and the influence on other values are shown.

3.3 Transparency and Operational Maintenance

Buchanan [1] points out that *transparency* is the key idea for making the system understandable despite the complexity of the task. He argues that the system matures through incremental improvements, which require thorough understanding of previous versions and that the system improves through criticism from persons who are not familiar with the system specific details. One very important aspect for making a transparent system is that we must give the user the opportunity to examine *how* and *why* a certain rule is fired. Thus the ability to trace the line of reasoning in this way makes it possible in the future to let the user of this system take greater part of the refinement of the knowledge base without having thorough understanding of all implementation details. The engineer himself might be capable of expanding the capacities of the system.

---

4. For further discussions on the subject of learnings systems many books and papers are available. For a brief discussion see [7]

4. CONCLUSIONS

We have briefly presented a computer supported method to choose tools and operational sequences for hole-machining. Initially we described the type of knowledge that we considered to be essential for this knowledge-processing system. This knowledge, i.e. domain specific knowledge, was characterized as *tacit knowledge* that gradually grows from experience. We argued that our ambition was to extract this knowledge and incorporate it in a computerized system. Subsequently we described the basic characteristics of the system. We concluded that the system was to be regarded as a decision support system rather than a decision making system according to the definitions given in [11]. We made a distinction between two forms of representing facts namely the rule based representation and the process oriented representation. If we could distinguish some kind of control structure in a problem and express it as an algorithm, then the problem was suited for a procedural representation. If it was hard to find out in what way a problem was solved, what information that was needed and how to place the result within a context then we used rules. The system must be capable of producing a satisfying result within a few minutes. To make this possible we first minimized (or optimized) the data base contents Then we pruned the search tree so that any proper combination of tools would give a satisfying but perhaps not always an optimized result. The transfer and transformation required to represent expertise for a program has proven to suffer from communication problems. This causes the development of the system to be a strongly iterative process. To make possible further refinement of knowledge by future users we said that the system had to be *transparent*. This makes the system behaviour visible to the user. We mean that this would facilitate the learning process for future users.

The system performs the tasks described and produces a satisfying result which means that it presents an operational sequence that has been tested and modified in accordance with the knowledge available. In order to make the system usable in a larger scale several issues mainly concerning the operating environment remain. In addition to continuously maintain, update and expand the knowledge base, aspects of user acceptance have to be analyzed as the reliability of the system must be secured. Final testing of the system will evaluate the following areas:

- System scope adequacy.
- User friendliness.
- System validity.
- Help feature quality.

Practically we test the system in two steps:

1. By using test cases provided by experts to validate the knowledge base.
2. By using IHOPE under actual operating conditions.

REFERENCES

[1]   Bruce G. Buchanan and Edward H. Shortliffe, *RULE-BASED EXPERT SYSTEMS, The MYCIN Experiments of The Stanford Heuristic Programming Project*, Addison Wesley (1984).

[2]   Alex d'Agapeyeff, *Guidelines on Know-How Programming*, Expertech Ltd, 1988.

[3]   Department of Production Technology, "Integrated Expertsystem for Planning of Hole-making Operation (Statusreport)", 1989.

[4]   Edward A. Feigenbaum and Pamela McCorduck, *The Fifth Generation*, Pan Books (1984).

[5]   Bo Göranzon, *Datautvecklingens Filosofi*, Studentlitteratur (1983).

[6]   Paul Harmon and David King, *Artificial Intelligence Business-Expertsystems*, Wiley&Jons (1985).

[7]   Paul Harmon, Rex Maus, and William Morrissey, *EXPERT SYSTEMS, Tools&Applications*, Wiley (1988).

[8]   Anna Hart, *Knowledge Acquisition for Expert Systems*, Kogan Page (1986).

[9]   Clyde W. Holsapple and Andrew Winston, *Expert Systems using GURU*, Dow Jones-Irwin (1986).

[10]   Peter Jackson, *Introduction to Expert Systems*, Addison Wesley (1986).

[11]   Bengt G. Lundberg, "On the Evaluation of Heuristic Information Systems", *To be published in Decision Support Systems*, 1988.

[12]   Hans G. Vogt, "Choice of Tools and Operational Sequences for Machining of Holes", *IVF Result 77629*, Mekanförbundet, Stockholm, 1977.

[13]   Hans G. Vogt, "Beeinflussung der Zerspanung bei der Innenbearbeitung insbesondere beim Gewindebohren", *Diss. CTH Department of Production Technology*, 1985.

Experience of Mediating Representation in an Industrial Application

Sarmad Alshawi and Garret Quigley
Department of Computer science
Brunel University
Uxbridge, Middex.
UB8 3PH
UK

Abstract

A major activity in Expert System development is the process of eliciting and analysing expert knowledge so that it can be suitably represented for implementation. Systemic Grammar Networks represent a domain independent mediating representation which provides an empty structure into which a domain of knowledge may be fitted. The aim of this paper is to demonstrate an approach based on constructing a mediating representation of elicited domain knowledge in the development of a knowledge-based system in an industrial engineering application. The value of constructing a mediating representation of domain knowledge is discussed, and the use of Systemic Grammar Networks notation as a representational tool in this application is evaluated.

1. Introduction

The authors were engaged in research and development of expert systems technology for business applications (ALVEY Project Business Applications of Expert Systems).

Cost estimation is a key stage of any production process of which an important component is the estimation of machining times. Work in this paper has originated from an attempt to build a prototype knowledge based system for estimating metal machining times for bid estimating purposes.

The overall task domain which forms the context of this work is the bid estimatingfunction in the engineering company Dowty Rotol. The bid estimator (domain expert) must estimate the cost of manufacturing a subsystem or part in the company. The bid estimator is supplied with a schematic engineering drawing which he assesses to identify the features that will require specific machining operations. The manufacturing of each part breaks down into a sequence of operations, and for each operation, the estimator writes down a sequence of actions which comprise that operation. The estimator associates times for each of these actions which will add up to the estimated time of each operation. These times are then used to estimate the cost incurred.

2. Mediating Representation

In the traditional approach to expert system development, knowledge elicited from the expert(s) was directly represented in a formalism for implementation - be it a knowledge representation scheme implemented in a symbolic processing language such as LISP or PROLOG, or an expert system shell abstracted from a previous application. Problems with this methodology have been identified in the literature (Johnson 1985; Breuker and Weilinga 1987; Clancey 1985; Newell 1982). These problems can be summarised as follows:-

a- Elicitation and acquisition are not distinguished, thus allowing for the confusion of issues separate to each stage.

b- There is no principled analysis of the knowledge prior to implementation details such as target representation and language. On the contrary, limitations of the target representation constrain the scope of the analysis of the knowledge in the first place.

On the basis of the above arguments, the need for some kind of implementation independent analysis has been argued for. Keravnou and Johnson (1986) argue that such an analysis would form the basis of a competence model of the expertise. In a similar vein, Breuker and Weilinga (1987) argue for an `epistemological analysis' independent of implementation considerations, and Newell (1982) speaks of the `knowledge level' descriptions missing in the traditional approach. Such a description of the expertise will yield a mediating representation of the knowledge that can be used during the knowledge elicitation process to help guide elicitation and interpretation of the resulting verbal data and decisions about an appropriate machine representation (Kidd 1987).

A major activity in expert system development , then, is the process of eliciting and analysing expert knowledge so that it can adequately be represented as a competence model or other implementation independent representation.

3. Systemic Grammar Networks (SGNs)

The use of systemic grammar networks for the analysis of verbal data began with Halliday (Halliday 1961, 1978), who approached the study of language not from a formal syntactic perspective, but from the perspective of analysing the social functions of language. Thus, the emphasis is on the importance of context and situation in the analysis of each utterance of text.

As functional grammar attempts to characterize utterances at different levels of functional abstraction. The representational tool used for expressing the functional grammar is the systemic grammar network which is a choice system that expresses the alternative roles of utterances(for a fuller treatment of this topic see Winigrad 1983, chap. 6). More recently, the technique of analysing qualitative data by constructing SGNs which characterize that data has been proposed (Bliss et al, 1987). The relevance of this work to the task of knowledge elicitation and analysis has been made by Johnson and Johnson (1987).

If we were to map the framework of functional grammar for a language to the problem of constructing a grammar which characterized a domain of expertise, the entities in the domain would correspond to the sentences (or 'clauses', etc) in the language. Since it is the test of a grammar if it can generate all of the sentences in a language, and no sentences which do not belong in it, then, correspondingly, the test of a good grammar which characterizes expertise should be that the entities which the grammar generates should comprise the set of possible entities in the domain and only those entities, i.e. it should not be possible to generate entities which do not exist in the domain, or nonesential entities. For instance, in an expert system we do not want rules which could not be applied. Thus in terms of knowledge elicitation, this means that we place a certain discipline on our activities in so far as our SGN,s must 'fit' the data in a special way judged through how appropriate the 'sentences' generated are. "Systemic grammar networks provide an empty structure into which a chosen domain of knowledge may be fit. The content free nature of networks is the most appealing feature in the search for ways of representing qualitative data emanating from interview transcripts" (Johnson and Johnson 1987).

The notation used comprises the following:
- terms - which may be terminal or non-terminal
- co-occurrance - which is represented as a curled bracket
- mutually exclusive choice - which is represented by a bar
- entry conditions - which is represented by a reversed bar or bracket.
- recursion - which is represented by a curled arrow

3.1. SGNs Representation in Time Calculation of Machining Operations

In constructing our SGNs we used the collection of data and information from early knowledge elicitation interviews transcripts, notes, and teachback transcripts.[1]

SGNs will be used primarily in the definition of the domain concepts and their static relations. Due to space constraints we will describe only some of the SGNs used in the time calculation work which will show the power of SGNs as a mediating representation tool. There are more than twenty metal removal operations in Dowty rotol, and to simplify matters we will only refer to Turning operations.

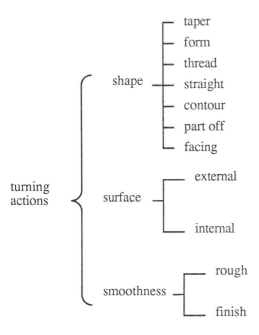

Figure 1a Action types

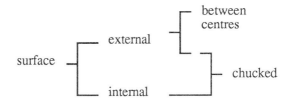

Figure 1b Relation between surface and fixing

Figure 1a above characterizes those aspects of turning operations on a lathe or machining center which are relevent to machining time estimations, and the network is to be read from left to right. The shape of the cut may take a number of different forms, metal may be removed from the external or internal surface of the work-piece, and smoothness of the cut may be rough or finish. This simple network summarizes a large

---

[1] For more about teachback technique see Johnson and Johnson (1987).

smoothness of the cut may be rough or finish. This simple network summarizes a large range of possibilities since any shape can be combined with any surface and smoothness. The network neatly draws out the important distinctions to be made in turning operations in relating to time calculations.The network in figure 1b charachterizes the relationship between the surface from which the metal will be removed and how the work-piece is fixed to the machine.This network is read from both left and right sides, since during removing metal from internal surface the work-piece is always fixed to the machine with a chuck (a securing tool), while during external turning the work-piece can either be fixed to the machine with a chuck or between the machine centres.

At this stage of our knowledge elicitation process we were primarily interested with characterizing the data not in extracting rules from the domain.

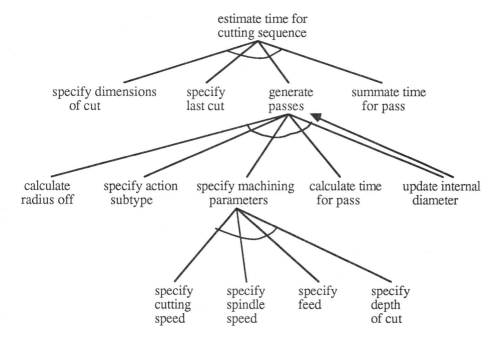

Figure 2 Task tree in estimating the time for a cutting sequence

Figure 2 represents the task tree used to depict the tasks involved in estimating the time for a cutting sequence. We will only describe two of the SGNs used for the subtasks. In the following SGNs (figs 3,4) some of the subtasks have enabling and disabling conditions. Conditions are evaluated using the problem specific data. A strategy may be selected if it's enabling condition is satisfied and it's disabling condition is not satisfied (see Keravnou and Johnson 1986)

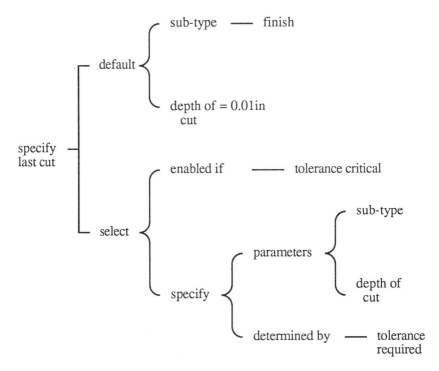

Figure 3 Specification of last cut

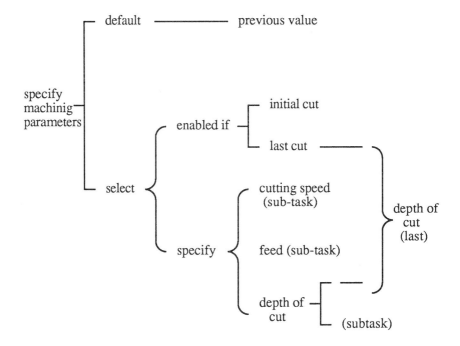

Figure 4 Specification of machining parameters

Figure 3 summarizes a decision process. This decision is to be made in the task of specifying the last cut in a cutting sequence,and the network is to be read from left to right . The sequence of rough cuts generally ends with a lighter cut in order to obtain a smoother surface on the work-piece. This is normally specified as a 'finish' cut with a default value for the depth of cut set to 0.01 inches. If, however, the required tolerance of the surface finish is higher than usual, then a lower depth of cut might be specified for the last cut in the sequence This requires specification of the cutting parameters (sub-type depth of cut) which are determined by the tolerance required.

Figure 4 illustrates the task of specifying the machining parameters for one cutting pass on a lathe, and the network is to be read from left and right sides. The specification of the spindle speed (not shown in the network) is compulsory for each cycle since the outer diameter of the work-piece is changing after each cut. The conditions for the invocation of the tasks of specifying the other three machining parameters (cutting speed, feed, and depth of cut) can be characterized in the network. Each of these tasks is enabled if the current cut is initial or last cut in the machining sequence. In the case of the last cut, the depth of cut will already have been specified (see figure 3). Otherwise the value of each of these three parameters will remain as it was in the previous cut. Where a sub-task appears this is broken down into it's own SGN network.

The above two SGNs have been constructed using knowledge from several knowledge elicitation interviews transcripts. This shows the ability of the networks to capture a large amount of knowledge, and show it in a short, clear, and useful way.

3.2. Evaluating the SGNs Approach

A significant characteristic of SGNs is that the representation should expose the constraints which exist in the domain. In so far as the exposition of constraints is concerned, it is a defining feature of the SGN that it should characterize all and only the possible entities which may arise in a domain. It is therefore an important test of the validity of the network that all the combinations of terminal nodes are sensible to the expert. The process of validating a network can itself be a valuable technique in knowledge elicitation since it is only by generating the combinations that it can be seen if the network adequately characterizes the domain. It was found to be useful in our elicitation to show the networks to the experts (estimators) who readily understood them and, in some cases, suggested modifications to them.

An issue related to the one of constraint, is the degree to which the network highlights the relevant detail in the domain and suppresses irrelevant detail. It is the task of the knowledge engineer to extract from the data those aspects of the knowledge which are relevant to the task in question. Invariably there is a great deal of information either in the data or in text books which is either not used by the experts or lies outside the scope of their considerations. For instance, there is a wealth of formal and empirical theory associated with the metal cutting process. Estimators, however, do not consider such a level of detail in their tasks. Those aspects of the domain which are relevant to their tasks must be brought out in the network if it is to successfully characterize their knowledge. The boundaries of the knowledge in the final system will be set by its proposed functionality and its operational environment as well as the nature of the experts' knowledge. Since these considerations should guide the knowledge elicitation process in general, they should also be reflected in the construction of the network.

The formal structure of the SGNs notation is very simple. There are benefits and losses in using such a basic formalism. A benefit is that there is no epistemological or cognitive theory associated with the formalism. Thus the formalism is neutral with respect to such theories. The justification for such neutrality is that it prevents the foisting of any preconceived epistemological theory on the data.

Any concepts derived from the data should therefore ideally be data-driven and insofar as any such theories are discernable in the analysis of the knowledge, the formalism itself cannot be held responsible. This is probably the most important motive for the use of such a simple formalism since it is consistent with the aim of achieving an implementation independent analysis of the data. From the networks which have been presented, it can be seen that the notation succeeds to a greater or lesser degree in characterizing the data at different levels of abstraction and from different perspectives e.g. taxonomies of objects, characterization of objects and description of task control. One might argue that a formalism which adopts different functional characteristics depending on the network does so at the expense of rigour. The reply would be that one is willing to sacrifice formal rigour if it enables one to say something meaningful about aspects of the data which would otherwise be difficult to express.[1]

One of the limitations experienced with the notation is context free nature of the choice system. Because selection in the network is context free, it can be difficult to construct useful networks which are not too powerful in the sense that they might allow the generation of combinations which are either meaningless or impossible. While it may be possible to express the legitimate combinations in a suitably large network, one is led to sacrifice economy and clarity for exactitude. An example of where this occurs in the networks presented is in figure 1a which characterizes the possible action types. In this network, all shapes are allowed to combines with either surface (internal or external) and either smoothness (rough or finish). In fact this network is slightly too powerful since in the case of (parting off) the (internal/external) distinction does not arise. To make the network exact, however, would have introduced unnecessary complexity and for the purposes of clarity, the network presented is to be preferred. Another example illustrating this issue is in the following network in figure 1b depicting the relation between surface and fixing. If the choice fixing (between centres/chucked) had been given as a separate selection, this would have allowed the combination of surface (internal) and fixing (between centres) which is exactly what is not allowed. But in expressing this constraint in SGN form, the convention of the combinations of terminals being the salient information is violated since in this case it is the nodes along the path from the root to the terminal which is the salient information (as in an AND/OR tree). Bearing in mind the desire for economy of expression in the formalism, a possible way out of this difficulty is to allow the network to be over-powerful and to describe any constraints, which restrict the possible combinations, outside the network.[2]

As regards the issue of communicability, networks appear to be successful. Their diagrammatic nature make them simple to understand once the notational conventions have been understood. An example of where an abstraction is simply depicted using the notation is in figure 4 which depicts the task control for the specification of machining parameters. If this network is compared with the realization of this control structure in the prototype, it will be found that its expression is distributed between the declarative and procedural semantics of the programming language PROLOG (the time calculation software was developed in PROLOG). Thus the program would be a poor starting point for understanding the conceptual structure of the task control. Furthermore, there is not a direct mapping from the networks to the implementation which is precisely why the networks are appropriate for a mediating representation as opposed to an intermediate representation where such a mapping is more direct. For instance the realization of those processes expressed in other lower level diagraming representation tools such as HIPO diagrams (see Martin and McClure 1985) are much more readily discernible in the PROLOG code.

The network appears to be most useful in the early stages of the knowledge elicitation cycle. During our initial interviews, we found that any mention of rules merely served to antagonise the experts (estimators). We think this is beacause imposing high level knowledge representation schemes in the early stages of the knowledge elicitation cycle limits the conceptual richness of the elicitation dialogue. Our SGNs approach gave us the freedom of conducting knowledge elicitation sessions with no strong epistimilogical

---

[1]See Winograd (1983) ch.6 for a comparison of Functional grammars with Chomskian grammars. For a rigorous account of Systemic grammar see Patten and Richie(1986).

[2] Grisham (1986) discusses these points in relation to context-free syntax analysis.

theory, and served to focus the expert's attention without constraining their individual cognitive process.

Furthermore, using SGNs allowed us to separate the different aspects of the domain knowledge (e.g. taxonomical, conceptual, control) without inforcing a knowledge representation scheme at too early a stage in the knowledge elicitation cycle. Once these aspects of knowledge have been adequately drawn apart, decisions can then be made about which representation(s) are most appropriate for implementation.

5. Conclusion

In the light of our experience, it was found that the approach of constructing a mediating representation in the early stages of the knowledge elicitation cycle was valuable in the process of developing software for the cost estimation task of metal machining operations. The usefulness of SGNs notation was proved as follows:
a- SGNs represented a valuable tool for the purpose of achieving a clear, high level, and communicable representation of the domain knowledge.
b- SGNs provided a useful way of documenting the information in the knowledge acquisition stage, and helped us cope with the mass of information gathered in such a complex engineering domain.
c- We found that SGNs can be used as a knowledge elicitation tool since it generated enthusiasm from the expert and helped both expert and elicitor to focus on important issues during interviews.

References

Bliss, J., Monk, M. and Ogborn, J.M. (1983). Qualitative Data Analysis for Educational Research: a guide to the use of systemic networks.: Croom Helm.

Breuker, J.A. and Wielinga, B.J. (1987). Use of Models in the Interpretation of Verbal Data. In Kidd, A. (Ed.) Knowledge Acquisition for Expert Systems: A practical handbook.: Plenum Press. pp 17-42.

Clancey, W.J. (1983). The epistemology of a rule-based expert system - a framework for explanation. Artifial Intelligence , 20, pp. 215-251.

Grishman, R. (1986). Computational Linguistics. An Introduction.: Cambridge University Press.

Halliday, M.A.K. (1961). Categories of the theory of Grammar. Word 17, pp. 241-292.

Halliday, M.A.K. (1978). Language as a Social Semiotic.: University Park Press.

Johnson, L. (1985). The need for competence models in the design of expert consultant systems. Int. J. Systems Research and Information Science, 1, No.1, pp. 23-36.

Johnson, L. and Johnson, N.E. (1987). Knowledge Elicitation Involving Teachback Interviewing. In Kidd, A. (Ed.) Knowledge Acquisition for Expert Systems: A practical handbook.: Plenum Press. pp. 91-108.

Johnson, N.E. (1987). Knowledge Elicitation. SDL-Insight report.

Keravnou, E.T. and Johnson, L. (1986). Competent Expert Systems: A case study in fault diagnosis.: Kogan Page.

Kidd, A. (1987). Knowledge Acquisition - An Introductory Framework. In Kidd, A. (Ed.) Knowledge Acquisition for Expert Systems: A practical handbook.: Plenum Press. pp. 1-15.

Martin, J. and McClure, C. (1985). Diagramming techniques for Analysts and Programmers. : Prentice Hall.

Newell, A. (1982). The knowledge level. Artificial Intelligence, 18, pp. 87-127.

Patten, T. and Richie, G. (1986). A Formal Model of Systemic Grammar. Department of Artificial Intelligence Research Paper No.290. University of Edinburgh.

Winograd, T. (1983). Language as a Cognitive Process. Vol. 1. Syntax. : Addison-Wesley.

REPRESENTING KNOWLEDGE AS ARGUMENTS: APPLYING EXPERT SYSTEM TECHNOLOGY TO JUDGEMENTAL PROBLEM-SOLVING

Peter Clark (pete@turing.ac.uk)
Turing Institute
36 N. Hanover St.
Glasgow G1 2AD.

Abstract

In many domains, it is not possible to easily gather a definitive body of expertise for problem-solving. A particularly well-known problem is that, when experts disagree, it is not easy or even possible to identify the 'right' answer, a characteristic particularly true of problems involving human judgement. In such domains, the process of argumentation between experts plays a crucial role in pooling knowledge, locating inconsistencies and focusing attention on areas for further examination.

In this paper we recognise this process of argumentation – reasoning about *why* inferences are valid – as important in problem-solving, and present techniques for using AI technology to assist experts in this process. In the implementation we present, models of different opinions are represented separately rather than combined. The user and system interact to solve a given problem, the system arguing its case on the basis of consistency with previous decisions and the user supplying extra knowledge which the system is unaware of. Dialog focuses on the meta-level justifications for inferences which are made, not normally represented in the usual expert system methodology. By exploiting the computer's power of memory and search a powerful decision support tool can be constructed. We illustrate this with a full-scale system, named Optimist, for assisting geologists in oil exploration.

1   Introduction

Many expert systems are constructed on the principle of assembling a body of expertise, representing it within the system and then using it to solve the task at hand. Domains where a well-defined body of knowledge exists are particularly suitable for this methodology as reflected by applications which have been successful [Andrews, 1989], and criteria of having a well-defined domain and agreement among experts have become established guidelines for selecting applications (eg. [Buchanan, 1985, Prerau, 1989]).

However, it is also recognised that not all domains are as 'neat' as to allow a definitive body of expertise to be easily gathered and then straightforwardly applied. A particularly well-known problem, which is the topic of this paper, is that in many domains there can be considerable variation of opinion among experts due to their differing knowledge and judgement. Experts sometimes disagree with each other and may change their opinion over time and with experience, and an expert's personal knowledge of previously solved problems can strongly influence his or her solutions to new problems.

In this type of domain, human problem-solving additionally involves retrieving similar previous cases and discussion among experts. The process of **argumentation** between experts serves to pool knowledge together and enforce consistency, and plays a crucial role in many problem-solving tasks. This feature is particularly prominent in tasks involving risk assessment [Alexander and Evans, 1988].

It is also clear that the value of such discussions in solving problems is dependent on the availability of experts, and their knowledge of and ability to recall relevant previous cases. Assistance in this process would thus be valuable, and as Reboh points out [Reboh, 1983] expert system research offers precisely a technology in which this expert reasoning can be captured and, by combining this with the computer's power for faithful memory and extensive search, provide a useful decision-support tool.

In this paper, we highlight the problems in constructing such a decision-support tool and present the techniques we have developed for dealing with them. These techniques are based on the modelling of differing expert opinions within a single system, and then using these records to involve the computer in the argumentation process. This work is framed in the context of risk assessment in oil exploration, and a full-scale implementation named Optimist is described.

2   Problem Description

2.1   Risk Assessment in Oil Exploration

We briefly describe the salient characteristics of expert reasoning in our illustrative domain to highlight the problems which our techniques address.

In the search for hydrocarbons such as oil and gas, the sites of potential prospects need to be appraised to assess the probability that hydrocarbons are present, and if so in what quantities. This task of **prospect appraisal** is formidable. Typically it takes a small team of highly trained experts several weeks of work, involving the sifting of a large amount of data to produce a final estimate of the probability of there being hydrocarbons present.

Some of the characteristics of reasoning in this domain are as follows:

1. Discussion or 'argumentation' among experts plays a central role in problem-solving, involving the retrieval of similar previous cases and forming hypotheses about unobservable features of the prospect. This process serves to pool knowledge together and enforce consistency, and is essential in risk assessment.

2. Experts frequently disagree; it is often impossible to identify the 'correct' answer, as the accuracy of probability judgements can only be assessed over sets of cases rather than in any single case.

3. Retrieval of previously drilled, similar cases is essential to making accurate risk assessments. The cases form a focus for discussion.

As a reflection of the differences in expert opinion in this domain, Table 1 presents some of the prospects appraised by different experts. As can be seen, there is often substantial disagreement.

Table 1: An illustration of differing expert opinions, showing assessments of the likelihood of finding oil at three real-world prospects by different experts (each figure is the conclusion of a detailed appraisal process).

	Opinion 1	Opinion 2
Prospect 1	72%	40%
Prospect 2	9%	17%
Prospect 3	1%	7%

2.2   Other Domains

The characteristics of disagreement among experts, the need for discussion and the important role of similar cases also hold for a large number of other real-world domains, particularly those where judgemental reasoning is involved. Some examples in the AI literature are business decision-making [Premkumar, 1989], financial risk analysis [Alexander and Evans, 1988], financial marketing [Castner et al., 1986] and legal reasoning [Rissland et al., 1984]. A particularly interesting case was the development of the Prospector system [Duda et al., 1981], where its encoded models were originally developed with and tested by a single (same) expert. Towards the end of the project, it became apparent that experts did often disagree, and Gaschnig optimistically raised the hope that discussion about Prospectors' models would smooth out the disagreements [Gaschnig, 1982]. Finally, in 1983 Reboh argues in favour of modelling (rather than seeking to eradicate) conflicting expertise and speculates on some of the mechanisms for doing this [Reboh, 1983]. The techniques which we present are thus also relevant to other domains such as these.

2.3   Applying Expert System Technology

The above problem characteristics make it particularly difficult to apply the normal expert system methodology of identifying and encoding the 'right' expertise for solving the problem. Instead we have had to develop alternative methods for assisting in problem-solving in this domain. In particular, we have made three atypical design decisions:

1. Conflicts between different opinions are not resolved during knowledge-base development, but instead the **different opinions are represented** separately within the system. Often the different opinions and methods of different experts constitute substantial domain-specific knowledge, and the location of conflict an important method of focusing attention during problem-solving [Klein and Lu, 1989].

2. The system's role is not the usual one of autonomous, explainable problem-solving but instead is to provide **decision support** by identifying, retrieving and presenting relevant information to the expert by 'arguing' with him or her. For knowledge-based systems to assist human *experts* rather novices, a decision support role is often more appropriate than one of autonomously repeating what the experts are already good at [Mittal and Dym, 1985].

3. **Specific, previous cases** constitute an important source of knowledge for problem-solving as well as that in a general knowledge-base. The importance of case records is also reflected in a number of other expert systems, where cases act as 'anchor points' for guiding decisions and knowledge-base evolution (eg. Garvan-ES1 [Compton et al., 1989], Prospector [Duda et al., 1981]).

The basic principle underlying these design decisions is that, in some domains, expert reasoning should be viewed as the processing of **arguments** rather than the application of a well-defined body of knowledge. We now briefly elaborate on these design decisions.

3   From Rules To Arguments

3.1   Meta-Level Knowledge for Justifying Arguments

We can define an argument simply as an inference (or chain of inferences) whose validity is open to question. Reasoning with arguments includes the use of **meta-level** knowledge about the justification for inferences being used, and thus this meta-level knowledge must be represented. This is in sharp contrast to the normal expert system methodology where the justification for a rule's validity is not represented. While in a normal system the proof of a rule's conditions can be queried, the justification for the presence of the rule itself is not represented. For example, consider a hypothetical rule

```
IF hightemp THEN meningitis cf 0.2.
```

The justification for expecting a weak correlation (0.2) between `hightemp` and `meningitis` is inaccessible to the user; this statistical and/or theoretical evidence is not represented in a normal expert system approach as the user is not expected to question inferences. However, in real-world problem-solving, reasoning *about* the justifications for inferences plays in important role.

3.2   The Dynamics of Argumentation

In the system we present, argumentation is incorporated in a framework of **interactive problem-solving**. The interaction involves an exchange of information between the system and user, discussing *why* a particular risk is valid. There are several strategies for this, but the over-riding principle (for both parties) is the **principle of consistency**: the same decisions should be made in the 'same' circumstances. There are several sources where consistency information be sought, including similar previous cases, statistical evidence and other experts' opinions.

4   Tools And Techniques

4.1   Tool Requirements

There are three major requirements of an implementation which must be met to allow the above functionality, which we now list.

1. **Ability to compare.** In order to construct justifications for risk, it must be possible to make easy comparisons between details of different user's opinions.
2. **Ability to modify.** As experts opinions may change, they must be able to easily modify the system's model of their opinions without the intervention of a programmer every time.
3. **Ability to argue.** In order to justify conclusions, there must be some internal representation of *why* something is believed.

We now describe the representational methods used in Optimist and how they fulful these requirements.

4.2 Representing Different Opinions

In order to represent different opinions it is necessary to keep the different opinions separate in some way. A simple (if time-consuming) method is to engineer a separate knowledge-base for each user, rules and 'facts' tagged with the believer's name. This approach has been adopted in the several systems, including Negoplan [Matwin et al., 1989] and LeClair's multi-expert knowledge system [Alexander and Evans, 1988].

For our particular requirements, however, there are two disadvantages with this approach. Firstly, given the known bottleneck of formalising expert knowledge, the time involved to separately engineer (and maintain) knowledge-bases for each user is likely to be impractically long. Secondly, the problem of making meaningful comparisons across knowledge-bases with completely different structures is formidable.

To overcome these problems we restrict this general approach to a more tractable version which we describe as a **'skeleton + certainty sets'** representation. First, a *single* rulebase for risk appraisal is developed, and then the *body* of the rules are separated from the *certainty measures* attached to them. As a result, a set of certainty values for the rulebase can be loaded, modified and stored under a different name. Thus multiple 'rule' sets (ie. sets of certainty values) can evolve. As there is a single common rulebase to which each set of certainty values attaches, the task of making comparisons and isolating points of disagreement is made possible. We show this schematically in Figure 1.

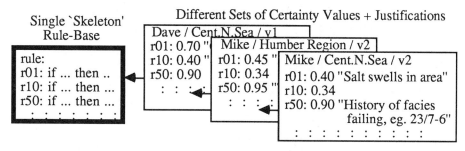

Figure 1: The separation of a single rule-base from sets of certainty values

Figure 2: The use of sliders for displaying and changing certainty values. The sliders are attached to a rule which, given a particular type of trap (ie. dip, facies, etc.) is present in the prospect, concludes a contributing probability of oil being present (ignoring all other factors).

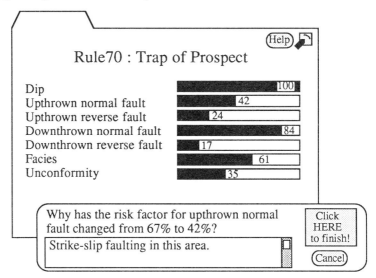

4.3   Human-Computer Interaction Issues

A second requirement of our representation (Section 4.1) is that the users should be easily able to modify the system's model of their opinions. Given our adoption of a 'skeleton + certainty sets' framework, we have a simple method by which the users can alter the system's conclusions: simply by changing the certainty values, along with a textual justification for the changes they make. This is implemented by allowing the user to drag graphical sliders, as shown in Figure 2.

This method allows users to easily maintain the system's record of their risk judgements themselves, thus reducing the need for intervention from a 'knowledge engineer'. Engineering of the knowledge-base thus requires enumerating all the possible sources of risk, while the details and degree of risk are tuned by the users. More structural changes to the knowledge-base still requires intervention from a programmer, but such interventions are infrequent and users are able to perform the day-to-day maintenance of the system's model of their opinions themselves.

4.4   Representation Details

4.4.1   Skeleton + Certainty Sets

While this described method is independent of our particular rule format and certainty calculus, we briefly overview the details here.

The calculation of the probability of finding oil is divided up into six loosely independent risking sub-problems relating to the probability of finding an oil-retaining rock structure and its connection to an oil-producing source. The overall probability is thus the product of the probabilities for each of the six conditions.

For each of the six conditions, there are a number of possible factors which may cause the condition to 'fail' (ie. be absent). Each of these is represented by a different rule with an attached 'probability of success' or **risk factor**. For example a very simple rule is:

```
rule03 ::
        if trap(DirnX) of new_prospect =   downthrown_reverse_fault
        then oil_present cf 65%.
```

The risk factor here is 65% (note that 'certainty factor' and 'risk factor' are used synonymously here). We adopt a simple certainty calculus in which these risk factors are again considered loosely independent. The probability for a condition is thus the product of the applicable risk factors.

It should be noted that these rules are high abstractions of the much more complex reasoning of experts in assessing risk. They should be thus be regarded as typical or **normative** risk values, rather than as absolute. The conclusions of the system thus represent a normative risk judgement.

Other rules are used to derive the conditions of the risk factor rules. These rules have no certainty measures attached (ie. are logical).

4.4.2   Representing Justifications

Risk factors are then stored separately from the rules, parameterised by rule number and attribute value, along with an attached textual justification as shown below.

Certainty Set: Mike, Humber Region, version1

rule	attribute	risk factor	date	justification
rule03	dip	90%	16.10.89	"Dip histories good here"
rule03	d.r.fault	65%	16.10.89	"Evidence of calcification in well 23/2 worrying"
:	:	:	:	:

Other tests besides equality on attribute values can be used to select a risk factor from this set.

In addition to using rules, some risk factors are derived instead by applying special-purpose statistical **procedures** based on available well data. This is described in detail in [Clark, 1988].

Because geological properties vary over regions, users can set up a number of 'rule sets' (ie. certainty sets) each for a different geographical region.

4.4.3   Storing Case Histories

In addition to storing personalised 'rule sets', we also record the *application* of those rules in solving particular problems. These history records are used extensively by the system during appraisals of other prospects. The stored history is akin to a proof tree, the tree depicting the formal structure of the argument while the textual justifications within the tree representing domain-specific knowledge. Smolensky et al. have described languages making this 'divide' between formal structure and 'informal' (ie. textual) content as **semi-formal languages**, and illustrate the power of this technique in their system Euclid [Smolensky et al., 1987].

5   Example

5.1   Initial Risk Calculation

At startup, the user gives their name and can enter/view a prospect using a map and graphical drawing tools, and providing values for the prospects' attributes.

   To perform a risk evaluation, the user selects their 'rule set' (ie. certainty set) which they have configured for that region, and then selects one of the six top-level risk components to work through. If statistical procedures are to be used to calculate risk (Section 4.4.2), plotting tools are called up. Otherwise, rules are applied to the prospect's description and a summary of those which fired given. A numerical **risk factor** denotes the *probability* of finding oil given the prospect has a certain feature, ignoring all risks due to other features. Thus a *high* risk factor implies a *low* risk. Risk factors range from 0% (zero probability of oil, ie. infinite risk) to 100% (oil certain, ie. no risk). For example:

> Risk for trap effectiveness:
> 1. Faulting is more recent than the seal   risk factor: 60%   (1 in 1.7)
> 2. Trap in dirn 1 is an unconformity   risk factor: 35%   (1 in 2.9)
> 3. Trap in dirn 2 is upthrown norm. fault   risk factor: 87%   (1 in 1.1)
> 4. Trap in dirn 3 is a dip   risk factor: 100%   (1 in 1.0)
> 5. Trap in dirn 4 is a dip   risk factor: 100%   (1 in 1.0)

> From this I'd conclude a likelihood of 1 in 5.5...

This likelihood ($1/\prod(r_i/100)$) represents the normative value according the rule-base which Mike loaded.

5.2   Argumentation Options

At this point, various options (in addition to normal explanation facilities) are available to discuss this risk value. Below we present loose textual equivalents of the graphically-presented information (using a HyperCard-like interface) which the user can inspect. The user's actions are underlined. Some of these functions are incorporated in the current system while others are still under development. We consider below the user querying/disagreeing with the normative risk of 87% caused by the faulting in the oil trapping structure.

> <u>Why faulting risk?</u>
> The initial fault risk factor as set at 70% (12-Oct-89).
> You raised it to 80% (14-Dec-89) because: good fault seals proven in wells 33/46g and 35/39k nearby.
> You raised it again to 87% (3-Feb-90) because: well 55/6y, involving upthrown normal faulting, struck oil.
>
> <u>Other appraisals?</u>
> Searching...

Dave's already appraised this prospect (12-Dec-89), he gave a risk factor
of 85% for the downthrown normal fault. He re-appraised it on 3-Jan-90
but didn't change his opinion here.
Hey! Steve appraised this prospect on 3-Feb-90 and gave the faulting risk factor as 25% because: seismic sections s34313-7 indicate the
faulting here is abnormally also strike-slip, a considerable risk to the
prospect.

Try other rulesets?
Searching...
Hey! According to the general region rules, Steve and Dave would have
pretty much agreed, but Andrew considers the fault much more risky!
According to my stored rule sets, the normative risk factors should be:
85% (Tim) because: good region for faults (eg 3/3r, 34/3w both sealed)
85% (Dave) because: similar to Humber region risks.
60% (Andrew) because: p65/32 was dry; I reckon faulting was to blame.

Here the user might call up Andrew's appraisal of p65/32 for inspection.

Search cases?
Searching...
You've previously appraised downthrown normal faults in nearby prospects
24/37y, 32/11w and 33/34d. You risked them as 80%, 85% and 50%.
Do you want to see the record for 33/34d?

The risk factor assigned for prospect 33/34d is in greatest conflict with the one
assigned here. The user is asked if he or she wishes to view this appraisal record.

Statistics?
Please sketch an area on the map to take statistics over. (User does so)
Searching...
According to my records, in this region there are 74 prospects,
13 with downthrown normal faults, 8 which struck oil.
Of those 8, 2 had the faulting as the major source of risk to the prospect.
Of those 2, 2 struck oil and 0 did not.

At this point the user might choose to inspect the appraisal records of the 13
prospects with downthrown normal faults.

5.3   Arguing Back

The user may, after this consideration, disagree with the risk factor and change it.
This change is effected by using graphical sliders (as shown previously in Figure 2).

Disagree.
What do you want to change the risk value to? 65%
Please justify this change from the normative value:
Seismics show strike-slip faulting. Andrew's appraisal of p65/32 and
its subsequent failure to strike oil suggests this factor is problematic.

This change and justification is stored in the user's appraisal of this prospect. If the change was for more general, ie. regional, reasons then the user would request that his or her ruleset for the geographical region *also* be updated.

Now the risk appraisal is redone with this changed risk value, and the dialog continues. In this way the user is able to 'argue back' with the system, providing more information which differentiates the current case from other cases, thus removing it from the common context which the system has suggested. This information is stored and hence is available to experts when performing other appraisals.

6   Evaluation

Following an initial prototype in 1988, a full-scale system named **Optimist** has been developed, installed and is now in use. We report from our experience of its use by geologists for real-world risk appraisal problems.

We first note that evaluation of the system is difficult for two reasons. Firstly, the system's role is not stand-alone problem-solving but to assist the user in producing a (machine-readable) argument for his/her risk by encouraging consistency. As the risk factors attached to rules are maintained by the users themselves, it is meaningless to compare them with the users' judgements (they are the same thing). Secondly, assessments of the practical utility of applications depend not only on the underlying theory but also on many aspects ancillary to AI, a point made also by other authors eg. [Gaschnig, 1982].

Following its installation, Optimist has been regularly used so far over a period of about five months and most importantly the users remain highly enthusiastic about its value to the appraisal process. Most fundamental to the system's operation has been finding a pragmatic solution to the 'knowledge maintenance' problem, by which users can maintain the system's models of their risk judgements without regular intervention of a knowledge engineer. The fact the system is now in use, away from its development environment, best testifies to the practical usefulness of the 'skeleton + certainty sets' method for representing and modifying different models of reasoning. During the system's development and following installation the system has been used to varying degrees by 8 different exploration experts, all of whom were able to dispute and correct the system's reasoning to their satisfaction.

One important question concerns the adequacy of experts sharing a single 'skeleton' rule-base and differing only in the attached risk factors. In practice, experts can disable rules which they consider irrelevant by setting the risk factor to 100% (no risk) and thus it is only important rules cover all *potential* sources of risk. It also should be noted that rules represent abstract summaries of more complex reasoning (Section 4.4.1); experts thus may still disagree about details of assessing a feature's risk, reflected in their textual justifications, without requiring two different rules to be encoded. During Optimist's use so far it has only been necessary once to extend the rulebase itself, reflecting the relatively high independence of the system from a trained programmer to maintain models of different opinions.

Logs of the system's usage support the claim that there can be substantial disagreement between experts. Table 1 earlier showed the breakdown of risk values for three of the real-world prospects where more than one geologist had made an appraisal. As can be seen, substantial disagreement can exist. This illustrates the difficulty of attempting to form a single, agreed-on body of knowledge for risk appraisal, as required by a more traditional ES methodology.

Finally, a significant observation is that experts will often 'work back' from a partially pre-conceived risk value. Thus, the expert does not only work through the six risk components in turn but may also return to a particular component to alter the risk value, reflecting the use of the system to *construct* rather than *derive* a structured argument for a conclusion. This observation agrees with the 'interpret-then-justify' model of reasoning, reported in other domains [Compton et al., 1989] and with major implications for knowledge engineering [Compton and Jansen, 1989]. It also reflects a degree of arbitrariness in the numerical measures and partly explains why violations of the independence assumption do not cause serious problems in Optimist. However, the numbers are not meaningless: In particular the *relative* risks are important to geologists, reflecting statements 'A is more risky than B'. The experts can make these qualitative judgements easily, and thus the numeric risk framework can be viewed as an approximately fitting model of these judgements.

7   Conclusion

In this paper we have presented a system for supporting experts in risk assessment, based on modelling different expert opinions and involving the user in argumentation about the validity of different risk judgements. Our main conclusion is that the process of argumentation can be made accessible to both skilled and 'computer-naive' users using the techniques we have described, and be used to provide a valuable decision support tool in domains where discussion and pooling of experience plays an important role. This work is significant as it enables expert system technology to be applied in domains where a single, agreed-on body of knowledge cannot be easily assembled.

From our observations of the system's usage following installation, three directions for future work are indicated. Firstly, it has become clear that the most useful argumentation options are those which deal with specific appraisal records rather than the more general regional risk values, suggesting that risk values always need to be presented along with specific appraisals to make them meaningful. Secondly, from users' comments, there is still potential for further developing knowledge-based methods for analysing the appraisal records, and involving the computer more in the location of inconsistencies. Finally, improvements to the user-interface and the graphical presentation of risk comparisons are possible.

Acknowledgements

This research and application was funded by Enterprise Oil plc, and I particularly thank our exploration experts Mike Whyatt and Dave Rhodes of Enterprise Oil for their involvement and continuing enthusiasm. Thanks also to Tim Niblett for valuable discussions on earlier versions of this paper.

References

Alexander, S. M. and Evans, G. W. (1988). The integration of multiple experts: A review of methodologies. In Turban, E. and Watkins, P. R., editors, *Applied Expert Systems*, pages 47–53. North-Holland, Amsterdam.

Andrews, B. (1989). *Successful Expert Systems*. Financial Times Business Info., London.

Buchanan, B. G. (1985). Expert systems. In *Knowledge-Based Systems and Their Applications: Texas Instruments AI Satellite Symposium*. Texas Instruments. (Seminar Notes).

Buchanan, B. G., Barstow, D., Bechtel, R., Bennet, J., Clancey, W., Kulikowski, C., Mitchell, T., and Waterman, D. A. (1983). Constructing an expert system. In Hayes-Roth, F., Waterman, D. A., and Lenat, D. B., editors, *Building Expert Systems*, pages 127–167. Addison-Wesley, Ma.

Castner, J., Apteé, C., Griesmer, J., Hong, S. J., Karnaugh, M., Mays, E., and Tozawa, Y. (1986). A knowledge-based consultant for financial marketing. *AI Magazine*, 7(5):71–79.

Clark, P. (1988). Exemplar-based reasoning in geological prospect appraisal. TIRM 034, Turing Institute, Glasgow, UK.

Compton, P., Horn, K., Quinlan, J. R., Lazarus, L., and Ho, K. (1989). Maintaining an expert system. In Quinlan, J. R., editor, *Applications of Expert Systems*, volume 2, pages 366–384. Addison-Wesley, Sydney.

Compton, P. and Jansen, R. (1989). A philosophical basis for knowledge acquisition. Tech. Report TR-FD-89-01, CSIRO IT Division, Sydney.

Duda, R., Gaschnig, J., and Hart, P. (1981). Model design in the Prospector consultant system for mineral exploration. In Webber, B. L. and Nilsson, N. J., editors, *Readings in Artificial Intelligence*, pages 334–348. Tioga, Ca.

Gaschnig, J. (1982). Application of the Prospector system to geological exploration problems. In Hayes, J. E., Michie, D., and Pao, Y.-H., editors, *Machine Intelligence 10*, pages 301–323. Horwood, Chichester.

Klein, M. and Lu, S. C.-Y. (1989). Conflict resolution in co-operative design. *AI in Engineering*, 4(4):168–180.

Matwin, S., Szpakowicz, S., Koperczak, Z., Kersten, G. E., and Michalowski, W. (1989). Negoplan: An expert system shell for negotiation support. *IEEE Expert*, 4(4):50–62.

Mittal, S. and Dym, C. L. (1985). Knowledge acquisition from multiple experts. *AI Magazine*, 6(2):32–36.

Premkumar, G. (1989). A cognitive study of the decision-making process in a business context: Implications for design of expert systems. *International Journal of Man-Machine Studies*, 31:557–572.

Prerau, D. S. (1989). Choosing an expert system domain. In Guida, G. and Tasso, C., editors, *Topics in Expert System Design*, pages 27–43. North-Holland, Amsterdam.

Reboh, R. (1983). Extracting useful advice from conflicting expertise. In *IJCAI-83*, volume 1, pages 145–150.

Rissland, E. L., Valcarce, E. M., and Ashley, K. D. (1984). Explaining and arguing with examples. In *AAAI-84*, pages 288–294.

Smolensky, P., Bell, B., Fox, B., King, R., and Lewis, C. (1987). Constraint-based hypertext for argumentation. In Smith, J. B. and Halasz, F., editors, *Hypertext '87 Proceedings*, pages 215–245, NY. Assoc. Computing Machinery.

KNOWLEDGE-BASED SYSTEMS FOR MULTI-CRITERION DECISION-MAKING

David McSherry
Department of Computing
School of Engineering, Computing and Mathematical Sciences
Lancaster University
Lancaster LA1 4YR

Abstract

This paper examines the limitations of expert systems for applications which involve multi-criterion decision-making, including countless problems in business, commerce and industry. The unsuitability of production rules for such applications is illustrated. The need to explicitly model the priorities and preferences of the decision-maker, an issue which has been largely neglected in knowledge-based systems research, is emphasised. An approach to multi-criterion reasoning is proposed, based on a combination of applied systems theory and knowledge-based systems techniques. The proposed methods have been implemented in an integrated knowledge elicitation and consultation environment, incorporating tools for the elicitation of priorities and preferences.

1. Introduction

The explicit representation of knowledge is an essential characteristic of expert systems. Attention has recently been drawn, however, to the relatively limited effort which has been made to explicitly represent *preferences*. The neglect of this issue limits the effectiveness of knowledge-based systems for many applications (Bradshaw & Boose 1990). The present paper examines the limitations of expert systems for a particular class of applications, namely those which involve multi-criterion decision-making (MCDM). Countless problems in business, commerce and industry involve MCDM and so do most of the important decisions which people make in their daily lives, such as buying a car or a house, or choosing a holiday. The development of techniques to support this kind of decision-making would greatly extend the usefulness of knowledge-based systems.

Production rules based on attribute-object-value triples are widely used in expert system shells. The limitations of such rules as a method of knowledge representation for MCDM are discussed in section 3. The need to explicitly model not only the preferences but also the *priorities* of the decision-maker is emphasised. The *analytical hierarchy process* (AHP) provides a method of representing the priorities and preferences of the decision-maker and synthesising this information to produce an overall rating of the alternatives (Saaty 1980). Section 4 describes how the AHP can be adapted for the purposes of knowledge elicitation for MCDM.

Many knowledge elicitation environments, such as AQUINAS (Boose & Bradshaw 1988), its predecessor ETS (Boose 1985), and KITTEN (Shaw & Gaines 1988) use techniques based on personal construct theory. The *repertory grid* technique (e.g. Hart 1986) involves the elicitation of constructs by triads. Elements are presented in groups of three and the subject is asked to name a distinction with respect to which two of the elements are alike and the third distinct. The subject is then required to name the poles of the construct and to rate the elements, typically on a scale of 1 to 5. This is a painstaking process compared with the AHP, which does not involve triadic elicitation and requires the decision-maker only to name the relevant criteria and not their extreme values. Provided that the decision-maker can identify the relevant criteria unaided, it may provide a more realistic basis for knowledge elicitation for many applications.

A Prolog implementation of the proposed methods in an integrated knowledge elicitation and consultation environment is described in section 5.

2. Characteristics of MCDM

The following list of questions summarises the elements and reasoning processes which characterise MCDM.

1. What is your **objective**?
2. What are the **alternatives**?
3. Which **factors** will influence your decision?
4. Which of these factors are your main **priorities**?
5. What are the basic **criteria** for comparison of the alternatives?
6. What is your relative **rating** of each of the alternatives w.r.t. each of the decision criteria?
7. What relevant **data** about the alternatives is available?
8. Which of the decision criteria are **costs** and which are **benefits**?

If the objective is choosing a career, the alternatives might be law, medicine, and teaching. Factors influencing this decision might include job satisfaction, salary, prospects and status. Before the alternatives can be meaningfully compared, the decision-maker must identify his or her priorities (i.e. the relative importance of the factors). He or she may wish to decompose the problem further by identifying subsidiary factors. Factors influencing job satisfaction might include intellectual challenge and social interaction. By identifying subsidiary factors, the decision-maker builds a *decision-making hierarchy*. The leaves of this hierarchy are the basic criteria w.r.t. which the alternatives can be compared.

Questions 5 to 8 are concerned with the preferences of the decision-maker. Preferences w.r.t. criteria which involve subjective judgement are often expressed in terms of a relative rating of the alternatives. For example, the decision-maker may consider a career in law to be a better choice in terms of status than teaching. The absolute rating of alternatives w.r.t. such criteria is unnecessary (and may not be possible; one may prefer the taste of apples to oranges though be unable to describe the taste of either).

The evaluation of alternatives w.r.t. certain criteria does not involve subjective judgement. For many decisions facing the consumer (such as buying a car), relevant data (such as mpg recorded in independent tests on cars) may be available from consumer magazines or other sources. When the number of alternatives is large, this may be the only feasible method, but possible only when the criterion in question is an objectively measurable attribute of the alternatives being compared. If so, preferences can be expressed in terms of the preferred *values* of the attribute. Often it is sufficient to distinguish between benefits (such as mpg) and costs (such as price).

3. Limitations of production rules

In MCDM there is often a large number of alternatives, all of which must be evaluated before an informed decision can be made (although it may be possible to eliminate alternatives which fail to meet absolute constraints, such as an upper price limit). The limitations of production rules for problems involving selection from a large number of alternatives (even on the basis of a single criterion) are illustrated by the following rule from an expert system for selecting the motor insurance company which offers the most competitive premium.

> **if**   adjusted premium of company one = AP1
> **and** adjusted premium of company two = AP2
> **and** adjusted premium of company three = AP3
> **and** AP1 < AP2
> **and** AP1 < AP3
> **then** recommended company is company one

When there are only three companies to choose from, only three such rules are needed (if the possibility of ties is ignored). But if there are 100 companies to choose from, then 100 rules will be needed and each rule will have 199 conditions.

It is now widely recognised (Clancy 1983) that the implicit encoding of strategic and structural knowledge in rules limits the quality of explanations which expert systems can provide. Often rules also contain implicit assumptions about the preferences of the decision-maker, for example that *people prefer lower premiums*. Few would dispute the soundness of this assumption. But not all people prefer higher temperatures, say, when choosing a holiday destination. Failure to explicitly represent such individual preferences is a serious limitation in many applications.

In the above example, an insurance company is selected on the basis of just a single criterion. Another factor which the decision-maker may wish to consider is the company's reputation for efficiency of claims settlement. With the same three alternatives, three rules would be enough to deal with the case of a *clearcut* decision, for example:

> **if**   recommended company w.r.t. adjusted premium is company one
> **and** recommended company w.r.t. efficiency of claims settlement is company one
> **then** recommended company is company one

But which company should be recommended if company one is best w.r.t. adjusted premium and company two is best w.r.t. efficiency of claims settlement? The answer depends on the priorities of the decision-maker. In the absence of the necessary knowledge, expert systems often rely on heuristics which make implicit assumptions about the user's priorities, for example:

> **if**   recommended company w.r.t. adjusted premium is company one
> **then** recommended company is company one

By assuming the adjusted premium to be the overriding factor, the above rule ignores the possibility that the proposer may be prepared to pay a little more for the greater security of being insured with a more reputable company. Without such assumptions, the number of rules required rises rapidly with the number of criteria. In the above example, the introduction of a third criterion would increase the number of possible permutations to 216.

4. The analytical hierarchy process

The AHP was developed by Thomas Saaty (Saaty, 1980), who describes it as a general method for dealing with unstructured problems and shows how it can be applied to a great variety of business, personal and domestic, and public policy decisions. It provides a method of eliciting the decision-maker's priorities and preferences and synthesising this information to produce an overall evaluation of the alternatives.

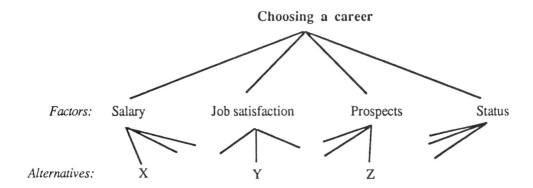

Choosing a career

Factors: Salary   Job satisfaction   Prospects   Status

Alternatives: X   Y   Z

Figure 1: A decision-making hierarchy for choosing a career.

Figure 1 shows a simple hierarchy for the objective of choosing a career. The factors which influence the decision are salary, prospects, and job satisfaction. The alternatives X, Y and Z (e.g. law, medicine and teaching) are also shown. In the AHP, the decision-maker's priorities are established through pairwise comparison of the factors. A matrix of priorities is constructed of which each element represents the relative importance of the corresponding row and column factors. If the row factor is considered by the decision-maker to be more important than the column factor (or of equal importance), then he or she enters a number between 1 (equal importance) and 9, indicating *how much* more important. If the row factor is considered less important than the column factor, then the reciprocal of a number between 1 and 9 is entered. In the example of Figure 2, the entry of 1/4 in row 3, column 4 of the matrix means that prospects are considered 4 times less important than status.

Choosing a career	Sa	J	P	St
Salary (Sa)	1	1/4	2	1/2
Job satisfaction (J)	4	1	8	2
Prospects (P)	1/2	1/8	1	1/4
Status (St)	2	1/2	4	1

Figure 2: Matrix of priorities constructed by the decision-maker.

Provided the decision-maker is consistent, much of the information contained in the matrix will be redundant, for the ij^{th} element of the matrix must be the reciprocal of the ji^{th} element. For example, if status is twice as important as salary, then salary must be 1/2 as important as status. Moreover, if job satisfaction is 4 times as important as salary and 8 times as important as prospects, then salary must be twice as important as prospects. Saaty's justification for requiring the user to fill the complete matrix is that it enables the *hypothesis* of consistency to be tested. In a consistent matrix, however, all the necessary information is contained in a single row.   Moreover, the row corresponding to the most important factor will contain only numbers between 1 and 9, the elicited priority for that factor being 1.

The following simplification of Saaty's prioritisation procedure may therefore provide a more realistic basis for knowledge elicitation for applications in which consistency may reasonably be assumed:

1. *Ask the decision-maker to identify the MOST important factor and assign this factor an elicited priority of 1.*

2. *Ask the decision-maker how MUCH more important this factor is compared with each of the remaining factors and assign them elicited priorities between 1 and 9 depending on his or her responses.*

The decision-maker's ratings of the alternatives w.r.t. to the decision criteria are elicited by the construction of similar matrices (Figure 3). Saaty (1980) describes a simple arithmetic procedure for weighting the alternatives by the priorities and preferences of the decision-maker to produce an overall rating of the alternatives on a percentage basis.

Job satisfaction	X	Y	Z
X	1	1/2	1/4
Y	2	1	1/2
Z	4	2	1

Figure 3: Rating the alternatives w.r.t. job satisfaction.

5. The McExpert environment

McExpert (Multi-criterion Expert) is written in LPA MacProlog™ for the Apple Macintosh™. It uses the Macintosh interface of windows, menus, graphics, and dialogs to provide an integrated knowledge elicitation and consultation environment for MCDM.   Whereas the role of the user in a conventional expert system consultation is merely to provide case-specific information necessary for application of the domain knowledge, McExpert extends the knowledge elicitation process into the consultation environment.   Elements of the problem (objectives, factors, criteria, alternatives, facts and rules) which do not depend on the priorities and preferences of the decision-maker may be elicited from a domain expert in advance and stored in the knowledge base. The priorities and preferences of the decision-maker, however, are directly elicited in the course of a consultation.   Additional factors or criteria which the decision-maker wishes to consider may also be elicited.

5.1 Knowledge representation and inference

There are two complementary knowledge representations in McExpert and two corresponding inference mechanisms. An hierarchical representation of objectives, factors and decision criteria is supplemented by domain knowledge represented in the form of Prolog facts and rules. The inference mechanism which drives the consultation is a logic programming implementation of the AHP. This is complemented by a Prolog meta-interpreter enabling domain rules and facts to be applied in the reasoning process.

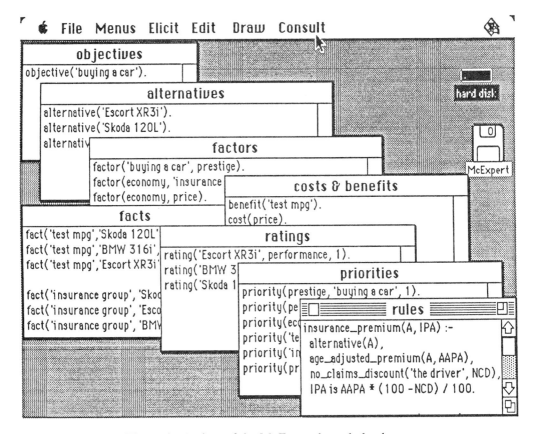

Figure 4: A view of the McExpert knowledge base.

An abstraction of the AHP (applicable to an unbalanced hierarchy of any depth) is represented by the following rules (which are implemented in Prolog):

if   F is a factor which influences X
and   the elicited priority of F w.r.t. X is EPFX
then the weighted priority of F w.r.t. X is the reciprocal of EPFX divided by the sum of the reciprocals of the elicited priorities of all the factors which influence X

if   O is an objective
then the overall priority of O is 1

if   F is a factor which influences X
and   the overall priority of X is OPX
and   the weighted priority of F w.r.t. X is WPFX
then the overall priority of F is WPFX * OPX

if   A is an alternative
and   C is a criterion
and   the elicited rating of A w.r.t. C is ERAC
then the weighted rating of A w.r.t. C is the reciprocal of ERAC divided by the sum of the reciprocals of the elicited ratings w.r.t. C of all the alternatives

if   O is an objective
and A is an alternative
then the overall rating of A w.r.t. O is the sum over all the decision criteria of the
      weighted rating of A w.r.t. each decision criterion multiplied by the overall
      priority of that criterion

Factual knowledge necessary for the evaluation of alternatives is stored in
the **facts** window (Figure 4) and used by the Prolog meta-interpreter. The following rule
provides the necessary link between the separate inference mechanisms. It distinguishes
between those criteria (such as mpg) whose values the decision-maker would wish to
maximise and those (such as price) whose values he or she would wish to minimise. The
necessary information is stored in the **costs & benefits** window (Figure 4). Weighting
of alternatives w.r.t. a cost criterion is on the basis of the reciprocals of their values.

if   A is an alternative
and C is a criterion
and C is a benefit
and the value of A w.r.t. C is VAC
then the weighted value of A w.r.t. C is VAC divided by the sum of the values
      w.r.t. C of all the alternatives

The evaluation of certain criteria may depend on additional case-specific
information e.g. about the intended use of an item to be purchased, or the needs and
circumstances of the consumer. One factor which influences the economy of a car, for
example, is the insurance premium which its owner will have to pay. This will depend not
only on the insurance group of the car but also on the type of insurance required, the age of
the driver, and the amount of the driver's entitlement to no-claims bonus. Such knowledge
can be elicited from a domain expert and stored in the **rules** window (Figure 4) in the form
of Prolog rules. The meta-interpreter provides the necessary extension to Prolog to ensure
that the user will be asked for case-specific information (such as the age of the driver)
needed to satisfy a goal for which no rule can be found in the knowledge base.

5.2 Eliciting factors, priorities and ratings
Figure 5 shows one of the modal dialogs used for eliciting factors which
influence the decision-making objective or subsidiary factors which influence another
(previously elicited) factor. A graphical display of the decision-making hierarchy (obtained
by selecting the objective from the **Draw** menu) is also shown.
The priorities of factors are elicited by comparison with the most important
factor. The decision-maker must first select the objective (or other factor) w.r.t. which
priorities are to be elicited. He or she is then is offered a menu containing all the factors
which influence that objective and invited to select the most important factor. The chosen
factor receives a priority w.r.t. the objective of 1. The priorities of the remaining factors
are elicited in a series of dialogs (e.g. Figure 6) in which the decision-maker is asked how
much more important this factor is in comparison with each of the remaining factors. The
options available to the decision-maker correspond to the standard priority values 1,3,5,7
and 9 of the AHP. If the user selects two adjacent radio buttons, the factor in question will
be assigned one of the intermediate priority values 2,4,6 or 8. In the example of Figure 6,
the factor of economy would be assigned a priority of 8.
Although the decision-maker's ratings of alternatives could be elicited by a
similar process, it is desirable to distinguish between the activities of prioritising factors
and rating alternatives. Additional advantages of an alternative approach are the provision
of a more interesting and varied user interface and greater efficiency in the case of a large
number of alternatives.

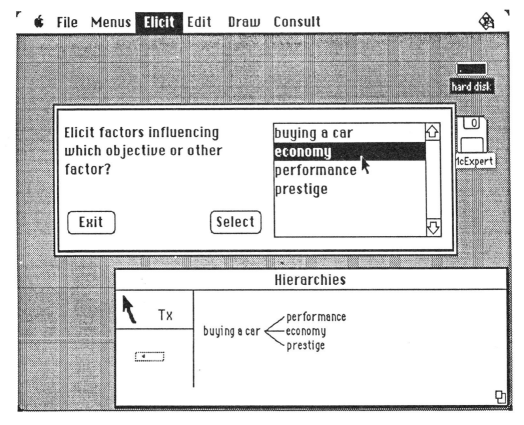

Figure 5: The decision-making hierarchy grows dynamically as new factors are elicited.

The decision-maker must first select the decision criterion w.r.t. which the alternatives are to be rated. By selecting from a scrollable menu containing all the known alternatives (Figure 7), the user is asked to indicate which of the alternatives he or she considers best w.r.t. the selected criterion. By shift-clicking the mouse, the user may select more than one alternative, indicating that the selected alternatives are rated equally highly. The selected alternatives are assigned a rating of 1 and removed from the menu. The user is then invited to indicate which of the remaining alternatives he or she considers to be best. The alternatives selected by the user on this occasion are assigned a rating of 2 and these in turn are removed from the menu. This process continues until no further alternatives remain (or just one remains). This technique enables *approximate* ratings of the alternatives to be elicited very rapidly.

5.3 The ratings editor

The ratings editor (Figure 8) provides an interactive graphical interface for increasing the precision of elicited ratings. The previously elicited ratings of the alternatives w.r.t. the selected criterion are displayed in a graphics window. Having selected the appropriate tool from the *tool pane* at the left of the window, the user can increase or decrease the rating of any alternative by clicking its button. In the example of Figure 8, the user has selected the tool (highlighted in the tool pane) for decreasing an alternative's rating and is about to decrease the prestige rating of an alternative. The effect of this action will be to move the alternative and its button to the right by one place and decrease its rating w.r.t. prestige by one.

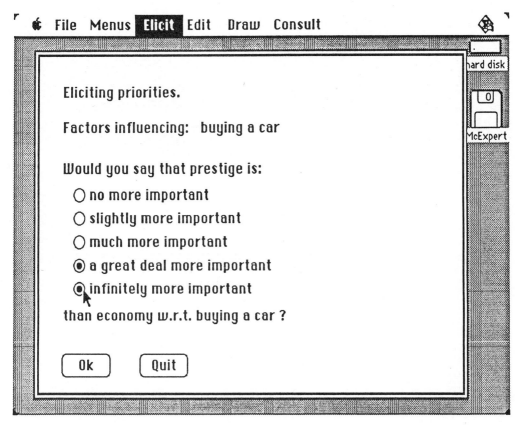

Figure 6: The priorities of factors are elicited by comparison with the most important factor.

5.4 Consulting the knowledge base

The decision-maker's priorities (unless elicited previously) are elicited during the course of the consultation. The method of evaluating alternatives depends on the nature of the decision criteria. In the case of a criterion w.r.t. which values for the alternatives are stored as facts in the knowledge base, no information will be required from the user. In the case of a criterion for which rules for evaluating the alternatives are found in the knowledge base, the user will be requested to provide any case-specific information necessary for their application. The user's ratings of the alternatives w.r.t. some of the criteria may have been elicited prior to the consultation, in which case they are retrieved from the knowledge base. Finally, in the case of a criterion for which no relevant facts, rules, or previously elicited ratings are found in the knowledge base, the user's ratings of the alternatives are elicited during the consultation.

At the end of the consultation, the conclusions are displayed graphically in the form of a bar chart (Figure 9) showing the overall ratings of the alternatives on a percentage basis. Rather than accepting the conclusions as final, the decision-maker can use the knowledge elicitation tools for interactive sensitivity analysis. Using the ratings editor, for example, he or she can review the ratings of alternatives elicited during the consultation and change the ratings to test how the conclusions are affected. The decision-maker may also examine the effects of introducing additional factors.

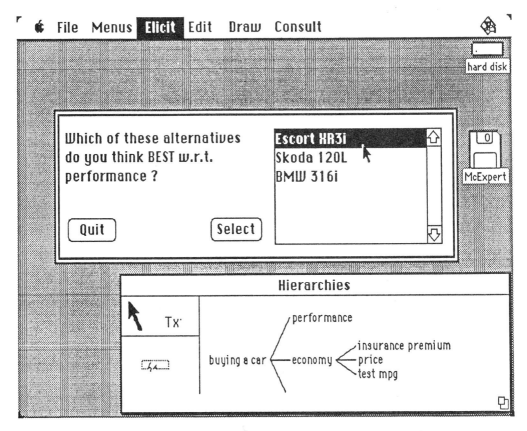

Figure 7: Eliciting the decision-maker's ratings of alternatives.

6. Discussion and future development

McExpert is a smaller and less complex environment than Aquinas (Boose & Bradshaw 1988) which incorporates a much greater variety of tools and techniques, including AHP tools. Unlike Aquinas and similar environments, its intended purpose is not the creation or prototyping of knowledge bases for rule-based expert system shells. It has been argued here that rules are unsuitable for applications involving MCDM. Instead of generating rules, McExpert combines an hierarchical representation of knowledge with logic programming to provide an integrated knowledge elicitation and consultation environment. In McExpert, the AHP is extended to include criteria for which the evaluation of alternatives is based on domain rules and facts (rather than pairwise comparison by the decision-maker).

McExpert elicits knowledge directly from the decision-maker. Much of the knowledge is elicited at consultation time and not entirely in advance as in Aquinas (Boose & Bradshaw 1988). For repertory grid elicitation in Aquinas and other tools, users are required to enter numbers representing their ratings of alternatives. An exception is KITTEN (Shaw & Gaines 1988), which provides interactive graphical tools for repertory grid elicitation. In McExpert, decision-makers can express their priorities and preferences qualitatively rather than quantitatively. It combines a linguistic approach to rapid elicitation of preferences with the use of interactive graphics for increasing the precision of the elicited preferences.

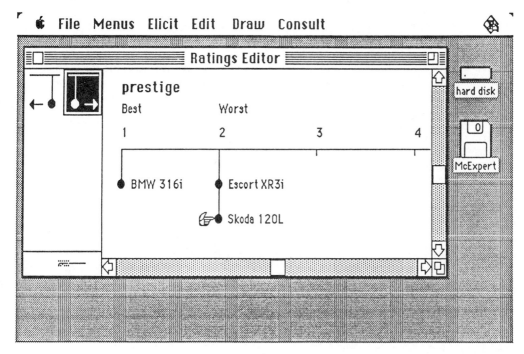

Figure 8: Increasing the precision of elicited ratings.

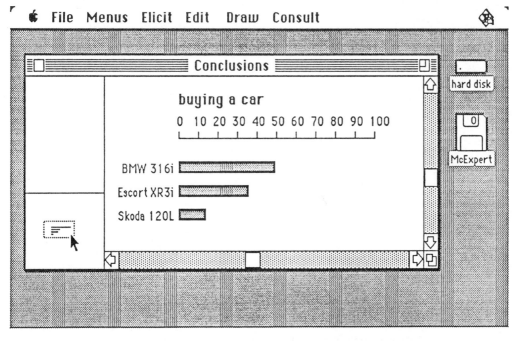

Figure 9: Overall ratings of the alternatives, based on the
priorities and preferences of the user.

Although McExpert distinguishes between costs and benefits, decision criteria are assumed to be *preferentially monotonic* in the sense that either a larger value is always preferred to a smaller one, or *vice versa*. Techniques for the elicitation of preferences w.r.t. criteria which are preferentially non-monotonic are being developed. It is also intended to develop techniques for eliciting absolute constraints (such as upper price limits) since in many problems the decision-maker may be prepared only to consider alternatives which satisfy such constraints.

Future research will investigate the suitability of McExpert for applications requiring large amounts of factual domain knowledge. A prototype expert system for the estate agent's office is being developed. Its role would be to elicit the priorities and preferences of prospective house purchasers in order to match their requirements with suitable properties on the estate agent's list.

References

Boose, J. H. (1985). A knowledge acquisition program for expert systems based on personal construct psychology. International Journal of Man-machine Studies, 23, 495-525.

Boose, J. H. & Bradshaw, J. M. (1988). Expertise transfer and complex problems: using AQUINAS as a knowledge-acquisition workbench for knowledge-based systems. In Knowledge acquisition tools for expert systems, eds. Boose, J. H. & Gaines, B. R., pp. 39-64. London : Academic Press.

Bradshaw, J. M. & Boose, J. H. (1990). Decision analysis techniques for knowledge acquisition: combining information and preferences using Aquinas and Axotl. International Journal of Man-Machine Studies, 32, 121-186.

Clancy, W. J. (1983). The epistemology of a rule-based expert system - a framework for explanation. Artificial Intelligence, 20, 215 -251.

Hart, A. (1986). Knowledge acquisition for expert systems. London : Kogan Page.

Saaty, T. L. (1980). The analytical hierarchy process. New York : McGraw-Hill International.

Shaw, M. L. G. and Gaines, B. R. (1988). KITTEN: Knowledge initiation and transfer tools for experts and novices. In Knowledge acquisition tools for expert systems, eds. Boose, J. H. & Gaines, B. R., pp. 309-338. London : Academic Press.

STRUCTURING FINANCIAL EXPERT SYSTEMS TO DEFEND AGAINST NEGLIGENCE

Vijay Mital and Les Johnson
Knowledge Based Systems Group
Department of Computer Science
Brunel University
Uxbridge,
Middlesex   UB8 3PH

Abstract

Reliance on an expert system carrying out complex reasoning, yet dispensing onerous advice at the boundary of a financial services organization, may potentially cause loss to a client and result in a legal challenge. The structure of the knowledge-base should be such as to facilitate the rebuttal of the challenge - a matter that has not been dealt with before.

Conduct-orientated legal reasoning plays a significant role in expert systems for comprehensive financial planning under the regulatory regime of the Financial Services Act. Such systems differ from rule-based systems used to select "suitable" financial products - where explicit modelling of legal reasoning is not essential. They also differ from most legal expert systems, in which the reasoning is from primary legal sources with minimal heuristic content. Those financial planning heuristics that are founded in precedents and hypothetical cases cannot easily have pertinent reasons attributed to them from primary sources. Explanatory or explicatory facilities, therefore, do not reveal sufficient cogent information to enable the user to readily decide whether an expert system has carried out valid reasoning to reach a purported solution.

Reasons or warrants articulated by experts to defend decisions are not coincidental with the reasons for reaching decisions; but both defensive and problem-solving knowledge is expressed in identical terminology. Defensive heuristics can be used to dynamically test solutions, but the reasonableness test requires that defensibility of a solution cannot itself be a primary criterion during problem-solving.

In this paper we present a methodology to acquire and differentiate defensive knowledge.

1. Introduction

Advice is available to the non-professional investor from various sources and in various forms. At the highest level of skill, a solicitor or accountant may arrange the affairs of a wealthy client to minimise tax liability using complex devices like customised trusts and off-shore companies. At the lowest level, a "product recommender" may advise a person of moderate means to buy a particular off-the-shelf financial service (product) as being tax-efficient or otherwise suitable for him. An adviser who undertakes a review of the entire circumstances of a client and formulates an overall strategy to meet qualitative goals such as inheritance tax provision and capital gains tax minimisation, but uses mainly standard products and devices to do so, falls somewhere in between the extremes. We will call him a "financial planner", even though mere product recommendation is sometimes styled as financial planning. The ability to provide a financial planning service is well recognised as giving an adviser (whether an agent tied to a particular product provider or independent) a distinct commercial advantage.

1.1.   Product recommendation without explicit legal reasoning

It is necessary for a product recommender to have some knowledge of the laws applicable to the financial products and human affairs. But, generally, the legal knowledge is given to him in a pre-digested form during training. In a computer model of his expertise, the lack of explicit representation of the legal knowledge appears not to have serious import.

It is possible to train operatives "from scratch within six to nine months at no great cost" to adequately carry out product recommendation (Howard, 1990). But expansion and staff turnover means that even such short training is not always available before they start dealing with customers. There are now several expert systems available, including some that the authors were involved with, to assist in selecting financial products like life insurance, unit trusts, mortgages, etc. (Anon., 1988; Bramer, 1988; Breeze, 1990). Essentially, *these systems classify the client - identified by means of certain personal, financial and attitudinal indicators - as being a "suitable" recipient for one or more of the products being considered.*

1.2.   Financial planning

Rather than classifying the client into predefined   "suitability-for-product" categories, *the objective during financial planning is to design a coordinated plan of action using, mainly, standard building blocks, to meet the demands of the situation* (Behan & Lecot, 1987).

Even where his role overlaps with that of the product recommender, reasonableness demands a higher standard of skill from a financial planner because he holds himself out as being capable of providing a more sophisticated service that has more serious consequences for the client. While financial planners do not need the same command of the taxation and other laws as do solicitors and accountants, the form of their knowledge has an intimate connection with legal knowledge, and their expertise is partly constituted by their grasp of those concepts. The presence of legal reasoning should be explicitly considered (Schlobohm & Waterman, 1987).

1.3.   Different emphasis of prior work

Most of the work on legal reasoning in expert systems has involved reasoning in and about the law, in an adversarial or notionally adversarial manner, with other knowledge playing a peripheral role, perhaps as aid to interpretation, or as basis of applicability of legal concepts to a factual situation (Berman and Hafner, 1989). This may conveniently be termed "litigation-related" reasoning. There are inherent difficulties in making the knowledge tractable and the concentration has been on the problems of computationally representing the formally recorded legal knowledge found in statutes, reported judgments, treatises, etc. (McCarty, 1977; Sergot et al, 1986). There is minimal heuristic content (Susskind, 1987). Most developers have acted as their own experts, not needing to encounter the problem of eliciting knowledge (Greenleaf et al, 1987).

In contrast, the financial planner's legal reasoning is aimed at determining his conduct. This conduct-orientated reasoning has a substantial heuristic element. There has been previous work in conduct-orientated legal reasoning. The major work was by the Rand group (Waterman et al, 1987). However, the issues that concern us here, viz., the significance of non-coincidence of justificational and decision-making reasons in spite of identical terminology, and the prohibition against using defensibility as a primary decision-making criterion, have not been dealt with.

When primary legal rules run out and no previous case fits the situation, a litigation-related system is expected to "produce at most some arguments relevant to the choice [of a] just conclusion" from a set of technically defensible possibilities (Gardner, 1987). The role of conduct-orientated systems is obviously wider. In fact, it has been envisaged that an expert system "should be able to interact directly with clients (possibly with the assistance of trained paralegals) to create their estate plans" (Schlobohm and Waterman, 1987). However, the issue of modelling knowledge in such a manner that a legal challenge resulting from an error in a knowledge-base can be met more readily, has not been considered by researchers in conduct-orientated legal reasoning. Nor has it received any attention from developers of financial expert systems in general (Humpert & Holley, 1988; Leinweber, 1988; Akelsen et al, 1989).

It can be foreseen that such erroneous advice produced by a financial planning expert system as is not obviously wrong, may be relied upon by a financial adviser. Due to the difficulty in attributing reasons to some of the heuristic knowledge, explanation facilities do not reveal sufficient information for the adviser to decide, without rigorous cross-checking, whether or not a valid reasoning path was followed. The legal issues of extent and apportionment of liability flowing from errors in expert systems have been mooted in abstract by a number of analysts (Frank, 1988; Turley, 1988), but there has been virtually no attempt to relate the legal issues to a concrete technological context or to the paradigms used by knowledge engineers to model expertise. We consider these aspects, in a domain-specific manner.

We will show that if a client suffers loss as a result of erroneous advice originating from a financial planning expert system and seeks to recover from the financial services organization using the system, the reasoning process employed by the expert system will be judged by the reasonableness test. We will characterize the reasonableness test and then go on to show that it contributes to the decoupling of defensive from problem-solving reasoning. It will be claimed that this decoupling must be identifiably maintained in the knowledge-base so that certain defences normally available to a human expert are also available when an expert system is relied upon. We will propose the active testing of financial plans by the selective use of defensive heuristics.

2.   Liability for loss resulting from reliance on an expert system

In the absence of decided cases, analysts have attempted to predict the manner in which the legal liability for errors may attach to and be apportioned between the various involved parties including the developers, contributors of knowledge, marketers, and system-owners. There is much controversy about whether an expert system can be treated as a 'good' or 'product', rather than as a 'service'; and whether some form of liability without proof of fault can be attracted. Mykytyn, et al (1990) have gone as far as to suggest that corporations seeking to develop or use expert systems should appoint "special counsels" to investigate the means of limiting legal liability before it arises. The analyses of issues in controversy have been summarized by Cook & Whittaker (1989) and Turley (1988).

2.1.   Fault-based liability for financial planning system

This is not the place to speculate upon the legal position of financial planning expert systems in general. It is sufficient to consider the following case which, for practical purposes, is the one with most relevance for us:

A custom-built financial planning expert system, developed in-house to forestall allegations of customization being a sham, is used by an adviser employed by a financial services organization ("the organization"). The adviser relies wholly upon a plan produced by the system and conveys it to the client who suffers loss as a direct result. The client seeks to recover damages from the organization.

In the above scenario it is difficult to hold the expert system to be a good or product (Turley, 1988; Mykytyn et al, 1990). Also, there is no question of any danger of physical damage or injury. In such situations, courts in the common law countries are essentially agreed that the occurrence of the damage itself is not sufficient to establish liability and the skills employed to perform the service need to be tested for reasonableness (Feldthusen, 1984). Further, the reasonableness test is relevant whether the suit is framed in contract or in tort, though the stringency of the test may vary (Feldthusen, 1984, pp. 140-163; Dugdale and Stanton, 1989, section 4.02). If resort is had to the remedies provided by the Financial Services Act 1986 which has set up a regulatory regime that binds a financial planner, the reasonableness test is again relevant. Substantial non-compliance with the rules of regulatory bodies is actionable under the Act. However, the rules are couched in wide terms, and import the reasonableness test from common law by the use of phrases like "reasonable grounds for believing that the transaction is suitable" and "using reasonable care" (Lownicka & Powell, 1987). The oft-cited umbrella concept of "best advice" encompasses these issues. The fault-based nature of liability in relation to certain financial expert systems (including financial planning systems) is discussed in more detail by Mital & Johnson (1990b).

2.2.   Unauthorized delegation
The self-regulatory bodies in U.K. have not yet objected to the use of expert systems by authorized financial advisers; though, in U.S.A., the Securities and Exchange Commission has left open the possibility that an expert system designed to recommend specific stocks may need registration as a financial adviser (Warner, 1988). However, provided that a system does not interface directly with clients, and the user accepts responsibility for all decisions, the matter of unauthorized delegation of duty need not trouble us (Willick, 1985), particularly because financial planning is not an *individually* regulated profession in the U.K., unlike law, medicine, and accountancy. It is highly unlikely that a higher standard can be required from a system used as a tool than from a reasonably competent human expert acting unaided (Frank, 1988).

2.3.   Different kinds of errors
Under the reasonableness test, the route taken to arrive at the advice has to be investigated, or it has to be seen whether there were any external factors that provided an excuse. There can be several causes of wrong advice:
(a)   although the knowledge is efficacious, factors unknown to the system (and the adviser) make the advice wrong;
(b)   there are programming errors in the knowledge-base; or
(c)   the knowledge is not efficacious because: (i) the knowledge of the contributing experts is inadequately represented or is used in a manner that the court finds unacceptable; or (ii) the knowledge is adequately embodied, but the source of the knowledge was not a reasonably competent expert.

Case (a) would generally be excusable. Case (b) is highly problematical and is concerned with the wider issues of whether expert systems should be relied on at all by professionals in the present fallible state of the art; the inertia inherent in the legal system will surely cause programming errors in expert systems to be treated, at least at first, just like errors in other computerised decision-making aids used by professionals (Willick, 1985). It is unreasonable to demand any more than that developers use the best practices available in the state of the art. Case (c)(ii) is not relevant here. Case (c)(i) is the important case, affecting our modelling.

2.4.   What the court can look for
The only attempt to relate paradigms used to model expertise and the legal issues of liability is a statement by Frank (1988) that "deep expert systems can generally be expected to deliver acceptable results over the entire useful range of the underlying causal model. Courts will undoubtedly expect greater vigilance from developers of shallow systems (or deep systems based on models that are not

robust) simply as a consequence of the diminished reliability implied by program design."

In the financial planning domain there is no semblance of an underlying causal model, but this does not really matter as the court too does not have any way of accessing the internal workings of the human mind. The court can merely receive evidence as to the supposed reasoning process so that it can eventually *ascribe* a reasoning process to a reasonably competent expert (Johnson & Mital, 1990). As such, it is possible to reconcile Frank's above statement with the practicalities in the domain of our concern by construing deepness as a relative term predicated on explicitness and competence (Keravnou & Washbrook, 1989).

If the knowledge-base is a mere "performance model" of expertise, aimed at reproducing, by means of synthesized knowledge, the results arrived at by experts in particular situations, without relating to the discernible form and dynamics of the expert's knowledge, then all that the court can see is that given certain facts the system arrives at a solution that reasonably competent experts would not. A small, excusable error may have led to a substantial deviation from the appropriateness target, but the protection of the defendable penumbra cannot be available.

But if the knowledge-base is a "competence model", then the organization of the conceptual structures of the knowledge, as articulated by the contributing experts, would be maintained during representation (Keravnou & Johnson, 1985) and would identifiably relate to the structure of the knowledge ascribed to human experts by the court. Then the court can more easily see whether the error is of a type that a reasonably competent expert could excusably make (Johnson & Mital, 1990).

2.5. A conceptual structure significant to reasonableness

There are many conceptual structures of the reasoning ascribable to a human expert that are significant to the finding of reasonableness (Johnson & Mital, 1990). In this paper *we are concerned with but one conceptual structure: the separation of defensive reasoning from problem-solving reasoning coupled with a restricted role for the former.* We will illustrate why this distinct structure needs to be maintained in the knowledge-base if the protection of the defendable penumbra under the reasonableness test is not to be lost.

3. The reasonableness test

The concept of reasonableness is the major cause of decoupling between the *a priori* problem-solving reasoning and *post hoc* justification. This is a very complex concept with varying meanings in different situations, but we can draw out some broad principles.

A *notional* peer review is applied to see whether the standards employed by reasonably competent professionals of equal standing have been met. In practice, the distinction between what domain experts actually would do in practice and what the court thinks they ought to do, is frequently blurred as it is the court that decides who is reasonably competent and that decision may or may not select practitioners of average competence (Jackson & Powell, 1987, p. 15).

The test is stringent as to the skills employed in appraising real world facts. Widespread disagreement is not countenanced and the decision needs to conform to that which would be taken by a *majority* of domain experts (Chapman v Walton). Skills in applying financial and legal knowledge to world facts are treated differently. Financial services organizations have different market positions and perspectives, and their interest in the outcome of problem-solving in identical factual situations can vary fundamentally. For instance, collective investment houses and life assurance organizations often provide similar services, but their underlying investment spreads and policies can differ. A portfolio manager may hold personal positions in situations connected with the solutions. The law recognises commercial realities to an extent, and it is normally sufficient that a *significant minority* of experts would do as the expert in question did. In any case, external conditions may be such as to make extremely difficult the task of establishing that something was actually unreasonable, e.g., advice about future performance of a volatile market (Stafford v Conti Commodity Services Ltd.)

3.1.   Missing narrowly is excused, aiming to miss is not

Around the recommendations that are considered to be acceptably achieving some qualitative goal, there lies a "defendable penumbra" of recommendations that are justifiable in the sense that it is difficult to conclude that they are actually unreasonable. However, the presence of the defendable penumbra should not be thought of as a licence to err. It is essential that an expert is not biased and considers all the facts of the situation before him. It is possible to lose the protection of the defendable penumbra if it can be shown that he has a fixed policy or heuristic such that, whenever a particular subset of facts is encountered, it invariably triggers a certain solution which is within the defendable penumbra but cannot be considered as acceptably achieving the qualitative goal. Equally so, if the heuristics are not sensitive to all the facts.

4.   Defendable penumbra illustrated

With experience, organizations form a shrewd idea as to what they - with their own peculiar interests and perspectives - can ultimately justify as being within the defendable penumbra, but that is obviously not open to public scrutiny prior to an actual challenge being made. We need not, however, rely on heuristics specific to a particular organization in giving the following realistic illustration of the principles.

The case involves a man aged 55, who has inherited an unencumbered house worth £95,000 and a cash sum of £45,000. He earns £14,000 per annum and, at the age of 65, will retire with an index-linked annual pension of about £6,500. He is a widower with independent, adult offspring. He previously had £7,000 capital, invested in National Savings Capital Bonds maturing in four years. He did not previously own a house. He is not averse to equity-related investments but does not seek to actively manage them. The plan recommended by the expert system and relied on by the financial adviser (a tied agent of a unit trust organization) is as follows:

The advice is to put £6,000 in a Personal Equity Plan, £7,500 in a high interest building society account with six months notice for withdrawal, and £7,500 in a building society instant access account. The system recommends that the balance, £24,000, be put in a selection of capital growth unit trusts offered by the adviser's organization, 80% being U.K. equity-based and 20% specializing in Far East equities. It is added that, should the client feel a need for more caution, index-linked Government stock be bought for £4,000 and only £20,000 be put in unit trusts. Other recommendations are not relevant.

It is possible to find various stereotypical justifications showing the reasonableness of the plan. One such justification is given below to *conditionally* justify the solution. In the illustration certain exceptional concepts which would disable the justification are not known. As such, justification has to be conditional on those exceptional concepts not actually being instantiated.

Basic justifying concepts:
U.K. resident; tax-payer; no income required from solution; no dependants; age over 50; suggested PEP and UT have "high" growth record; suggested PEP and UT have "wide" spread; client will have "secure" and accessible cash equal to over 50% of present income.

Exceptional concepts negated:
>   Client says he is "cautious"; client says he wishes to "speculate"; client
>   is an "active" investor; stagnant equity market forecast; direct purchase of
>   shares also recommended.

Exceptional concepts not known:
>   May need to liquidate at short notice; is changing resident status; likely
>   to become unemployed.

But the recommended plan is not qualitatively appropriate. Most experts would have considered the impact of inheritance tax (IHT) as the estate is already over the threshold figure of £128,000, and the client is old enough. They might have recommended insurance policies in trust or utilisation of the annual gift exemption.

If the concepts forming part of the above stereotypical justification were expressed as selectional criteria in the knowledge-base, then a court would quite likely find the advice negligent on the basis that a reasonably competent expert would not have such a coarse fixed policy. Instead, it may be that the problem-solving knowledge searched through the entire solution space and, due to an error of judgment during the chain of reasoning (e.g., ignoring IHT when the estate is fairly close to the threshold IHT figure), consciously ruled out steps to mitigate IHT liability. In that case the court would most likely find the advice within the reasonableness penumbra, on the basis of the instantiated stereotypical justification and, probably, on other grounds too.

This decoupling of defensive from problem-solving knowledge exists at the epistemological level, and has to do with the nature of the domain.

5. Epistemological distinctions

It is possible to give warrants or supposed reasons for a decision that do not reveal the decision-making process:
"... a judge functions ... as an engineer does. He has to make both an intellectual decision about which party has the better case ... and also a practical decision about whether to award judgment for that party. The two decisions are easily confused ... because precisely the same string of words may express both the intellectual decision and also the declaration of award. But [an intellectually] dishonest judge makes the two decisions differently, and correspondingly ... 'a has a good cause of action versus b' may be said to justify awarding judgment for a versus b. Now the proposition 'Any bridge built according to specification R is stable' may equally be said to justify an engineer's action in building such a bridge. However the justification here is based on a prediction about what will happen rather than on an evaluation of what ought to be done. Consequently the engineer has an opportunity to be borne out by what happens while the judge does not. But this difference arises from subject-matter, not logic - from being concerned with empirical facts rather than rules." (Cohen, 1970).

However, unlike in litigation-related situations, *defensibility or justifiability of the solution cannot itself be chosen as a guiding criterion during the a priori reasoning process*, which must be based on other qualitative criteria of appropriateness. Therefore, it is necessary to analyze the character of warrants or supposed reasons.

6.   Characterizing warrants

Much of the expertise of a financial planner can be articulated only in terms of cases and hypothetical examples. This is not surprising and the theoretical foundations of this phenomenon can be found in Kant's analysis of the concept of concept (Johnson, 1984). For Kant, concepts were categories of judgment kinds, some of which may only be illustrated through examples and cases. However, knowledge engineers and, at their instigation, domain experts, often seek to draw out deductive principles or rules from the articulated knowledge. Sometimes the principles which can be abstracted from the more frequently applied precedents come close to deductive rules (Ehrenzweig, 1971). More often, one can obtain no more than *presumptive* heuristics that are defeasible away from the context in which they were articulated. In other words, seeing concepts as nodes in a deductive framework is an abstraction; it may be a harmless abstraction provided that we realise that it is indeed an abstraction from a more complex situation.

It is difficult to pertinently attribute reasons (in the *explanatory*, let alone causal, sense) to heuristics derived from precedents (Gardner, 1987, p. 33) or from knowledge articulated in the particularised form of hypothetical cases. However, when pressed by a knowledge engineer, a financial planner will readily give "grounds" and "warrants" for the decision-making process. An example given by Toulmin, et al (1979) can be paraphrased to illustrate the nature of warrants:

Knowledge engineer ("KE"): What is the best policy of the company regarding this liquidity?

Expert's assertion: The company's best interim policy is to put this money into short-term municipal bonds.

KE: What is your ground for saying that?

Expert's "ground": Short-term municipal bonds are the best interim investment.

KE: What makes you give that ground?

Expert's "warrant": Short-term municipal bonds are easily traded and bring in decent interest, and the income is free of federal tax.

Particularly knowledgeable KE: That does not strike me as much of an argument - surely, we could obtain a much higher interest rate from private bonds without much loss of liquidity?

Expert's "backing": [examples, derived "rules", other principles].

Some warrants may be predominantly defensive in nature. Others may provide valid principles for problem-solving. Yet others may be spurious. We can state the principles behind the methodology for differentiating defensive from problem-solving knowledge, though with no claims to being exhaustive of this rich domain.

7.   Differentiating and augmenting defensive warrants

Some of the warrants are predominantly orientated towards deriving a higher level description of the situation from world facts, as opposed to deriving a concept more closely related to a component of the solution. There is no firm dividing line and it is a question of remoteness from concepts describing the situation itself, though simple illustrations can be given:

Situationally orientated warrants:

Income derived from the capital of a minor child is likely to be treated as that of the parent *because* the capital was provided by the parent, and...

The client is likely to have carried forward capital gains allowance *because* in the previous year the assets disposed off fetched a price lower than they were acquired at, and...

Solutionally orientated warrants:

An already held insurance bond should not be surrendered by a minor with substantial capital *because* the income produced is not treated as taxable, and...

Moving money from high technology shares into Swiss francs is beneficial *because* the latter are forecast to appreciate sharply term, and...

If a solutionally orientated warrant keeps occurring in various problem-solving situations in substantially similar guises, then it is possibly defensive in nature. The warrant can be further tested by seeing if it continues to be said to apply in spite of what are usually quite significant variations in those real world or circumstantial concepts that are not part of the warrant.

For instance, one may come across a warrant in the following form: "The client is not resident in UK; he is not liable to U.K. income or capital gains taxes; he is not planning to change residence; he does not need a regular income from the investment; solution XYZ does not have corporation or capital gains taxes deducted at source; and growth is forecast". The warrant can be tested by putting to the expert some hypothetical variations in the client's situation, e.g., changing age by 20 years, changing income from moderate to high, assuming that he has or does not have a family, and so on. Similarly, the combinational mix or quantitative spread of the solution set of which XYZ is a part, can be varied hypothetically. But the expert would insist that the warrant continues to provide support to the solution XYZ. The knowledge engineer would thus be able to see that though the warrant is *not capable of narrowing the solution space significantly, it is nevertheless felt to be inordinately important by the expert.* This would suggest strongly that the warrant is defensive or justificatory in character.

A stereotypical justification is defeasible by the presence of exceptional concepts. However, those exceptional concepts that are not immediately relevant may not be articulated during knowledge acquisition in a particular problem-solving context. In the above example, none of the suggested variational tests would have caused the expert to reveal that the illustrated warrant cannot be a sufficient justification if on-shore money funds existed in the solution set. There are many other exceptional concepts associated with this warrant, but they would come to light only when the warrant is made the focus of the knowledge acquisition, rather than via the usual technique of studying problem-solving reasoning. One may then also discover those alternative or complementary solutions that the warrant can support but which were not encountered earlier.

8.   Justificational knowledge to provide assurance

It has been mentioned above that justificational knowledge may not be used for problem solving. We propose to use justificational knowledge to provide assurance to the system-owner that a solution for which stereotypical justifications can be found will potentially be upheld by a court if challenged. Conversely, and perhaps more importantly, if a purported solution cannot be matched with a stereotypical justification, then there is need for greater caution before relying on the advice. System-owner organizations have to formulate their own peculiar policy in this matter.

To put the work presented here in its proper context, it may be added that we are extending the work done on second generation architectures by the Knowledge Based Systems Group at Brunel University. As part of this enterprise we are building a justificational task-model for expert systems in finance, including the financial planning application (Mital & Johnson, 1990a).

9.   Conclusions

The recognition of the decoupling of defensive from problem-solving reasoning has implications for the analysis and acquisition of knowledge in financial domains in general. Further, the knowledge-differentiation methodology presented above is directly applicable in many areas where conduct-orientated legal reasoning plays a significant role, such as discretionary portfolio management where allegations of churning are likely, and the monitoring of financial transactions for compliance with regulations. The development of second-generation expert systems, at least in the financial domains, requires modelling the conceptual structures of expertise. We have shown in this paper that - leaving aside the technical reasons - there are sound legal and commercial reasons for doing so. It is practically important for user organizations and developers to take these matters into consideration when thinking strategically about expert systems.

Acknowledgements

The authors wish to thank Prof. M.A. Bramer and Mr. C. Church for their helpful suggestion as to the structure of this paper.

References

Akelsen, S.; Hartvigsen, G.; & Richardsen, P.W. (1989). Knowledge_based systems for commercial line insurance. *AI Communications, 2,* 2, 98-109.

Anon. (1988). News. *Expert Systems,* **5**, 1, 58-59.

Behan, J. & Lecot, K. (1987). Overview of financial applications of expert systems. *Proceedings of The Western Conference on Expert Systems,* 223-229.

Berman, D.H. & Hafner, C.D. (1989). *Communications of the ACM,* **32**, 8, 928-938.

Bramer, M.A. (1988). Expert systems in business: a British perspective. *Expert Systems,* **5**, 2, 104-117.

Breeze, P. (1990). Be your own expert. *Money Management,* January, 47-49.

Chapman v. Walton (1833) 10 Bingham 57, per Tindal, C.J.

Cohen, L.J. (1970). *The Implications of Induction.* Methuen & Co.

Cook, D.F. & Whittaker, A.D. (1989). Legal issues of expert system use. *Applied Artificial Intelligence,* **3**, 1, 69-81.

Dugdale, A.M. & Stanton, K.M. (1989). *Professional Negligence.* Butterworths.

Ehrenzweig, A.A. (1971). *Psychoanalytic Jurisprudence.* A.W. Sijthoff-Leiden.

Frank, S.J. (1988). What AI practitioners should know about the law. *A.I. Magazine,* Summer 1988, 109-113.

Feldthusen, B. (1984). *Economic Negligence.* Carswell Legal Publications.

Gardner, von der Leith, A. (1987). *An Artificial Intelligence Approach to Legal Reasoning.* MIT Press.

Greenleaf, G.; Mowbray, A.; & Tyree, A.L. (1987). Expert Systems in Law: The DataLex Project. *Proceedings of The First International Conference on Artificial Intelligence and Law,* 9-17.

Howard, E. (1990). Testing time for the rule-makers. *The Sunday Correspondent,* 13th May, 23.

Humpert, B. & Holley, P. (1988). Expert systems in finance. *Expert Systems*, **5**, 2, 78-101.

Jackson, R.M. & Powell, J.L. (1987). *Professional Negligence*. Sweet & Maxwell.

Johnson, L. (1984). Medical Concepts. **In** *Knowledge Representation in Medical and Clinical Behavioral Science*, eds. L.J. Kohout & W. Bandler, 27-35. Abacus Press.

Johnson, L. & Mital, V. (1990). Developing second-generation architectures for financial-legal KBS: a modelling approach, Technical Report no. CSTR-90-3; available from authors, Brunel University, Uxbridge, Middx. UB8 3PH, U.K. To be published in *International Journal of Systems Research and Information Science*.

Keravnou, E.T. & Johnson, L. (1985). *Competent Expert Systems*. Kogan Page.

Keravnou, E.T. & Washbrook, J. (1989). An analysis of the architectural requirements of second-generation expert systems. *The Knowledge Engineering Review*, **3**, 4, 205-233.

Leinweber, D. (1988). Knowledge-based systems for financial applications. *IEEE Expert*, **3** (3), 18-31.

Lownicka, E.Z. & Powell, J.L. (1987). *Encyclopaedia of Financial Services Law*. Sweet & Maxwell. Regularly updated.

McCarty, L.T. (1977). Reflections on TAXMAN: An experiment in Artificial Intelligence and legal reasoning. *Harvard Law Review*, **90**, 837-893.

Mital, V. & Johnson, L. (1990a) Structuring financial expert systems to defend against negligence, *Technical Report* no. CSTR-90-1; available from authors; the report is closely related to the present paper.

Mital, V. & Johnson, L. (1990b) Professional negligence and the reasonableness defence in financial-legal expert systems: a developers' perspective, *Technical Report* no. CSTR-90-4; available from authors.

Mykytyn, K.; Mykytyn, P.P., Jr.; & Slinkman, C.W. (1990). Expert systems: a question of liability? *MIS Quarterly*, March, 27-42.

Schlobohm, D.A. & Waterman, D.A. (1987). Explanation for an expert system that performs estate planning. *Proceedings of The First International Conference on Artificial Intelligence and Law*, 18-27.

Sergot, M.J.; Sadri, F.; Kowalski, R.A.; Kriwaczek, F.; Hammond, P.; & Cory, H.T. (1986). The British Nationality Act as a logic program. *Communications of the ACM*, **29**, 370-383.

Stafford v Conti Commodity Services Ltd. [1981] 1 All. E. R. 691.

Susskind, R.E. (1987). *Expert Systems in Law*, Clarendon Press.

Toulmin, S.; Rieke, R.; & Janik, A. (1979). *An Introduction to Reasoning*. Macmillan.

Turley, T.M. (1988). Expert software systems: the legal implications. *Computer/Law Journal*, **8**, 455-477.

Warner, E. (1988). Expert systems and the law. *High Technology Business*, October, 32-35.

Waterman, D.A.; Paul, J.; & Peterson, M. (1987). Expert Systems for Legal Decision Making. **In** *Applications of Expert Systems*, ed. J. Ross Quinlan. Turing Institute Press.

Willick, M.S. (1985). Professional malpractice and the unauthorised practice of profession: some legal and ethical aspects of the use of computers as decision-aids. **In** *Computing Power and Legal Reasoning*, ed. C. Walter, 817-863. West Publishing Company.

ON CONCEPTUAL MODELS FOR DISTRIBUTED
OBJECT ORIENTED DATABASES

D R McGregor
Department of Computer Science
University of Strathclyde
26 Richmond Street
Glasgow G1 1XH

Abstract

To-day even more extensive computer systems are required by complex,
multi-centre organisations. This paper discusses why a Distributed Object Oriented
Systems Model matches well to these requirements. The Object Relational Database
Model is introduced, combining the attractive properties of Persistent Object Model
with the contents addressability of the conventional Relational Model. Multi-level
systems architecture for the support of the Object Relational Model in a concurrent
distributed processing environment is outlined.

1. Introduction

This paper is the result of recent studies of the requirements for a number of large-scale systems. These included a detailed analysis of the requirements for the support of healthcare, from the individual patient's personal, biochemical, medical and administrative data to the hospital, district and larger groupings.

While not particularly glamorous areas of operation, they are large, and reasonably characteristic of many applications in administration, government, and commerce.

They are also areas for which a clear commercial demand exists, because current conventional technologies are proving inadequate in at least three respects.

1. Accommodation to change
2. Implementation correctness
3. System performance.

Our earlier work [McGregor 1987], in collaboration with Deductive Systems Ltd., resulted in the Generis System, an Expert Database. This paper discusses the design of the Object Oriented Database Management Systems (OODBMS) aiming to exploit the processing capabilities of large arrays of MIMD processors with message sending capabilities, but distributed memory.

2. Application of Object Oriented Concepts - the users' view

Until recently Object Oriented Programming, has been mainly limited to languages and systems suitable for constructing sophisticated prototype systems, but not well matched to the needs or culture of the commercial world.

In particular, the single-thread, single address space, synchronous-message-passing model (as in SmallTalk) has been the general architectural model.

However in recent years increased attention has been given to the development of Distributed and Concurrent Object Systems [Agha 1986] [Yonezawa 1987]. Our aim in this paper is to discuss the application of the Object Oriented model in large-scale concurrent distributed database systems.

A typical large human organisation exists as a set of semi-autonomous centres, each responsible for a different facet of the organisation's activity, and communicating via messages. This matches the Distributed Object Oriented Model very closely.

In designing a really large scale and complex system such as a major healthcare application, the simplest approach is to build a model of the existing human organisation. Fortunately, with to-days' technology this is also a cost/effective approach.

3. 'Knowledge Centre Objects

Departments and sub-departments can be very readily modelled as objects to which messages are sent to effect appropriate actions. Often such departments are basically databases, for example a hospital's medical records archive. People trust such databases as objects, e.g. when a patient is admitted to hospital, the admissions section request the archives section to transfer the patient's records to the ward.

4. 'Knowledge Integration' Objects

A particular user application, may be conceptually to a single task, but may well involve general access to information throughout the entire system. Here the concept of a 'knowledge integration' object is useful (see figure 1). This may give access to local data, but its main function is to know 'who to ask' in order to extract required information from other high-level objects in the system. Clearly this concept is not limited to the outermost level of the system, but may in fact be carried out by any 'knowledge centre' object as required to fulfil its responsibilities. A key advantage is that they provide defined interfaces, enhancing modularity and imposing localisation of knowledge.

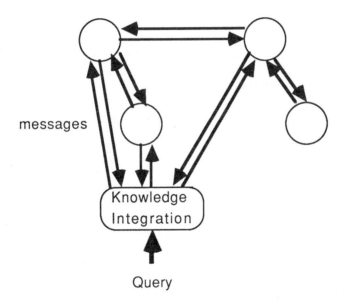

Figure 1. Architecture: A user's view

It seems clear, therefore, what users want from a distributed Object Oriented database model. They want modularity and modifiability which the Object model provides, combined with the clear identification of responsibility and ownership of data which the Knowledge Centre provide, and the system-wide access to information supplied by the Integration Objects. They also want the robustness which the hardware separation of the individual systems provides, and the narrow message protocol interface leads to trustworthy software.

5. Distributed Object Systems - a System Designer's View

The system designer is frequently concerned to find new ways of improving performance. Many current database and knowledgebase systems become grossly overloaded, and perform totally inadequately. The attraction of multi-processor distributed systems is that they open up the possibility of greatly improved performance. This can only be obtained however if ways can be found to allow multiple operations in parallel. The placement of logically and physically disjoint subsystems in separate processor hardware allows then to run asynchronously. A message sending protocol provides a narrow, formally-defined interface. Such a design thus captures the natural coarse-grain parallelism of the overall system. Such systems, however, only supply a limited degree of parallelism.   What is required is a means of load balancing between processors, and also of splitting large tasks into a number of sub-tasks to be tackled in parallel on multiple processors. In the case of a Knowledge Centre Object, standard database operations on large volumes of information may be candidates for this.

We shall now explore the basic functionality required of an OODBMS and compare it to a Relational Database Management Systems (RDBMS).

6. OODBMS and RDBMS - some comments

OODBMS's intended to take over the functions that to-day are typically undertaken by a Relations DBMS (RDBMS). It is a distinct datamodel in much the same way that Relational, Network, and Hierarchical are recognisably different datamodels.

The functions of the OODBMS are as follows:

1.   To provide a Persistent Object Store[Atkinson 1983];a means of storing the state of objects independent from the process which creates them, such that they can be sent messages etc. from different processes, via a 'handle' or object identifier, which too, must be persistent and unique.

2.   To provide an Associative Object Store; a means of selecting a set of objects by an associative access using the contents of the object's attributes known to OODBMS. (This corresponds to Relational contents addressing).

There is what at first appears to be a contradiction in treating objects in a contents addressable fashion [Tsichritzis 1988]. One of the important elements of the object paradigm is the notion of data hiding, and the private nature of the internal contents of an object.

This contradiction is resolved if we allow contents addressing only using the public message interface of the object. We can thus have a quasi Relational view of objects, each object being represented by a virtual tuple of values each value in the domain of values returned by a message function (or of course, an inherited message function) of the Object. Given this virtual Relational representation of the Object Database, clearly Relational Operations can be applied.

This Object Relation Model (Figure 2) is significantly different from the conventional Relational Model. The differences are due, of course, to the hidden data and built-in semantics of the objects, and provide the composite model with attractive properties.

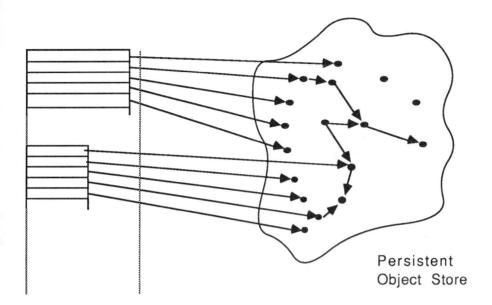

Persistent
Object Store

Virtual Relational view
of Persistent Object Store

Figure 2. The Object relational Model.

The public interface of Objects revealed in associative mode need only include an abstraction of general interest, not the full details of their internal data. There is no need to reveal this private data as it is acted upon only by the object's methods. For example, while an object representation for a robot manipulator might have internal information concerning the angles of its joints, oil pressures and so on, its public interface could be restricted to only items of general interest such as the manipulator position, its reach, its capacity, and its current load. The whole process of accessing the information necessary to manipulate the robot is rendered private, and the details hidden. In turn this makes it easier to maintain a stable virtual schema for the public interface.

As an Object is a single integrated representation of a single real-world entity, it follows that the OODBMS is not a 3NF format database, but each object effectively includes all associated repeating groups or relations necessary to its representation of the single real-world entity which it models. *The OODBMS is thus equivalent to a Non First Normal Form Relational Database.*

From the above it follows that the OODBMS is effectively in the 'all joined' from. Join is not required to collect data belonging to a single object.

Direct access via the object name is an important operation. Restriction is the main operation required to select appropriate sets of objects, with the set operations such as Union and Difference to combine results. The result of such database operations is to prepare a set of Object Names in an output register of the OODBMS.

7. The Programmers view - two possibilities

It is unequivocal that explicit accesses to an object via its handle or name should be handled automatically by the DBMS system. It is also clear that in general an access from an applications program to an OODBMS should be probably some form of hardware firewall to avoid inadvertent corruption of the OODBMS by applications program errors.

Two distinct views of the functionality of the OODBMS have emerged with regard to associated access to sets of objects:

a)   associative access to objects is handled explicitly by the programmers

b)   associative access is a built-in function of the OODBMS.

In the first case the philosophy is that the application should model human data handling strategy as far as possible. We can illustrate this by an example: in order to easily look up my telephone number, the telephone company maintains a telephone directory in which my number may be associatively looked up. This is a cheap and efficient process. However, if I have decided to remain ex-directory I cannot be located this way. If I have changed my name or address it is my responsibility to see that the directory is updated. Thus the directory is a separate explicit object for the purpose of ensuring efficient associative access. It is not in principle necessary as we could ask every telephone subscriber explicitly, however if there are many associative accesses and relatively infrequent changes, access to information can be facilitated low cost and will be greatly speeded-up.

The view which we have adopted in this paper however is that there would be significant advantages in an OODBMS going further than this in automatically providing associative access objects within it.

The alternative is thus to make associativity of access to an automatic property. How this is actually achieved is a matter of implementation, from the abstract model viewpoint, we neither know or care how this is being done - either by maintaining an attribute index, (a cache of virtual tuples representing the current public interface states of Objects) or by explicitly asking each object its property values.

8. The Architecture

This paper takes the term 'architecture' and applies the metaphor of a building more directly than usual to the domain of Object Databases. The model is concerned with systems for large scale applications using multiple distributed systems with interprocessor message-passing capability but without the necessity of a shared store (see figure 3).

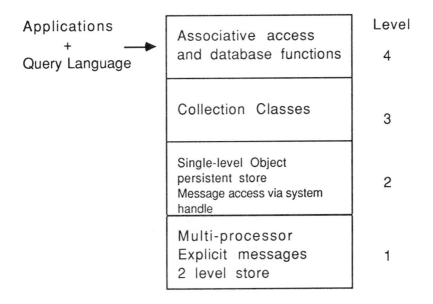

Figure 3. Four level model for Distributed OODBMS

The applications at which it is aimed require multiple simultaneous interactions, and the system must be capable of providing a highly reliable service, with protection of the data against accident or unauthorised access.

The 'top floor' of the database is as a collection of collections of objects providing

- associative access to each object via its public method interface. The basic result of this is a collection of objects.

    The most important operation is Restriction of a set, using Search Resource Objects. Effectively the Object Base is equivalent to a Non First Normal (Relational) Form.

- access to every object via its handle

- insertion

- deletion

- assignment of collections, union, difference, intersection, join and division.

It is to this level that applications interface including particular applications, and general query/display interfaces.

The 'first floor' provides a basic kit of parts to construct the 'top floor'. Typical parts are:

- objects
- collections of classes including:

  : sets

  : ordered collections

  : sorted collections
- standard interface classes for each of the basic classes of object

The 'ground floor' level is an 'ideal' simple object store providing:

- a single storage level persistent object store
- direct access to every object via its 'name' (an extended handle)

The basement 'floor': a distributed multi-processor system.

This supports the ground floor providing:

- virtual object store dealing with two-level physical storage
- concurrent objects with asynchronous message sending
- system-wide object handling
- exchange of messages requires the cooperation of both caller and receiver. Message queues etc. are not implemented at this level (at the next level, if required). For example a queue would be implemented as a queue object with push and pull primitives. A particular example could be a tuple store mechanism to manage the execution of messages by multiple processors, on the Linda model
- message sending at object level maps to local message sending and interprocessor message sending (as required by the virtual object store).

The code objects are defined theoretically as molecules and obeyed or interpreted dynamically. This would be one solution to the heterogenous processes distributed system.

An alternative is to treat each object as having code and data segments, and handle them suitably. As Objects belong to Classes in our system, and there will typically be many objects per Class, and these will have the same code segment, a separation of code from data is desirable. The ultimate extension of this is the code is permanently mounted, only data being in two-level store.

Dynamic code inheritance of methods from more general classes may be unduly expensive in a distributed processing environment.

Hardware store protection, limiting access and providing means to separate new unreliable applications from the database except via the message sending mechanism. The concept of each object running with its separate address space is attractive, but may prove too expensive for every situation. The alternative is to have some messages implemented by a heavyweight mechanism providing interprocessor communications with secure addressing limits, while a lightweight mechanism deals with messages sent between trusted objects within a single address space.

An alternative and more extensive treatment of the operating systems support required is given in [Russo 1989] describing the Choices system developed at the University of Illinois.

9. Distributed Object-Oriented Database Implementation

Access to an Object in the OODBMS is via a 'handle' or 'identifier'.. As this 'handle' must exhibit uniqueness and persistence it is a 'name' not an address and can be used as a means of tracking the object to its current environment. The analogy is virtual address to real address translation in segmented paging systems. More precisely we view the handle as a Capability allowing particular protocol (if desired) restricted access to its object. Following this we can envisage objects being paged to and from secondary storage, or migrating from on processor environment to another to achieve load balancing, and minimise inter-machine message passing. It is the job of the underlying system to position, move and maintain the physical address of each object.

There will only be one active representation of any individual object anywhere in the universe.

Like a real-world object, the object model can move about to different locations and machines, and can have itself photographed as often as it likes (i.e. have backup copies taken). Wherever it is, however, it is to that location that a message must be directed (even though the object can be moved to a convenient location prior to receiving the message).

Essentially Objects inhabit the machines. In fact every object will have quiescent periods when its stored representation is on a backingstore, and its current representation will reside in RAM and its methods will be activated by a processor.

10. Locating the physical address of an Object, given its name

In single-machine object oriented programming systems, the object's identifier is often the memory address of the object, or the address of a table entry which in turn contains the address of the object (to permit easier garbage collection).

In systems which permit 'persistent storage' of objects a look-up table, often implemented in fast hardware is used to turn the object's name into a real machine address. The Rekursiv machine (Linn Products Ltd.) has this facility for a single-processor, single memory system. The frequency of message sending, relative to other code obeyed determines how necessary such a hardware facility is, to obtain reasonable performance. If a typical method involves a significant portion of code between messages such a facility is less necessary, and a software-based associator may suffice in some situations.

11. Mapping the architecture to a Transputer Array

The Transputer is a microprocessor device intended as a node processor array. It is supplied by INMOS. A Transputer array permits fast interprocessor message sending via the Transputer's 4 hardware links. The machines can each have their own memory RAM, but there is no shared memory access. Whatever the physical network topology adopted for the inter-transputer network, message sending from any processor to any other processor is implemented as a virtual function, by a low-level of the system software.

Objects reside on different machines distributed according to various strategies.

For the distributed Object Database systems prototype we are concerned with here, message translation via software associator will be used. Only some messages will require to use real message-sending (if they are to an object on a different machine), otherwise the message will be to an object on the same machine, which will incur lower overheads.

Each machine manages its storage by some acceptable technique, such a relegating Least Recently Used objects to a backing-store. When an object currently on backing store is sent a message, it is activated and brought into the store of a convenient machine. (In many ways this suggestion is analogous to a demand paged capability-based architecture). There may be many strategies which will have to be evaluated, and it is well to recall how many plausible paging schemes were found to be disastrous to performance when paged operating systems were a new development. An initial and simple strategy is to transport each object to the machine from which it received the message. Some objects are permanently located because they represent physical devices attached to a particular machine, and hence in a machine with many external objects this immediately ensures considerable initial parallelism.

This strategy:

a)   brings cooperating objects into the same machine, where message sending costs will be minimised

b)   puts processes which are forced to be sequential into the same machine.

If, however, an object is already in the system, a message will be routed to it. At this stage it must be left to decide whether LRU should differentiate between externally routed messages and internally routed ones, and whether code should be treated separately from data (in some systems it may be acceptable to have the primitive classes permanently compiled into each machine).

When an object is removed from active store, or moved to another location,the name/address tables in each machine will require to be updated consistently. This will, of course require message sending, but the messages are essentially a broadcast. which visits all machines. This is less inefficient than might at first be supposed in many common physical network topologies and is analoguous to the action of 'snoopy caches' on shared memory parallel machines.

12. Consistent Updating

An object is responsible for the consistency of its methods i.e. it is effectively a 'monitor' in the classical sense. Many inconsistent update problems occur because the representation has more degrees of freedom than the real-world object. This cannot occur in the object oriented model described above.

13. Concurrent Implementation of Database Primitives

Parallelism is frequently classified as *functional* in which different functions are handled by different sub systems e.g. communications or disk controllers, or *non-functional* in which the processing of an individual function is split among a set of parallel processes. Object parallelism is different from either of the above. In the above scenario we have already (hopefully) split the database resources between a number of distinct database objects, some of which can call on others as subsystem objects to deliver answers to queries. At this stage therefore there is already a degree of functional parallelism. Let us now consider the maintenance of a single intelligent database object, and the execution of its functions. A number of objects representing major subsystems will cooperate in answering a query. As we are not dealing with a shared store machine, however, each processor would either have to hold a different portion of the data, or the processor would first have to read in data for example from a RAM "backing store", or from a genuine backing store transfer. It is suggested that a cache object should be responsible for maintaining frequently required results according to a Most Recently Used algorithm. Beyond this we envisage data parallelism in which say different portions of an array are considered as separate objects, and activated concurrently. This will occur when the data required exceeds the storage of a single machine, or the computation becomes too heavy. This type of parallelism deals with the heaviest computation demands on the system.

The Associative Tuple Store Mechanism of the Linda programming system appears to be an attractive model for implementing the inter-process message passing. The Linda conceptual computational model of parallelism is well suited to the implementation of distributed systems. The Linda model can be viewed as a way of activating ready-to-run object processes, as available processors (with appropriate code and data) pick up messages to implement.

14. Conclusion

The aim of our work is to advance the state of technology of large Object Knowledgebases so as to be capable of handling the operations of a large organisation in an integrated and cohesive way, while providing the minimum restriction on its flexibility to meet future development needs.

We have discussed the Distributed Object Oriented Database from a number of viewpoints. The attraction of the concept from the users' standpoint, where the system can be seen as a combination of largely independent systems, were noted.

We have presented an abstract model - the Object Virtual Relational Model for Object Oriented Database Systems. This combines the concepts of a Persistent Object Store, with those of the Relational Datamodel.

A multi-level architecture for such a Distributed Object Relational Database was outlined.

The architectures of multi-processor arrays (such as Transputer arrays), and collections of workstations connected by the LAN provide a good implementation base for the inherent potential parallelism of the Distributed Object Oriented Database Model, which provides an environment for application of problem-oriented techniques to large scale systems.

References

Agha, G. (1986). A Model of Concurrent computation in Distributed Systems. MIT Press .

Atkinson, M.P. Bailey, P.J., Chisholm, K.J., Cockshott, W.P. & Morrison, R. (1983). An Approach to Persistent Programming. The Computer Journal, 26 (4) pp 360-365.

Cox, B. (1986). Object Oriented Programming: an Evolutionary Approach. Addison Wesley.

McGregor, D. McInnes, S. & Henning, M. (1987). An Architecture for Associative Processing of Large Knowledge Bases. Computer Journal, Vol. 30, pp 403-412.

Russo, V.F & Campbell, R.H. Virtual Memory and Backing Storage Management in Multiprocessor Operating Systems Using Object Oriented Design Techniques. Proceedings of OOPSLA/1989, pp 267-278.

Tsichritzis, D.C. & Nierstrasz, O.M. (1989). Fitting Round Objects into Square Databases. Gjessing S & Nygard, K. (editors). Proceedings of the European Conference on Object Oriented Programming. Springer Verlag.

Yonezawa A. & Tokoro M. (Editors). (1987) Object Oriented Concurrent Programming. MIT Press.

Default Information in Database Systems

Peter King[†], Alexandra Poulovassilis[‡] and Carol Small[†]

Abstract

Recent work in database systems has proposed the use of default rules to extend the apparent information content of a database using explicitly stated assumptions. This work, carried out in the context of the logic paradigm, is briefly reviewed. We then also review how such defaults can be coded in FDL, a recently introduced database language which follows the functional paradigm. The paper concludes with some comparative comments and suggests further work.

1. Introduction.

Conventional database systems provide facilities for the storage and management of time dependent factual information. Deductive databases provide also for the specification and use of *derivation rules* which allow the inference of implied information from stored information. In some application areas there is also advantage in allowing *default rules* which are based on assumptions in addition to stored data. Consider, for example, the sending of mailshots to potential customers. If retired people are being targeted but the quality of the "occupation" data is not high and/or has many missing values, but there is age data available, then a reasonable assumption would be that any person over 65 is retired. Other assumptions of this type commonly made are that income level is associated with location and that some forenames are associated with age bracket.

In all these cases we are effectively extending the information content on the basis of the usefulness of being right versus the cost of being wrong. Clearly one should not make such assumptions where to be wrong would have serious adverse consequences even when the probability of being right is very high e.g. that blood taken from a random donor is not HIV positive.

In this paper we address the provision of database facilities to handle default assumptions and show how these assumptions can be made explicit and incorporated into the database schema as opposed to being coded into application programs. We take the view that a database comprises information about entities, their attributes, relationships among them, and constraints and rules reflecting the real world situation of which the database is a model. Such a database can be formulated in the conventions and notations of logic and this is one of the two approaches we adopt in the present work - the database is then seen as comprising a collection of clausal form formulae. The other approach we adopt here is an entity/functional viewpoint in which the database is seen as comprising a

---

[†] Department of Computer Science, Birkbeck College London, Malet Street, London WC1E 7HX
[‡] Department of Computer Science, University College London, Gower Street, London WC1E 6BT

collection of entities and functions over them.

In Section 2 of the paper we discuss how default information can be handled from the logic viewpoint and in Section 3 we consider the provision of the same functionality from the entity/function viewpoint. We give our concluding remarks in Section 4.

2. Default Information from a Logic Viewpoint.

With deductive databases we can have a derivation rule such that if all antecedents hold then the consequent must necessarily also hold. For example, using a logical style notation, for any α and β such that father(α,β) holds then a necessary consequence of

$$parent(X,Y) \leftarrow father(X,Y)$$

is that parent(α,β) also holds.

In addition to implied information it is frequently useful for a database system to enable *assumptions* to be made where data values are unknown. Given a *default rule* such that the prerequisites hold and the consequent is consistent with the database content, then the consequent can be assumed. For example, again using a logic style notation we may use the default rule

$$married(X,Y) \twoheadleftarrow father(X,Z) \wedge mother(Y,Z)$$

to specify the assumption that if α is the father of γ and β is the mother of γ then, unless there is information to the contrary, α is married to β.

Taking the logic view of the relational model, the intention of each relation is seen as an n-ary predicate and the extension as a set of n-tuples for each of which the predicate is true. For each such relation either the *Closed World Assumption (CWA)* or the *Open World Assumption (OWA)* can be made. The former assumes that *all* n-tuples for which the predicate is true are present in the extension, and thus for any other n-tuple the predicate is false. The Open World Assumption allows there to be further n-tuples not in the extension satisfying the predicate, and thus for any other n-tuple the truth or falsity of the predicate is unknown. These two assumptions are commonly made in database practice, although often implicitly in terms of the context and embedded in the functionality of the application programs.

Reiter's default logic (Reiter 1980) provides a more flexible approach to missing and incomplete information than either the OWA or the CWA. We can adapt Reiter's default reasoning to the database environment in order to provide a mechanism for making assumptions about data which is neither recorded nor can be inferred using the derivation rules, based upon what is usual, or on statistical considerations, weighted according to the penalties incurred should the assumptions be wrong. The defaults will be explicit and specified at schema or sub-schema level and not embedded in program code as hitherto.

Adapting Reiter's notation we express an assumption as a default in the form :

A(X) ⟵ P(X) & M C(X)

where A(X) is the assumption to be made (about X), P(X) is the prerequisite which must be true for the assumption to be made, and M C(X) expresses the consistency requirement. The notation may colloquially be read : "if P(X) is true then in the absence of information to the contrary assume A(X)", the information to the contrary being that C(X) is false. For example, we can express the assumption that persons aged over 65 are retired with the default :

Retired(X) ⟵ AgeOver65(X) & M Retired(X)

In this paper we discuss only those cases like this one where A(X) and C(X) are identical, which is thought to cover the majority of practical cases; consequently we omit the consistency component when writing defaults. Persuasive arguments that most defaults are of this form are given by Reiter, although the need for the more general form has been demonstrated by several authors including Reiter (1981), Touretsky (1986) and Etherington (1987).

It is possible to write defaults which, in some circumstances, are contradictory. Thus, if we allow more than one profession for an individual the two defaults :

Male(X) ⟵ Soldier(X)
Female(X) ⟵ Nurse(X)

are ambiguous when taken in conjunction with the derivation rule

¬Female(X) V ¬Male(X)

If the defaults are activated sequentially rather than simultaneously then the activation of the first would cause Male to be assumed which would then prevent the activation of the second; and vice versa. If, on the other hand, the defaults are activated simultaneously then two inconsistent assumptions will be made. Given a set of default rules the problem of detecting whether such inconsistencies can arise is discussed by King and Small (1989) and a solution given. The inconsistency in defaults once detected can always be removed by modification of the prerequisites to prioritise them.

For example, consider the following database :

nurse(bob)
nurse(mary)
soldier(bob)
soldier(jim)
¬soldier(X) ⟵
¬nurse(X) ⟵
male(X) ⟵ soldier(X)
female(X) ⟵ nurse(X)

In this case there is only one extension (the information after applying the default and derivation rules to the stored data) which contains the following clauses :

female(bob)
female(mary)
male(bob)
male(jim)

Note that our definition allows a database to have more than one distinct extension, as would arise if we add the following rule to our example database :

¬male(X) V ¬female(X)

Now we obtain two distinct extensions :

female(bob)	male(bob)
female(mary)	female(mary)
male(jim)	male(jim)

In many practical cases the user will require a database to give rise to only one extension, and will believe the database to be in error if it supports contradictory extensions. By extending one or other of our defaults we can ensure that conflicts do not arise by giving priority to one of the defaults :

male(X) ⟵ soldier(X) ∧ ¬nurse(X)

Here we have given priority to the default which allows us to assume that someone is female since we cannot use the above default to draw the conclusion that bob is female since we cannot show ¬nurse(bob). Alternatively, we can re-express *both* defaults to ensure that *no* conclusions are drawn regarding the sex of someone who is both a soldier and a nurse :

male(X) ⟵ soldier(X) ∧ ¬nurse(X)
female(X) ⟵ nurse(X) ∧ ¬soldier(X)

3. Default Information from a Functional Viewpoint.

Taking the view of an entity/function data model of Shipman (1980) and Poulovassilis (1989), the domain of discourse is modelled by means of entities and functions between them. Queries are formulated by applying functions to arguments, and query evaluation consists of repeatedly *reducing* (Peyton Jones 1987) function applications until none remain in the query. Each function is declared as taking zero or more arguments of a given type and returning a value of a given type. For example, we can declare the single-argument functions "age" and "retired", and the 0-argument function "retirement_age" :

age	: person → integer
retired	: person → bool
retirement_age	: integer

Each entity is declared as a uniquely named *constructor function* (Peyton Jones 1987) where a constructor function is a tag of a union type or, equivalently, a function with no rewrite rules (we distinguish between functions and constructor functions by giving the former names which begin with a lowercase letter and the latter names which begin with an uppercase letter). For example, we can declare the union type "person" and the people "Jim", "Mary" and "Bob" :

    person :: sum
    Jim   : person
    Mary : person
    Bob : person

We can also extend the "person" type with a sub-domain of null values by declaring a constructor Unknown_person which takes an integer argument and returns a value of type "person" :

    Unknown_person : integer $\rightarrow$ person

Each function is defined by a number of equations (to be used as reduction rules) with distinct left hand sides. For example, the 0-argument function "retirement_age" can only have one defining equation :

    retirement_age = 65

say, while the functions "age" and "retired" may have a number of defining equations :

age	Bob	= 70	(1)
age	Mary	= 67	(2)
retired	Mary	= false	(3)
retired	v	= (age v) > retirement_age	(4)

During query evaluation, a *pattern-matching algorithm* (Peyton Jones 1987, Field and Harrison 1988) determines the single equation which the defines a function for a given set of arguments; the function and its argument then reduce to the right hand side of this equation with its variables appropriately instantiated. For example, in the query

    retired Mary

the function application "retired Mary" matches the left hand side of two equations, (3) and (4) above, and the pattern-matching algorithm must chose one of them in some deterministic fashion. If, as we assume from now on, the pattern-matching algorithm regards a constant as a preferable match for itself than a variable, the equation chosen would be (3) and "retired Mary" would reduce to "false".

It is clear that given such a pattern-matching strategy, equations with variables on their left hand side can be used as default equations which may be over-ridden by more specific equations. For example, equation (4) may be used to derive a value of "true" for the query "retired Bob" while equation (4) is over-ridden by equation (3) for the query "retired Mary".

This is not quite the whole story for, clearly, given the incremental definition of functions by the insertion and deletion of equations, it may be the case that the equations currently defining a function do not cover the entire domain of the function. For example, equations (3) and (4) cover the entire person domain for the function "retired" but equations (1) and (2) do not for the function "age". Assumptions analogous to the CWA and OWA of logic databases are made about partially defined functions such as "age" - these assumptions may be termed *error-as-failure* and *null-as-failure*. The former strategy is adopted by most functional programming languages : it assumes that all the arguments for which the function is defined are covered by the current equations and that an attempt to apply the function to any other argument results in the query aborting with an error message. The latter strategy is adopted by the functional database language FDL (Poulovassilis 1989, Poulovassilis & King 1990) and reduces function applications which do not match any current equation to a null value "@", denoting "currently undefined". @ is a first-class member of all types and can be used in equations and queries just as any other constant.

It follows from the above discussion that from the entity/functional viewpoint a database consists of a set of declarations of types, functions and constructor functions, and a set of equations which are type-correct with respect to the declarations. Equations can be partitioned into facts (ground equations) and derivation rules (non-ground equations) both of which are used as reduction rules during query evaluation. Since the semantics of pattern matching are deterministic, there is no need for a further category of default rules since these can be expressed as derivation rules. There can only be one extension to any functional database.

As a final example in this Section, consider the soldier/nurse example of Section 2. Given the functions

$$
\begin{array}{lll}
\text{male} & : \text{person} \rightarrow \text{bool} \\
\text{female} & : \text{person} \rightarrow \text{bool} \\
\text{nurse} & : \text{person} \rightarrow \text{bool} \\
\text{soldier} & : \text{person} \rightarrow \text{bool}
\end{array}
$$

we can define the following default equations for them :

$$
\begin{array}{llll}
\text{female} & v & = \text{nurse } v & (5) \\
\text{male} & v & = \text{soldier } v & (6) \\
\text{nurse} & v & = \text{false} & (7) \\
\text{soldier} & v & = \text{false} & (8)
\end{array}
$$

If we also have the following definitions for "nurse" and "soldier"

$$
\begin{array}{lll}
\text{nurse} & \text{Bob} & = \text{true} \\
\text{nurse} & \text{Mary} & = \text{true} \\
\text{soldier} & \text{Bob} & = \text{true} \\
\text{soldier} & \text{Jim} & = \text{true}
\end{array}
$$

then

  female Bob = male Bob   = female Mary = male Jim = true
  male Mary = female Jim   = false

If it is unacceptable to infer that a person is both male and female because they are both a nurse and a solder then we can choose for them to be either male or female (by default) by adding an extra condition to either (5) or (6), respectively :

  female v = (nurse v) and (not (male v))   (5´)
  male   v = (soldier v) and (not (female v))   (6´)

Then, with (5´) and (6) we have

  male Bob = true
  female Bob = false

and with (5) and (6´) we have

  female Bob = true
  male Bob = false

We note that we must chose between these two default configurations since with both (5´) and (6´) the queries "male Bob" and "female Bob" would fail to terminate. Finally, it is worth noting that if we modify (5) and (6) as in Section 2 :

  female v = (nurse v) and (not (soldier v))   (5´´)
  male   v = (soldier v) and (not (nurse v))   (6´´)

then both "male Bob" and "female Bob" reduce to "false". This is where functional defaults differ slightly from the default rules of Section 2 since with the latter no information would be derived about the status of Bob as male or female.

4. Conclusions.

  In this paper we have discussed how DBMS based on the logic and functional paradigms can encompass default information. We have shown how in both cases default assumptions can be stated explicitly as part of the schema information rather than by being coded within application programs. The main difference between the two formalisms is that with the functional approach a query either reduces to a definite value or fails to terminate, whereas with the logic formalism either the required property is shown to hold, or we fail to show that the property holds, or again the query may fail to terminate.

  We foresee applications of database systems with default facilities particularly in areas such as marketing where action on the basis of probabilities is reasonable. The ease with which default rules can be changed is important in this context since it facilitates change between broadly based and narrowly focussed targeting. Notice that this activity, at its most simple the selective printing of mailing labels from a serial pass of the database entities, will frequently be fast batch processing rather than an on-line activity.

For such activity the print/non-print decision must be taken automatically for every database entity whatever data is missing and a "don't know" or "can't decide" outcome is impracticable. Moreover, marketing information is typical of application areas where useful information comes to be stored on an incremental basis and incomplete information is of the essence. Useful information on particular entities will be stored when there is no prospect of such information becoming available for every database entity.

Our work also has a more prosaic but important application in easing data entry and thus improving the human/computer interface in screen-based applications. Consider, for example, a form-filling interface in which the user gives the values of attributes of an entity by completing fields on the screen. Rather than initially displaying these fields as blank, default values can be placed in them which are derived from the default rules; these values can then be overwritten if they do not apply. It should be stressed that the defaults displayed are calculated dynamically, possibly changing as fields are completed.

The developments we are pioneering follow in the established route of the long-term evolution of DBMS, the objective being to remove as much of the problem specification as possible from application programs and into the schemas and sub-schemas. This approach makes systems more readily modifiable and so more maintainable and amenable to prototyping and evolutionary development.

Acknowledgements.

This work was carried out in the context of the TriStarp project, and the authors are grateful to IBM U.K. Laboratories, Hursley, and the SERC for support.

References.

Etherington, D.W. (1987). Formalizing Non-Monotonic Reasoning Systems, Artificial Intelligence (31).

Field, A.J. Harrison, P.G. (1988). Functional Programming, Addison Wesley.

King, P. and Small C. (1989). Default Databases and Incomplete Information, submitted for publication.

Peyton Jones, S. (1986). The Implementation of Functional Programming Languages, Prentice Hall.

Poulovassilis, A. (1989). The Design and Implementation of FDL, a Functional Database Language, Ph.D Thesis, Birkbeck College, University of London, 1989.

Poulovassilis, A. and King, P. (1990). Extending the Functional Data Model to Computational Completeness, EDBT-90 proceedings, Springer-Verlag 1990.

Reiter, R. (1980). A Logic for Default Reasoning, Artificial Intelligence (13).

Small, C. (1988). Guarded Default Databases : An Approach to the Control of Incomplete Information, Ph.D Thesis, Birkbeck College, University of London, 1988.

Touretsky, D.S. (1986). The Mathematics of Inheritance Systems, Morgan Kaufmann.

AN OODB WITH ENTITY-BASED PERSISTENCE: A PROTEIN MODELLING APPLICATION

P. M. D. Gray[1] and G. J. L. Kemp[1,2]
Departments of Computing Science[1] and
Molecular and Cell Biology[2]
University of Aberdeen
King's College
Aberdeen
Scotland

Abstract

An object-oriented database (P/FDM) which is based on an extension of semantic data model concepts, has been implemented in a combination of Prolog and C. This database is being used to store protein structure data. An application of this database is the construction of models of proteins, based on knowledge of the structures of proteins with related sequences. In this work, the database is used for the storage of working data, including abstract design concepts and molecular fragments. As modelling proceeds, there is often a requirement to introduce new kinds of data. Examples are given of how the database can be extended "on the fly" to contain new object classes and relationships which will persist. Code for functions defined on object classes is also stored in the database, and can be shared by all users. It is conjectured that this form of persistent storage is suitable for many expert system applications, and better than either relational tuples or persistent heap storage.

1. Introduction

At Aberdeen we have built an object-oriented database (P/FDM) as a natural extension of Shipman's Functional Data Model (FDM) (Shipman 1981) which is itself founded on entity-relationship concepts. Most of the database system is written in compiled Prolog; this calls to C routines which access UNIX file structures. We are using this to store 50 Mb of protein structure data (Gray et al. 1990), including the coordinates of every non-hydrogen atom in over 80 proteins. The database is mainly used to search for fragments of protein backbone that are of interest, either because of their shape, or because of their relationship to other substructures (helices, sheets, loops). P/FDM also has a completely general query language (Daplex), which is founded on set-abstraction, list comprehensions and functions. Daplex can call out to functions which may do arbitrary computations, combined with database search and updates. The Daplex language is compiled into Prolog (Paton & Gray 1990), and one can also write complex searches directly in Prolog.

The architecture is described in (Gray 1988). An early version (Gray et al. 1988) used persistent storage in PS-Algol (Atkinson et al. 1983). However, we have found that we were not needing the full persistent storage facilities of PS-Algol, but instead were using "entity based persistence". We have found this to be extremely useful and easy to work with. It fits nicely with modern data-modelling concepts, and is much more general than normalised relations. It also fits very well with the Prolog language, and seems to overcome much of the "impedance mismatch" between programming languages and a database language like SQL. It allows one the flexibility of Prolog, to declare new entity and relationship types dynamically, and also to give these structures long term persistence for shared access and efficient search.

First let us describe the basic structures, and then let us see why they are so useful and important. We shall illustrate them with reference to the protein application (Gray *et al.* 1990). The protein structure domain provides a very useful test of these ideas, because it is not realistic to store over 50Mb of data as a single virtual memory image. Furthermore, it has a lot of natural structuring and sub-type information. Finally, most protein structure queries combine some geometrical calculation with data search; thus they are particularly suitable for an object-oriented database, which stores calculation code along with data.

2. Data Structures

The basic structure is an object representing an entity of some class which is declared beforehand (possibly dynamically). If the class is declared in Daplex syntax we write e.g.

> **declare protein_structure ->> entity**
> **declare helix ->> protein_structure**
> **declare strand ->> protein_structure**

This declaration names *protein_structure* as an entity class. New instances of this class can be created, each of which is given a unique and unchanging *internal object identifier* by which it can be accessed directly. At any time one can enumerate the identifiers of all instances of a given class created so far.

The declarations of *helix* and *strand* also name them as entity types, but as *sub-types* of *protein_structure*, and these instances also permit extra or more specialised methods to be defined on them. In the original Daplex, one was only allowed to store extra attribute values, but in our OODB one can also declare functions considered as methods, whose code is held in the database with the class descriptor.

Attribute values are associated with entity types by declaring functions e.g.

> **declare start(protein_structure) -> integer**

This declares a single-valued function *start*, such that if p is a variable representing a protein structure object (e.g. a particular strand or helix) then *start(p)* returns the ordinal position of the start of the structure in the sequence of residues forming the protein backbone chain.

Unlike the relational model, relationships are represented by functions (which may be multi-valued). Thus

> **declare parallel(strand) ->> strand**

declares a function which returns a list of those strands (zero or more), which are adjacent and parallel to the given strand, in a beta-sheet. Thus a relationship is represented as a function which maps an object into a list of related objects. Thus, instead of having to match an external object identifier with a large B-tree holding index values, one has a simple direct list of pointers which can be clustered with the object much as in the pointer-array implementation of Codasyl network databases.

As another example, we have

declare structure_chain(protein_structure) -> chain

This gives the chain to which a particular protein_structure belongs. However, automatically associated with it is an inverse function

structure_chain_inv(chain) ->> protein_structure

This function gives the list of protein_structures which form part of any given chain. Thus the symmetry of a relation R(A,B) is represented by a function from A onto B and one from B onto A.

Another type of function is a two-argument function, which can be used to give the effect of an auxiliary index to a large set. Thus we have

declare absolutepos(chain, integer) -> residue
declare res_by_name(chain, string) ->> residue

The first function when applied to a chain object and given an integer (which may have been obtained from *start(p)*), returns the residue object at that position in the chain, from which one can find its amino-acid type, atomic coordinates, etc.. The function does **not** do a sequential search down the chain, it uses direct access. It is invaluable for protein queries, many of which need to compute the value of the second argument e.g. absolutepos(c, start(p) + k). The ability to do this is vital because the order of amino-acid residues in a chain is extremely important when analysing protein structures. We frequently want to go directly to a particular residue and then examine others at an offset from this position.

The other function (*res_by_name*), when applied to a chain object, enables one to find quickly all the residues of a particular amino-acid type in a chain, again without a sequential search.

The schema diagram for the protein structure database is shown in Figure 1.

3. Persistence by Entity

The functional data model gives us very directly most of the operations used in semantic nets by AI researchers (Shipman came from MIT). Thus it has a good data modelling pedigree. It also has a very simple and elegant type structure which is easily extensible. The types are either primitive (integer, bool, float, string) or lists thereof, or entity types, or lists thereof. Every function has a domain and a range type, and its application can be type-checked.

The difference in philosophy with a language like PS-Algol (Atkinson *et al.* 1983) is as follows. In PS-Algol the unit of persistence is an individual unit of storage allocation such as an array or list cell. Effectively one is making persistent the state of an arbitrarily complex computation. In P/FDM one is making persistent the state of an entity. This restricts the kinds of things one can hold onto, but not very much so! If you want to hang onto a value, then make it an attribute value given by a function on some entity instance (possibly newly created). If there are a group of such values, then make them into a list of values of a multi-valued function. If the values are of different type, then make them into distinct attribute values of the same entity instance. If one has a list of objects, then consider it as a kind of relationship. Lastly, if one has a piece of code, then store it as a method defined over an entity class!

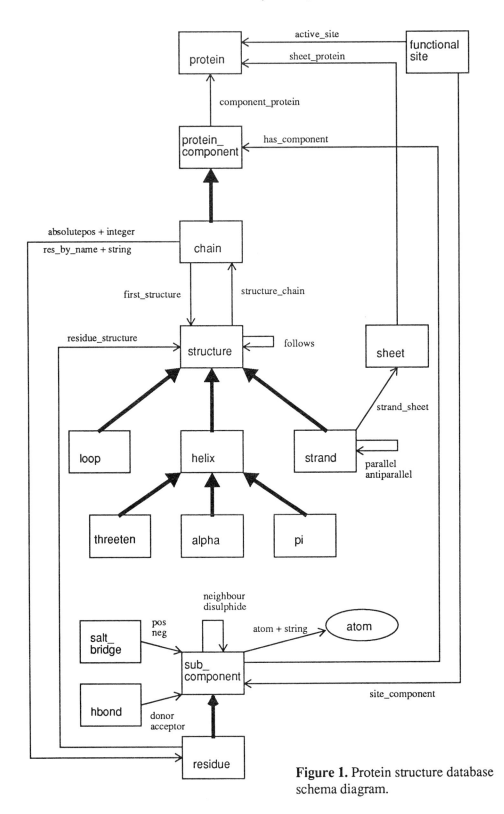

Figure 1. Protein structure database schema diagram.

This may sound restrictive, but consider it another way. If there is something that cannot be modelled in this entity-relationship fashion, then do you really wish it to be persistent? Does it have some *raison d'etre*? We have yet to find a counter example. We have used entities and relationships to represent abstract design concepts, intentions and plans of modellers, as well as concrete things. We have the three classic data structure constructors known to computing: aggregation to form objects, repetition to form lists and generalisation to form super-types with variants. It should suffice.

4. Simple Type Structures for Persistence

Donahue (1987) argues strongly for a simple type structure for persistent objects, without the complexity found in Eiffel or PS-Algol. He makes several very good points.

The first is that the type structure must allow full space reclamation and stop the long term build up of unreferenced data. The beauty of FDM is that deletion is well defined and can be made to leave no dangling references and to return all space to free without using a complex garbage collection algorithm.

His second point is that if one is accumulating data over a long time then one doesn't want to tie it to a particular programming language and to restructure it to match each subtle nuance in new programming languages. By contrast, entity-relationships and sub-types are well established and are likely to stay so.

His third point is that long term persistent data must have fast access structures in order to give logarithmic or constant time access. In P/FDM we have constant time access by internal object identifier and logarithmic time access by an external prime key formed from a combination of object attribute values and relationships. We can have fast access to related objects by a kind of pointer array structure. We also have a kind of secondary structure index through the use of two-argument functions. Our main shortcoming is the cost of access of super-type methods via a chain of descriptors even though these are cached in main memory.

For all these reasons, based on experience in building databases for network mail, Donahue concludes that programming languages and databases should have separate type systems, and suggests that this may lead to a mismatch. However, in our case, the use of Prolog fits well with objects.

5. Match between Prolog and Object Types

We simply use the following generic Prolog predicates to access the database. Where they return multiple values they are written to do this by backtracking, which fits the Prolog control structure and provides an opportunity for lazy evaluation. Thus they work basically "tuple at a time" rather than "set at a time". The predicates are :-

```
getentity(+ClassName, -Instance)
getentity(+ClassName, +KeyValues, -Instance)
getfnval(+FunctionName, +Instance, -Value)
```

Getentity enumerates instances of classes or else gets a specific instance given an external key. **Getfnval** gets attribute or method value(s) from an instance. Thus given the following Daplex query :-

> **for each c in chain such that num_residues(c) > 200**
> **for each s in protein_structure such that structure_chain(s) = c**
> **print component_name(c), structure_name(s);**

we can translate it into very concise Prolog :-

> **(getentity(chain, C),**
> **getfnval(num_residues, [C], Num), Num > 200,**
> **getfnval(component_name, [C], CName),**
> **getfnval(structure_chain_inv, [C], S),**
> **getfnval(structure_name, [S], SName),**
> **write([CName, SName]), nl, fail;**
> **true)**

Note that the generated Prolog has been optimised to use an inverse function, and the order of the goals are carefully chosen. An optimiser written in Prolog does much of the work of a relational query optimiser which re-orders joins. We have also found that even hand-written queries in Prolog fit very well with entity-relational storage.

We also have primitives to create new entity classes or subclasses, create new instances, add new functions to a class descriptor, extend, reduce or modify the value of a multi-valued function on a particular instance, move an instance across to another sub-type, and so on. The beauty of these predicates is that they hide the internal representation of objects in the object store, whilst giving enough information to allow efficient implementation.

6. Protein Modelling Application

One application of the protein structure database is the construction of models of proteins, based on knowledge of the structures of proteins with related sequences. A full understanding of the activity of a particular protein requires knowledge of its three-dimensional structure. While protein sequences can be determined relatively easily, the experimental determination of a protein's three-dimensional structure is a slow and difficult task. Therefore there is a demand to be able to construct hypothetical models of proteins which may give rise to scientific insight, where no experimentally determined structure is available.

There is an underlying assumption in protein modelling that if two proteins are configured from a similar sequence of amino-acid residues, then they will have similar three-dimensional shapes. Thus, if we have the amino-acid sequence for a protein, and an experimentally determined three-dimensional structure for a protein with a related sequence, then a hypothetical model of the protein with known sequence can be constructed, based on the known structure. Amino acid residues common to both sequences are usually expected to occupy the same positions in the model and the known structure. Also, regularly repeating conformations of protein backbone such as helices are often found to be conserved over a family of related proteins. Differences in two protein chains with closely related sequences mostly occur in surface loops.

Since a modelling exercise is typically continued over a number of sessions, perhaps by different people, it is important that working data generated and *ad hoc* functions introduced during one session can be retained for use in subsequent sessions. This persistence can be achieved by extending the database to include objects representing design concepts and molecular fragments. Therefore, in this application the database is used not just for static protein structure data, but also for storage of dynamic working data.

The first step in generating a protein model based on the known structure of a molecule with a similar sequence is to align the two sequences, introducing gaps where appropriate into either sequence in order to improve the alignment. We are interested in the residue names and numbers at each alignment position in both the old and new sequences. We model the concept of an alignment position as an object class in our database and store residue names and numbers as scalar attributes of this class. Note that an *alignment_position* is a modelling concept, and not a physical entity such as a protein residue or a chain.

Consider now a surface loop containing an insertion. This variable region can be defined by the range of alignment positions which it spans and can be represented within our database as a *backbone_range* object. In fact the entire model can be partitioned into insertions, deletions and other ranges which are conserved in length. Like *alignment_position*, a *backbone_range* is a modelling concept, rather than a physical entity. However, we find it convenient to store abstract design concepts like this as objects in our database — there are a number of scalar attributes associated with them, derived functions can be defined over them, and they are related to other objects in the system (both concrete objects and other concepts).

In our modelling procedure the polypeptide backbone for regions containing insertions or deletions of residues are remodelled using a "cut and paste" approach proposed by Jones and Thirup (1986). This involves identifying regions of the known structure's backbone which we expect to be conserved in the model, then discarding loops with insertions or deletions and replacing these with fragments of protein backbone taken from other structures stored in the database. For each variable region, the database is searched initially for fragments which have the correct number of residues and a suitable geometry to fit onto "anchors" in the model template. This search typically identifies a number of candidate fragments for each variable region. These are represented by *candidate_fragment* objects which are related to the corresponding *backbone_range* by the function *for_range*.

These working objects and the relationship between them can be declared in a new module using Daplex, as shown in Figure 2. These objects and relationships are shown graphically in Figure 3. The multi-valued inverse function *for_range_inv* is declared automatically in our implementation of Daplex. The value of *from_residue* is the residue object, in the native structure, from which a particular fragment starts. *Rms_error* is a measure of how well a particular fragment fits the anchors in the model.

Chain and *residue* are both object classes in a module of protein structure data, whereas these working objects and relationships have been declared in a new module called *protmod*. The ability to partition data into modules is important for developing applications of this kind. While all users of the database can share the same core of protein structure data, each is able to augment the database by adding their own modules with objects and relationships useful for their individual applications, such as protein modelling or the identification of microdomains in hydrophobic protein cores (Kemp and Gray 1990). These objects can reference those in other modules. It thus provides a simple form of concurrency for multiple users.

```
create private module protmod

declare protein_model ->> entity
declare model_name(protein_model) -> string
declare based_on_chain(protein_model) -> chain
key_of protein_model is (model_name)

declare alignment_position ->> entity
declare in_model(alignment_position) -> protein_model
declare position(alignment_position) -> integer
declare old_name(alignment_position) -> string
declare new_name(alignment_position) -> string
declare old_number(alignment_position) -> integer
declare new_number(alignment_position) -> integer
key_of alignment_position is (key_of(in_model), position)

declare backbone_range ->> entity
declare start_position(backbone_range) -> alignment_position
declare end_position(backbone_range) -> alignment_position
declare range_type(backbone_range) -> string
key_of backbone_range is (key_of(start_position), key_of(end_position))

declare candidate_fragment ->> entity
declare for_range(candidate_fragment) -> backbone_range
declare from_residue(candidate_fragment) -> residue
declare rms_error(candidate_fragment) -> float
key_of candidate_fragment is (key_of(for_range), key_of(from_residue))
```

Figure 2. Daplex declaration of working data.

The next step in constructing a protein model is to select from the candidate fragments identified for a particular backbone range the one which should be included in the model. One possible selection criterion is to use the fragment which has the smallest value for *rms_error* of all the candidate fragments identified for that range. This value can be derived using the following Daplex function :-

```
define smallest_rms_error(r in backbone_range) -> float in protmod
minimum(rms_error(for_range_inv(r)));
```

Note that this function has been defined in the module *protmod*. The Prolog code generated for this function definition will be stored in this database module on disc.

To identify the particular candidate fragment which has smallest value for *rms_error* for a given range we can define another Daplex function :-

```
define best_fragment(r in backbone_range) -> candidate_fragment
 in protmod
the c in for_range_inv(r) such that rms_error(c) = smallest_rms_error(r);
```

Again the code for this function will be stored in the database and can be shared by all users who open the *protmod* module.

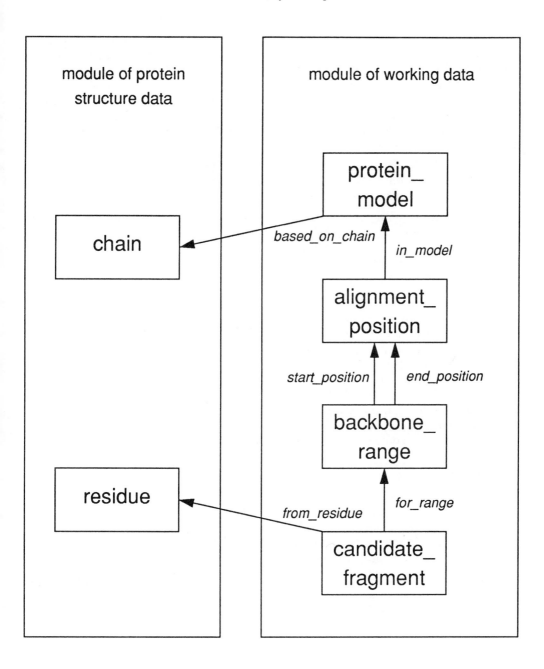

Figure 3. Schema diagram showing working data objects. The panel on the right shows the objects used for storing working data generated when constructing models from homologous structures. Object classes are represented as rectangular boxes. Labelled arrows represent relationships between objects. The panel on the left shows two object classes in a module of protein structure data which are related to the working objects.

Other fragment selection criteria may make use of information about the sequence of residues of the fragments in their native structures. While each amino-acid residue has the same backbone atoms, side chains can influence the conformations which the backbone atoms can adopt. For example the side chain of a proline residue imposes particular constraints on that residue's backbone. Therefore, if we are modelling a loop which is to have a proline residue in its fourth position, then we may choose to examine those fragments which have a proline in their fourth position in the native structure.

More generally, we can define a function in Daplex which finds those candidate fragments for a given range which have a residue of a particular kind at a specified position in their native structure :-

define frags_with_res_at_pos(r in backbone_range, s in string, i in integer)
 ->> candidate_fragment in protmod
c in for_range_inv(r) such that
 name(absolutepos(has_component(from_residue(c)) as chain,
 pos(from_residue(c)) + i - 1)) = s;

Returning to the example of fragments with a proline residue in their fourth position, a proline residue can occur in two different conformations — *cis* or *trans*. Which of these two conformations a residue is in can be determined by measuring the rotation around the backbone C-N bond (the "peptide bond"). This torsion angle is denoted by ω and can be derived using a function defined on the class *residue*. Rather than calling *frags_with_res_at_pos* to identify fragments with proline residues in their fourth position in several different queries, it would convenient to identify this set of fragments once and store them in a "hit list" which can then be used in subsequent queries, or even subsequent modelling sessions. The ω torsion angle of the proline could also be stored with each fragment in the hit list.

Such a hit list can be implemented by declaring a new object class in our database. This can be done in Daplex "on the fly" during a modelling session.

extend module protmod
declare proline_four_fragment ->> entity
declare a_fragment(proline_four_fragment) -> candidate_fragment
declare peptide_conformation(proline_four_fragment) -> float
key_of proline_four_fragment is (key_of(a_fragment));

Suppose that the loop which contains a proline in its fourth position lies between positions 34 and 41 in our new sequence. Then we can populate the *proline_four_fragment* object class using the following Daplex program :-

program populate_pffs is
for the r in backbone_range such that
 new_number(start_position(r)) = 34 and
 new_number(end_position(r)) = 41
 for each c in frags_with_res_at_pos(r, "pro", 4)
create a new proline_four_fragment with key = (key_of(c));

The following Daplex command calculates and stores values for the function *peptide_conformation* :-

```
for each p in proline_four_fragment
let peptide_conformation(p) = omega(
    absolutepos(has_component(from_residue(a_fragment(p)))) as chain,
    pos(from_residue(a_fragment(p))) + 3));
```

Subsequent database queries can iterate over the instances of this class, thus we access those fragments which are of interest quickly and conveniently.

7. Conclusions and Future Directions

So far, we have been able to use entity-relationship concepts to represent all kinds of working data generated when modelling proteins. This has been achieved by extending the database, adding new object classes representing both physical entities and abstract design concepts. Further object classes and relationships can be added in an *ad hoc* fashion. All working data persists on disc and can be used in subsequent sessions. The code of functions defined on these working object classes also persists.

The schema as described works well, but it needs a number of extensions. Firstly, the code is currently stored as the text of Prolog predicates, which may call out to compiled C or Fortran object code. The beauty of this is that Prolog predicates have no non-locals and a simple type structure compared to raw C or Fortran. However, we do need the concept of *mixins*, which are classes with no instances which can provide procedures via multiple inheritance, as in ADAM (Paton 1989). Secondly, we need to consider whether Prolog predicates should be held in a semi-compiled form, instead of being consulted at the start of a session. Lastly, we need to consider the use of *integrity constraints* expressed in some form of Prolog syntax, and again attached to class descriptors in much the same way that facets are used in Frame-based systems.

References

Atkinson, M.P., Bailey, P.J., Chisholm, K.C., Cockshott, P.W. and Morrison, R. (1983) An Approach to Persistent Programming. *The Computer Journal*, **26**, 360-365.

Donahue, J. (1987) What's a Database. *Research Report*, Olivetti Research Center, Palo Alto, CA.

Gray, P.M.D. (1988) Expert Systems and Object-Oriented Databases: Evolving a new Software Architecture. In Kelly, B. and Rector, A. (eds.), *Research and Development in Expert Systems V*, Cambridge University Press, pp 284-295.

Gray, P.M.D., Moffat, D.S. and Paton, N.W. (1988) A Prolog Interface to a Functional Data Model Database. In Schmidt, J.W., Ceri, S. and Missikoff, M. (eds.), *Proc. EDBT-88*, Springer-Verlag, pp 34-49.

Gray, P.M.D., Paton, N.W., Kemp, G.J.L. and Fothergill, J.E. (1990) An object-oriented database for protein structure analysis. *Protein Engineering*, **3**, 235-243.

Jones, T.A. and Thirup, S. (1986) Using known substructures in protein model building and crystallography. *The EMBO Journal*, **5**, 819-822.

Kemp, G.J.L. and Gray, P.M.D. (1990) Finding hydrophobic microdomains using an object-oriented database. *CABIOS* (to be published).

Paton, N.W. (1989) ADAM: An Object-Oriented database System Implemented in Prolog. In Williams, M.H. (ed.), *Proceedings of the Seventh British National Conference on Databases (BNCOD 7)*, Cambridge University Press, pp 147-161. ˜

Paton, N.W. and Gray, P.M.D. (1990) Optimising and Executing Daplex Queries Using Prolog. *Research Report*, Department of Computing Science, Aberdeen.

Shipman, D.W. (1981) The Functional Data Model and the Data Language DAPLEX *ACM TODS*, **6**, 140-173.

TOWARDS LARGE KNOWLEDGE BASES: AUTOMATING
KNOWLEDGE ELICITATION, KNOWLEDGE VERIFICATION
AND KNOWLEDGE BASE BUILDING

Peter Alan Swaby
BP Research International,
Chertsey Road, Sunbury-on-Thames,
Middlesex, TW16 7LN, UK.

Abstract

Large knowledge bases are a prerequisite for most real-world expert system applications. Traditional methods for eliciting, checking, and representing knowledge tend to be time consuming and labour intensive, and therefore threaten to render large scale applications cost ineffective. This paper describes how, by computerising knowledge elicitation, providing a series of verification tools, and constructing knowledge bases automatically, it is possible to substantially reduce development time and cost. The techniques were applied in the development of an expert system for microfossil identification for use in the petroleum industry.

1 Introduction

Expert system applications have been developed since the early seventies, but despite initial enthusiasm large scale applications are still few and far between. Systems in the petroleum industry were regarded as a particularly promising application area, but large scale systems were found to be very expensive to develop and maintain. Naturally, this has led to suggestions that such systems can never be cost effective (see Walker, 1988).

When faced with the task of building an expert system for microfossil identification for use in the petroleum industry, developing methods which reduced time and cost of traditional approaches was a prime concern. The expert system (for an overview see Williams, 1990; and for a description see Swaby, 1989 and 1990) was to incorporate textual and graphical information on thousands of fossils.

A knowledge base for fossil identification on that scale had never been attempted before. After reviewing the initial stages of knowledge elicitation and knowledge base building, methods were developed which helped to automate the process. With these methods, it was possible to build knowledge bases for Phylum Conodonta fossils (see Higgins & Austin, 1985) and Phylum Foraminifera fossils (see Haynes, 1981) each in three months, with one expert and one knowledge engineer.

The paper describes the methods that were developed for automating knowledge elicitation, knowledge verification, and knowledge base building (see Figure 1). They were developed with the particular application in mind, but the approach as such can be applied to expert systems in other domains.

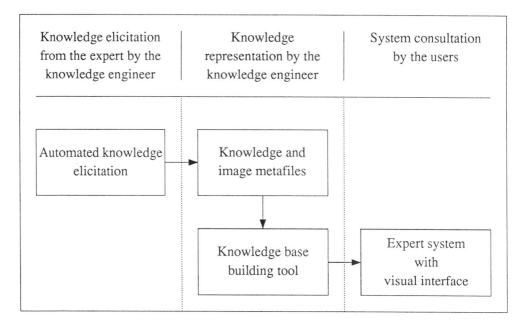

Figure 1 The Stages of the Development Process

2 Knowledge Elicitation

Knowledge elicitation is often described as the biggest problem in expert systems development (Liebowitz, 1988) and is referred to as a *bottleneck* (see Feigenbaum & McCorduck, 1984) in the development process. Capturing the knowledge and skills which constitute expertise in a particular domain is a difficult undertaking for several reasons (Greenwell, 1988), even when the full cooperation of the expert(s) is ensured.

For any successful knowledge-based application the knowledge elicited, and eventually embodied in the system will have to be correct, consistent and complete. This is a prerequisite for the success of even the most simple system operating in a narrow well-defined domain. For large knowledge bases, the knowledge elicitation techniques employed have to be parsimonious: the experts in question should have to spend as little time as possible in actual knowledge elicitation sessions. Knowledge elicitation techniques which are time-consuming and require experts to work through repetitive exercises are not only cost-ineffective, but also threaten to stretch the patience of the experts. and thus undermine the cooperation between them and the knowledge engineers. To avoid this problem with the application presented here, the knowledge elicitation process was reviewed after a series of initial sessions had supplied sufficient data to determine the type and form of the knowledge needed. The initial knowledge elicitation process, and subsequent refinements, designed to automate the process to a large extent, are described below.

2.1 Initial knowledge elicitation procedure

At the beginning of the knowledge elicitation process the expert - a palaeontologist - introduced the knowledge engineer to the problem of microfossil identification. The initial session was conducted in an unstructured manner: the expert explained the classification of microfossils by example of two genera (*Gnathodus* and *Scaliognathus*) to the knowledge engineer. The knowledge engineer asked questions in order to determine the criteria by which microfossils are classified. The session was recorded on video, and the video served as a basis for the knowledge engineer's first attempt to model the expert's knowledge. The model was refined after a review by the expert - again, the review session was filmed to provide a record for the knowledge engineer.

On the basis of the first two genera it was decided that the knowledge needed for the identification of microfossils should be modeled in the form of a table of species, attributes, and attribute values (for an example of such an attribute-value table see Table 1). Moreover, the analysis of the filmed sessions revealed that the process of microfossil identification is inherently a visual one: the expert would always draw a picture of the attributes and their values to distinguish fossils, and only then assign verbal descriptions to them. Clearly, if the system was to be employed as a tool by palaeontologists, it would have to allow them to describe the object to be identified in pictorial rather than textual form. Consequently, while the textual information incorporated in the attribute-value tables provided the symbolic representation necessary for the inference mechanism, a corresponding image for each attribute value is stored to allow users to describe the objects to be identified by consulting pictures rather than text.

In agreement with the expert, it was decided to proceed with knowledge elicitation in a very structured form: the expert would supply attribute value tables, a description of each attribute, and a drawing and description for each attribute value, as well as a drawing and a description for each fossil. Thus, the initial informal unstructured explanation of the expert's knowledge was transformed into a highly structured, domain-specific approach which now allows the expert to supply his knowledge in the form of tables, drawings and descriptions which in turn can be immediately utilised by the knowledge engineer.

2.2 Automating the knowledge elicitation process

The complete knowledge base for a phylum of several thousand species contains hundreds of attribute-value tables, thousands of images, and tens of thousands of lines of additional information in text form. When information on this scale has to be elicited and transferred into machine readable form, manual methods would be time-consuming and expensive. Moreover, manual entry of images and selection of attribute value images from them is a routine task, nevertheless requiring considerable knowledge and utmost vigilance, and therefore error-prone. Consequently, it was decided that a lot could be gained from automating this process.

In the initial knowledge elicitation sessions, hand-drawn sketches of the fossils were provided by the expert. One of the earlier considerations was to replace these sketches by photographs. These would, of course, provide better images, but it was found

CAVUSGNATHIDAE	Platform Blade	Blade Position	Prominent Denticles
Cavusgnathus	present	right only	present
Adetognathus	present	right or left	present and absent
Cloghergnathus	absent	right or left	present
Clydagnathus	absent	right only	present
Rhachistognathus	absent	right or left	absent
Taphrognathus	absent	right, left or median	present
Patrognathus	absent	right or left	posterior only

Table 1 An attribute-value table for Family Cavusgnathidae

```
genus name
    attribute name
        attribute value
            description
            .
        description
        .
    species name
        author
        brief description
        attribute
            value
            .
            .
        basin
            environment
                range
                .
                .
                .
        detailed catalogue description
        .
    knowledge base type
    group name
        subgroup name
```

Figure 2 Knowledge Metafile Structure

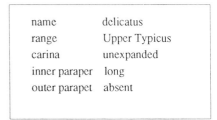

Figure 3 Frame Structure

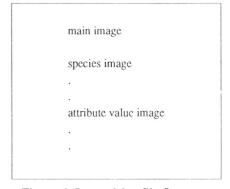

Figure 4 Image Metafile Structure

that the quality was impaired due to the fact that ordinary light photography of minute objects such as microfossils (typically less than a millimetre) loses some of its resolution. The expert therefore decided to use high-quality drawings of fossils, which are available to palaeontologists via manuals and catalogues. These drawings are translated into machine readable form by an image scanner. Special program routines now allow images to be processed automatically: the images are read in, enhanced by removing small marks (e.g. caused by dust on photocopiers), scaled, named and placed in an image file. The images of a taxon (approximately 30) can now be entered in a matter of hours rather than days.

The attribute-value tables and additional text descriptions are now supplied in electronic form (via electronic mail) by the expert. The knowledge engineer converts the information provided into a knowledge metafile, employing routines to ensure validity and completeness. Further routines provide feedback for the expert with regard to the discrimination power of the knowledge provided for each taxon (see Section 4).

The system of knowledge elicitation is now very efficient. The expert produces information in a form that is very close to that required by the knowledge engineer. This means that the knowledge engineer has to make few modifications to this information, and hence, that it can be entered into the system very quickly and few mistakes, if any, will be made.

3 Knowledge Representation

Choosing an appropriate form of representing the knowledge contained in an expert system is always a crucial decision in the development process (Brachman & Levesque, 1985). Representations should be chosen with the eventual use of the knowledge in mind: firstly, the representation has to allow speedy retrieval of relevant facts from the knowledge base; secondly, the representation has to be flexible to allow for extension and modification of the knowledge contained; and thirdly, the representation has to be compatible with the inference mechanism chosen. Possible representation schemes have to be evaluated to ensure that their characteristics match those of the knowledge acquired (e.g. scope and grain size, modularity and understandability, explicit versus implicit, and declarative versus procedural - see Barr & Feigenbaum, 1981).

The knowledge representation of the system described here is strongly influenced by the way in which palaeontologists classify and identify fossils. Incorporating their classification scheme in the knowledge representation structure of the system ensures that the characteristics of the domain knowledge are represented appropriately. This does not, however, mean that the system is a simple automation of identification procedures performed manually to date. Traditionally, palaeontologists make use of taxonomic keys, which basically consist of a series of structured rules. While it is not difficult to translate these rules into a rule-based representation or shell (e.g. Wiley, 1987), simply computerising taxonomic keys has two serious limitations. Firstly, such a system would not address the advantages of visual identification: the information in the keys is purely text-based. Secondly, the very nature of these keys enforces a strictly sequential identification procedure, and therefore compels the user to choose an option even in cases of uncertainty. One of the earlier decisions made by the expert and the knowledge engineer was that the representation must allow flexible access to the knowledge, and not impose a rigid identification procedure on the user.

Text-based information and images are stored in separate parts of the system. Textual information for each taxon is stored in a *knowledge metafile*. Fossil groups are classified in a tree structure from the phylum level down to species level. Consequently, the metafile contains all of the attributes and attribute values, and their descriptions; and all of the related taxa with their attributes and attribute values, which describe them, and other relevant information (see Figure 2). The knowledge in the metafile provides the basis from which frames (see Figure 3) are generated (by the *knowledge base building tool*, see Section 5). A set of reduced metafiles contains the knowledge of higher level taxa. Their characteristics are more distinct, and the fossils can be identified without working through attributes and attribute values. The user can therefore differentiate between the fossils simply by comparing their images.

The images for each taxon are stored in an *image metafile*. These contain the main image, all of the species images, and images of their attribute values (see Figure 4). Again, the image metafiles for the higher level taxa contain only images of related taxa, since these can be identified by simply matching fossils to their appropriate image.

4 Knowledge Verification

It is essential that the knowledge within any expert system's knowledge base is consistent, complete and correct (see Mars & Miller, 1987) otherwise incorrect inferences will be produced. Inconsistencies can be introduced into a knowledge base for a variety of reasons ranging from simple typing mistakes through to conflicting use of terminology if knowledge is being entered from more than one expert. Whilst it may be relatively straightforward to manually check for inconsistences within small knowledge bases which typically contain only a few hundred rules, it is very difficult if not practically impossible to check for errors in large knowledge bases. However, it is desirable to detect such errors early on in the knowledge base construction cycle before the knowledge base testing phase (see Nguyen et al., 1987; and Preece, 1989). One solution to this problem is to provide a series of computer-based tools which can verify the knowledge structures automatically before they are incorporated into the knowledge base.

A simple tool has been produced which simply takes a knowledge metafile (see Figure 2) and checks each of the attributes and attribute values of each entry with the attributes and attribute values that have been defined for that group:

Checking Eotaphrus For Attribute Errors...

There Are 0 Attribute Errors and 0 Attribute Value Errors

Another tool prints an attribute table using a knowledge metafile for a given category. It is very readable even by a non-computer expert. The top left corner contains the category name, the elements within the category are listed down the left hand side, the attributes are listed along the top and the attribute values are entered within the table. The expert can then be presented with a series of tables and quickly check them for obvious mistakes:

CAVUSGNATHIDAE	Platform_Blade	Blade_Position	Prominent_Denticles
Cavusgnathus	present	right_only	present
Adetognathus	present	right_or_left	present_and_absent
Cloghergnathus	absent	right_or_left	present
Clydagnathus	absent	right_only	present
Rhachistognathus	absent	right_or_left	absent
Taphrognathus	absent	right_or_left median	present
Patrognathus	absent	right_or_left	posterior_only

An important factor in determining whether good attributes and attribute values have been chosen is to see how well they can be used to discriminate between the different objects within a group. A tool has been developed which does this. It assumes that all attributes have a value entered for them and then works out if it is possible to discriminate absolutely in each case. The objects for which this is not true are printed out. This will instantly show if a bad choice of attributes has been made or if some attribute values have been entered incorrectly:

Category CAVUSGNATHIDAE

All attributes are present

Cloghergnathus and Taphrognathus cannot be distinguished

Each fossil existed for a certain period of time; this is described by its range, which consists of a possible qualifier such as Lower or Upper and the name of a time zone. This information is used when fossils are being selected by their range or when the time span of existence is shown on a stratigraphic column. Neither of these functions will be possible if there are errors in the ranges. A routine has been developed that checks these descriptions and prints out the results of erroneous occurrences:

Checking ANCYRODELLA for Range Errors...

Range List for IOIDES is... ((Upper_A_Triangularis) (Lower_Gigas))

Range is... Upper_A_Triangularis   ...ERROR in Biozone name

Range List for NODOSA is... ((Lower Asymmetricus) (Middle_Gigas))

Range is... MIDDLE_GIGAS   ...ERROR in Biozone name

There are 0 Qualifier errors and 2 Biozone errors

Once the knowledge has been checked it can be converted into a knowledge base. The following section describes how the knowledge base building tool draws on the knowledge and image metafiles to generate the actual knowledge bases used in the consultation process.

5 Automatic Knowledge Base Generation

During an identification session, the user enters information about a fossil by consulting images of the species. There are two different ways in which the knowledge bases presented to the user can be generated from the metafiles. One way is to convert the information only when needed - this would be quite efficient in terms of storage space, but would increase the system response time up to several minutes in some cases. The other way is to convert the information beforehand and store it in (KEE - see Fraser, 1987) knowledge bases - this approach is less efficient in terms of storage space, but allows the user to move quickly between information in different parts of the classification structure. In the interests of usability the second approach was chosen.

The conversion of metafiles into knowledge bases is done by a Lisp program - the *knowledge base building tool*. This program creates all of the code and data structures that the expert system needs. It also produces all graphical windows complete with images and descriptions. Once a knowledge base has been completed it is saved and can be used by the expert system. It was necessary to write a program to build knowledge bases automatically rather than producing them manually for several reasons. Firstly, alterations might be made to the information used. Once they are made a knowledge base can be rebuilt with almost no effort. Secondly, the format of the output might be changed. It would be feasible to manually modify a knowledge base if it were small, but if it was large, i.e. contained many entries, even small changes would take weeks. However, modifications can be made to the building tool, which only has to be done once, and a whole knowledge base can be rebuilt incorporating the changes.

6 Discussion

The process of knowledge elicitation, the form of the knowledge representation, and the methods by which the knowledge bases are built automatically have been developed specially for this system, and have been applied to Phylum Conodonta (see Higgins & Austin, 1985) and Phylum Foraminifera (see Haynes, 1981). The knowledge elicitation process, which was developed by the expert and knowledge engineer together, initially consisted of very informal techniques and later converged to specific methods which are more efficient (see Kitto & Boose, 1989). The methods now employed are very convenient for both the expert and the knowledge engineer. The expert can supply all of the necessary knowledge for the system, and prepare it in his own time - independent of the knowledge engineer. The knowledge engineer is provided with the information in a way which can easily be converted into the form of the knowledge representation i.e. the knowledge and image metafiles.

Once the knowledge has been elicited and placed in a machine readable form it must be verified before it is finally converted into a knowledge base. It is relatively straightforward to check a small number of facts for consistency and correctness, but it is much more difficult to check tens of thousands of facts. However, if only a small number of facts are erroneous the whole knowledge base could be rendered useless. It is therefore desirable to provide a series of computer-based checking tools which are capable of verifying the knowledge and pointing out mistakes at an early stage. Mistakes identified early can be corrected much more easily than those found later on e.g.

when the expert system is being used by palaeontologists.

The generation of large knowledge bases containing all of the knowledge necessary for microfossil identification for complete phyla would be a very time-consuming process for the knowledge engineer. It would involve the entry of many thousands of rules and images, and many tens of thousands of lines of textual descriptions. Also, the manual construction of knowledge bases would be very error prone due to the repetitive nature of the problem. This was automated through the *knowledge base building tool* which makes this step as efficient as possible in terms of time and ensures that no mistakes are made.

The knowledge required to identify each group of fossils is known by only a few experts. Training each expert to the high degree necessary takes many years and is expensive, and this knowledge is lost when the experts retire. Also, since the experts are few in number it is not always possible for them to be at the rig site where the information is needed. Often, fossils have to be flown to the experts, this creates delays and leads to less accurate drilling. Using the techniques developed here each expert's knowledge can be captured permanently, copied, and distributed to less specialised palaeontologists at the decision site, e.g. the oil rig. Fast, accurate identification at the drilling site saves time and considerable cost in petroleum exploration.

With a knowledge base it is possible to select and present information in ways that would be almost impossible by manual means. Although experts can identify fossils quickly and analyse results effectively they cannot, for instance, easily list all fossils that existed in certain time ranges, environments or basins. It would be equally difficult to review all of the literature relating to a fossil group and choose such a subset. However, it is relatively straightforward to search through the knowledge base and present information according to certain selection criteria. This in turn will make the analysis of results easier, quicker and more accurate.

7 Conclusions and Further Work

The system described here was developed using techniques from the field of artificial intelligence to provide complete knowledge bases for fossil phyla. These knowledge bases are part of a microfossil identification expert system intended for use by palaeontologists to help them identify fossils more quickly and accurately than is currently possible using traditional manual methods. The system differs from previous fossil identification expert systems in that all of the knowledge for each phylum is being elicited and not just a few example cases to provide a demonstration. In order to elicit, verify and represent knowledge on this scale, it is imperative that methods are employed which are more efficient than traditional ones.

Computerised tools were developed to replace traditional, less efficient approaches. These tools are not general-purpose ones, but were designed for the specific problem domain. I would like to suggest that tools developed to suit the problem domain will usually be more efficient than general-purpose ones. The specific tools should be designed after careful review of the problem domain i.e. after initial knowledge elicitation sessions, some experimental coding, and joint review by the expert and knowledge engineer. This provides a good basis for focussing the techniques employed and automating steps of knowledge base construction wherever possible.

There is still scope to improve on the current tools. A *knowledge elicitation tool* could be developed which would allow the expert to enter knowledge into the knowledge base interactively. Such a tool could check for logic errors and knowledge base consistency, and provide immediate feedback reducing the time needed to enter the knowledge. At present, the knowledge has to be converted into machine readable form by the knowledge engineer.

References

Barr, A., and Feigenbaum, E. A., (Eds.) The Handbook of Artificial Intelligence, Vol. 1, Pitman, London, 1981.

Brachman, R. J., and Levesque, H. J. (Eds.), Readings in Knowledge Representation, Morgan Kaufman, California, 1985.

Feigenbaum, E. A., and McCorduck, P., The Fifth Generation, Michael Joseph, London, 1984.

Fraser, J., Some Aspects of Programming in KEE, Airing, AIAI, University of Edinburgh, 1987.

Greenwell, M. (Ed.), Knowledge Engineering for Expert Systems, Ellis Horwood Series in Expert Systems, Chichester, 1988.

Haynes, J. R., Foraminifera, Macmillan, London, 1981.

Higgins, A. C., and Austin, R. L., A Stratigraphical Index of Conodonts, Ellis Horwood, Chichester, 1985.

Kitto, C. M., and Boose, J. H., Selecting Knowledge Acquisition Tools and Strategies Based on Application Characteristics, International Journal of Man-Machine Studies, Vol. 31, pp. 149-160, 1989.

Liebowitz, J., Knowledge Acquisition Approaches in Expert Systems Development. Interface: The Computer Education Quarterly, Vol. 10, pp. 13-17, 1988.

Mars, N. J. I., and Miller, P. L., Knowledge Acquisition and Verification Tools for Medical Expert Systems, Medical Decision Making, Vol 7, pp. 6-11, 1987.

Nguyen, T. A., Perkins, W. A., and Laffey, T. J., Checking an Expert Systems Knowledge Base for Consistency and Completeness, Proceedings of the 9th International Joint Conference on Artificial Intelligence, pp. 375-78, 1985.

Preece, A. D., Verification of Rule-Based Expert Systems in Wide Domains, BCS Expert Systems Conference, London, 20th - 22nd September, 1989.

Swaby, P. A., A Graphical Expert System for Microfossil Identification, BCS Expert Systems Conference, London, 20th - 22nd September, 1989.

Swaby, P. A., Integrating AI and Graphics in a Tool for Microfossil Identification for use in the Petroleum Industry, Second Annual Conference on Innovative Applications of Artificial Intelligence, Washington, 1st - 3rd May, 1990.

Walker, M. G., Expert Systems in Geological Exploration: Can They Be Cost Effective? Geobyte, pp. 18-23, August, 1988.

Wiley, P. A., To Evaluate the use of the Expert System Builder 'CRYSTAL' for use in Conodont Identification, unpublished information technology MSc thesis, Kingston Polytechnic, 1987.

Williams, S., Identifying Fossils by Computer, Science, American Association for the Advancement of Science, Vol. 248, p. 1080, June 1st, 1990.

Acknowledgements

The author would like to thank Dr. Richard Howarth of BPRI for his support and encouragement, Dr. Alan Higgins and Professor Fred Banner of BPRI for their expertise and help, and Angela Sasse of Philips for her assistance in writing this paper.

An Information Engineering Methodology for the Development of
Knowledge-Based Systems

Alex I. Horvitz
University of Lausanne (HEC) and
Banque Cantonale Vaudoise, Lausanne, Switzerland
Andre R. Probst
University of Lausanne (HEC) and IBM Switzerland
Dieter Wenger
Swiss Bank Corporation, Basel, Switzerland

Abstract

This paper describes a methodology for the construction of information
processing systems that is specially suited for the development of knowledge-based
systems (KBS). A case taken from the world of banking is used to describe the use of the
methodology. The case is also used to describe the manner in which the methodology
supports all the phases present in the life cycle of a KBS.

1. Introduction

The construction of a knowledge-based system (KBS) is an information
engineering endeavour. Therefore the use of a well defined development methodology is
an essential requirement. The methodology that we propose, called the **Agent Concept
(AC)** Methodology, supports all the phases of the construction of a KBS's namely,
knowledge acquisition, knowledge analysis and structuring, system's design and
implementation and finally the maintenance of the system.
The methodology is described by presenting its use in a case taken from the
world of banking. The case has been simplified such that the complexity of the problem
does not represent an obstacle in the understanding of the AC methodology.

2. Overview of the Problem
2.1. Description of the Personal Loan Assessment Problem
The case selected to present the AC methodology is the assessment of personal
loan requests. Personal loan requests are evaluated by loan officer that generally have a
long experience in performing this task. Personal loans can be deceived in very general
terms as follows :
* Loans are given to private persons older that 20 years of age.
* The maximum and minimum amount for loans has been pre-determined
by the loan department.
* A person asking for a loan must have a stable income, address, and
residence status (working permit).
Once all relevant information has been obtained the loan officer asses the
loan application in three areas :

2.1.1 Completeness of the application
The completeness of an application consist in checking that all relevant
information is present. Clients should not be ask unnecessary question, but all crucial
information must be available to the bank officer. It must be noticed that the completeness
of an application is case dependent since the information required in one kind of
application might not be required in another. For instance, if a client requests a loan for
purchasing an object (car, machine, TV, etc), then the value of the object and its intended

use become crucial information. This is due to the fact that there are some specific legal restrictions regarding this kind of loans. Another example regards divorced clients where information regarding alimony and age of minor children is very important. Depending on the kind of information missing, and also depending on the kind of credit requested, the loan officer determines wether the application can be considered completed or not. If the application is not completed additional information is requested from the client. Once all relevant information has been obtained the coherence of the application is determined.

2.1.2 Coherence of the application
All the information regarding the application is cross examined in order to detect possible incoherences. Incoherences can be trivial such as the case where an applicant has stated that he is not married but he has included "his wife's salary" as part of his total revenue. Incoherences can be more complex for instance, a client could claim to have a type of working permit that given his nationality and the time of residency in the country is legally impossible to obtained.
If the loan officer determines that the there are some serious incoherences, the application is rejected. If the incoherences found are not critical then additional information is gather in order to clarify the confusion. If no incoherences are found, or all incoherences found are clarified, a financial analysis of the client is performed.

2.1.3 Financial Analysis of the applicant
The financial analysis of the client is performed in three parts.
a) Financial Capacity : This aspect regards mainly the client's financial capacity to pay back the loan he is requesting.
b) Financial Credibility : This criteria concerns the stability of the client in areas such as employment and residency.
c) Financial Personality : This area the client's spending patterns and his reasons for borrowing funds are analyzed.
The financial analysis of the applicant is based on the combination of the three factors mentioned above (capacity, credibility, and personality). The way these factors are combined to arrive to a decision is based on the experience of the loan officer's experience.
Once the analysis is completed, the loan officer, has four alternatives. First, the loan can be approved without any conditions. Second, the loan can be denied. Third, the loan can be approved provided some conditions are meet. And fourth, not enough information is available therefore the loan officer must asks for additional information (either the client is asked for more information or the loan officer's superiors are asked to authorize the loan).

3. Complexity of the problem.

From the description of the problem one can notice that, the amount of information that has to be analyzed for assessing a personal loan application is not very large. The difficulty of the problem comes from all the possible kinds of inferences that can be performed upon this information. For example, the "financial personality" of a client can be inferred from the client's reasons for requesting a loan, his age and his employment stability. The employment stability can be inferred from the reputation of the client's employer, the quality of the client's professional training, and his years of working experience. On the other hand, the "financial personality" of a client can also be inferred from the client's credit history, his current salary, and the portion of his salary that he spends in rent. The decision of which inference is performed is based on the information available, and the loan officers experience.

We believe that even for a small problem like this, a strong and systematic development methodology is required. This need comes from the fact that a **strict knowledge modeling framework is vital** to capture all the knowledge used by the expert in performing his task. And also, from the fact that **modifications and extensions** to a system like this would become very difficult without the support of a well defined development methodology.

4. The Justification and Benefits derived from building a knowledge-based system for the Assessment of Personal Loans.

The feasibility study for the construction of a loan assessment KBS showed that the main benefit of implementing a system like this was the improvement in the quality of the service offered by the bank. This improvement is due to four factors, which are the following :

First, the KBS can decrease the number of applications rejected due to the absence of a human expert. As it can be imagined, the image of the bank is hurt if a client requesting a personal loan is told that his application cannot be processed because there is nobody that can treat it. By having a KBS process loan applications, an employee of the bank that is not an expert in the area of personal loans can provide the client with an answer to his request.

Second, the KBS can minimize a loan application's processing time. The KBS will be able to make a decision regarding the acceptance or rejection of loan applications in a large number of situations. Cases that are more difficult to asses will be handle by human experts, but the KBS will make sure that all relevant information has been collected.

Third, the bank wishes that all its clients are treated with the same high quality standards, therefore a KBS is a way to enforce these standards. A KBS will also guarantee that any changes in the knowledge used to asses a personal loan request are automatically and uniformly made available to all the appropriate personal throughout the bank.

Fourth, the KBS can decrease the amount of training required for the loan officers. The time saved can be used for education in more complex areas. This is mainly due to the fact that an educational version of the KBS can be used for training personal.

5. Overview of the methodology

5.1. User Centered Systems

The type of applications (Norman 86) that we envision are user centered knowledge-based system intended for decision support. In this type of applications, the user and the system work on a partnership to accomplish certain task (i.e to make a decision regarding a problem or a situation such as the investment of funds, or credit evaluation, etc). The user must be able to control the operations that the system performs as well as the order in which these operations are performed. It is clear that this requires the system to be extremely flexible and also that the dialogue between user and system be accomplished through the use of a very sophisticated user interface. These two requirement imply that : the user must be able to guide the system's operations; and that, since user and system are to work in partnership, the system must possess enough domain knowledge in order to guide the dialogue with the user as well as to solve problems that the user presents at his own initiative.

In order to fulfil the two requirement mentioned above, we propose the following solution :

First, the flexibility of a system can only come from the way the system is designed. Furthermore, the design of a system is the result of the application of a methodology's underlying principles. Based on these facts, we propose the **AC methodology**. This methodology support the development of flexible systems. Since the tasks performed by a system are seen as the **result of the independent work of multiple agents.**

Second, in order for the user to perceive the system as a partner we propose an "intelligent interface" that resembles the user's mental image of the problem he is trying to solve. This topic will not be discused in this paper but it is described in (Probst & Horvitz 89; Probst and Wenger 90).

6. The AC Methodology

The AC methodology has been the result of experiences gained in the development of multiple knowledge-based systems mostly in the banking area. The methodology uses concepts from software engineering as well as from artificial intelligence.

Software engineers have long realized the fact that software systems cannot be developed without a strict methodology, for them this is as obvious as the fact that one cannot construct a building without blueprints. The AC methodology tries to provide the blueprints for the development of knowledge-based systems. The actual implementation technologies that knowledge engineers select to construct these systems are independent of the use of the AC methodology. We believe that **a good design can be implemented with many different tools but, no tool can substitute the lack of proper design.**

6.1 The Knowledge Model

The knowledge model represents the set of *activities* and *concepts* necessary to perform some task in a certain domain. The knowledge model organizes these activities and concepts by **identifying the dependencies between activities and concepts**, and by **recognizing the relationships among concepts**. The building blocks of the knowledge model are **concepts, agents, and events**. Concepts and their relationships are organized in structures. Agents are organized in global views and their functionalities are described in local views.

6.1.1 Concepts / Concept Structures.

Concepts are used to model the **static knowledge** needed to accomplish a specific task. Concepts can represent abstract objects such as *a loan, a client, or a car*. These are referred to as object-types. Concepts can also be used to refer to specific information regarding the attributes of an object-type such as *the amount of a loan, the name of a client, or the colour of a car.*

Concepts are related by relationships, the AC methodology provides three types of relationships :

1) **Generalisation (is_a)** : This relationship is used to express the idea that one concept could be use to describe a set of concepts with similar characteristics (subclass/class relationships). For example "a car is_a vehicle" or "A truck is_a vehicle".

2) **Aggregation (is_part_of)**: Use to describe the fact that a concept can be made up of other concept. For example, "A wheel is_part_of a car" and "an engine is_part_of a car".

3) **Association-Relation (as in ER models)** : This is the same kind of relationship used in the Entity Relationship models [CHEN76]. It is used to express a special kind of relation between concepts. For instance, "a client *owns* a vehicle" this statement expresses the relationship owns between the concept client and the concept vehicle.

The collection of all the modelled concepts and their relationships form the **Concept Structure**. Figure 1 is the concept structure for the loan assessment case study. The concept structure represents a map of all the static knowledge that a system contains.

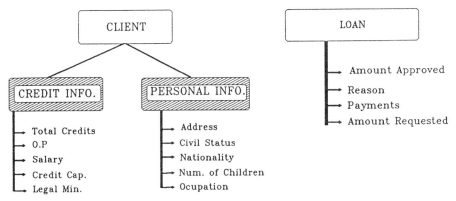

Figure 1: Conceptual Structure for Client and Loan

As it was mentioned above, concepts represent object-types, the instances of these object-types are called **objects**. For example "John's BMW" is an object which is an instance of the object-type car. The simplest form of information in the AC methodology is called **information-unit** (info-unit). Info-units are made up of an object, one of its attributes and the value of this attribute. For example, "John's BMW is red" which implies that the *attribute colour* of the *object John's car* has the *value red*. A generalisation of an information-unit is called an **information-type** (info-type). For example, every car has a colour. A set of info-units of the same info-type is called an information-set (info-set). It is clear that in some circumstance an info-set would be composed of one info-unit, for instance, "the amount of the loan requested by Mr. Smith", since the system processes one loan application at the time then there is only one instance of this info-unit. On the other hand, if we were to model the credit history of Mr. Smith as the amount of funds borrowed and the time to repay them, then this info-set would be made up of all the info-units "amount of credit and re-payment time".

Info-sets are related among themselves by **dependency relationships**. This type of relationship indicates the logical dependency between one dependent info-set and one or more causal info-sets. The dependent info-set is produced based on the information contained in the causal info-sets. The actual processing required to produce a dependent info-set from its causal info-sets is model using **agents**, this is explained next.

6.1.2 Agents

Agents are the active elements in the AC methodology, they are used to express the relationships among dependent and causal info-sets. More specifically, they describe the processing required to produce a causal info-set. There are five types of knowledge needed to perform this processing:

1) **Activation Knowledge** : the information specifying when the agent has to become active.

2) **Input Knowledge** : information regarding the causal info-sets that the agent has to process.

3) **Constraint Knowledge** : information regarding special circumstances under which some info-units of the causal info-sets have to be selected.

4) **Processing Context Knowledge** : information regarding the processing of info-sets (processing parameters).

5) **Functional Knowledge** : functional description of the processing of causal info-sets.

It is important to notice that agents are self-contained, they possess all the knowledge to control themselves and to process the info-sets that are sent to them. Agents do not "know" about the existence of other agents. The only communication among agents takes place through info-sets. This principle is what permits systems developed with the AC methodology to be extremely flexible. Agents can be implemented using very distinct technologies (rule-programming, object-oriented programming, procedural programming, etc). Agents can be modified or replaced with out affecting the activities of other agents.

6.1.3 Events

Events represent the information or the stimulus coming from the environment that surrounds an application. They depict external request for processing or external submission of information to the system. There are 3 kinds of events, namely :

1) **User-Interface Events** : Information coming from the user.

2) **Machine-Events** : Information coming from other application.

3) **Domain-Events** : Information coming directly from the domain (such as input coming from real-time sensors).

As it can be seen events are used to model the interaction of a system with the external world. The interaction includes dialogue with the user, query requests to DBs or messages coming to the system from external instrumentation. In order for the interaction between a system and its environment to be flexible, it must be model at the **right level of abstraction**. This is the purpose of using events for modeling system-environment interactions. For example, the communication between a user and a system can be implemented using mouse and menu technologies or a natural language interface, but the modeling of this communication would be **equivalent at the event level**.

6.2 Views of the Knowledge Model

The role of Agent and Concept Views of the knowledge model is to represent the **system's behaviour** and the knowledge structures used to produce this conduct. The views also serve as an intellectual map of an application. They put in evidence the relationships among concepts, as well as the behaviour of the application at the macro and micro level.

6.2.1 Agent View

6.2.1.1 Global View

This view shows the application's reaction to an event. More specifically, when the system receives a stimulus from the environment, this activates one or more agents, these agents in turn produce info-sets that are used as causal info-sets by other agents, therefore causing their activation. This chain reaction goes on until no more agents are activated. The Agent Global View is a map of this activity propagation.

6.2.1.2 Local View

This view describes the knowledge enclosed in an agent. This knowledge is used by an agent to be able to process the different info-sets in order to produce a dependent info-set.

6.2.2 Conceptual View

Is a representation of all the system's concepts and all the relationships that link them. This view provides a map of all the static knowledge contained in the system. That is, if the system contains any knowledge regarding a concept, then this concept must be part of the conceptual view.

7. How to use the AC methodology.

This section describes the four phases that compose the application of the AC methodology for the development of a KBS. It must be bear in mind that the phases are not applied sequentially and that the boundaries of each phase are very flexible. Figure 2 describes how the different phases are applied. Notice the fact that the analysis of the system must be started from phase 1. The remaining phases are applied in a cyclical fashion, such that the results from one phase can be recycled by the previous phase or used by the next one.

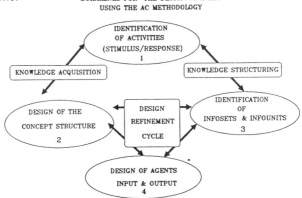

Figure 2: Application of Different Phases of the AC Methodology

7.1. Identification of activities. Phase 1.

The purpose of this phase is to identify the main activities performed by the expert and then to guide the knowledge engineer in performing knowledge acquisition based on these activities. It is important to notice that the objective of this phase is the acquisition of knowledge and not the structuring of it. The structuring of knowledge is the purpose of the second phase.

The expert in assessing personal loan requests with whom the KBS was developed, is also in charged of training new loan officers. Therefore, he has already structure a great deal of the knowledge required to asses a loan application. The knowledge has been structured reflecting the different tasks that have to be performed to asses an application. As it was described above, there are three areas in which a loan request is analyzed, and these are: assessment of a client's repayment capacity, his financial personality, and his financial credibility. Based on the way the expert has structure his knowledge, it is clear that the main activity of the system must be:

* assessment of client's repayment capacity,
* assessment of the client's financial personality,
* assessment of the client's financial credibility.

Based on this decomposition the first mission that we had as knowledge engineers was to perform knowledge acquisition guided by these three activities.

The activities identified in this phase serve as a navigation assistance through the knowledge used by the expert. Activities are also useful for identifying the boundaries of the domain. It is clear that the domain of personal loans is very vast, but the intended KBS should only be concerned with the activities required to perform the task of assessing a loan application.

As knowledge is acquired, there is a need for structuring this knowledge. This is the point when the second and third phases are started, but due to the cyclical nature of the development process in the AC methodology, this is not when phase 1 is finished. The processes performed in phases 2 and 3 will cause the knowledge engineer to go back to the expert and ask additional questions regarding the activities that he performs, and this of course will trigger the acquisition of additional knowledge.

7.2. Design of Conceptual Structure. Phase 2.

The functions of this phase are: to **structure** the knowledge acquire in the previous phase; and to **detect possible incompleteness** in this knowledge. The missing knowledge is acquired with the aid of the knowledge structured in this phase, and the activities identified in the first phase.

In applying the second phase of the AC methodology to the loan assessment problem, two structures were identified. The first one is the information regarding the client and the second one, the information regarding the loan. Under the structure client, two sub groups were identified : credit information, and personal information (see figure 1).

7.3. Identification of Info-sets. Phase 3.

The objective of this phase is to identify the data that the system will have to process. As its is described in figure 2, this phase is done in parallel with phase number 2. The idea here is that as the designer structures the knowledge acquired from the expert (phase 2), at the same time, he can identify the instances of the data that will be process by the system (phase 3).

7.4. Design of Agents. Phase 4.

The purpose of phase 4 is to identify the agents that compose the system. Agents as it was mentioned before, are in charged of performing the processing of info-units in order to produce the response of the system to a given stimulus. Phase 4 must be executed in a cycle that involves phases 2, and 3

Phases 2, 3, and 4 make up a cycle that we have called, the **Design Refinement Cycle (DRC)**. This cycle takes place as follows: in phase 2 the designer identifies the concept structures that compose the system; this triggers the identification of info-units and info-sets, which is done in phase 3. These info-units are used to identify the agents that will perform the processing, this is done in phase 4. The identification of an agent's dependant and causal info-units, in turn, might cause the update of the concept structure (done in phase 2), which in turn might trigger the discovery of new info-units (phase 3).

As it can be seen DRC is a refinement cycle and not the result of the sequential execution of three phases. An appropriate concern at this point would be to know when should the designer stop the DRC. It is a difficult to give very strict rules on when to stop the DRC, but we can say that this is largely based on the experience of the designer. Nevertheless, the following guide-lines can be used :

1. As the knowledge model tends to be more stable the discovery of new *concepts* tends to decrease or disappear. This implies that phase 2 of the DRC is completed.

2. Once phase 2 is completed, the identification of info-sets and info-units should also be concluded.

3. Once phases 2 and 3 are completed, the purpose of phase 4 should be to refine the agents that have already been identify. Phase 4 should also have as an objective to detect possible contradictions in the knowledge extracted from the expert. For instance, if under the same circumstances two agents produce the same info-unit, and they have different causal info-sets, then this should hint the possibility of combining the two agents to perform the same task. Phase 4 is concluded once agents have been specified to a level of detail appropriate to the technology used for implementing the system.

Once the designer has completed the DRC, the **agent's local view** must be described. This implies an effort of **very fine knowledge engineering**. This is due to the fact that one must model the actual intellectual operations that the expert performs to deduce atomic pieces of information. This is not to say that, while phases 2, 3, and 4 were carried out there was no knowledge what so ever regarding the fashion in which the expert preforms his task. The difference here is that at this point the knowledge engineer must ask <u>very specific questions</u> regarding the inferences that the expert performs in order to specify how this process will be automated. For example, in the loan assessment problem, some characteristic questions to his phase would be : *"Based on a client's Credit Capacity and the Amount of a Loan, how is the Amount to Guaranty determined ? "*, and *"Under what circumstances should the Amount to Guaranty not be calculated ? "*. The answers to these questions lead to the design of the internal knowledge contained in the agent in charged of this particular task.

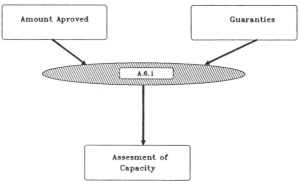

Figure 3: Agent for Producing Assessment Capacity

The following is a description of how the DRC was applied to the loan assessment case study. (The DRC for the other two areas: financial personality and financial credibility is analogues).
        1) First pass :
            a) The assessment of the client's capacity is produced by the agent A.6.1 (figure 3). In order to produce this info-unit, two input info-units are needed, *amount-approved* and *guaranties*.
            b) All the info-units identified so far are part of the concept structure (figure 1) therefore no changes to the concept structure are needed.
        2) Second Pass:
            a) The output info-set amount approved is produced based on 4 input info-sets (figure 4). All of them have already been modelled in the conceptual structure except for the concept **type-of-loan**.
            b) The concept structure for loan does not contain the idea of **type-of-loan**. Therefore this has to be created as an attribute or as a subset of the general concept "loan".
            c) The expert is questioned about the concept "type of loan" and he points out that due to some legal consideration, he must know the type of loan in order to determine the amount of credit that he can approve.
            d) This new information causes the creation of two specialisation (is-a) links. That is, the concept "loan" is transformed into a generalisation with two specific types of loans, namely **personal loan** and **sales loan** (see figure 5).
The DRC was performed 6 times to produce the final agent's global view shown in figure 4 and the concept structure for loan (figure 5) and for client (figure 6).

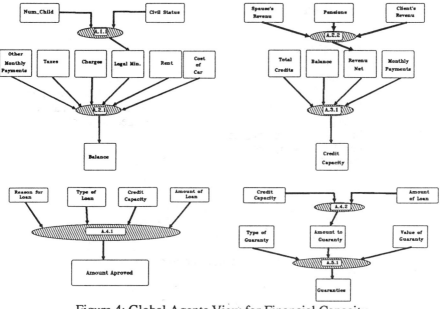

Figure 4: Global Agents View for Financial Capacity

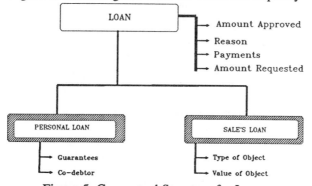

Figure 5: Conceptual Structure for Loan

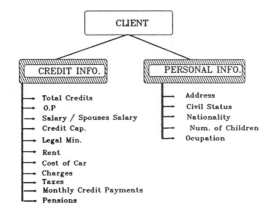

Figure 6: Conceptual Structure for Client

8. Verification and Validation

   Knowledge-based systems as any other software system must be verified and validated. The verification of a KBS entitles the confirmation that the system has been implemented according to specifications. The validation of the KBS consist in checking whether the system perform the task that is supposed to.

   The verification of a KBS is supported by the AC methodology by providing a map of the behaviour of a system (the agents global view) and a map of the knowledge contained in the system (concept structure). The agents global view permits the tracing of the behaviour of a system since each task that a system performs can be traced back to an agent. By the same token, the concept structure along with the agents global view allows the tracing of the usage of each concepts.

   The validation of a KBS is akin to the validation of any other software system. Validation usually involves the comparison of system's results with the expected results or the solutions provided by experts in the case of a KBS. The AC methodology provides some support in this area by helping in the conduction of test. This is based on the fact that, by using a system's agents global view, one can segment the system and test particular areas of it individually. It must be notice that this is not similar to the testing of one subroutine at the time in conventional programming. The segmentation supported by the agents global view reflects the logical subdivision of the system.

9. The use of AC in the maintenance of the system.

   Even though the AC methodology involves the users in the entire spectrum of the life cycle of a KBS, as soon as a system is deployed, it is very likely that users will request changes and improvements. One of the differences between the maintenance of a traditional information system and a KBS is that changes and their side effects tend to be more complex in a KBS since the information that a KBS processed and the way this information is process is more complex. The AC methodology tries to ameliorate this problem by providing some support to the person doing the maintenance of a KBS.

   The information produced in each of the phases described in section 7 are used to guide the maintenance process. The output of phases 2 (**conceptual structure**) is particularly important in the maintenance process since it provides a blue print of the concepts that the KBS manipulates. The information generated in phase 4 (**agent's global view**) is also critical for the maintenance of a KBS since it provides a map of the behaviour of the system.

   The manner in which AC supports the maintenance of a KBS is better seen through an example. For instance, imagine that in the loan assessment problem the following change was requested : "*the credit capacity of a client must be related to his age, therefore clients under 30 years of age should get 20% less credit than clients older than 30*". The first thing to do is to examine the conceptual structure produced in phase 2. This check reveals that under "personal information" the attribute age is not present, then the new attribute is added. The next step is to examine the agent's global view (produced in phase 4) looking for the agent that produces the client's credit capacity. The agent that produces this info-unit has as input the info-units Total Credits, Balance, Net Revenue, and Monthly Payments. At this point is obvious that the new info-unit **client@age** must be added as input, and that the logic inside the agent (agent's local view) must be changed to include the requested change.

   This example is simple, but it does show how a system's conceptual structure, and its agent's global and local view can be used to detect the system's components that must be modified to accommodate a change as well as to isolate the areas affected by the change.

10. CONCLUSIONS

During the 1970s we saw in the information processing field the famous spaghetti mess where the lack of proper design lead to the chaos in many software systems. As KBS become more popular in industry we must be very careful not to create the **knowledge mess** which could be much worse than the crisis of the 70s since KBSs are usually implemented in very sensitive areas of an organization.

The AC methodology in an attempt to provide a sound development methodology for the construction of KBSs. The methodology tries to provide support to all the phases that compose the life cycle of a KBS. The real acid test of any development methodology is to actually use it to construct commercial systems and then evaluate the results. This is precisely what we have been doing and so far, the results have been encouraging. Our current work is addressing the issue of expanding the AC methodology to support the integration of KBS to conventional information processing systems. We are also exploring the possibilities of combining the AC methodology with other techniques such as KADS (BREUKER & WIELINGA 88) (for model driven knowledge acquisition) and International Business Machine's AD/Cycle and Repository (for conventional information engineering development technology).

The Knowledge-based systems group at the Swiss Bank Corporation, Basel in collaboration with the Advanced Software System's Group of IBM Switzerland are currently developing a CASE tool that automates the AC methodology. This tool is called **EMA** for Executable Methodology for the development of knowledge-bases systems Applications.

REFERENCES

Chen, P.P. (1976). "The entity-relationship model: Toward a unified view of data", ACN Transactions in Database Systems, 1, No 1.

Breuker, J. and Wielinga, B. (1988). Models of Expertise in Knowledge Acquisition. University of Amsterdam, Department of Social Science Informatics, Memo 103, VF-Project.

Norman D.A, and Draper S.W. (1986). User Centered Systems Design. Lawrence Erlbaum Associates, Publishers.

Probst A.R., and Horvitz A.I (1989). Man-Machine Interfaces and Knowledge-Based Systems. First Swiss Meeting on Artificial Intelligence and Cognitive Science, Yverdon, Switzerland.

Probst A.R., and Wenger D. (1990). Knowledge-Based Systems : Towards a design methodology which smooths away interface problems. Third International Symposium in Commercial Expert Systems in Banking and Insurance, Lugano, Switzerland.

SCALING UP KNOWLEDGE SYSTEMS:
An Architecture for the GigaKnowledge-Base

T. R. Addis and M. C. C. Nowell

Knowledge Systems Group,
Department of Computer Science,
University of Reading,
Whiteknights,
Reading,
Berkshire RG6 2AX.

Abstract

    It is argued here that Systems Analysis and Knowledge Engineering are strongly influenced by the different components of the underlying computer architecture to which they are directed; influenced to the extent that it sets bounds on what kinds of knowledge can be represented. It is both the computer architecture and the representation language which will eventually set limits on the size and complexity of knowledge-based systems. One possible solution is proposed that includes an example of a family of front end processors based upon the transputer. Three transputers are formed into a pipeline that supports a content addressable relational mass storage system (1.6 Gbytes). This relational system is used to support a Functional Database (FDB) language called FAITH. It is shown that the Functional Database has formal coherence and is the appropriate vehicle for developing knowledge systems. The major objective has been to produce an inexpensive knowledge-base accelerator for the intelligent accessing of mass storage (CARDS).

1. Introduction

    The description of scientific activity in terms of progressive and non- progressive development has been used by analogy to describe both systems analysis and knowledge engineering (Addis, 1985, 1987). Progressive development involves the acknowledgement of new attributes and relationships in a task domain whereas the non-progressive development is a process of refinement. The end result of both activities is a model.

    Ultimately these models must be implemented on machines; machines that impose their own characteristics through limitations on performance and constraints on representation. These limitations are particularly marked when considering secondary (mass) storage. The question now arises as to how best to advance the computational machinery we have available when knowledge engineering will no doubt be extended to include databases and company-wide expertise.

    Research into PROLOG databases has highlighted the need for close control of expensive database operations. This need will exist despite the predicted increases in the size and speed of both primary and secondary storage devices. On the other hand, the research reflects the necessity for a powerful (high-level) and elegant (simple) representation that will support a large knowledge-base. Only with such a representation and its associated technological support will it be feasible to envisage a knowledge-base that embodies the growth and history of a company, provides the response to change and can capture and retain its best expertise.

2. Systems Analysis and Knowledge Engineering

The systems analyst will produce a conceptual model that is static. This static model relates to 'scientific theory' in the sense that it will describe the bounds of all future states of the domain and it will also form the basis for the calculation of data which is not held explicitly. The knowledge engineer, on the other hand, will create an active model that will describe the behaviour of an expert.

The significant difference between the systems analyst's task and the knowledge engineer's task is that the systems analyst is constrained by the representation of mass storage. Mass storage implies disc or tape; both these media depend upon electro- mechanical devices for processing. In both disc and tape, the data is arranged in a line and thus is principally one dimensional. This linear arrangement can easily support simple structures that are based upon order and grouping. Any other structure will result in considerable processing overheads because of the more frequent need to physically move the media in order to access data that may be scattered over the surface of one or more discs or tapes.

Access is not the only consideration since the cost of change of data values or of the data reorganization to accommodate new views both have high performance overheads. It is thus not surprising that the 'knowledge' on which the systems analyst focuses tends to be static, of a simple uniform structure and extensive. Other kinds of 'knowledge' that are equivalent to 'rules' and 'heuristics', knowledge that tends to be dynamic, of a complex variable structure and compact are confined to the programs that access the data. For example, the COBOL program that processes salaries contains expert knowledge. However, this knowledge is not conveniently expressed and hence is usually restricted to simple procedural knowledge.

Relational analysis, one of the major tools of the systems analyst, provides a means of representing data independently of accessing and storage. It is a formulation that expresses most easily the data component of knowledge and confines the rules and heuristic knowledge to the program (e.g. the query).

Relational analysis has an advantage over all other formulations in that it provides a technique of reducing a domain to its most useful primitive elements by eliminating all but the most elementary constraints. This process of normalization (viz. TNF, BCNF, 4NF, 5NF) can then be reversed under the control of the systems analyst to create a conceptual model (Addis, 1985); a conceptual model that illustrates the existence constraints between data. However, the underlying physical limitations of mass storage necessarily re- emerge when implementation is considered. The tool for designing the physical layout of data on the storage media and controlling the implementation is the technique that translates the conceptual model into a logical model; a model that reflects the limitations of the media.

Knowledge engineering has not been bounded by these limitations of mass storage. Knowledge engineering has developed from Artificial Intelligence which is mainly concerned with problem solving. Artificial Intelligence programs have their major physical realization in main memory (primary memory) and they are usually implemented in functional or logic languages such as LISP and PROLOG; these are languages designed to represent complex structures and cope with involved inferential search patterns. In this case, the accessing of information and its processing has relied upon pure electronic devices (e.g. RAM).

3. Large Knowledge-Based Programs

Large knowledge-based programs that go beyond the limitations of main memory have relied upon mass storage through the paging facility; a technique that eventually restricts the operational size of the knowledge-base.

Other approaches that endeavour to expand the knowledge-base through linking directly to a database have had some success (e.g. PROSQL, PROGRES, MU-PROLOG). The main problem with all these arrangements, referred to as loosely coupled systems, is that it forces the designer to consider query and inference as entirely separate tasks (Rybinski, 1987. Stonebraker et al, 1987). Further, these loosely coupled systems must be built around a pre-determined static conceptual model; a model that, once specified and implemented, cannot be dynamically modified except in a trivial way (i.e. the non- progressive changes).

The alternative tightly coupled (provides a unified view) PROLOG systems make the integration of the database management (typically a Relational Database Management System - RDB) transparent to the user; the database management merely replaces the normal memory-based PROLOG database (e.g. EDUCE - Bocca, 1986). The greatest advantage of the tightly coupled database is also its critical weakness. The entirely implicit nature of database operations means that the programmer can forget the database altogether, but then any control over database operations must also be forgotten. In particular there is a tension that exists between 'tuple at a time' and 'set at a time' processing and this difference between the PROLOG and the RDB is a primary source of inefficiency (see Table 1). As an example of these efficiency problems, consider the following (simplified) PROLOG clause:

sibling(X,Y) :- *father_of*(X,Z),*father_of*(Y,Z).

In a tightly coupled system, one would not expect to change this representation according to how it may be used if the *father_of* predicate is held extensively (as a set of tuples) on the database. However, if this predicate is held as a large relation then the manner of evaluating the *sibling* clause becomes dependent upon the way it will be employed and hence the employment, if not properly supervised, is critical to the performance. In this example, the PROLOG code allows several possible constructions (uses) of the *sibling* clause, including:

- Finding all pairs of *siblings* where the conjunction in the clause becomes a relational join.
- Finding all *siblings* of a given X or Y where the projection should be carried out before the join whichever of X or Y is instantiated in the head.

- Finding a pair of *siblings* or a single *sibling* of a given X or Y.

Each of these constructions implies a different optimization of the database operations which can only be determined at the time of calling the clauses; PROLOG abstracts out this information which should be part of the programmer's conceptualization of the problem. It should be part of the programmer's conceptualization because of the procedural component of the knowledge.

Another approach, based upon the lambda calculus and functional programming, also provides a unified view of data and computation. This unified view, the functional database (FDB) does not require the additional features to manipulate sets since it is computationally complete whereas the logic approach (i.e. PROLOG in its pure form) is incomplete. Experiments with a functional database language have shown that it possesses all of the properties necessary for expressing knowledge-based processes in a clear and succinct manner (Poulovassilis, 1988). In particular, its uniformity of expression of data and processes ensures that no artificial distinctions are introduced into the system design; it provides a language that is unconstrained by the distinctions between data and its manipulation.

It is the functional database approach that has the representational power; this approach we eventually chose. The functional database retains the important unification property (pattern matching) of PROLOG but, in addition, has the explicit control over the processing strategy without loss of generalization. However, can this representational power be transformed into machinery that will support very large knowledge systems?

So far, the spectacular advance of computer technology has kept pace with the requirements of knowledge engineering. It has been presumed that this advance would match and overtake the electro- mechanical mass storage mechanisms so that all data would be stored in solid state devices. This presumption has not been realised and the electro-mechanical device is still the best means of storing large quantities of data. So the machinery we need to support a functional database would depend upon mass storage. Further, the advent of optical discs will provide robust mass storage of considerable density. It is a storage medium that can now be optionally supplied with the advantage of providing an indelible trace of activity; a trace that can be used for auditing.

4. Knowledge-Base Machines

Developments of hardware in response to the demands of knowledge-based systems are of two kinds:

- machines that are primarily engineered as extensions to main memory.
- machines that extend the use of mass storage (secondary storage).

The argument for the main memory extensions, such as the Intelligent File Store (Lavington, 1987) and the Connection Machine (Hillis, 1985) is that they provide a system that is not only very fast but is organised in just the right kind of way for modelling large scale complex systems. In these cases, the systems work in conjunction with mass storage where the data is retrieved for processing.

The alternative kind of machine is orientated around the mass storage unit(s) and is designed to access information directly from disc and process the information "on the fly". The main features of these machines are the ability to act as a fast information filter (content addressing) and to provide a balance between search area indexing (does not look where the information is known not to be) and exhaustive search. Examples of these are the ICL CAFS and the GEC CARDS (Foster, 1987).

The development of the two kinds of machine has converged towards a single concept. The main memory types have had to introduce improved methods for accessing and processing data from mass storage and the mass storage types have had to introduce more parallelism to improve the real time performance. The result in both cases is a mechanism that performs highly parallel processing of data streams from mass storage (also see Lavington, 1987).

This convergence of ideas suggests that there is a family of knowledge-based machines that ranges from complex parallel processing to intelligent access of mass storage. This family of machines should ideally be based upon a single architectural element that can easily be put into different configurations; configurations which are sufficiently flexible to jointly exploit the parallelism in both the search task of data access and the computational task of query evaluation (pattern matching and inference). One such architectural element is the transputer.

5. CARDS: A Knowledge-Base Accelerator

The awkwardness of many large knowledge-based systems is, in part, due to the incoherence of the different 'technologies' that have come together to manipulate knowledge. Experts in hardware design do not necessarily have the breadth of understanding of data-base structures to create the 'best' kind of machines to support large data-bases and experts in data-bases are not completely aware of all the issues involved in manipulating and representing knowledge. Both these classes of experts may be forced to modify greatly their approach to their designs in the light of a complex application.

The objective of the CARDS project (Alvey Project IKBS140) has been to focus a wide range of expertise on to the construction of a viable very large knowledge-based system. GEC (Hirst Research Laboratories) were the principal investigators and were responsible for the overall management of the project. GEC also designed and implemented the transputer pipeline, modified the operating system of the SUN workstation into a special device server and incorporated other functions in response to demands from the theory and the application (viz. Pattern Matching of text and the BANG search area indexing).

Reading University provided much of the theory and supporting software for the Functional Database (FDB). In particular, a method for knowledge-base design had been developed that integrated hardware considerations with data and knowledge-base demands.

The Functional Database language FAITH was also developed at Reading University from ML and from work done at Birkbeck College (London) by C. Small and A. Poulovassilis (Poulovassilis 1988). FAITH provides a coherent functional language which forms a common link to many knowledge representation schemes (viz. PROLOG, Semantic Nets, Production Rules, Frames and Relations).

The application chosen was the protein folding problem of the Imperial Cancer Research Fund (ICRF). Work already carried out by Rawlings (Rawlings et al 1987) at ICRF before the CARDS project commenced involved a large knowledge-base that had all the problems of size and complexity. This knowledge-base described what was then known about the three dimensional folding behaviour of some proteins. Most of the original work was written in PROLOG. However, ICRF were unable to extend their work due to the limitations imposed by the available hardware and methods.

6. From Relations to Functions

The Conceptual and Relational Database Server (CARDS) was originally proposed to harness the power and flexibility of transputers as a special front-end processor (server with an accelerator) to mass storage.

The CARDS was conceived as a complete system that would include its own schema (Conceptual Model) processor which would ensure data integrity. In the initial stages of the CARDS development a conceptual modelling interpreter (ERA2) was constructed as a front end to the transputer accelerator. The interpreter provided a language (CL) that would describe 'knowledge' in terms of constraints and concepts. The language also had a graphical form called Rfd Graphs.

The principles that formed the foundations of the language CL are derived from a development of a conceptual modelling scheme that is used in the relational technique called Sfd analysis (Addis, 1985); a technique that has some similarities with Entity Relationship modelling. The language CL represents 'knowledge' of the subject environment in the form of constraints (selected from a base set) between normalised relations. The objective was to describe all 'knowledge' in terms of a fixed set of primitive constraints that could be constructed to form complex 'ideas'. Although a set of primitive constraints was defined that covered a range of possible worlds (Addis & Bull 1988) the pursuit was shown to involve a much longer research programme than could be contained within the scale of the project.

The language CL, having emerged from the realm of the Relational Database (RDB), inherited many of the relational calculus features. In particular, the Group A features shown in Table 1 primarily relate to the storage and access of mass information. Group A in Table 1 shows the principal features that make the relational calculus sympathetic to mass storage and compatible with the transputer accelerator. It is these Group A features that any language, such as CL, based on the relational paradigm, will naturally inherit. However, as can be seen from Table 1, all the important modelling features of PROLOG and RDB are diametrically opposite. It is the inverse of the RDB Group A features that encapsulate the basic modelling principles of PROLOG; the language in which the ICRF protein folding and much of the knowledge-base work has been developed.

The relational calculus (without further development such as suggested by the CL work) is representationally too weak to replace PROLOG except in trivial cases and it is too incompatible to be integrated satisfactorily as a sub-language.

Functional languages, such as ML, HOPE and MIRANDA, are compatible with PROLOG but are more primitive. They are more primitive because they are not committed to the full 'logic' paradigm. However, it is this non-commitment that allows

Group	Features	PROLOG	FDB	RDB
A	Tuple at a time processing	*yes*	*yes*	no
	Set at a time processing	*no*	*no*	yes
	Binary or few-nary relationships	*yes*	*yes*	no
	Unification-based retrieval	*yes*	*yes*	no
	Data and program co-exist	*yes*	*yes*	no
B	Polymorphic Types	possible	yes	no
	Strong Typing	no	yes	*yes*
	Negation as failure	yes	*no*	*no*
	Null values	no	yes	yes
	Decidable	no	yes	*yes?*
	Backtracking	yes	*no*	*no*

Table 1 Comparison of FDB, PROLOG and RDB models
(Modified from a table by C. J. Rawlings, 1990)

the functional language to readily accept a wide range of 'knowledge' representation schemes (these also include relational representation).

Work on extending the functional languages to have 'persistence' through the notion of a Functional Database (FDB) has overcome the incompatability of the Group A features shown in Table 1. This was done through the mapping of all functions on to a set of n-tuples through the graph reduction of Lambda calculus expressions. For example, consider the definition of a function PLUS84 in the CARDS FDB language FAITH.

                fdec
                    PLUS84 ::= Int -> Int;
                fdef
                    PLUS84 ?0 ::= SUM ?0 #84;

FAITH is a strongly typed language that has a similar but extended syntax to Standard ML and MIRANDA both of which are described by C. Read (Read, 1989). The extensions provide for database operations (Poulovassilis A, 1988) and regular expression pattern matching in string data. The function is declared (fdec) to be a mapping of an integer (Int) into an integer. The function is then defined as the addition (SUM) of the parameter of PLUS84 (?0) to the number 84.

The declaration is translated into a set of 3-tuples for the mass storage media that records the arity, domain type and range type of the function. In this simple case only three 3-tuples are needed:

                [Arity   PLUS84   1]
                [Domain PLUS84   Int]
                [Range   PLUS84   Int]

The definition of the function is more complex in that it represents the 'apply' structure of the expression (see Figure 1). The left hand side of the expression simply identifies the function with a number (in this case 401). The storable 3-tuple becomes:

[PLUS84 fdef 401]

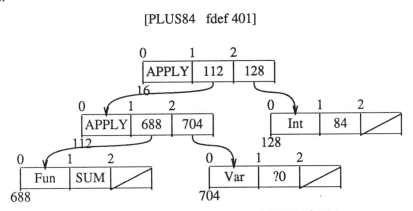

Figure 1 The APPLY structure of SUM ?0 #84

The right hand side of the expression is normally transformed by the interpreter into an apply tree so that it can be used. The apply tree structure is shown in Figure 1. This structure is then converted into a form that can be stored and retrieved by rewriting it as a set of 4-tuples. The elements of the 4-tuple are:

[Function_Identifier, Relative_Address, 3-tpl_elmnt_No, Element]

and in this case the function expands to:

[401 16 0   APPLY]
[401 16 1   112]
[401 16 2   128]

[401 112 0   APPLY]
[401 112 1   688]
[401 112 2   704]

[401 128 0   Int]
[401 128 1   84   ]

[401 688 0   Fun]
[401 688 1   SUM]

[401 704 0   Var]
[401 704 1   ?0   ]

7. The Functional Database System

The Functional Database system can be used either through the standard disc accessing mechanism or with the aid of the CARDS accelerator. Figure 2 shows the different functions that are removed from the CARDS (server) program and built into the transputer accelerator. Figure 2 also shows a proposed development called the ZF accelerator that would incorporate most of the functions into the accelerator through the ZF-function (Peyton-Jones S L, 1986).

Prototype functionally-based database systems (FDB's) that use standard disc accessing through UNIX have been implemented at both the University of Reading and Birkbeck College (London University) and have proved successful for small data-bases up to 20 Mbytes in size. The FDB has been tested on the ICRF's genetic database where many of the PROLOG functions that describe protein folding (Rawlings C J, 1987) have been reproduced in the Functional Database language FAITH.

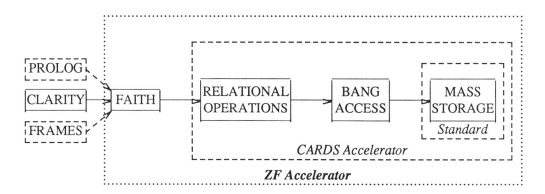

Figure 2 Variants of the Functional Database System

The FAITH interpreter interfaces a search area indexed system that is based upon the Balanced And Nested Grid (BANG) technique (Freeston M W, 1987).

Every function in the language is stored (and in practice this has been implemented in combinator form) as a set of n-tuples (records) on the disc. Performance of this technique is improved by using a Lexical to Token Converter (LTC) as used in the IFS (Lavington S H, 1987) in order to standardise the physical layout of the disc. Perfor-mance is also improved by *caching* selected functions (e.g. those concerned with transformations) in main memory during interpretation.

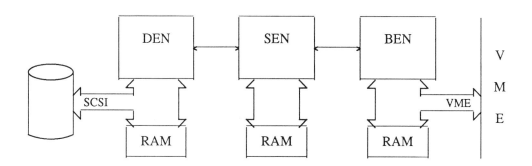

Figure 3 The Physical Pipeline Structure

8. The Accelerator

The CARDS hardware (the transputers) has been constructed and installed into a SUN3/160 with 1.6 Gbytes mass storage unit. The CARDS search and filter engine provides mechanisms for *on-the-fly* filtering of information read from the storage units. The information is passed through the search and filter engine as sets of records (tuples) which may be modified by a multi-stage filtering unit (see "logical" pipeline below).

The CARDS search and filter engine is implemented as a pipeline of three transputers each with a total cache store of 6 Mbytes.; this is the **physical pipeline** (see Figure 3). One of the transputers, the Disc Engine (DEN) is used primarily for disc access and has a DMA interface to the SCSI disc controller. This connects to the Spare Engine (SEN), which handles the majority of a pool of filter elements (see logical pipeline below). Finally, the SEN connects to the Bus Engine (BEN) which interfaces to a VME-bus and is attached to the backplane of a SUN. The role of the BEN is primarily to act as the interface to the Server host processor, but can also handle some of the pool of filter elements.

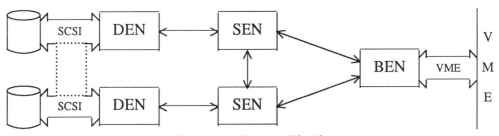

Figure 4 A Parallel Pipeline

Complex pipelines can be built by combining the basic physical pipeline in parallel. For example several discs may be read simultaneously using parallel pipelines (see Figure 4). The pipeline is extensible through the addition of further transputers both in parallel and in sequence; thus a family of CARDS devices may be constructed where each is organised according to the demands of the application.

The physical disc access makes use of a DMA device (customized) with a SCSI controller (NCR 53C90). Transfer rates of up 2 Mbytes/sec. have been achieved using the DMA control with memory mapped I/O.

Databases are stored on the disc systems in contiguous files. Each database consists of four files: BANG File, BANG File directory, Lexical Token Store (LTC), LTC Directory. The directories for a particular database are maintained in DEN memory (see Figure 3) while that particular database is active. This ensures that the access to the database is not delayed by directory activity.

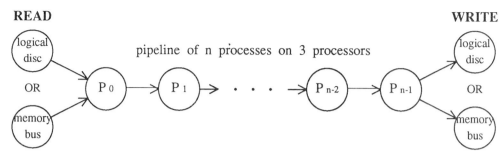

Figure 5 The Logical Pipeline Structure

9. The Logical Pipeline

The CARDS behaves as a multi-stage pipeline processor (see Figure 5) through the **logical pipeline** (tested up to 1000 co-processes for a single transputer) that can be programmed to process a data stream coming directly from the disc. The logical pipeline consists of a number of pipeline elements. Each of the pipeline elements performs a single filtering operation. The information to be filtered, processed as a sequence of records, is passed along the pipeline through each of the filter elements in turn.

Three types of basic operations can be performed by a filter element: 'Project', 'Select' or 'a VML function'. The VML language provides, amongst other possibilities, the mechanisms for arithmetic operations to be performed on the field of the records as they pass through the filters. The structure of the **logical pipeline** of filter elements is built over the **physical pipeline**.

Each of the filter elements is implemented as a pair of INMOS processes. One of the processes acts as a local control for the filter element and the other provides the filter operation. The two processes are connected by a pair of data channels which provide communication between the control process and the filter operation. Each record can be processed as either tokens or field values. The operation of each filter element can be represented by a function applied to fields within the record or to aggregations over a number of records. The aggregation facility enables sums, averages, etc. to be calculated.

All of the filter elements assigned to the network of transputers that make up the physical pipeline are chained together via a control channel which carries all of the pipeline control information. The control information for each of the filter elements is generated by a master control process which is located in the BEN (see Figure 3). This process keeps track of the status of each of the filter elements, decodes pipeline creation requests, generates the pipeline commands and deals with unusual events such as error reports.

A logical pipeline can be created dynamically from a pool of filter elements. The control channel is used to select the filter elements for a logical pipeline from the filter elements' pool and assign them to the transputers in the physical pipeline.

The operational CARDS device is under the access control of a BANG process and is operated through the FAITH interpreter. The CARDS also uses the BANG interface with the LTC and it is possible to switch the FAITH interpreter between the standard disc controller and the CARDS. The main application and test base has been the ICRF's genetics database.

10. Conclusions

The full potential of the CARDS has not yet been explored. The performance can be radically improved by both the physical organisation of the records and the migration of many of the FAITH functions into the transputer pipeline. The current organisation is that:

- the functions (including data as functions) are all stored on the disc as 3-tuples and 4-tuples. This is wasteful of both space and processing since many of the functions can be more efficiently expressed as n-tuples where n > 4;

- the only operations performed by the transputers are 'Select' and 'Project'. More complex functions are possible through the VML. However, this requires the construction of a set of (possibly parallel) filters in the form of a pipeline.

It should be noted that the ZF function is a syntactic transformation of the functional language (Peyton-Jones S L, 1986) that maps directly into the transputer pipeline. Such a mapping would provide considerable processing power at the very source of the data stream. It is thus possible to extend the CARDS by developing a "second phase" prototype which can support a Functional Database an order of magnitude larger than the current device. To achieve this objective the CARDS, developed by GEC (Hirst) Research Laboratories, could be used as an intelligent "back-end" database machine, into which FAITH statements could be *compiled*.

The CARDS accelerator represents a class of inexpensive devices that can be used to expand the performance and size of a knowledge-base system. This work has also shown that the functional database (with or without an accelerator) provides a sound basis for any knowledge representation scheme in that it bridges the gap between formal coherence and the architectural demands of mass storage. This firm base is very valuable from the standpoint of quality assurance considerations.

11. Acknowledgements

The CARDS project involved many people from GEC (Hirst), ICRF and Reading University. Each of the individuals contributed ideas that have merged into a successful project. The three Team Leaders were Arthur Foster (GEC), Chris Rawlings (ICRF) and Tom Addis (Reading University). Arthur Foster was also the overall Project Manager. However, particular acknowledgement should go to Carol Small for introducing us to the delights of the Functional Database. The CARDS project was supported by the SERC grant number GR/D73065-IKBS140.

12. Bibliography and References

Addis, T. R. (1985) *Designing Knowledge-Based Systems*, Kogan Page, London.

Addis, T. R. (1987) *A Framework for Knowledge Elicitation*, Proceedings of the First European Workshop on Knowledge Acquisition, Reading, ppA1/1 - A1/16.

Addis, T. R. & Bull, S. P. (1988) *A Concept Language for Knowledge Elicitation*. Proceedings of the Second European Workshop on Knowledge Acquisition, Bonn, pp1/1 - 1/11. June.

Addis, T. R. (1989) *The Science of Knowledge: A Research Programme for Knowledge Engineering*, 3rd European Workshop on Knowledge Acquisition for Knowledge-Based Systems, Paris, July.

Bocca, J. (1986) *EDUCE - A Marriage of Convenience: Prolog and a Relational DBMS*, Proceedings of the Third International Conference on Logic Programming, Springer-Verlag.

Codd, E. F. (1970) *A Relational Model of Data for Large Shared Data Banks*, Comm ACM, 13(6) pp 377-387.

Darlington, J. & Reeve, M. (1981) *ALICE - A Multiprocessor Reduction Machine for the Parallel Evaluation of Applicative Languages*, Proc ACM Conf on Functional Programming Languages and Computer Architecture, New Hampshire, pp65-75.

Date, C. J. (1981) *An Introduction to Database Systems*, Addison-Wesley, London.

Foster, A. (1987) *The CARDS Project*, SIGKME 1, Reading University.

Freeston, M. W. (1987) *Data Structures for Knowledge Bases*, Proceedings of the first Workshop of the Special Interest Group on Knowledge Manipulation Engines (SIGKME 1), Reading University.

Hillis, W. D. (1985) *The connection machine* (Cambridge MA: MIT)

Lavington, S. H. et al. (1987) *Memory Structures in the Intelligent File Store*, SIGKME 1, January, Reading University

Lavington, S. H. (1987) *Architectures for Large Knowledge-based Systems: Future Research Directions Based on Graph Paradigms*, SIGKME 2, May, Brunel University.

Lea, R. M. (1987) *VLSI/WSI Associative Processors: Overview, current status and future prospects*, SIGKME 1, Reading University.

McGregor, D. R. et al. (1987) Parallel Network Architectures for Large Scale Knowledge Based Systems, SIGKME 1, Reading University.

Peyton-Jones, S. L. (1986) *The Implementation of Functional Programming Languages*, Prentice-Hall, London.

Peyton-Jones, S. L. et al (1987) *GRIP - A High-Performance Architecture for Parallel Graph Reduction*, Functional Programming Languages and Computer Architecture, ed Kahn, G., Springer Verlag LNCS 274, pp98-112.

Poulovassilis, A. (1988) *FDL: An Integration of the Functional Data Model and the Functional Computational Model*, BNCOD6, CUP, pp215-236.

Rawlings, C. J. et al (1987) *Large Knowledge Bases: an example from molecular biology*, SIGKME 1, Reading University.

Read, C. (1989) *Elements of Functional Programming*, Addison-Wesley.

Rybinski, H. (1987) *On First-Order-Logic Databases*, ACM Trans on Database Systems, Vol 12, No 3, pp 325-349.

Stonebraker, M. et al, (1987) *Extending a Database System with Procedures*, ACM Trans on Database Systems, Vol 12, No3, pp 350-376.

Augmenting the RETE network to efficiently compile a blackboard system.

Thomas CHEHIRE

Thomson-CSF/RCC
160 Boulevard de Valmy. BP 82
92704 COLOMBES Cedex
FRANCE
tel: +33 (1) 4760 3892
Email: T_Chehire@eurokom.ie

Abstract:

Commercial expert system builders are widespread on the market and well designed for applications with simple control strategies. These toolkits focus more on the richness of the knowledge representation formalisms and the graphical development facilities than on the ability to adapt the behaviour of a large knowledge-base to a particular problem.

The lack of sophisticated control primitives entails bad performance for large applications and the user has to embed in his domain knowledge control declarations that make the rule-base less readable and difficult to maintain.

On the other hand, blackboard systems have shown their efficiency in such hard problems because of the neat separation between the control and the domain knowledge. But the explicit control primitives of blackboard systems are usually very cpu intensive and unnatural for many applications. In this article we show how to combine the blackboard concepts for tuning the control of an application and the RETE algorithm for efficiently compiling a rule-base.

After a short presentation of the RETE technology, we present the rule packet concept that extends the knowledge source paradigm of blackboard systems, and the multiple agendas system associated to the rule packets that provide a convenient formalism for specifying the control of an application. We finally describe the extension of the RETE network to increase its efficiency in applications where control is crucial to reduce the combinatorial explosion and where it is sufficient to execute a small portion of the selectable rules to solve the problem.

1. The RETE network:

The work presented in this paper has been implemented in an AI toolkit called KIRK (Knowledge Interpretation and Representation Kernel). The KIRK forward chainer relies on a RETE network. This means that the condition part of all forward chaining rules are compiled into a network with two parts: a discrimination network and a join network.

The role of the discrimination network is to determine which facts unify with each rule pattern. It will thus create local fact-bases associated with the patterns they match. This can be viewed as a mean of indexing the fact-base by the rule patterns.

The join network determines which combinations of facts (tuples) simultaneously fulfill all conditions of the rules. The join network thus maintains the partial and total instantiations of all rules.

The inputs of the RETE network are the modifications to the fact-base and the outputs are the modifications to the conflict set (or the agenda). The addition of a fact to the fact-base will eventually add instantiated rules to the conflict set, and the deletion of a fact from the fact-base will eventually remove instantiated rules from the agenda.

The basic operation of a forward chaining engine is as follows:
- The rules are compiled into a RETE network,
- Adding facts yields some rule instantiations,
- The inference engine enters, upon request, a selection-execution cycle:
    If the agenda is not empty, it selects the instantiated rule with the highest priority, and it executes its right-hand side actions. These actions may add new facts which will eventually instantiate more rules.

Let us write, for example, a rule to execute some processing on each candidate who is younger than thirty:

Rule_1:   *If*   (candidate ?name)
           and   (age ?name ?number & < 30)
           Then   <action>

After the rule has been compiled and some facts have been added to the fact-base, we end up in the following configuration:

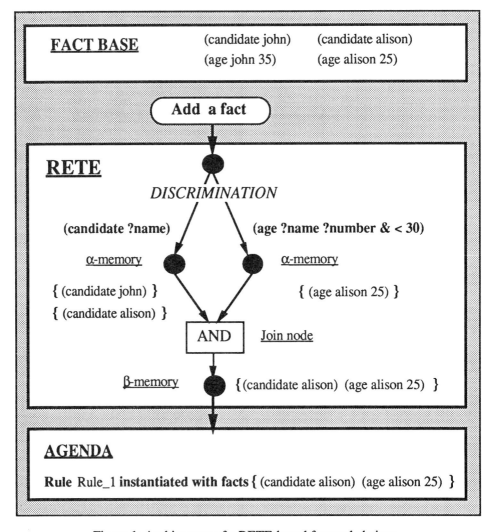

Figure 1: Architecture of a RETE-based forward chainer.

The network for rule Rule_1 starts with a dicrimination part which directs instances of relations "candidate" and "age" towards nodes called alpha-memories, associated with the two patterns (candidate ?name) and (age ?name ?number & < 30). When adding a fact, the discrimination network will store it in the nodes associated with the patterns it matches.

The AND node succeeds in combining the facts stored in its parent nodes when the shared variables match, and stores the resulting tuple in a node called beta-memory. In this example, (candidate john) and (age alison 25) cannot be combined.

The beta-memory is the terminal node for rule Rule_1. Thus, as soon as a tuple of facts is received by the node it is forwarded to the agenda with the name of the rule for future selection and execution of its right-hand side actions.

2. Architecture of the join network:

The join network is the place where most of the expert system execution time is spent. The basic RETE algorithm generates the following join network for a rule with n patterns:

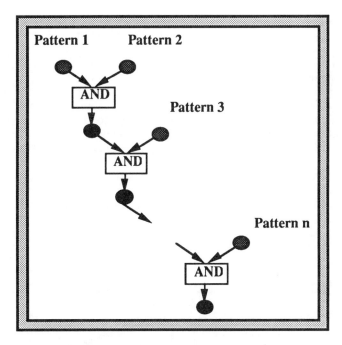

Figure 2: Architecture of the RETE network.

The terminal beta-memory stores the rule instantiations which are computed incrementally in the intermediate beta-memories.

Sharing nodes among rules is a crucial mean of improving global performance. But in order to ensure the maximum sharing between rules, the user has to write them very carefully: patterns that are common to several rules should appear in the same order at the beginning of each rule.

Another mean of improving global performance is to rewrite the rules in order to place the most constrained patterns first, thus minimizing the size of the memories and reducing the cost of combining their content. However, this will sometimes conflict with the maximum sharing of nodes between rules.

Hand rewriting of an important rule-base with these two optimization techniques in mind is not an easy task. Optimisers have been proposed that take a rule-base and run-time statistics collected on the RETE memories and that automatically propose a new rule-base with an improved global performance. The problem being similar to the query optimization in data-base systems, such optimizers are not always satisfactory, the optimization heuristics are contradictory and the problem is NP-hard

Other compilation techniques have been proposed, such as TREAT and OFLAZER. But the choice between one of these algorithms cannot be made a priori, the optimality of a rule-base compilation technique being not only rule-base dependant but essentially problem dependant. And since the initial state of the fact-base and its evolution over rule executions are arbitrary, it is very difficult to propose a general optimization scheme.

We will further develop two aspects of the optimization of the RETE network:
Maximizing node sharing between rules while minimizing coding constraints.
Minimizing unnecessary work involved in instantiating rules that will never get selected.

3. Rule packets:

When rules have some patterns in common, the tuning of large knowledge-bases may become extremely cumbersome, especially when it is necessary to modify these patterns. In addition, one has to write the common patterns in the same order and at the beginning of all relevant rules in order to share, among the rules, the RETE computations induced by the patterns.

KIRK provides the **rule packet** concept as a knowledge representation formalism to handle both rule-base tuning and common patterns sharing.

A rule packet has a name and may have a condition part. When a rule is attached to a rule packet, it automatically inherits the rule packet condition part as the beginning of its own condition part. Therefore, all rules share the RETE nodes of their rule packet.

Consequently, whenever a pattern is modified in the rule packet, the modification automatically extends to all relevant rules. Such global handling alleviates tuning and debugging and maximum sharing among rules is insured without bearing the burden of careful coding.

In addition, a rule packet can itself contain rule packets. A rule-base can thus be structured as a hierarchy of operators (rules or rule packets).

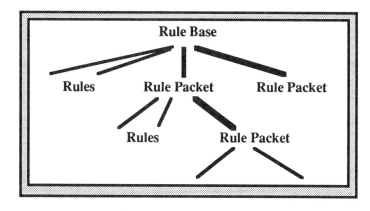

Figure 3: Rule-base organisation.

Organizing the rule-base as a hierarchy of operators does not modify the RETE network. The only difference with an OPS-like rule-base is that the rule condition part is split over its rule packet ancestors. This reduces the average number of conditions in an operator left-hand side and makes the rule-base more readable. A tree editor will let the user browse in the operator hierarchy in a convenient way.

Controlling OPS-like rule-bases is very difficult and unnatural, but in some applications the specification of sequences of rule execution, or even the grouping of rules and the specification of the preference of one group over another in certain contexts, is more important than the rules themselves.

Blackboard systems propose some solutions to the problem of focusing an application on the most relevant task at a certain point in a problem space. But usually, in a blackboard system, the deductive knowledge is separated in a list of Knowledge Sources, there is no notion of operator hierarchy.

Drawbacks of blackboard implementations include:
- a rule language not as rich as the one of OPS-like systems,
- an inefficient rule-base compilation,
- very cpu-intensive control primitives.

KIRK merges the RETE algorithm known for its efficiency and blackboard concepts for organizing and controlling an application. The rule packet and multiple agendas concepts that we propose were shown to be convenient, natural and efficient in many applications. Their use is enforced by the fact that the specification and tuning of the control of an appplication can be mapped to the organisation of the rule-base.

4. Multiple Agendas:

Rule packets extend the notion of knowledge sources to any level in the tree. At each depth in the operator hierarchy, rules and rule packets will compete to modify the blackboard.

Whenever a rule packet condition part is verified, an agenda is created for this particular instantiation of the rule packet. The agenda is placed in the agenda of the parent packet. This will dynamically organise the conflict set as a hierarchy of agendas.

Whenever a rule is instantiated, it is placed in its rule packet agenda.

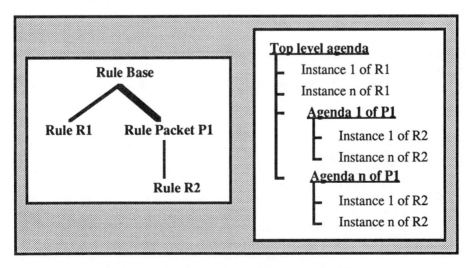

Figure 4: Operators and conflict set hierarchies.

However, rule packets do not need to have an agenda mechanism, the user may restrict the agenda hierarchy to the top-level agenda and have an OPS-like conflict resolution strategy or he may attach an agenda mechanism only to the rule packets that need a sophisticated control.

Moreover, it is not necessary to create an agenda for each of the instantiations of a rule packet (as shown in figure 4), the user can decide to create just one agenda for a rule packet and this agenda will store all the instantiations of its operators.

Expensive control strategies will thus only be deployed for those rule packets that require it. The overhead of the multiple agendas mechanism can thus be minimized, and the cpu intensiveness of a control blackboard or any other mean of creating an opportunistic control of an application can thus be reduced to the portions of the rule-base that require it.

In the configuration where only one agenda is attached to each rule packet, the agenda hierarchy is isomorphic to the rule packet hierarchy and the conflict set is not dynamically organized and thus easier to trace.

Another advantage of this configuration, when using decreasing priority agendas is that rule priorities become local to their rule packet. This is of prime importance for large rule-bases: when defining a new rule one has to compare its priority to the operators belonging directly to the same rule packet, and not to all other rules (as done in most inference engines).

5. Modifying the RETE network:

A standard RETE algorithm compiles the rule-base in a network which constructs the total and partial instantiations of all operators. But, in applications that require a blackboard architecture, the system is focused on important tasks and the selection-execution cycle terminates when a solution is found, not when the conflict set is empty. The problem with the RETE network is that the expensive operations in the join nodes are undertaken even if the operators never get selected. Large performance gains can be obtained with a fine partition of the network and the disabling of portions that are not relevant to the current state of the problem space.

But if it is necessary to enable back those RETE nodes, large computations may have to take place since all the tuples of facts that were blocked should be readily transmitted and eventually combined to instantiate previously disabled operators. This overload is unacceptable for some applications and especially in real-world real-time applications.

We propose a better way of minimizing the load of the network:
- the rule packet organisation of the rule-base allows a fine grain partition of the RETE network,
- the agenda mechanism allows a fine tuning of the computations in the RETE network, thus minimizing the unnecessary work for instantiating rules that will never get selected for execution.

The RETE network is partitioned is such a way that a join node can be shared only by operators of a same rule packet:

Whenever a rule packet is defined, it is compiled into nodes that are added to (or shared in) the RETE network. The terminal node for that rule packet is a memory node that will compute its total instantiations, but that may be shared by other operators extending the rule packet condition part.

In order to break the node sharing algorithm of the RETE network, we sprout **a special RETE node** from that terminal node and we call it a **rule packet node**. This particular node will serve as the leftmost node of the RETE network of all the rule packet operators and will thus belong only to the rule packet and to its operators and cannot be shared by any other operator.

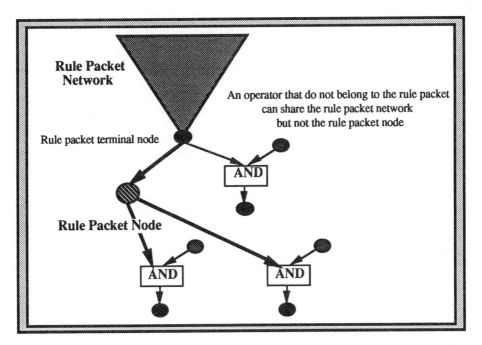

Figure 5: Partitionning the RETE network.

An agenda will not transmit the facts which enabled its creation, until it is selected:
          When a fact tuple reaches the rule packet node, it is not forwarded to its successors but an agenda is created that holds that fact tuple. The agenda is placed in the agenda of the parent packet for an eventual selection. But since the fact tuple has not been transmitted, it could not instantiate the operators of the rule packet and the agenda is thus empty. When the agenda is selected and becomes the current agenda, the fact tuple is transmitted to the successors of the rule packet node.
          Therefore the computation needed to instantiate the rule packet operators are only undertaken when needed, and the join nodes are not completely frozen: they just do not receive fact tuples from the rule packet node until the selection of the agenda they created.

          The rule packet node acts like a filter, it contains a memory the size of which is always smaller than the size of the memory node it was sprouted from. The memory of the rule packet node can even be empty, and the difference in size with the parent node is equal to the number of agendas created for the rule packet and not yet selected.
          In combinatorial rule left-hand sides, the size of the memory nodes is an exponential function of the node's depth in the network and of the size of the rule's alpha-memories. Therefore, a carefull organisation of the rule-base and association of adequate agendas may reduce dramatically the computations undertaken in the RETE network in applications where the selection-execution cycle stops before the conflict set is empty.

6. Operations defined on agendas:

The agenda mechanism modifies the selection-execution cycle of the inference engine: it starts at the top-level agenda and selects the operator with the highest priority.

If it is a rule, its actions are executed.

If it is a rule packet agenda the selection-execution cycle moves to the sub-agenda and sets it as the current agenda. When the current agenda is empty, the selection-execution cycle moves back to its parent agenda.

An agenda can be interrupted if a rule execution creates new facts that instantiate operators of higher priority than the one of the selected agenda. Moreover the user can set a limit to the number of rule firings in an agenda or set a lower limit to the priority of a selectable operator in an agenda.

The user can define for each rule packet the kind of agenda that is best suited. He can specialize the behavior of the rule packet agendas by attaching actions to be executed at the different phases of an agenda life cycle. The actions will be specified with the language used for the rules right-hand side and will of course make reference to the variables matched in the condition part of the rule packet. But while a rule has one action part executed after the rule instance is selected, an agenda has many action parts that will be executed when the agenda is created, deleted, selected, interrupted, etc...

To obtain flexibility, the multiple agendas mechanism is implemented in an object oriented language. A predefined set of agenda classes can be proposed, from the simple and efficient FIFO, LIFO or decreasing priority conflict resolution strategies to more complex methods for adding and selecting an operator. The user can create new classes of agendas, and specialize their behaviour using all the multiple inheritance and method combination possibilities of the object oriented language.

7. Control example:

Let us write a short example that illustrates how one can separate control knowledge from domain knowledge with the agenda mechanism:

The domain knowledge is on the selection of candidates, it is organised in two operator hierarchies: one for the selection of female candidates and the other for the selection of male candidates. We will describe only the roots of the two hierarchies for the sake of the example:

```
Rule Packet:      Female_selection
   conditions:       (candidate ?name)
              and   (age ?name ?age)
              and   (sexe ?name Female)

Rule Packet:      Male_selection
   conditions:       (candidate ?name)
              and   (age ?name ?age)
              and   (sexe ?name Male)
```

The control knowledge will consist for example in prefering the younguest candidates and otherwise prefering female candidates to male candidates:

```
(Attach-agenda-to-Packet    Female_selection  :priority      0
            :when-created    Assert (Agenda @current_agenda Female ?age) )

(Attach-agenda-to-Packet    Male_selection    :priority      0
            :when-created    Assert (Agenda @current_agenda Male ?age) )
```

When the fact-base is initialized with candidates data, an agenda of priority 0 is created for each candidate. The creation of an agenda fires the when-created actions and creates a new fact of the form:

(Agenda <name-of-the-created-agenda> <Female-or-Male> <Age-of-the-candidate>)

Those control facts will not instantiate any rule of the domain knowledge, they are created for the sake of the following control rules:

<u>Rule:</u>   Prefer_Younguest
        Priority: 100
If   ?fact : (Agenda ?agenda ?sex ?age)
   and   NOT (Agenda ~?agenda ? ?other_age & <= ?age)
Then   Change-agenda-priority (?agenda 1000)
   and   Retract (?fact)

<u>Rule:</u>   Prefer_Female
        Priority: 10
If   ?fact : (Agenda ?agenda Female ?age)
   and   (Agenda ?other_agenda Male ?other_age)
Then   Change-agenda-priority (?agenda 1000)
   and   Retract (?fact)

The priority of the Prefer_Younguest rule is higher than the priority of the Prefer_Female rule, it will thus be selected first.The priorities of the control rules are higher than the initial priority of the agendas created for each candidate, they will thus be selected before any processing is undertaken on any candidate.The control rules will pick an agenda and raise its priority above their own priority. This ensures that whenever a control rule is fired, the next cycle will process the corresponding agenda and therefore apply the domain knowledge to the selected candidate. When a candidate's agenda is exhausted and is withdrawn from the global conflict set, the control rules will have the maximum priority and their execution will select the next candidate's agenda.

As shown in the section on the modification of the RETE network, if we want to retain only a small number of candidates, then only a small portion of the agendas created for the Female_selection and Male_selection rule packets will get selected and therefore the join nodes of their operator hierarchies will not get overwhelmed by all the candidates data, only by those of the happy few.

Acknowledgements:

KIRK is part of the SPIRITS environment for generating highly interactive graphical man machine interfaces and building expert systems. SPIRITS is a commercial product resulting from the ESPRIT project P96.
I would like to thank my collegues, Geneviève BAILLY and Antoine MENSCH for their contributions to the final version of this paper.

References:

Bond, A.H. & Gasser Les. (1988). Readings in distributed artificial intelligence, Morgan Kaufmann.

Corkill, D.D.& Gallaher, Q. (1988). Tuning a blackboard-based application.
A case study using GBB, AAAI 88.

Chehire, T. (1988). KIRK Un environnement de développement de systèmes experts. Conference internationale les systèmes experts et leurs applications. Avignon.

Engelmore, R. & Morgan, T. (1988). Blackboard Systems, Addison-Wesley.

Erman, D.L. & al. (1980). The HEARSAY II speech understanding system: integrating knowledge to resolve uncertainty, ACM Computing Surveys, 12.

Forgy, C.L. (1982). RETE a fast algorithm for the many pattern / many object pattern match problem. Artificial Intelligence, vol 19.

Garvey, A. & Hewettt, M. & Vaughan , J.M. Jr. & Schulman , R. & Hayes-Roth, B. (1987). BB1 User manual, Stanford University, Report No KSL 86-61.

Ghallab, M. (1982). Optimisation de processus décisionnels pour la robotique. Thèse d'état, UPS, Toulouse.

Gilmore, J.F. (1987). GEST : The anatomy of a blackboard expert system tool. Conference internationale les systèmes experts et leurs applications. Avignon.

Gupta, A. & Forgy, C.L. (1983). Measurements on Production Systems.Tech. Report, CMU-CS-83-167; Carnegie-Mellon University.

Gupta , A. & Forgy, C. & Newell , A.(1989). High-Speed Implementations of Ruled-Based Systems, ACM Transactions on Conputer Systems

Haton, J.P. (1989). Panorama des systèmes multi-agents, Architectures avancées pour l'intelligence artificielle. EC2.

Hayes-Roth, B. (1984). BB1 : An architecture for blacboard systems that control, explain and learn about their own behaviour. HPP-84-16. STANFORD.

Ishida, T. (1988). Optimizing rules in production system. AAAI 88

Laasri, H. & Maitre, B. & Mondot, T. & Charpillet, F. & Haton J.P. (1988). ATOME A Blackboard Architecture with temporal and Hypothetical reasoning,ECAI, Munich.

Lesser, V.R. & Corkill, D.D. (1983). The distributed vehicle monitoring testbed: a tool for investigating distributed problem solving networks. AI magazine 4.

Dermott, J.Mc & Newell A. & Moore, J. (1978). The Efficiency of certain Production System Implementations. Pattern-directed Inference Systems. Academic Press.

Miranker, D.P. (1987). TREAT: A Better Match Algorithm for AI Production Systems. AAAI. 87.

Nii , H.P. (1986). Blackboard Systems . AI Magazine 7(2) & 7(3)

Schorr, M.I. & Daly, T.P. & Lee, H.S. & Tibbits, B.R. (1986). Advances in RETE pattern matching. AAAI 86.

Scales, D.J. (1986). Efficient Matching Algorithms for the SOAR/OPS5 Production System. Knowledge System Laboratory, Report N° KSL 86-47

UNIFYING COMPUTING: INDUCTIVE LEARNING AND LOGIC

J Gerard Wolff

Andrew J Chipperfield

School of Electronic Engineering Science, University of Wales, Dean Street, Bangor, Gwynedd, LL57 1UT, UK. Telephone: +44 248 351151 ext 2691. Electronic mail: j.g.wolff@uk.ac.bangor.sees.

Abstract

The paper introduces a new theory of computing, called 'SP', and describes a prototype of a new kind of computing system (also called SP) which is based on the theory. The focus of the paper is on how the SP theory and the SP system may integrate two kinds of computing which are not normally related: inductive learning and logic.

The SP theory is based on the conjecture that all kinds of computing and formal reasoning may usefully be seen as a search for *efficiency* in information, where the concept of efficiency is defined in terms of the concept of *redundancy* in Shannon's information theory.

The SP prototype (SP6) provides a simple language intended for the representation of diverse kinds of knowledge. The prototype is dedicated to searching for redundancy in knowledge and extracting it wherever it is found. Elements of this process are pattern matching and unification of patterns combined with a hill-climbing search amongst alternative sets of unifications.

The paper describes examples showing how SP6 performs the induction of a grammar from examples, the induction of a class hierarchy from examples, simple syllogistic reasoning and logical reasoning with a transitive relation ('equals'). Issues for future research are discussed.

1. Introduction

What has inductive learning got to do with logic? "Not much" is the answer implied by most research in these two areas. The two topics are not normally connected.

This paper introduces a theory of computing within which learning and logic may be integrated. The theory is relevant to several other areas of computing - including probabilistic inference, information retrieval, natural language processing, pattern recognition, object-oriented design, problem solving and automatic planning - but these topics will not be considered here. The focus in this paper is on how inductive learning and logic may be seen as two facets of one computing process.

In the paper, we first give an outline of the theory, called 'SP'. Then we describe a prototype of a new kind of computing system - also called SP - which is based on the theory. Last, we describe and discuss examples from the prototype showing how inductive learning and logical inference may both result from one unified computing process.

2. The SP Theory

The central idea in the SP theory (described in Wolff (in press) and Wolff (1989)) is the conjecture that all kinds of computing and formal reasoning may usefully be seen as a search for *efficiency* in information, where the concept of efficiency is defined in terms of the concept of *redundancy* in Shannon's information theory.

In the SP theory, the efficiency of a body of information (I) is defined as:

$$efficiency = power \, / \, size$$

Power is defined as the information content of I (in bits), **excluding** any redundancy in I.

Size (otherwise known as *simplicity*) is defined as the information content of I (in bits), **including** any redundancy in I.

2.1. The SP Search Space

The SP search space is illustrated in figure 1 below.

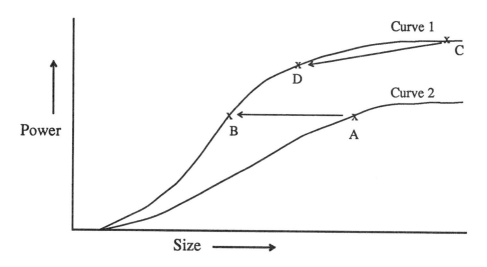

Figure 1. The SP Search Space

Each point in figure 1 represents a body of information or a knowledge structure with its own measure of size and power.

Each curve in the figure illustrates the trade-off between size and power: big knowledge structures are usually more powerful than little ones and *vice versa*.

Curve 1 represents a set of relatively efficient knowledge structures at varying levels of size and power while curve 2 represents relatively inefficient knowledge structures varying in a similar way.

2.2. Pattern Matching, Unification and Hill-Climbing Search

Searching for efficiency in a body of information means, in large part, searching for redundancy in the information and extracting the redundancy wherever it is found:

1   Redundancy means repetition of information. Where a pattern of information repeats more often than other patterns of the same size, there is redundancy.

The elements of a 'pattern' are not necessarily contiguous. In many bodies of information, especially natural language, a significant part of the redundancy is due to constraints and contingencies which bridge other structures.

2   Redundancy in a body of information may be detected by comparing or *matching* patterns.

3   Redundancy in a body of information may be reduced by the merging or *unification* of repeating instances of a pattern to make just one.

4   The complication is that there are often many alternative ways in which a given pattern or part of a pattern may be unified. Finding a good set of unifications for the repeating patterns in a body of information amongst all the many possible sets of unifications means a process of *searching*. Because the search space is usually very large, often infinite, it is necessary to use a *hill-climbing* technique - or something equivalent - to achieve an effective search in a reasonable time.

To find and extract as much redundancy as possible means searching for the largest possible value of **R** where:

$$R = \sum_{i=1}^{i=n} (f_i - 1) . s_i \, ,$$

f is the frequency of the **i**th member of a set of **n** patterns and **s** is its size in bits.

2.3. Variations

The process of searching for efficiency in information can take a variety of forms:

- **Preserving power or sacrificing power.** The search may be constrained to preserve all the power in the body of information I. In the diagram, a transformation in a knowledge structure which moves it from A to B means increasing its efficiency without reducing its power. If the circumstances are right, the knowledge structure may be moved 'down market' by sacrificing power in order to gain an overall increase in efficiency. In the diagram, a transformation in a knowledge structure which moves it from C to D reduces its power but increases the ratio of power to size and thus increases efficiency.

- **Breadth of search.** Small knowledge structures may be searched exhaustively. As already indicated, most realistically large knowledge structures cannot be searched exhaustively - but the thoroughness of the search may vary. *Broad* searching is hungry for computing resources and is likely to need high levels of parallelism in processing to achieve adequate speed. The benefit of broad or thorough search in a computing system is that the system can be relatively flexible and intelligent. *Narrow* searching reduces computational costs but means that the computing system has less flexibility and more of that 'brittleness' and stupidity which characterises current systems.

- **One path or multiple paths**. The search process may thread one path through the search space and give one 'best' answer. Alternatively, the search process may follow two or more paths through the search space and give a set of answers, graded in terms of the efficiency they represent. These parallel paths may be followed in sequence - in which case we have the effect of 'backtracking'. If there are sufficient resources, they may be followed in parallel.

2.4. Related Work

The SP theory originated in a programme of work on language learning by children, with research in inductive learning of grammars as a major part of the programme (Wolff, 1987, 1988). The similarity between the processes needed for the inductive learning of grammars and processes at the heart of resolution theorem proving is what lead to the SP theory.

The idea of searching for economical structures, which is a central part of the SP theory, features in some research on 'neural' computing (see, for example, Campbell, Sherrington & Wong, 1989, and Hinton & Sejnowski, 1986) and also in research on cluster analysis and numerical taxonomy. The SP theory presents a view of computing which is not tied to any particular architecture (such as neural networks) and which is in several other respects different from work on neural computing or cluster analysis. There is potential in the theory to integrate the 'connectionist' and 'symbolic' views of computing.

The idea that all kinds of formal system and computing system may be seen as information has been developed as 'algorithmic information theory' (see, for example, Chaitin,1987). That work focuses on issues of completeness and decidability in formal systems whereas the SP theory focuses on how an analysis of formal systems in terms of information and redundancy may illuminate issues in knowledge representation and the process of computation itself.

The SP language (described below) owes its greatest debt to Prolog (see, for example, Clocksin & Mellish, 1981) but differs from Prolog in several ways. There is some resemblance between SP and 'unification grammars' (see, for example, Shieber, 1986) but also significant differences. Unification concepts are reviewed in Siekmann (1989). The most important difference between SP and these kinds of system is that the pattern matching and unification processes in SP are much more general and they are set within a broader theoretical frame. This generalisation gives SP capabilities - like an ability to learn - which are not exhibited by Prolog or by systems of that type.

SP incorporates many of the concepts associated with object-oriented design (reviewed in Cook, 1986).

Although extraction of redundancy in information is a key part of the SP theory, the SP system is **not** a *reduction* system in the technical sense of that word (see, for example, Robinson, 1988).

Although SP can imitate the effect of a re-write system it does **not** use any re-writing technique in the technical sense of that term (see, for example, Beaten, Bergstra & Klop, 1987).

The SP system may be loosely classified as a 'knowledge manipulation engine' like the FACT database system (McGregor, McInnes & Henning, 1987), the 'Intelligent File Store' (Lavington, 1988) or the integrated database and expert system (Syntel) described by Risch, Reboh, Hart & Duda, 1988) but there are many differences between SP and these systems in orientation and expected capabilities.

3. SP6

SP6 is a software simulation of SP, written in C, which runs on a Sun workstation. The following subsections describe the elements of this prototype and some of its internal workings.

3.1. The SP Language

In the SP system, all kinds of information or knowledge - 'data', 'programs', 'results' - are expressed in one simple language.

A formal syntax for this language is given in Wolff (in press) and repeated (with small changes) here:

```
Object --> Ordered-AND-object | Unordered-AND-object
          OR-object | Simple-object
Ordered-AND-object --> '(' , body , ')' ;
Unordered-AND-object --> '[' , body , ']' ;
OR-object --> '{' , body , '}' ;
body --> (Object, body) | NULL ;
Simple-object --> symbol | '_' ;
symbol --> (character , symbol) | character ;
character --> 'a' | 'A' | ... | 'z' | 'Z' | '0' | ... | '9' | '%' ;
```

Less formally, any item of information or knowledge in the SP language is represented as an *object*. SP objects come in four main types:

- (...). Zero or more objects enclosed in round brackets are an *Ordered AND Object (OAO)*. In an OAO, the order or sequence of the constituent objects is significant.

  At some stage in the research programme, it is likely that the OAO construct will be generalised to two- or three-dimensional structures as well as simple sequences. This will mean that the SP language can be used to represent such things as maps or three-dimensional models of real world objects.

- [...]. Zero or more objects in square brackets are an *Unordered AND Object (UAO)*. In a UAO, the order or sequence of the constituent objects is not significant. The concept of a UAO is similar to the concept of a 'set' in mathematics or, more accurately, a 'bag' because two or more of the constituents of a UAO may be identical.

- { ... }. Zero or more objects enclosed in curly brackets are an *OR Object (ORO)*. In an ORO, the constituent objects are treated as alternatives in the context in which the ORO is found.

- *Simple objects* come in two sub-types:

  - A *symbol* is one or more alphanumeric characters. If the symbols are always one fixed length, boundary markers are not needed. In current prototypes, the symbols can vary in length and boundary markers (spaces and commas) are used.

  - A *variable*, represented by an underscore ('_'), functions as a place marker for information which is missing from a structure. It is similar in some ways to the concept of an unnamed variable in Prolog. There is some discussion, below, of what the SP variable means.

Unlike Prolog, and most systems of that kind, SP does not have named variables. The effect of naming can be achieved in SP by bracketing a 'name' with an object to be named inside a UAO or OAO, eg [Fred _]. Normally, a name will be a SP symbol but other kinds of objects may be used as names.

Every symbol in an SP object has a frequency value which shows how many identical copies of that symbol were unified to create the given symbol. In the examples presented later, frequency values are not shown in full because this makes the examples difficult to read. Instead, symbols with a frequency of 1 are shown in plain type and symbols with any frequency greater than 1 are shown in bold type.

Sets of symbols used in versions of the SP language may vary from large sets of variable-length character strings down to the familiar binary set of single characters, 0 and 1. The symbol set used in any given SP object controls the 'granularity' of the operations in SP.

3.2. Processing in SP6

The 'search' function provides the semantics of the SP language and expresses the SP theory of computing, as currently understood. In terms of the options described earlier, the search process in SP6 works like this:

- The search for efficiency in SP6 means searching for redundancy in the corpus and extracting it wherever possible but without removing any non-redundant information. In other words, the search process is designed to preserve all the power in the corpus. Exploring how power may be sacrificed to improve efficiency has not been attempted yet in this research programme.

- The search process is systematic but not totally exhaustive. There are some kinds of redundancy which it cannot detect.

- SP6 produces one 'best' answer rather than a set of alternative answers (which future versions of SP will aim to produce).

- A simple and relatively unsophisticated kind of hill-climbing technique is being used.

3.2.1. Finding Redundancy

SP6 searches for redundancy by searching for patterns which match each other. To do this, it makes systematic comparisons (all-or-nothing matches) between all the constituent objects of the corpus and all sub-sets of the OAOs in the corpus, where the members of each sub-set are contiguous within the OAO from which they are drawn. SP6 does not compare sub-sets of UAOs although it would be relatively easy to extend the search in this way.

Notice that, although the matching process gives a simple all-or-nothing result, **SP6 detects partial matches between objects.** This is because the all-or-nothing matching process is applied to sub-sets of OAOs as well as whole OAOs.

3.2.2. The Unification Process

Where two patterns match, they may be unified. This is achieved in four main ways:

- Where two objects match and are siblings within a UAO or ORO, they may be unified to give an object which replaces them within the parent. For example:

    [A A B] => [A B]

(The symbol '=>' is not part of the SP language. It is used to show how the SP system may transform one SP object into another.)

- Where two objects match and have an 'uncle / nephew' relationship within a UAO (or grand-uncle / grand-nephew relationship, etc.), they may be unified and replaced by an object in the location of the nephew. In effect, the uncle 'moves' to merge with its nephew. Here is a simple example:

    [A (A B) C] => [(A B) C]

The argument here is that if the uncle moves to join the nephew then there is no loss of non-redundant information but if the nephew moves to join the uncle then there is loss of non-redundant information. The uncle is merely 'associated' with the other objects and this association is not destroyed by the unification. But if the nephew moves then there is loss of information about its position relative to other objects: the fact that it precedes B within (A B) in the example.

- Where there is a partial match between two OAOs which are siblings within a UAO, the parts which match are merged to make one pattern and the parts which do not match are formed into an ORO. For example,

    [(A B C D E F) (A B C X Y Z)]
    =>
    (A B C {(D E F)(X Y Z)})

In SP6, there are constraints on when this kind of unification can be done which are designed to ensure that there is no loss of power in the corpus.

- In cases where the other three kinds of unification cannot be applied, SP6 may achieve unification by the creation of 'references' and 'definitions'. A reference is a UAO containing a 'reference tag' and a variable like this: [%1 _]; the corresponding definition is a UAO containing the same reference tag and another object - the 'body' of the definition - which is typically an OAO. The following example illustrates how references and a definition may be used to effect the extraction of redundancy in an object:

    (A B C D E F G H I J K L X Y Z A B C D E F G H I J K L)
    =>
    ([%1 (A B C D E F G H I J K L)] X Y Z [%1 _])

The general idea is to record the repeating pattern once within the body of a definition, leaving references to mark where the original patterns came from. With this mechanism, redundancy may be extracted without losing the non-redundant information about where the original patterns were located within the corpus.

References and definitions are only created where the redundancy which is extracted is greater than the information 'cost' of the symbols which are introduced by the transformation.

With one qualification, references and definitions do not have any formal status in the SP theory. A reference tag is simply a 'pattern' with the same status as any other pattern. The mechanisms in SP for pattern matching and unification are used to bring the body of a definition back into the context whence it came.

The qualification, just mentioned, is that the SP system knows when it has added reference tags to a structure. Any tags added in this way are distinct from information supplied to the system by the user. For this reason, the system can undo references and definitions which it has created at one stage in the search for efficiency if, at a later stage, they are no longer needed.

3.2.3. Scheduling of Processes

The compress function of SP6 extracts redundancy in an iterative way like this:

While no more extractable redundancy in the corpus do
BEGIN
    1 Search for redundancy in the corpus by identifying matching
      patterns.
    2 Select the pair of matching patterns which represents the greatest
      amount of redundancy.
    3 Unify the selected pair of matching patterns.
END

The iteration of these three operations constitutes a simple form of hill-climbing search.

4. Examples

The examples described in this section are intended to illustrate how SP6 may perform both inductive learning and logic. We stress that **these two contrasted kinds of computing result from one unifying concept: a search for efficiency in knowledge.**

As already mentioned, bold type is used in the examples to highlight symbols which have been created by unification of two or more other symbols. And the symbol '=>' used in the examples is not part of the SP language but is used to show how one SP object is transformed into another in the course of computing.

4.1. Inductive Learning

We are using the term *inductive learning* to mean a process of organising knowledge which is done without explicit instruction or intervention from a (human or non-human) 'teacher' and without any other knowledge apart from the learning processes themselves.

4.1.1. Example 1: Discovering Word Segments, Classes and Shared Structure

[

        (petermeetsjane)
        (peteradmiresjane)
        (petermeetspeter)
        (peteradmirespeter)
        (janemeetspeter)
        (janeadmirespeter)
        (janemeetsjane)
        (janeadmiresjane)

]

=>

([%1 {(peter)(jane)}] {(meet)(admire)} s [%1 _])

The first example illustrates how, from examples of a simple sub-set of English, the SP system infers a structure which is equivalent to a grammar for the sub-set.

The OAOs in the first SP object may be seen as 'sentences'. By analogy with the way people normally talk, there is no explicit marker for the end of one word within a sentence and the beginning of the next. Likewise, there is nothing explicit in the example sentences to mark classes of syntactically equivalent words.

SP6 transforms the first object into the second by searching for redundancy and removing it wherever possible. The effect of this search is to identify the words within the sentences as discrete entities and to group the words into syntactic classes. The search process also has the effect of isolating the terminal 's' in 'meets' and 'admires' rather in the same way that a linguist would identify that terminal 's' as a distinct sub-structure ('morpheme') within these words.

SP6 recognises that the ORO {(peter)(jane)} occurs in two contexts, at the start of each sentence and at the end. It removes the redundancy by placing the structure arbitrarily in one of the two locations (first in the example) giving it a label ('%1') and leaving this label as a 'reference' at the other location (last) where the structure can occur. A tag like '%1' is equivalent to a label like 'NP' used in conventional grammars.

4.1.2. Example 2: Induction of a Class Hierarchy

```
[
        (backbone cold-blooded scaly lungs dry-skin limbless
                wide-gape snake)
        (backbone warm-blooded fur milk whiskers purrs retractile-claws cat)
        (backbone cold-blooded scaly lungs dry-skin limbs lizard)
        (backbone warm-blooded feathers beak wings flightless ostrich)
        (backbone cold-blooded scaly swims gills fresh-water small minnow)
        (backbone warm-blooded fur milk barks dog)
        (backbone warm-blooded feathers beak wings flies
                small brown sparrow)
        (backbone cold-blooded scaly swims gills sea-living aggressive shark)
]
=>
(backbone
        {(cold-blooded scaly
                {(lungs dry-skin
                        {(limbless wide-gape snake)
                        (limbs lizard)}})
                (swims gills
                        {(fresh-water small minnow)
                        (sea-living aggressive shark)}})})
        (warm-blooded
                {(feathers beak wings
                        {(flightless ostrich)
                        (flies small brown sparrow)}})
                (fur milk
                        {(whiskers purrs retractile-claws cat)
                        (barks dog)}})})})
```

This example illustrates how SP6 may create a class hierarchy or taxonomic hierarchy in the manner of numerical taxonomy or cluster analysis. The example also illustrates how SP6 can create a 'discrimination net' like the ones produced by Quinlan's ID3 (Quinlan, 1983).

The first object shows a set of animals, each with some distinctive attributes. OAOs have been used rather than the more appropriate UAOs because SP6 lacks the ability to look for patterns and sub-groupings within UAOs. Future versions of SP will plug this gap.

The second object is, in effect, a class hierarchy or discrimination net with attributes at appropriate levels. In the spirit of object-oriented design (Cook, 1986), redundancy is minimised by placing each attribute at a level in the hierarchy where it applies to all the lower levels and none of the higher levels.

4.2. Logic and Logical Inferences

The two examples in this section illustrate how the SP language may be used to express logical propositions and how, as a by-product of its search for efficiency in information, the SP system may do the kinds of things which are normally regarded as logical inference.

In this area, SP6 has a weakness which we believe we can cure in future versions. SP6 is designed so that variables (shown with the symbol '_') will match and unify with one SP object and only one object. We now believe that the number of objects to be matched and unified with any given variable should not be set at an arbitrary value but should be determined by the search for efficiency. This would mean that any given variable would match and unify with zero or more SP objects.

4.2.1. Example 3: a Simple Syllogism

[[mortal [man _]] [man Socrates]]
=>
[mortal [**man** Socrates]]

This example is modelled on the well-known syllogism: "All men are mortal. Socrates is a man. Therefore, Socrates is mortal." In logical notation the syllogism is written like this:

$$\forall x \in \text{man} \, . \, \text{mortal}(x) \land \text{Socrates} \in \text{man} \Rightarrow \text{mortal}(\text{Socrates})$$

Given the current meaning of '_' as 'one and only one', the object [man _] may be unified with any UAO which contains the symbol 'man' and one other object. Thus it may be read as "any man with one attribute" rather than the more general "any man" or "all men".

If we ignore the restriction on the meaning of [man _] then [mortal[man _]] should be read as "Any man is mortal" or "All men are mortal".

[man Socrates] should be read as "Socrates is a man".

The object created by SP, [mortal[man Socrates]], should be read as "Socrates is a man and he is mortal". This covers the meaning of the conventional conclusion ("Socrates is mortal") and also includes one of the premises of the syllogism - that "Socrates is a man". There are two things here which deserve comment:

- The first point is that any version of SP which is designed to preserve power in a knowledge structure - like SP6 - should preserve logical premises along with any inferences which may be drawn. The apparent difference between this style of working and the conventional style (where only the inference is shown) is more cosmetic than real. Conventional systems for logic do normally preserve logical premises but only display the inferences. The display mechanisms in SP could, perhaps, be designed to pick out inferences for attention in a similar way.

- The second point is that this version of SP6 has actually failed to preserve one of the premises in this example (that "All men are mortal") although, in designing the system, we intended that it should not lose power in its knowledge structures. We expect this weakness in SP6 to be cured in later versions of SP when the meaning of '_' is changed to become 'zero or more objects'. In this case, the SP system should work like this:

[[mortal[man _]] [man Socrates]]
=>
[mortal[**man** Socrates _]]

The variable remains in the final object because unification with 'Socrates' does not exhaust the 'or more' part of its meaning. The result should be read as "Socrates, and all other men, are mortal", a conclusion which covers the meaning of "Socrates is mortal" and preserves the meaning of both of the original premises.

4.2.2. Example 4: Transitive Relations

[[equals A B _ _] [equals B C _ _] [equals C D _ _]]
=>
[equals C D A B]

This example illustrates how, from the premises that "A equals B and B equals C and C equals D", the SP system can infer that A, B, C and D are all equal.

Like the previous example, this example is not completely accurate because the variable ('_') means 'one and only one' instead of 'zero or more'. Given the current meaning of the SP variable, an object like [equals A B _ _] means "A and B and two other unspecified objects are all equal". The two instances of '_' are needed in this example for unification with C and D.

If '_' had its proper meaning then a transitive relation like "A equals B" would be represented in SP as [equals A B _] which may be read as "A equals B and there may be other objects which are equal to A and B". The variable shows that unification may add other objects to the relationship and thus marks the relationship as transitive. By contrast, an intransitive relationship such as 'likes' may be represented as (likes A B) - the absence of a variable in this structure is what ensures that the relationship is not transitive. (This relationship is shown as an OAO because the fact of A liking B does not mean that B likes A.)

Notice that this example would not give a valid conclusion if the relationship were, say, 'not-equals'. This and other examples point to the conclusion that negation will require special treatment in SP, a point discussed below.

4.2.3. A Comparison with Prolog

To represent a transitive relationship like 'equals' in an established logic programming system like Prolog, it is necessary to include a rule like this:

equals(X,Z) :- equals(X,Y), equals(Y,Z).

This rule means "X equals Z if X equals Y and Y equals Z"; X, Y and Z are all variables. The inclusion of this rule along with 'facts' like equals(a,b) and equals(b,c) allows the system to infer that equals(a,c) is true.

This way of representing the transitive nature of 'equals' works well enough but is distinctly more cumbersome than what is needed in SP. In addition, a rule like the one just shown needs to generalized to cope with other transitive relations like 'ancestor', 'before', 'above', 'bigger' etc. and the generalization is relatively complicated.

SP seems to have a distinct advantage over established systems in this area.

4.2.4. TRUE and FALSE in SP

At present, SP has no explicit concepts of TRUE and FALSE. As with systems like Prolog, we may adopt the 'closed world hypothesis' and suppose that truth is whatever the system knows about and everything else is false. In this case, the answer to a 'query' is 'true' if the query unifies with an object in a given knowledge structure, otherwise it is 'false'.

In SP it is natural to generalise this model of truth to take advantage of the fact that SP can recognise partial matches between structures as well as full matches. Given this feature of SP, we may recognise degrees of truth and falseness. If a query unifies completely with an object in the knowledge base then it is unequivocally true in terms of that knowledge base. If it does not unify with anything in the knowledge base then it is unequivocally false. In all other cases, it has some degree of truth corresponding to the amount of unification which has been achieved.

Does SP need a negation operator ('not') and, if so, what is its status within the SP theory? In the spirit of 'simplicity and power' it would be nice if negation in SP could be a by-product of mechanisms which are already established in the system.

One possibility is that 'not' is simply a symbol (with the same status as all other symbols) which may be used as a 'spoiler' to prevent a given object unifying with any identical copy of that object. Thus [not TRUE] would not unify with TRUE and would therefore be 'false' in the terms which we have sketched.

One difficulty with this idea is that the 'spoiler' would never eliminate partial unification and would thus never have the meaning 'unequivocally false' as one would wish. Another problem is that [not [not TRUE]] would not mean the same as TRUE as one would wish.

These points and examples like 'not-equals', mentioned above, suggest that a special negation operator will be needed in SP. This and related questions are issues to be explored in the future.

5. Conclusion

In this paper we have tried to show how two sub-fields of computing which are not normally related may be seen as two facets of a more general set of principles. All the examples which have been shown - examples of inductive learning and examples of logical inference - are the product of a system which is dedicated to one goal: searching for efficiency in information by finding redundancy in the information and removing it wherever possible.

There are many issues still to be explored in developing this framework of ideas but there are also many potential benefits - in simplifying our thinking about computing and in the practicalities of using computers. The practical benefits and advantages which expect from the SP system when it is mature are described in Wolff & Chipperfield (submitted for publication).

Acknowledgement

We are very grateful to Paul Mather for helpful comments on earlier drafts of this paper.

References

Baeten J C M, Bergstra J A & Klop J W (1987). Term re-writing systems with priorities. Proceedings of the Conference on Re-writing Techniques and Applications, Bordeaux, France, May 1987. pp 83-94.

Campbell C, Sherrington D & Wong K Y M (1989). Statistical mechanics and neural networks. In I Aleksander (Ed), *Neural Computing Architectures*, London: North Oxford Academic.

Chaitin G J (1987). *Algorithmic Information Theory*. Cambridge: Cambridge University Press.

Clocksin W F & Mellish C S (1981). *Programming in Prolog*. Heidelberg: Springer-Verlag.

Cook S (1986). Languages and object-oriented programming. *Software Engineering Journal 1 (2)*, 73-80.

Hinton G E & Sejnowski T J (1986). Learning and relearning in Boltzmann machines. Chapter 7 in D E Rumelhart and J L McClelland (Eds), *Parallel Distributed Processing*, Vol I, Cambridge Mass.: MIT Press, pp 282-317.

Lavington S H (1988). An overview of knowledge manipulation engines and the Intelligent File Store. Proceedings of the IEE Colloquium on Knowledge Manipulation Engines, London. pp 1-4.

McGregor D, McInnes S and Henning M (1987). An architecture for associative processing of large knowledge bases (LKBs). *The Computer Journal 30(5)*, 404-412.

Quinlan J R (1983). Learning efficient classification procedures and their application to chess end games. In R Michalski, J G Carbonell and T Mitchell (Eds) *Machine Learning: an Artificial Intelligence Approach*. Palo Alto, CA: Tioga.

Risch T, Reboh R, Hart P & Duda R (1988). A functional approach to integrating database and expert systems. *Communications of the ACM 31*, 1424-1437.

Robinson J A (1988). Beyond Loglisp: combining functional and relational programming in a reduction setting. *Machine Intelligence 11*, 57-68.

Shieber S M (1986). *An Introduction to Unification-Based Approaches to Grammar*. Stanford, CA: Center for the Study of Language and Information.

Siekmann J H (1989). Unification theory. *Journal of Symbolic Computation 7*, 207-274.

Wolff J G (1987). Cognitive development as optimisation. In L Bolc (Ed), *Computational Models of Learning*. Heidelberg: Springer-Verlag, 161-205.

Wolff J G (1988). Learning syntax and meanings through optimisation and distributional analysis. In Y Levy, I M Schlessinger and M D S Braine

Wolff J G (1989). Information and redundancy in computing and cognition. *AISB Quarterly 68*, 14-17.

Wolff J G (in press). Simplicity and power: some unifying ideas in computing. To appear in the *Computer Journal*.

Wolff J G & Chipperfield A J (in preparation). SP: a new view of software engineering and computing.

PROGRAMMING INTELLIGENCE : TRENDS AND FUTURE DIRECTIONS IN AI LANGUAGES

Colin Shearer
Integral Solutions Ltd., Bramley, Basingstoke, UK

Abstract

This paper discusses the main programming languages used in expert systems development and artificial intelligence: Lisp, Prolog and POP. Desirable qualities of languages to be used in this field are presented, and the background and characteristics of the languages described. Past and current trends in implementations of these languages, and promising future directions, are discussed.

1. What makes an AI language?

Use of the term "AI language" or "expert systems language" is dubious at best. If an expert system is implemented using, say, COBOL or Fortran, does this not imply that these are AI languages? An answer to that question cannot be dissociated from more basic issues such as, "At what stage does a program which performs decision making qualify as an expert system", and as such is well beyond the scope of this paper.

The languages considered here - Lisp, Prolog and POP - are labelled "AI languages" because they share a common property which makes them particularly suitable for the implementation of knowledge-based or expert systems: they allow the programmer to work at a level which is not dictated by underlying machine considerations, and which is closer to the level at which problems are "visualised" and manipulated by human thought processes. This also has the benefit of easing maintenance of expert systems by helping the programmer to produce a clear and abstract representation of the encoded knowledge.

Two factors contribute to this. Data handled by these languages is not restricted by hardware constraints, unlike most "conventional" languages where the datatypes available and the operations supported upon them closely reflect their bit-level representation. This data also has more abstract and meaningful literal representation than in conventional languages. A nested list structure in Lisp, for example, is represented transparently and intuitively, while its equivalent in C would usually require constructing an opaque and possibly highly complex association of pointer chains and data.

The AI languages also offer execution models more useful for modelling varied cognitive processes, either by supporting a rich assortment of control strategies (with associated redundancy) (Lisp and POP), or by providing high-level, specialised facilities (Prolog).

Some of the representational formalisms provided by expert system shells could also be considered as AI languages. Their extreme specialisation and often highly specialised, restrictive nature, however, excludes them from use as general programming tools and from consideration here.

2. The Languages

2.1 Lisp

One of the most surprising things for newcomers to Lisp is discovering just how long it has been around. Developed in the late 1950s at MIT, Lisp is a contemporary of Fortran, and has been in use longer than almost any other general purpose language. A diversity of dialects have been implemented but for the last few years Common Lisp, a *de facto* standard implementing the best features of what had previously been the leading implementations, has dominated.

Based on lambda calculus, Lisp supports computation by function application ("functional programming"), but most dialects also support a procedural or imperative approach. Lisp stands for LISt Processing - the language was designed for symbolic computation, handling structures such as variable length lists and textual items.

Typing is dynamic; that is, type is a property of the data held in a variable, not of the variable itself. This means that a variable can hold different types of data at different times; say, a list, a number, or even a function (code is treated as first-order data by Lisp). A common misconception is that such languages are weakly typed. They aren't; type checking is strong, but is generally performed at run-time rather than compile-time. This is a trade-off, usually sacrificing some execution speed for increased scope and flexibility of programs.

Lisp has an immediately recognisable syntax, structured using nested parentheses. This relates to one of the prime aims of the developers of the language: to represent code and data uniformly. The bracket notation represents both literal lists and function application and definition.

This syntax is simple and uniform; once programmers have mastered the basic concept, they can work out the structure of large and complex programs. On the other hand, a common complaint is that this massive overloading of a single basic construct can actually place a much higher cognitive load on those learning Lisp than is the case for syntactically richer, more redundant languages. One much-used wisecrack is the acronym "Lots of Irritating, Silly Parentheses", often heard from those who would argue that the human eye was not designed to count brackets.

Lisp has, over the years, been extended with a wide range of features and facilities that make it a very powerful, general purpose programming language whose use is by no means constrained to artificial intelligence. In the most sophisticated dialects for example, symbolic and structured data types including records, arrays and hash-coded association tables, have been supplemented by rich numerical types. Those familiar with more mundane programming languages are often astounded the first time they see Lisp calculate an exact integer result for the factorial of 1000 (using arbitrary precision arithmetic) or, using ratio representations, calculate 39/1129 * 45/17517 with exact accuracy. It may seem heresy to state it (to programmers using conventional languages, that is!) but Lisp - originally conceived as a symbol-cruncher rather than a number-cruncher - is now far more appropriate for some types of numerical and mathematical application than Fortran.

Lisp has grown into a functionally rich language - Common Lisp includes around 800 built-in functions - while retaining the simplicity and elegance of its original concepts: this large collection of functions can all be defined in terms of a small subset of basic Lisp functions and constructs. A popular simile is that "APL is like a perfect diamond: if you add anything to it, it becomes flawed. In contrast, Lisp is like a ball of mud - if you add more to it, you get a bigger ball of mud".

2.2 Prolog

Prolog is a more recent and more specialised language than Lisp. The name stands for "Programming in Logic", and the language derived mainly from theoretical work at Edinburgh University in the early 1970's, the first implementation being carried out at Marseille University.

Prolog is based on predicate calculus. A Prolog program consists of logical rules ("predicates") and a set of facts ("unit clauses"). Execution of a Prolog program is an attempt to prove a goal by applying the rules to the facts. Because the programmer defines the rules which may be used in proving a goal, rather than the steps to take in proving it, Prolog is termed a declarative language, rather than procedural or imperative.

Goals, or queries, given to PROLOG can specify data explicitly or provide incomplete data. For example, the query "brother(fred,mary)" is explicit and asks PROLOG if fred is the brother of mary, the query "pensioner(X)" asks PROLOG to instantiate the variable X to someone who is a pensioner, the query "brother(X,Y)" asks PROLOG to instantiate X and Y such that X is the brother of Y, and so on. PROLOG may be able to match the query directly onto facts (unit-clauses) defined, or may need to invoke some rules and prove certain sub-goals first.

Another property of the language is that it is "non-deterministic"; alternative definitions ("clauses") of a rule may be provided and in the proof of a goal Prolog uses "back-tracking" to try each in turn to find a solution. This same mechanism makes it possible for Prolog programs to derive several different solutions, or a complete set of possible solutions. Prolog uses pattern matching on the arguments in the head of each clause to recognise which clauses are applicable.

Because a Prolog program can be thought of as a collection of rules and facts, and execution equates to goal-proving, Prolog is often considered as a "natural" choice for the implementation of systems which emulate human reasoning. Its mode of operation corresponds directly to what is commonly referred to in expert systems jargon as "backward chaining".

2.3 POP

POP was developed at Edinburgh University in the mid-1960's. Officially an acronym for "Package for On-line Programming", the name is also generally acknowledged to derive from that of its originator - Robin Popplestone.

The dominant dialect, POP-11, is similar in power and semantics to the most sophisticated Lisps, but the Algol-like syntax is generally considered more readable , making POP easily accessible to those who have previously programmed in more conventional languages.

POP is based around an open data stack, used for passing arguments and results to and from procedures. The stack makes it possible to work in either a procedural or functional style, and allows procedures to handle variable numbers of arguments and results.

POP has a structural pattern matcher, which allows matching of segment patterns against arbitrary length sequences in a list. The user can express sophisticated patterns, combining such concepts as "match with one item in this position, providing that item succeeds this test", "match with any single item", "match with any number of items" etc. This is often used in, for example, parsing application specific command line languages.

Another feature of the language is a co-routining mechanism, supporting "light-weight processes" or "multi-threading". This is very useful for applications which include a simulation element, or for solutions which have a parallel flavour.

Lexical and syntactic analysis tools are part of the POP-11 language, as are procedures which plant code for the underlying abstract virtual machine. This has made it a popular choice for compiler construction; it has been used both to implement general purpose languages and to build specialised, application-specific representation syntaxes.

These compiler tools also allow POP itself to be easily extended. An object-oriented extension, FLAVOURS, has been used extensively in simulation and modelling applications.

While POP has yet to achieve the widespread adoption of Lisp, the signs are that developers are finding it an increasingly attractive alternative. In a survey of projects funded by the UK Alvey Programme only three languages were rated "good" by users, on a scale of "good/indifferent/poor": C++, PARLOG and POP-11. Of these three, POP-11 had the most users. The complete list of languages mentioned included Prolog, Lisp, C, Pascal, Fortran, Ada and others.

2.4 Comparing Styles

Figure 1 shows the same problem implemented in all Lisp, Prolog and POP-11,, showing styles typical of the three languages. The example program is the "member" function - testing for the presence of a specified item within a linked list.

The Lisp version shows a recursive implementation in a purely functional style. (It also shows one of the historical peculiarities of Lisp; the overloading of the empty list to also represent the boolean false). The Prolog version shows the use of two alternative clauses (selected by matching arguments) and recursion. This Prolog predicate could be used both as a check for list membership and, using Prolog's backtracking, as a generator to return successive members of a given list. The POP-11 version illustrates the power of the pattern matcher: the test for list membership is simply expressed as, "Does the item occur anywhere in the list?").

Lisp :

```
(defun member (item list)
        (and
                list      ; list isn't empty
                (or
                        (equalp item (car list))
                        (member item (cdr list))))))
```

Prolog :

```
member(Item, [Item | _]).
member(Item, [_|Tail]) :-
        member(Item,Tail).
```

POP-11 :

```
define member (item,list);
        list matches [== ^item ==];
enddefine;
```

Figure 1 : "member" implemented in Lisp, Prolog and POP-11

3. Past Trends, Present and Future Directions

3.1 Dedicated Hardware

A few years ago, the main issue concerning AI languages was performance. Many implementations were notoriously slow and resource hungry. Because of the flexibility of data-handling provided by these languages, "garbage collection" of redundant store is essential, and this often presented major performance overheads.

This led to the development of specialised hardware, most notably "Lisp machines" - dedicated workstations with hardware or microcode support for symbolic processing. These provided sophisticated development environments, but were unable to operate as anything other than stand-alone, single user systems. The Japanese ICOT programme focused considerable effort on developing similar hosts for Prolog and related languages, but successful commercial results in this area have been slow to appear. Very high performance has been claimed for a prototype "Declarative Language Machine" (DLM), developed by British Aerospace.

In the last few years, the performance of conventional hardware has increased dramatically, while prices have plummeted. Techniques for implementing AI languages and the support they require have improved considerably. Efficient implementations are now available on standard computers, and low-cost graphics workstations are used to provide window-based development environments.

3.2 Standardisation

Standardisation is important for the recognition and large-scale adoption of any language. An ISO standard for Common Lisp is imminent, and a BSI/ISO standard for Prolog is in draft form. A "POP9x" committee is working to produce the first POP standard. With the current surge of interest in object-oriented programming, all three languages have acquired object-oriented extensions. Common Lisp has CLOS, POP-11 has FLAVOURS, and Prolog has a variety of object and frame-handling packages such as Flex.

3.3 Parallelism

As serial computer architectures approach physical limits on performance, parallel systems are seen as a route to making greater orders of magnitude in speed accessible. In AI and Expert Systems, where applications have traditionally been considered "expensive", this potential has been of particular interest.

Because Prolog programs consist of alternative clauses for the same rule, it was once thought that parallel hardware could be exploited in goal evaluation. However, due to the way most Prolog programs are written (that is, dependent on clause ordering), parallelism has been found to be largely inapplicable to standard Prolog, at least at a clause-processing level. It may prove useful, though, at a lower level (in the matching and "unification" of Prolog terms for example), or in the implementation of what are currently experimental derivatives of the language, the best known being PARLOG.

POP, through its co-routing mechanism, could be made to make use of parallelism, though this would involve significant modifications to an architecture which is currently based around sequential handling of lightweight processes. The same is true of Lisp systems which support a limited facility for multi-threading.

3.4 Prolog and Databases

One direction which holds great promise for Prolog is its integration with database technology. Because Prolog's internal representation of facts maps exactly onto the storage of tuples in relational databases tables, interfaces have been developed which allow Prolog applications to operate transparently over standard relational databases. This allows Prolog to be used as an extremely powerful, logic-based query language, and makes it possible for Prolog programs to share information and benefit from the use of persistent data.

3.5 Language Integration

One significant problem in applications development is that a typical problem is not necessarily 100% "Lisp-shaped", "POP-shaped", or "Prolog-shaped". Each language is ideal for tackling parts of the problem to which its strengths are suited, but clumsy and often inefficient for the remainder. This is particularly a problem for Prolog users, as Prolog is far less suited to general purpose programming than are Lisp and POP.

This problem is addressed by tightly-coupled mixed languages systems, such as POPLOG. POPLOG provides an architecture which supports the development of applications using any combination of Prolog, Lisp and POP, mixed to use the strengths of each language to best advantage.

A related issue is the integration of code written in AI languages with the software in more conventional languages, essential as many real expert systems will need to integrate with standard library packages and existing software systems to be truly effective. Most implementors recognise this and the best commercial implementations of Lisp, Prolog and POP provide such integration to varying degrees. Because of the special requirements of the AI language, however, it has always remained the master; that is, the application must be structured as, say, a Lisp program that calls out to C (which may or may not be able to call back to Lisp).

What has not yet been achieved is the general ability to embed individual Lisp or POP functions, or Prolog rules, in applications coded in, say, C or Fortran. This should serve to make the AI languages relevant to many applications areas in which they have not previously been deployed.

PROBABILISTIC INDUCTION BY DYNAMIC PATH GENERATION FOR CONTINUOUS ATTRIBUTES

A.P. White and W.Z. Liu
School of Computer Science
University of Birmingham
P.O. Box 363
Birmingham B15 2TT
United Kingdom

Abstract

The technique of dynamic path generation for the induction of decision rules in noisy domains is described briefly and then extended to deal with continuous attributes by optimal splitting. Methods of using the χ^2 test statistic to perform the three tasks of optimal splitting, attribute selection and branch termination are described in some detail. Difficulties arising from comparing attributes with different numbers of cutting points are discussed and solutions proposed. Features dealing with categorical variables, stepwise techniques, missing values, cross-validation and class grouping are described briefly.

1   Introduction

Knowledge acquisition by interviewing a domain expert is known to be a problem because of the "knowledge bottleneck" (Feigenbaum, 1977, 1981). For this reason, there has been much interest in the last two decades in the alternative approach of automatic induction of rules from examples. A number of systems have been produced which construct decision trees from actual cases. These decision trees can then be thought of as containing production rules which may then be used to classify new cases. Quinlan's ID3 algorithm (Quinlan, 1979, 1986) is one of the most representative systems in the TDIDT (Top-Down Induction of Decision Trees) family. Systems such as ACLS (Patterson & Niblett, 1983) and ASSISTANT (Kononenko et al., 1984) are directly descended from ID3. Other systems include Michalski's GEM (1978) and his AQ systems (1980, 1986).

Problems arise when the data is "noisy", i.e. when two or more cases are identical, apart from their class membership. Originally, approaches like that of ID3 did not deal adequately with these situations but merely reported a "clash" and requested further information to discriminate between the cases concerned. More recently, this problem has been approached by methods with a statistical aspect such as that described by Quinlan (1983, 1986) and that used in CART, described by Breiman et al. (1984).

Another approach to the problem of dealing with noisy data is dynamic path generation, used in PREDICTOR (White, 1987). Instead of generating the whole decision tree beforehand, the dynamic path generation method only produces the path required to classify the case currently under consideration. This technique offers greater flexibility in dealing with missing values than other methods.

The original ID3 algorithm only dealt with discrete attributes. An obvious extension to this family of techniques is to permit the use of attributes with a continuous range of values. This is done in ASSISTANT and also in CART. In the latter, each continuous attribute is examined at each point in order to decide the best possible binary split for that attribute. These attributes are then used in the tree in their binary form. A somewhat similar approach to dealing with continuous attributes is now incorporated in PREDICTOR.

The purpose of the present paper is to describe in some detail the current state of development of PREDICTOR and to give some technical information on the approaches used in dealing with the various theoretical and practical problems that have arisen with the implementation.

2   Path Construction for Binary Attributes

Machine learning algorithms of the ID3 type build case-classifying decision trees which are constructed along the following lines. (The explanation is given in terms of binary attributes and a resulting binary tree. This is partly for reasons which will become apparent later in this paper).

Building a decision tree from a set of training data involves utilising data on a number of cases whose classification is known. Thus, for a set consisting of k classes, n attributes and N cases, the training set consists of N data vectors, as follows:

$$(C, A_1, A_2, \dots, A_n)$$

$$\text{where} \quad C \in \{c_1, c_2, \dots, c_k\}$$

$$\text{and} \quad A_j \in \{a_1^{(j)}, a_2^{(j)}\}$$

To begin with, the algorithm searches through the set of attributes to find that attribute which discriminates best between the various classes. This attribute is then selected to form the root node of the tree. Thus, the cases are now partitioned into two subsets according to their values on the attribute at the root node. Similar operations are then performed separately on each of the subsets, with further attributes being selected for the two nodes immediately below the root. This process is then repeated in an iterative fashion until either a complete binary tree is built (in which each path down the tree passes through each attribute exactly once) or some premature terminating condition is encountered. (More will be said about terminating conditions later).

As mentioned in the previous section, during path construction, attributes not already branched on must be compared at each node in order to decide which attribute to branch on next. The precise method by which attributes may be compared leaves considerable room for choice. Quinlan's ID3 uses an information-theoretic measure which is algebraically equivalent to transmitted information, i.e. that attribute is selected which transmits the maximum information about class membership. Other possibilities exist, such as the Gini index of diversity and the "twoing rule". Both these are described by Breiman et al. (1984) and used in CART. However, they do not really concern us here.

The method used in PREDICTOR is to determine which available attribute has the largest interaction with class (as measured by the χ^2 test statistic) and to select that attribute for branching. This technique has been described elsewhere (Hart, 1985; Niblett & Bratko, 1987; Quinlan, 1986; White, 1985, 1987).

Another good reason for using χ^2 is that it provides a ready-made mechanism for implementing a stopping rule, i.e. a device to prevent a maximum-size binary tree from being generated. The full reason why this is a desirable feature is really a matter of mathematical statistics. It has been described elsewhere in various ways in some detail (Breiman et al., 1984; Niblett & Bratko, 1987; Quinlan, 1986; White & Reed, 1986). A brief explanation is, however, necessary here because of the greater technical detail on this topic that is to follow in Section 3.2.

Basically, when dealing with domains characterised by noisy data, it is possible to grow a tree which is too large and thereby lose predictive accuracy as a result. (In the field of mathematical statistics, this is a well-recognised phenomenon known as "overfitting", which refers to the equivalent practice of constructing a predictive equation with more terms than is optimal for best prediction). The remedy is either to grow a large tree and prune it back in the manner described by Breiman et al. (1984), or to use some sort of stopping rule to prevent an over-large tree from being grown in the first place. Similar remarks apply to the practice of dynamic path generation, except that we are only concerned with the number of nodes in the path that has been generated rather than the size of the whole tree.

An easy way of implementing a stopping rule is to use some sort of statistical significance test on the test statistic used for attribute selection. It is for this reason that the use of the χ^2 test statistic for attribute selection is a popular choice. Its use in this way (i.e. both for attribute selection and as a stopping rule) has been described elsewhere (Hart, 1985; Niblett & Bratko, 1987; Quinlan, 1986; White, 1985, 1987; White & Reed, 1986)

3   Extension to Continuous Attributes

Once we attempt to extend this method from binary attributes to attributes which may take three or more different values, we encounter difficulties. These difficulties are compounded if we extend our efforts to cope with attributes which are continuous. Let us explain the difficulty.

Suppose we wish to compare the discrimination power of two attributes of different arity, e.g. sex (two values) and social class (five values) in a problem with k classes. The technique of using the χ^2 test statistic runs into the immediate difficulty that the χ^2 values are not directly comparable. They have been derived from tables with different numbers of cells. Consequently, one χ^2 value has $k - 1$ degrees of freedom, while the other has $4(k - 1)$ and hence they should be compared with different χ^2 distributions. If the χ^2 value itself is used to determine attribute selection, then attributes of high arity gain an "unfair advantage". On the other hand, if the significance level is used for the purpose of attribute selection as well as for the stopping rule, then this means that selection is no longer governed by the *magnitude* of the association between attribute and class. None of the work cited in the previous section actually addresses this problem.

Continuous attributes pose an even greater difficulty. How are these best dealt with in the framework of a decision tree?

3.1   Optimal Splitting

Breiman et al. (1984) have employed a different approach which neatly circumvents the problem just described (although, as we shall see in the next section it leads to another problem which requires solution). Their technique is to work entirely with binary trees. Ordered discrete attributes which are not initially binary are converted into "pseudo-binary" attributes by the technique of "optimal splitting". This involves splitting the attribute between every possible pair of adjacent values to yield a number of derived binary variables. For such an attribute having m categories, this would mean generating $m - 1$ derived variables. The best of these $m - 1$ variables (as judged by one of the methods used for attribute selection) then becomes the pseudo-binary attribute which is used in place of the original attribute. Attributes which are discrete and unordered are dealt with in Section 4.1.

The same type of approach is used in PREDICTOR, except that the χ^2 test statistic is used. Thus, each of the variables derived from a given attribute is cross-tabulated against class for all the cases at the node under consideration and χ^2 calculated for each. That variable with the largest χ^2 (denoted by χ^2_{max}) is chosen as the pseudo-binary attribute to represent the original attribute.

At first sight, continuous attributes appear to present more of a problem because there are infinitely many places at which such an attribute may be cut to yield a derived variable. However, the number of cases *at a node* is definitely finite and the same technique as just described may be employed, using one fewer cutting positions than the number of values.

Perhaps it should be mentioned that this technique leaves open the possibility that a multi-valued attribute may legitimately be branched on more than once (at different cutting points) in the same path.

3.2   Attribute Selection and Stopping Rule

Unfortunately, the optimal splitting technique described in the previous section has one potentially serious drawback. It gives an "unfair advantage" during path construction to pseudo-binary attributes. This is seen most clearly in the case of the stopping rule. The stopping rule is based on a significance test, but this test will not have the same *actual* significance level for pseudo-binary attributes derived from attributes of different arity. This is because the test is applied to χ^2_{max} (as previously defined) rather than a straightforward χ^2 value. Under a null hypothesis of no association between attribute and class, χ^2 will be distributed as chi-square with $k - 1$ degrees of freedom but χ^2_{max} will not be distributed in this way and its c.d.f. (cumulative distribution function) is not known.

This problem was investigated with a large number of Monte Carlo simulation experiments, in which continuous attributes with no inherent discriminating power between classes were generated randomly and χ^2_{max} obtained for different numbers of cutting points (N'). Of course, we are interested in knowing the upper percentage points of the c.d.f. for χ^2_{max}. The simulation results revealed that a given upper percentage point depends on:

- the number of cases at the node under consideration, N_t (for node t).

- the class probabilities, p_i, where $i = 1, ..., k$.

- the number of cutting points, N'.

Furthermore, the results reveal that, if N_t, α (the significance level) and the various p_i are held constant, χ^2_{max} is approximated by a linear increasing function of $\log(N')$:

$$E(\chi^2_{\alpha,max}) = a + b\log(N') \tag{1}$$

Theoretical considerations dictate that the intercept, a, is actually χ^2_{α} with $k-1$ degrees of freedom, i.e. the upper percentage point of the c.d.f. for chi-square corresponding to a significance level of α. It is only the gradient, b, that needs to be estimated empirically. Thus we arrive at the following equation:

$$E(\chi^2_{\alpha,max}) = \chi^2_{\alpha,k-1} + b\log(N') \tag{2}$$

Unfortunately, the estimated value for the slope, b, depends on α, N_t and the class probabilities. However, at any given node, N_t and the various p_i will be the same for all attributes and α will have been decided as a parameter for the entire path generation process. One possible solution to the stopping rule problem is to perform a Monte Carlo simulation, in situ, at each node in the path, in order to estimate the slope, b, of the function in Equation (2). This function can then be used to compensate for the different values of N' possessed by the different variables.

Similar considerations apply to attribute selection. Once again, attributes with many cutting points have an "unfair advantage" over those with fewer. The simplest heuristic solution to this difficulty seems to be to extend the technique proposed in the previous paragraph for dealing with the stopping rule problem. Thus, we regard Equation (2) as a baseline for attribute selection. We simply select that attribute whose value for χ^2_{max} exceeds the relevant baseline by the largest amount. If none of the χ^2_{max} values is found to exceed the baseline, then branching is terminated.

Perhaps it is worth mentioning another related problem at this point. It concerns the validity of using the χ^2 test statistic as a stopping rule when N_t is small. Most statistics textbooks caution against the use of χ^2 when expected frequencies are low (e.g. around five or ten) because, at this levels, the distribution of χ^2 under the null hypothesis is only poorly approximated by the chi-square distribution. Niblett and Bratko (1987) point out that, for 2×2 tables, Fisher's exact probability test may be used instead. In the general $k \times 2$ case, a Monte Carlo significance test along similar lines could be employed as a stopping rule.

4   Further Features

PREDICTOR is currently in a state of continuous development. Many features have either been incorporated into the software, or are planned for inclusion at some future date. Those features thought to be of some relevance to this paper are described in this section. These are as follows:

- an extension to deal with categorical attributes.

- an option to determine how the path is constructed (i.e. whether growth is terminated using a stopping rule or a full-length path is generated and then pruned or whether some other, more esoteric, method is employed).

- facilities for dealing with missing values.

- a test versus cross-validation option.

- class grouping options.

Let us examine each of these features in more detail.

4.1   Categorical Attributes

For categorical (i.e. discrete and unordered) attributes, we simply need a variant of optimal splitting which chooses the best partition of the attribute into two subsets of its set of values. The number of such subset pairs available is simply $2^{n-1} - 1$. This corresponds to N' in the case of an ordered attribute. This allows us to make the adjustment for $\chi^2_{\max}$ in the same way as previously described.

Perhaps it should be mentioned that earlier versions of PREDICTOR used a different method of generating pseudo-binary attributes from discrete attributes. This approach simply partitioned the attribute into two values – one being the value of that attribute in the test case under consideration, while the other corresponded to all other possible values of the attribute. This method would appear to be non-optimal (and is not currently available in PREDICTOR) although perhaps it should be made the subject of some experiments.

4.2   Path Construction Options

It is instructive to consider methods for the inclusion of variables used in stepwise statistical procedures such as discriminant analysis. In the forward inclusion method, the procedure is started with an empty set of variables and independent variables are included, one at a time on each step, according to the increase in discriminative power obtained. This procedure is terminated when no further improvement in discrimination can be obtained.

The backward elimination method, on the other hand, starts with a full set of independent variables and eliminates the least useful one on each step and terminates just before eliminating a variable with some useful discriminating power.

These two techniques are combined in the full stepwise approach which, on any given step, may include or eliminate a variable according to preset criteria. This is an attempt to assemble a more nearly optimal subset of variables for prediction purposes than would be obtained from either the pure forward or the pure backward technique alone. A full stepwise approach may be arranged to start with either an empty set of variables, or a full set, (or, indeed, any particular subset specified by the investigator).

Now, the path construction process can be looked upon as a type of equation-building process. In fact, there is a formal correspondence between this type of approach and the logit model in mathematical statistics, as shown in White and Reed (1989). Thus, any of the equation-building approaches can equally well be used as path generation techniques. Currently, PREDICTOR has an option to choose between two techniques, both of which are variants of the forward inclusion approach. In one, the path is generated one step at a time and terminated by the stopping rule (in the manner described earlier). In the other, a full-length path is generated and then pruned back. The pruning is based on a significance test criterion, with termination occurring just before the deletion of an attribute with significant discriminating power. It should be noted that, even with the same test statistic and significance level, the two techniques are not guaranteed to produce paths of the same length. The pruning technique will never produce a shorter path than the other, but may produce a longer one.

The counterpart of the backward elimination method is more difficult to imagine in the ordered context of a path in a tree. However, it must be remembered that the effect of branching on a set of nodes in a path is a commutative process, i.e. the *order* of the nodes has no effect whatever on the resulting subset of cases which is filtered through to the terminal node. This enables us to imagine how the backward elimination procedure might be implemented in a dynamic path generation algorithm. Starting with a full-length path, say of length l (i.e. the number of terminal nodes), we obtain l re-orderings of that path such that each of the attributes appears in the lowest non-terminal node exactly once. In other words, each attributes is branched on last in exactly one of the re-ordered paths. Thus, it is possible to examine the effect of each attribute *as if it had been branched on last*. The effect of each attribute is then judged by the same χ^2 techniques as previously described. The attribute of least importance is then compared with the significance test criterion previously decided on and, if the significance is not met, the variable is eliminated. This entire process is repeated until no more attributes can be eliminated.

4.3   Facilities for Dealing With Missing Values

The advantages of the dynamic path generation in dealing with missing values have been described fully elsewhere (White, 1987). However, a brief description of the approach employed is given here for the sake of completeness. There are two types of missing values: those that occur in the database of past cases and those that appear in new cases requiring classification. Let us deal with each of these in turn.

The problem of missing values in the training set can be dealt with quite simply. When branching on an attribute, only cases which match the test case on the pseudo-binary attribute under consideration are passed down the path to the next node. Cases with missing values on the attribute are excluded from further consideration.

Secondly, let us consider missing values in attributes of new cases. Such an attribute is never branched on when classifying the case in question. In terms of conceptual tree structure, this means that path generation is now *strictly* dynamic. Without missing values, the entire tree *could* have been generated. Once missing values appear in new cases, however, this becomes impossible – at least without knowing in advance which attributes are missing. This contrasts with the method of surrogate variables used in CART, in which cases are classified using attributes which are statistically correlated with those attributes in the decision tree which have missing values for the case under consideration.

4.4   Testing and Cross-Validation Options

There is an option already incorporated within PREDICTOR which determines whether the program runs in test mode or cross-validation mode. In the former, new cases are classified. In the later, an internal N-fold cross-validation (Breiman et al., 1984) is performed on the database of training cases. This is a particularly thorough way of estimating the true predictive performance of a classification algorithm using only a single sample. Briefly, This involves classifying each of the N cases in the database by reference to the remaining $N-1$ cases.

4.5   Class Grouping Options

There are two ideas here which are worthy of consideration, though neither of them has yet been implemented in PREDICTOR. The first idea concerns the focus of discrimination. During the classification of a test case, a branch is constructed. If the program is running interactively, the branching process can be observed and some form of user intervention could be implemented. At some stage in the branching process, a user might wish to shift the focus of discrimination away from a global consideration of all k classes to a particular subset (perhaps two or three) which seem to be particularly relevant. This feature could be implemented simply by altering the χ^2 test used in the later stages of the branching process, to one based only on this subset of classes.

The second idea is one that arises from the observation by Breiman et al. (1984) that better trees can be grown in the case of multiple classes if attributes are chosen so as to either maximise or minimise the frequencies of each of the classes which are passed to the descendant nodes. One way to do this is to consider all possible ways of grouping the k classes into two supersets and to choose for branching that attribute which gives the largest association between class superset and attribute. With this technique, the optimal splitting for continuous variables should be treated by a similar approach. It should be noted that, if this technique is employed, some further adjustments to the stopping rule criterion will be required, along the lines specified earlier.

5   Concluding Remarks

Currently, PREDICTOR is being developed for use in a machine learning project in the field of medical diagnosis. However, the techniques described here are not specific to this one area of application. They should be equally applicable to noisy classification problems in other domains.

An important point concerns the use of the χ^2 test. Currently, heavy use is made of this procedure for three purposes:

- as a criterion for use in optimal splitting.

- as a criterion for attribute selection.

- as a significance test for the stopping rule.

There is an obvious economy in using the same procedure for these different functions but no absolute necessity for doing so. Should the need arise, different procedures could be adopted for any or all of these functions.

It is the intention of the authors to test many of the ideas described here by performing experiments. Some of these will be on specially generated synthetic data sets and others will be performed using medical data from the project. Results from these experiments will form the basis of future reports.

References

Breiman, L., Friedman, J.H., Olshen, R.A. & Stone, C.J. (1984). *Classification and Regression Trees*. Belmont: Wadsworth.

Feigenbaum, E.A. (1977). The art of artificial intelligence 1: themes and case studies of knowledge engineering. *Pub. no. STAN-CS-77-621*. Dept. of Computer Science, Stanford University.

Feigenbaum, E.A. (1981). Expert systems in the 1980s. In *State of the Art Report on Machine Intelligence*, edited by A. Bond. Maidenhead: Pergamon-Infotech.

Hart, A.E. (1985). Experience in the use of an inductive system in knowledge engineering. In *Research and Development in Expert Systems*, edited by M.A. Bramer, pp. 117-126. Cambridge: Cambridge University Press.

Kononenko, I., Bratko, I. & Roskar, E. (1984). Experiments in automatic learning of medical diagnostic rules. *Technical Report*. Jozef Stefan Institute, Ljubjana, Yugoslavia.

Michalski, R.S. & Larson, J.B. (1978). Selection of most representative training examples and incremental generation of VL_1 hypotheses. *Technical Report, 867*. Dept. of Computer Science, University of Illinois.

Michalski, R.S. & Chilausky, R.L. (1980). Learning by being told and learning from examples: An experimental comparison of the two methods of knowledge acquisition in the context of developing an expert system for soybean disease diagnosis. *International Journal of Policy Analysis and Information Systems*, 4, 125-161.

Michalski, R.S., Mozetic, I., Hong, J. & Lavrac, N. (1986). The multipurpose incremental learning system AQ15 and its testing applications to three medical domains. In *Proceeding of the AAAI Conference* (Philadelphia, PA).

Niblett, T. & Bratko, I. (1987). Learning decision rules in noisy domains. In *Research and Development in Expert Systems* III, edited by M.A. Bramer, pp. 25-34. Cambridge: Cambridge University Press.

Patterson, A. & Niblett, T. (1983). *ACLS User Manual*. Glasgow: Intelligent Terminals Ltd.

Quinlan, J.R. (1979). Discovering rules by induction from large collections of examples. In *Introductory Readings in Expert Systems*, edited by D. Michie, pp. 33-46. London: Gorden and Breach.

Quinlan, J.R. (1983). Learning from noisy data. In *Proceedings of the International Machine Learning Workshop*, pp. 58-64. University of Illinois at Urbana-Champaign.

Quinlan, J.R. (1986). Induction of decision trees. *Machine Learning*, **1**, 81-106.

White, A.P. (1985). PREDICTOR: An alternative approach to uncertain inference in expert systems. In *Proceedings of the Ninth International Joint Conference on Artificial Intelligence* (Los Angeles, 1985), edited by A. Joshi, vol. 1, pp. 328-330. Los Altos: Morgan Kaufmann.

White, A.P. & Reed, A. (1986). Some predictive difficulties in automatic induction. In *Proceedings of the International Meeting on Advances in Learning* (Les Arcs, 1986), edited by Y. Kodratoff and R.S. Michalski, pp. 132-139. Paris: Universite de Paris Sud.

White, A.P. (1987). Probabilistic induction by dynamic path generation in virtual trees. In *Research and Development in Expert Systems* III, edited by M.A. Bramer, pp. 35-46. Cambridge: Cambridge University Press.

White, A.P. & Reed A. (1989). Probabilistic induction and logit models. In *Machine and Human Learning*, edited by Y. Kodratoff and A. Hutchinson, pp. 221-225. London: Kogan Page.

ATENA, A KNOWLEDGE BASED SYSTEM FOR AUTOMATIC PAGINATION OF YELLOW DIRECTORIES[1]

João A. Câmara, João F. Martins, Margarida S. Jácome
INESC, Instituto de Engenharia de Sistemas e Computadores
Rua Alves Redol, 9
Apartado 10105
1017 Lisboa Codex
Portugal

Abstract

In this paper we describe the design, implementation and testing of the Knowledge Based System Atena, presently being used to produce automatically the portuguese yellow directories.

The rules followed by human paginators in order to achieve quality layouts (with minimum waste of space) are, typically, quite complex and full of intricate exceptions and somewhat "fuzzy" evaluation criteria. This explains why no software systems were developed (previously to Atena) able to deal automatically with the yellow directories layout composition problem[2].

Atena has been carefully designed in order to assure easy knowledge acquisition processes, with no lack of run-time efficiency. During the incremental development of the system, the authors had permanent feedback from pagination experts, that examined carefully and criticized each page produced by the system. All the necessary corrections and tuning were implemented in order to satisfy their demands.

Also, in order to achieve an approach with generality, several yellow directories from different countries were examined and their differences and communalities were taken into consideration when final decisions were made about Atena formulation and treatments of the pagination problem.

1. Introduction

Atena (Automatic Yellow Directory Paginator) is a Knowledge Based System for automatic pagination of yellow directories. The system operates in an entirely autonomous way, no kind of human intervention being required. Atena behaves like a human paginator, in the sense that it only generates intelligent[3] alternatives and evaluates them, in order to select the best solution.

Atena generic pagination rules and evaluation criteria were acquired from experienced pagination experts. Since Atena never discards any promising solution, there is the guarantee that the best one, i.e., the one corresponding to the best compromise among the different quality criteria is generated. Also, changes in the relative weights of these criteria are trivial to implement and, since the internal

---

1 This system was conceived and made at INESC (Instituto de Engenharia de Sistemas e Computadores, Lisbon), a portuguese research and development institute, in association with ITT-Portugal. Atena is presently being used by this company.
2 The typical scenario was the human paginators being supported by partially interactive systems, or systems able to deal only with a very simplified set of rules.
3 Intelligent generation means that certain alternatives, though correct from the pagination rules point of view, are never generated since the system knows for sure (from a rough context evaluation) that better solutions are being simultaneously generated.

description of the candidate pages is quite exhaustive, new quality criteria can easily be added to the system.

Atena was designed to be integrated in an environment of conventional (non A.I. based) systems, being the tool responsible for the unique non-systematic task of the whole process, and works at a level completely independent from the specific environment organization. This decoupling was achieved by imposing that the input file should contain all the information relevant to the pagination process. The input text file is currently being automatically generated from the costumer's data base (by means of a preprocessor system), according to a clearly defined format specification, prior to the pagination process. On the other hand, Atena's output is also a text file that describes appropriately the layout of the best solution found for every page of the current edition. The file format was carefully designed in order to simplify and optimize the subsequent systematic process of automatic composition of the actual pages, since it feeds directly the remaining chain of conventional systems.

Atena is running on a VAX[4] 8530 computer and producing all the editions of the portuguese yellow directories[5]. Compared with the average time of six minutes spent by a human expert to produce a solution for the layout of a pair of pages, Atena spends less than one minute on average to test exhaustively all the the interesting possibilities, in order to find out the layout that allies regularity and intelligibility with minimum waste of area. This performance transfers the bottleneck of book printing away from the page composition.

2. Why a Knowledge Based System?

The specifics of the pagination problem make it a suitable example for resorting to the expert systems technology. Actually, since the knowledge acquisition relies on oral information, provided by human experts, misunderstandings can easily occur. Furthermore, the knowledge engineer is almost entirely dependent on personal points of view: the criteria for selecting the best solution, among a set of alternatives, are subjective and involve personalized knowledge[6]. Moreover, these criteria are difficult to validate from other sources and the loose formulation of some of them makes the objective quantification and appreciation of results difficult. Finally, the permanent evolution which is predictable for such a dynamic field (graphic edition) is another factor that must be taken into account.

In a problem with characteristics such as the ones referred above, choosing an algorithmic approach, in which all knowledge must be available initially[7], is risky. It also leads to a very uncomfortable decision: to choose between a general but complex and inefficient algorithm and one algorithm which is efficient though tied forever to a very specific problem configuration. Otherwise, the iterative strategy inherent to the development of knowledge based systems permits to accompany the evolution and refinement of the acquired knowledge: the application itself and its results constitute an excellent instrument to collect and validate the information obtained so far. This happens because in these systems, the domain specific knowledge can be represented in an identifiable and separate part of the system, rather than being dispersed throughout it. Consequently, it becomes extremely easy to identify, access

---

4   VAX is a trademark of Digital Equipment Corp.

5   Directories already produced by Atena (total amount of pages of the last edition in brackets): Centro (1040); Sul (1040); Madeira (344); Açores (328); Norte (1456); Lisboa (2032); Margem Sul do Tejo (368); Linha de Sintra (304); Linha de Cascais (304); Zona Norte de Lisboa (304); Porto (1640).

6   Two paginators with the same degree of expertise can opt for different solutions.

7   Subsequent changes can question the adopted solution.

and modify particular chunks of information. The treatment of exceptions also becomes very easy to handle. Besides, the declarative forms of knowledge representation extensively used in this class of systems contributes to the structural flexibility and intelligibility exhibited by this type of systems.

In conclusion, the production systems technology[8] was chosen because it appeared to us as the most realistic and practicable (in terms of cost and efficiency) alternative which:
- enables the development of a complete system in an acceptable period of time;
- ensures an easy and cheap updating of the system, throughout the predictable evolution of the knowledge in the area;
- guarantees the possibility of integration of disperse (individual) knowledge.

3. Brief Overview of the Pagination Strategy

As said above, Atena behaves like a human paginator. So, its strategy consists basically in determining all the relevant alternatives for a given pair of pages, and in evaluating them according to a set of criteria.

For each new pair of pages, Atena starts deriving the interval of admissible advertisement[9] area and the maximum editorial text[10] area to be inserted in all the alternative solutions. This decision is taken consulting the input file, where several classifications[11] are concerned. The aim is to identify clearly the next pagination context and also to guarantee a well-balanced distribution of text and advertisements under the same classification, among the subsequent pages and to avoid the existence of too large fillers[12] in a page.

Another important aspect should be considered, before the generation of alternative solutions is started. Achieving maximum intelligibility and coherence, from the reader's point of view, requires that the text and advertisements under the same classification be geometrically adjoint. However, trying to maintain this quality criteria for pages that are going to include advertisements under many classifications can lead to chaotic dispositions, with the advertisements appearing confusingly dispersed among islands of text. In order to avoid this, at the beginning of a new cycle of a pair of pages generation, Atena chooses between two possible strategies: page- or classification-based (see figure 1 next page: the classification-strategy was used in the even page, while the page-strategy was used in the odd one). This decision is based on the computed ratio of advertisements and text areas, and advertisements configurations that are expected to be treated. If advertisements over too many classifications are detected the system decides to treat the different classifications involved as if they were a unique classification (page-based strategy), by grouping advertisements (for example, at the center of the page) and placing the text around them. Otherwise (classification-based strategy), the generation is classification-driven, involving partial cycles for advertisement placement and text insertion.

The different alternatives generated by the system correspond to the several legal dispositions that are available for placing a variable number[13] of advertisements in a page. These alternatives must therefore obey a certain number of restrictions: correct hierarchical ordering of advertisements (according to format,

---

8   Production rules as declarative forms.
9   Rectangular boxes bounded by a frame, with free composition.
10 Constituted by the editorial listings: text in various fonts, framed or not, with or without logotype.
11 Each of the groups of related information, appearing in the yellow directory.
12 Wasted area.
13 According to the validity interval.

sequence, which varies with format and comprehends some exceptions, and available free positions in the page grid), correct sequencing of classifications[14], necessity of immediate identification of text blocks by the reader (text should be continuous within a column), and so on. These alternative solutions can differ as far as amount and distribution of fillers, regularity of text and advertisements disposition, and so on, are concerned.

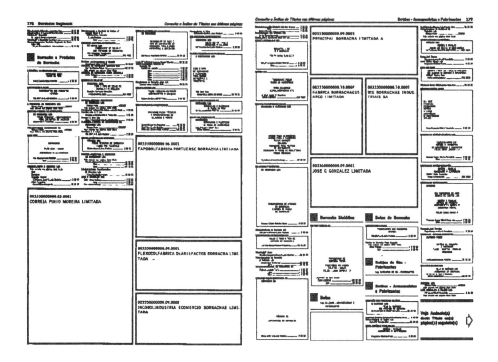

Figure 1: Example of a pair of pages produced by Atena for the Lisbon directory.

One purpose of Atena at this particular stage is not to waste time generating absurd hypotheses. Thus the system only considers those alternatives that correspond to acceptable advertisements and text configurations. Consequently, all the decisions concerning the position of the first entry in a column are carefully considered according to the sequence (number and type) of advertisements still waiting for insertion, the number of predicted changes of classification in the page and the viability of the insertion of the minimum acceptable area of advertisements. Furthermore, none of the horizontally symmetric alternative distributions is generated, unless changes of classifications occur in the relevant columns. The reason being that the horizontally symmetric alternatives do not differ from the existing ones in terms of filler area, definitively one of the most important criteria when evaluating a page. The previously horizontal symmetry avoidance (in specific circumstances) is one of the several Atena "intelligent" decisions when generating pages.

Once all the alternative solutions are generated, the system proceeds with the text insertion cycle. Atena is provided with knowledge about how to break editorial listings and what to repeat at the beginning of the next column and what to

---

14   Aspect particularly critical for the odd pages, were the reading direction (ordering) is inverse to the grid hierarchical prescriptions.

append at the end of the current one, in such cases. Atena also knows how to expand text in order to avoid small fillers and how to contract text, within given limits, in order to avoid the insertion of fillers.

At this stage the alternative solutions are completely defined, with respect to advertisements and text, and the selection cycle starts. The implemented selection set of criteria includes:

- Effective area, i.e., area occupied by "useful" information. It does not include filler area (even if the filler does not show due to expansion of the text) and repetition lines (which appear when an editorial listing is broken);
- Regularity and position of the advertisements configurations (favouring certain forms, as the "L" shape, and penalizing several isolated blocks of advertisements under the same classification in the same page);
- Pages filled with advertisements and without any editorial listing (billboarding).
- Regularity of text disposition, favouring the contiguity of blocks between columns;
- Contiguity of text and advertisement blocks under the same classification (several types of "touching" are considered: text on top of the advertisement; advertisement on top of the text; text and advertisement with lateral touching; lateral touching with the advertisement on the top of the page; lateral touching with the advertisement of this classification underneath another advertisement of a different classification);
- Fillers disposition, according to the hierarchy of the page grid positions;
- Fillers size and final format (dispersion of small fillers over the page can be penalized, since this make them less saleable);
- Number of classifications starting in each page.

These criteria are combined in a hierarchical way, according to their relative importance, in order to find the best solution. If necessary, other criteria can be easily added to these.

It may occur that the total filler area, in the best solution reached by the system, is larger than what is considered acceptable[15]. Atena tries to avoid such situations by deriving, at the beginning of the pagination of a pair of pages, the amounts of area that should be occupied by text and advertisements. However if this situation arises, Atena knows how to backtrack, going back a suitable number of pages (depending on the size of the filler and on the previous pages), repaginating them in order to distribute the filler along the pages, essentially repeating the same process as at the first time, but using some additional information. Text insertion can have in mind the configuration of the eventual fillers, when applicable. Finally, selected pages can still receive a final fixing (under specific circumstances), with the text disposition being modified in order to aggregate fillers and transfer them to less noble positions in the page.

The system is presently implemented according to the following framework: grid page with 48 positions (4 columns), 768 points per column, 10 advertisement formats and structured text without any restrictions (editorial listings with any size; breakable, not breakable, with frame[16] and without frame options are available). The so called geographic line, or postal district (sub-classifications), is also supported at any level, with the necessary repetition of sub-classifications names at the beginning of each column. According to what was said in the last section, this framework (namely, the page grid and the advertisements formats) can be easily adapted to other specific necessities.

---

[15] Typically when there are large advertisements and few listings under a classification.

[16] The frame is considered when some information advertisement is broken.

4. Brief Overview of the Development Stages

First of all, a prototype was written aiming to prove that the project was feasible. It included a simplified approach to the problem, satisfying only a subset of the pagination rules. The results of this prototype led to the conclusion that the right conceptualization and formalization of the problem were the chosen ones. So it was decided to proceed.

Initially all the work, was done in OPS5 and the system generated all the possible alternatives in order to guarantee that the very best solution would be created and chosen. This approach proved to cause an enormous combinatory explosion, which made it just not feasible. So it was necessary to study the results of the system, in order to induce which conditions could be added to the left hand side of the rules, to avoid the generation of solutions that obviously would not be chosen. These new conditions were implemented in the most careful way, to avoid unexpected side effects. As new restrictions were included in the rules, the program got faster, allowing a more exhaustive testing which has shown the need of new rules and changes to the existing ones. During the incremental development of the system, all the results were fully examined by human experts and the necessary corrections were implemented in order to satisfy all their demands.

The placement of text in the generated pages, was recognized as being a systematic task, so several procedures in Pascal were written to take care of this part of the work, in a more efficient way that OPS5 ever could. The introduction of this new procedures caused, naturally, considerable modifications in the nature and number of elements in the OPS5 working memory, since it was no longer necessary to keep so much information in it, and a set of messages between OPS5 and Pascal procedures had to be implemented.

It was also decided that the computations of the upper and lower bounds of the area to be occupied by advertisements and text[17], as well as the choice of pagination strategy[18], should be performed by Pascal procedures. This computations are made every time the pagination of a pair of pages starts.

5. Input and Output Files

The input file of Atena contains a list of all the classifications to be inserted on the current yellow directory[19]. The information contained in the specification of a classification comprises the total of advertisements (referred by type), the total text area (in "points") and a list of all the editorial listings, related lines (source file) and valid break points. As said before, this file can be easily generated from the costumer's data base.

The output file contains the layout for each page, organized in terms of text blocks, space advertisements and fillers. Text blocks are described by the correspondent height, entry coordinates and lines (source file). Advertisements are identified by their type, sequence number, related classification and entry coordinates. Fillers are described in terms of size (number of columns and height), type and entry coordinates.

---

[17] It is not possible to compute an exact ideal area.
[18] Page-based or classification-based strategy.
[19] The sub-classifications are embedded on the correspondent main classifications.

6. Implementation

Atena is a knowledge based system written in OPS5 and Pascal. Pascal routines are used on the program[20], whenever the related task is of the imperative type, being possible to perform it in just one execution cycle[21], or when some condition to be tested, or some basic operation to be performed, have more complexity than those easily handled by the OPS5 primitives. Some procedures were also written in Pascal to avoid the insertion of a large number of very similar rules; these procedures are used in some rules that work as if they were "parameter dependent rules".

The alternative solutions are generated according to a tree scheme. The root corresponds to a blank pair of pages. The tree is built from this root by the production rules for placement of advertisements. Each and every node is expanded towards a final alternative solution. The generation of new nodes is exhaustive, according to the set of those rules, which include the domain knowledge, enough to avoid absurd hypotheses. Because of efficiency concerns, Atena discards immediately non-relevant partial solutions.

Atena handles the pagination process by pair of pages. Again, due to efficiency concerns, the even pages are grouped in families, before the system proceeds to the odd page, thus avoiding repetition of generation cycles for similar pages. Each family consists of pages with the same advertisements and editorial text, but with a different layout.

A small file is produced for each pair of pages, containing its initial state. This allows the pagination process to be done in several stages (useful when dealing with very large directories). The facility to restart the process from any previously paginated pair of pages is also implemented.

The system evaluates the final solutions according to a predefined criteria hierarchy, being able to discard pages at every criteria level.

As said above, the input file consists of a text file. This file is preprocessed to generate a direct access file which is used during the pagination.

7. Knowledge Representation

Several types of rules were implemented. Some of them have knowledge about a particular advertisement type at a given page position; other have information about groups of space advertisements and page regions.

Some of the rules conditions are based in: minimum and maximum area previously computed for the placement units; possible advertisement configurations at this point; contiguity to previously placed advertisements; proximity to the text under the same classification; expected changes of classification in the current page and pair of pages; anticipation of some predicted pagination contexts.

The existence of typical sequences of advertisements under the some classification was detected. This knowledge was formalized in specialized rules that place those sequences, bypassing rules for individual placement, speeding up the program since the space of solutions is reduced.

---

[20] Called from both the LHS and RHS of the rules.
[21] For instance, the text insertion.

8.   Adaptability to Different Pagination Contexts

Atena contains embedded a general method to deal with any pagination context. Reconfiguration does not require any supplementary effort to derive new methods or strategies, but only the adaptation of the existing ones.

It is important to keep in mind that, at the time of best solution choice, there is a variety of alternative solutions in the working memory. So, eventually, most changes will probably concern the choice criteria and not the generation methods.

Some of the possible modifications[22] are:
- Evaluation parameters: Trivial modification and iterative adjustment.
- New formats of advertisements: New set of advertisement placement rules (systematic task) and small changes in one global precondition; Small adjustment in the computation of text and advertisement limits per page.
- Grid with less columns: Minor modifications in the text insertion procedure; Adjustment in the computation of text and advertisement limits per page.
- Pagination rules: Advertisements priorities - trivial modification; Grid prescriptions - trivial modifications in the whole set of advertisement placement rules.

9.   Conclusions

The system Atena offers several advantages that can be summarized as shown below.
- The pages generated by Atena present a quality at least as good as those obtained manually by the experts. And the notion of quality in Atena remains constant (consistent) through an entire book. The results were submitted to human experts, who considered that the set of possible solutions from which Atena chooses the best page, is wide enough to allow a satisfactory result when dealing with the different aspects of the pagination problem; the set of alternative solutions also allows different criteria of quality to be easily implemented and contains, for all the tested cases in 1988/89 Lisbon yellow directory (human made), the solution here presented.
- There is the guarantee that the best solution, i.e. the one that corresponds to the best compromise among different criteria (filler area minimization, better filler distribution and better regularity of text and advertisement placement), is generated.
- There is perfect coherence in the selection of the final solutions for similar cases.
- The system forces the optimal resolution ("point"). Expansion and contraction of text is implemented in order to achieve the optimal utilization of area. In a large directory[23] the program achieved a percentage of filler area as good as the one obtained by very trained human experts.
- The time required for the generation of the layout of a pair of pages is 1 minute on average on a VAX 8530 machine (about one sixth of the time spent by an experimented paginator). This result was only possible due to a constant care in the way the rules were written, in order to avoid the generation of solutions considered illegal or with bad quality. So every solution generated by the system is not only legal but also has the possibility of being the best one. The good temporal results have required a deep study of the matching process and the insertion of goals in the program code.

---

22   For example: Significant changes (20%) were made in 5 person day on 350 rules for advertisement placement and after an introductory explanation of half an hour.

23   The Lisbon directory has more than 2000 pages.

- The choice of alternative solutions guarantees the optimization of a pair of pages (those the reader sees at the same time, when he opens the directory book).
- Atena is the key link required for implementing a full automated production of yellow directories.
- In order to achieve these results it became necessary to write about 600 rules of OPS5 (120 000 lines of code) and several procedures in Pascal (25 000 lines of code). The executable file size is near 4 Mbytes, showing the complexity of the actual version.
- Atena performs a task in a domain where the number of existing human experts is typically very small, so it may be regarded as a way of preserving the knowledge it contains.

As a final comment, it can be stated that Atena has all the requirements to achieve a reduction of the total size of the directory book. This was demonstrated by the tests performed on the 1988/89 Lisbon directory: the solution for every pair of pages is either equal to the solution obtained manually or one with smaller filler area without compromising the quality of the subsequent pages. Atena is currently being used successfully in production environment, without any need of human intervention.

OBJECT-ORIENTED EXPERT DIAGNOSTIC SYSTEMS: DESIGN PRINCIPLES

Ajit Narayanan and Yuanping Jin[1]
Department of Computer Science
Old Library
University of Exeter
Exeter EX4 4PT

Abstract

The representation and use of *knowledge* about the dynamics and mechanics of a circuit board for inclusion in diagnostic hardware fault location systems is one of the central issues in developing artificial intelligence (AI) programs capable of the kind of problem solving skills exhibited by a technician or engineer who identifies and locates component faults. Because the area of AI which has received the greatest application during recent areas is that of (knowledge-based) expert systems, it is natural that an expert systems approach should be initially explored by researchers in order to embody technical expertise and emulate expert technician performance. We describe the theoretical foundations and assumptions of a different approach — *expert object-oriented diagnosis* (EXOOD) — which we believe is suitable for the domain under consideration. We then describe the specifications for a system based on the EXOOD approach and outline various design principles as well as an architecture for an expert object-oriented diagnostic system. Finally, we highlight the general features of EXOOD which distinguish it from other approaches in the knowledge representation domain.

1. Current approaches to fault diagnosis

Human fault diagnosis is a knowledge-intensive and experience-based task. Ideally, a computerized diagnostic system should provide critically required assistance for prompt detection and location of component faults (Jones & Burge 1987). A variety of systems based on the expert systems approach have been tried, with varying degrees of success (Pau 1986). Tzafestas (1987), in his overview of the essential characteristics of this approach to system fault diagnosis and supervisory control, stresses that, whilst there is no single methodology for building an expert system (ES) in this domain, various designs can be generally categorized as falling into one of two approaches — *deep knowledge*, and *shallow reasoning*. Shallow reasoning designs typically are used in evidentially-based domains (e.g. medical diagnosis), where there is a pre-specified relationship between fault symptoms and system malfunctions, i.e. between system behaviour irregularities and system faults.

---

[1]The authors are deeply grateful to Eby Zafari of the Department of Computer Science, and Dr Philip Barbonis of Digital (Nijmegen) for their valuable assistance and support during the project.

The ES typically uses production rules to mimic the deductive processes of the skilled expert and has the advantage that in domains where the underlying causal mechanisms are not completely understood (as in medical diagnosis) the rules can be used to capture, at the rule level, whatever evidential knowledge does exist. This makes knowledge acquisition and refinement difficult and can lead to large, unstructured rule bases. A deep-knowledge ES, on the other hand, attempts to capture the underlying principles of a domain explicitly, thereby making redundant the need to capture every fault scenario explicitly. As Tzafestas (1987) points out, such an approach seems appropriate for man-made technological system diagnosis.

Typically, three main deep-knowledge, or *model-based*, diagnosis methods have been tried: causal search method (which usually uses semantic nets or graphs to trace a process malfunction back to its source); mathematical model method (which relies on redundancy between process and state measurements); and hypothesis/test method (which follows the usual diagnostic path of postulating a cause of a system malfunction, determining the symptoms of the postulated fault, and comparing the result with actual system observations). All three methods have advantages and disadvantages, as identified by Tzafestas (1987) and Pau (1986).

However, the main problem is that a *measure* of diagnosability is not available with which to make comparisons between different deep knowledge approaches. It is therefore not possible to state with any degree of certainty exactly how far down the levels of principles we should go in order to ensure as comprehensive a deep knowledge system as possible or as required is provided. For instance, we theoretically can go down as far as the level of electronic principles, irrespective of what components there are on the board under test. The question of whether going down that far has any significant advantage over only a higher level description of principles (at the component level, for instance) is not clear, given current ES approaches in the domain.

2. Ontological structure analysis

We now introduce a particular knowledge engineering methodology which, after some reinterpretation, does provide a well-defined starting-point for a deep knowledge approach to knowledge-based hardware fault diagnosis and location. *Ontological structure analysis* (Freiling, Rehfuss, Alexander, Messick & Shulman 1986) proceeds in a step-by-step articulation of the knowledge structures needed to perform a task. The aim is to introduce a *knowledge engineering methodology* which proceeds in a principled way and thereby provides a set of 'good practice' principles.

The notion of ontological structure is decomposed into three levels: *static ontology*, *dynamic ontology*, and *epistemic ontology*. The aim of static ontology is to allow the knowledge engineer to get on with the business of declaring the physical objects in the problem domain, their properties and relationships, without having to worry about complex knowledge representation issues such as which inference strategy to use. Static ontology is normally unpacked in the domain of electronic instrument troubleshooting by means of:

physical objects, such as components and knobs of the instruments;

the physical *properties* of such objects, such as capacity and other physical object data; and

the *connectivity* of these objects (achieved, for example, by grouping objects (by means of an appropriate notation) into *blocks*).

The second step is to define the state space in which the problem solving must occur and the actions which transform the problem from one state to another. The dynamic ontology in this domain is typically unpacked in terms of *belief states* and *instrument states*:

belief states comprise diagnostics beliefs about the diagnostic conditions of each module (component, knob or block), which have associated *justifications*, e.g. fragments of evidence, user assumptions, test results and inferences; these justifications are fed down from the level of epistemic ontology

an instrument state consists of knob settings and signal inputs which are used to *simulate* the instrument under test.

Measurements are made of signals and other electrical parameters, and these measurements are grouped into tests which in turn are grouped into strategies. Each test and each strategy have *implications*, i.e. diagnostic beliefs implied by the test results.

The framework, as presented so far, involves a possibly exponential growth of possible states and transformation sequences. The final step is to define constraints and heuristics so that effective transformations are chosen which allow the problem state space to be navigated in a reasonable amount of time. The epistemic ontology in the domain of electronic troubleshooting defines appropriate types of diagnostic knowledge. For example, most experts diagnose a fault by proposing a set of hypotheses about which modules (i.e. objects and blocks) are good and bad. In order to test such hypotheses experts may use heuristic diagnostic strategies which relate each module to the method by which it may be tested[2].

The ontological analysis approach has the advantage that it has a clear starting point, namely, the level of static ontology which deals with actual physical objects (components). However, subsequent levels of analysis, as described by Freiling *et al.* (1986), are heavily dependent on a *state-space* approach, where fault diagnosis is interpreted as a typical AI problem-solving task (e.g. game-playing and planning a route). Defining the state-space (the level of dynamic ontology) would be relatively simple for heavily constrained domains, such as a simple circuit board with only a few components, but it is clear that the dynamic ontology requires the epistemic ontology in order to constrain exponential growth. In addition, using heuristics at the epistemic ontology level to control search of the space is not entirely consistent with the step-by-step approach advocated by Freiling *et al.* (1986). That is, one can imagine the level of static ontology being defined,

---

[2]Freiling *et al.* (1986) go on to propose a formal tool called SPOONS (SPecification Of ONtological Structure) which is an adaptation of *domain equations* used in denotational semantics (Gordon 1979). However, they admit that they have not been able to construct a complete ontological analysis with this formal tool.

implemented and evaluated without regard to the next level of dynamic ontology, but it is difficult to imagine defining, implementing and evaluating the level of dynamic ontology without using constraining heuristics, as well as justifications, at the level of epistemic ontology: the evaluation of the level of dynamic ontology, for instance, may itself be exponentially complex unless heuristics from the level above are used.

These considerations led to the following conclusions. *First*, we concluded that, whilst the ontological analysis approach is essentially correct with regard to its base level of defining *objects*, their properties and relationships, what was required was a much richer object representation at the base level than that implied by static ontology. *Secondly*, we concluded that, by re-opening the question of what the base level should look like, a much richer level of dynamic, as well as possibly epistemic, ontology could be attained — one which was not dependent on the traditional state-space paradigm and one which also took into account the nature of the domain we were working in.

Both the above conclusions led to the view that the design and implementation of a *structured-object knowledge representation scheme and architecture* for expert diagnosis should be examined further.

3. Theoretical foundations of EXOOD

We converged on the followings statements[3] as axiomatic of the domain.

(A1) Expert diagnostic knowledge should be organized around a set of primitive conceptual entities, in this case components (which represent the primitive replaceable objects), with associated descriptions and procedures.

(A2) A description of a component must be able to represent partial knowledge about an entity and accommodate multiple descriptors which can describe the associated entity from different viewpoints.

(A3) One important method of component description is comparison with a known component entity, with further specification of the desired component instance with respect to the component prototype.

(A4) Diagnosis is dominated by a process of recognition in which new component objects and events are compared to stored sets of expected component prototypes, and in which specialized diagnostic knowledge is keyed to these component prototypes as well as component instances.

We now present some justifications and explanations for the above axioms. First, there is the issue of *naturalness and expressibility*. If one expands on

---

[3]These axioms are closely related to a set of 'aphorisms', i.e. short pithy statements or maxims, and intuitions provided by Bobrow & Winograd (1985) when discussing language understanding systems. The underlying motivation to the above axioms is that the diagnosis and location of hardware faults are not naturally, or efficiently, or even effectively, modeled on the state-space, or game-playing, paradigm.

the proposals of Freiling *et al.* (1986), the natural organization for the declarative knowledge base in a hardware fault diagnosis system would be centred around a set of primitive conceptual entities which represent components (actual as well as prototypical), together with associated descriptions which provide *data* concerning the components as well as information concerning the *functionality* of the components. This leads to an object-oriented factorization of knowledge at the base level, rather than the more common factorization in which knowledge is structured as a set of facts, each referring to one or more objects. Object descriptions for components will need to include the following information:

(i) the assignment of a component object to be a member of a particular *class*, or prototype, of component;

(ii) if a component object is a complex one, the specification of the atomic component objects and their roles in the complex component object;

(iii) statements concerning the relationship that a component object has with other component objects, both functionally and topologically.

Secondly, there is the issue of *expectations*. Axiom A3 highlights the importance of describing an entity by comparing it with another entity. The component object being used as a basis for comparison is called a prototype and provides a *perspective* from which to view the component object being described. Details of the comparison can be thought of as further specifying the prototype. The standard method of comparison is with a *stereotypical* individual component which represents the *typical* member of a class. For instance, if an expert is told that a particular component is a power supply, that expert can immediately make comparisons between the actual power supply and a prototypical (even 'ideal') power supply. These comparisons can be made in several ways: physical size, functionality, component constituents, and so on. It is this type of activity that Axiom 3 is attempting to capture. Such a prototype has a description which may be true of no one member of the class, but combines the default knowledge applied to members of the class in the absence of specific information (Axiom A1). This default knowledge can be used to provide a set of particular *expectations* concerning the components and topology of the circuit board under consideration (Axiom A4). For example, if one is told that a particular component is a power supply, automatically a set of expectations is generated about the component, such as where it will be located on various boards, how it will be connected, and so on. Axioms A1 and A4 attempt to capture this expert ability.

Thirdly, there is the issue of *conceptual efficiency*. A single component can be described with respect to several prototypes, with further specifications from the perspective of each (Axiom A2). For instance, the default for one particular component class, say, a binary adder, may be to perform a certain function which, through experience, the expert knows that component typically performs given the board type and the nature of its connectivity to other components. Nevertheless, that component may have a different function in one particular context which has not been included in the prototypical information (Axiom A2). Such variance from normal expectations must be catered for, as must

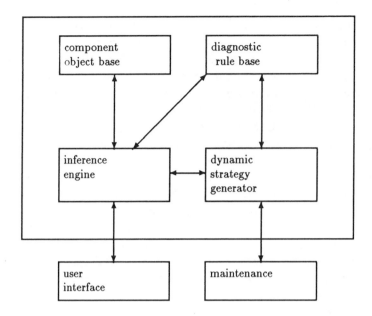

Figure 1 —The general architecture of an EXOODS

the principle that the use of typical and expected properties of components will be necessary when there is incomplete information about the board and its components (Axiom A2, Axiom A4).

And finally, there is the issue of *causal reasoning*. The main *inferencing* mechanism in a traditional object-oriented approach consists of 'property inheritance', where in the absence of information to the contrary an object inherits the properties of the prototype, or class of objects, to which it belongs. Such a *frame-based* approach does not cater well for *causal reasoning*, where knowledge is used of how a component or group of components causally influence, or are influenced by, other components or groups of components.

4. Design principles

The analysis above led to the following design principles for an expert object-oriented diagnostic system (EXOODS), the architecture of which is provided in Figure 1.

There has to be a *description* of the circuit board, in terms of both individual components and connectivity between components. The set of component and connectivity descriptions constitute the base-level object-oriented *model* of the board. For every component on the board there will be a component description instance of it, together with a description of the class of object to which it belongs. Described here will be not only the basic operational parameters of the component (which may be accessed via a database of some sort) and the connectivity between components (provided at both the class and instance levels) but also the *functionality* of each class of component. For instance, an individual component will be described according to manufacturers' specifications (e.g. basic data concerning permissible temperature range, maximum and minimum voltages allowed, and the number of pins for input and output), basic functional design (e.g. buffer, counter, RAM, ROM, and power supply), and connectivity via *connected* pins (e.g. pin 14 has input from a certain component, and pin 26 provides output to another component). The set of such descriptions we call the *component object base*.

The diagnostic expertise of an expert troubleshooter (technician or repairer) has to be stored so that the system has some basic diagnostic 'knowledge'. Such knowledge will be both *board-specific* as well as *board-general*. Board-specific diagnostic knowledge will usually consist of some description of previous experience with the particular board, or board-type, under examination. For instance, a particular component may, through experience, be the main cause for a particular type of fault on a particular type of board. Board-general diagnostic knowledge will usually contain descriptions of experience with types of component rather than boards.

Each diagnostic rule must be an object which is a member of a class of (rule) objects. In order to represent causal reasoning processes, classes of rule objects can be distinguished on the basis of different *types of causality*, e.g. sufficient cause, necessary cause, probabilistic cause, intermittent cause, and so on. By classifying items of diagnostic knowledge in this manner, we have a method for partitioning the diagnostic knowledge in a way which reflects human expertise in this domain. There may be other ways of classifying rules. For instance, two other ways are on the basis of *structure*, and on the basis of the *component objects* referred to in the rule. For instance, rules can be collected together and distinguished on the basis of being *if ... then ...* rules, *if ... then ... else ...* rules, multiple condition rules, multiple action rules, and so on. On the other hand, rules can be collected together and distinguished on the basis of being about components of memory boards, of vdu boards, of power supply units, and so on. No matter which class criterion or set of criteria is selected (and it may well be the domain that finally selects the criteria), the important point is that individual diagnostic rules are instances of a class of rules and therefore inherit many of the properties of the class, just as component objects do.

The inference engine has as its overall aim the knitting together of individual rules in the diagnostic base into an effective diagnostic *strategy*. This requires an *inference engine* of a type which is an extension of that found in traditional ESs, where the task of an inference engine typically is to identify candidate rules for firing and then to execute one or more rules according to some preprogrammed strategy. In addition to the above task, an inference engine in an EXOODS has others:

(a) to take a reported fault symptom and to extract the semantics of the fault so that an internal representation of the fault symptom is derived;

(b) to generate appropriate diagnostic strategies concerning possible causes of the fault symptom;

(c) to hand over the fault symptom, either in its entirety or in parts, to the diagnostic (rule) base so that the appropriate diagnostic knowledge is accessed and various requests, i.e. *messages*, are generated;

(d) to pass the requests (messages) of the diagnostic base either to the user (e.g. requests for further information or for some manual probing to be done) or to the component object base (e.g. requests for comparing the expectations of the diagnostic base with the information contained within components);

(e) to receive information back from both the component object base and user so that comparisons can be made with regard to its previously chosen diagnostic strategy and to choose another diagnostic strategy if appropriate;

The symptom is reported by a user via a *user interface*. It may be possible to replace the user-interface with a *system interface* so that faults can be reported to the EXOODS directly by the computer system in which the board is located.

Finally, there needs to be some *learning* module so that the results of the EXOODS can be used for updating its diagnostic base and inference engine, as well as for generating novel diagnostic strategies when the inference engine is stuck. Such updating need not be caused by the particular EXOODS in which the *dynamic strategy generator* is located: results from other EXOODSs located in other machines and at other sites can also be fed, via a *maintenance* module, into the dynamic strategy generator. Initially, the maintenance procedure is manual[4].

5. An example

In order to demonstrate the feasibility of EXOOD, we constructed an experimental version which concentrated on the heart of the system, namely, the component object base, the diagnostic (rule) base, and the inference engine. The experiments were run on a simple circuit consisting of an oscillator, a 4-bit binary counter, and a buffer (Figure 2). The oscillator produces pulses of a certain frequency and the counter increments in steps of one after receiving a pulse. The labels 'ga', 'gb', 'gc' and 'gd' represent the four bits output from the counter. The buffer simply amplifies the output of the counter, and 'A', 'B', 'C' and 'D' represent the four outputs from the buffer which are fed to leds.

In our experiments, a base class for other component object classes is defined and has the following form:

class object;
<some class information>;
check_input and <carry out action>;
check_function and <carry out action>;
check_condition and <carry out action>.

Any derived component class can redefine the check functions or simply inherit them from the base class. Usually a derived class needs to redefine these functions

---

[4]Issues concerning the user interface, dynamic strategy generator and maintenance fall outside the scope of this paper.

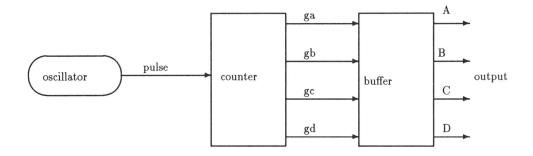

Figure 2 - A simple experimental circuit

to meet the requirement of specific objects. As far as base level fault diagnosis is concerned, **check_input** checks whether the input (via pins) to the object is correct, **check_function** the functionality of the object, and **check_condition** the working condition of the object (e.g. if the voltage is out of a specified range). So, for instance, given the above skeletal form of an object class definition we can define the class for **counter** as well as specify typical checks and actions to be carried out, by default, on all objects of the class. We can then use that class to declare various instances of counter as well as specify, if necessary, more, or different, checks and actions depending on the actual counter. The checks as well as other component information are *encapsulated* within the object, both at the class and individual level.

To be natural to use and easy to understand, a diagnostic rule in the system must have a simple form. Consequently, a rule has one of the following forms:

\<head_fault_name\>: IF \<option\> OF \<object\> OK
THEN \<then_fault_name\>
ELSE \<else_fault_name\>.

\<head_fault_name\>.

There are three options for **\<option\>**: INPUT, FUNCTION and CONDITION. These correspond to the three types of check in a component object. The rules of format (2) are terminal ones and of format (1) non-terminal ones.
\<head_fault_name\> also serves as an identifier of the rule. **\<then_fault_name\>** and **\<else_fault_name\>** must be the **\<head_fault_name\>** of some other rule that can be either terminal or non-terminal. A terminal rule tells the system to stop searching and a non-terminal rule guides the system to diagnose a fault in more detail.

Each rule is an object and is an instance of the class of rule objects. In the above case our class is simply one of sufficient condition, i.e. the satisfaction of the necessary conditions after *if* leads to the fault described after *then* which is sufficient for the main (goal) fault, otherwise diagnosing the fault described after

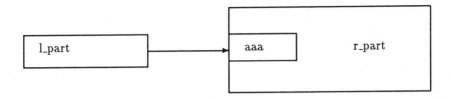

Figure 3 - Rule-form

else is sufficient. The idea is to allow each rule object to encapsulate at the class level and at the individual level a certain piece of diagnostic knowledge concerning casual relationships between component objects. These relationships can in turn be between component class objects or individual component objects[5].

Let us look at a simple example. Suppose a circuit can be subdivided into two parts, a left-hand part and a right-hand part. That is, we assume that we can distinguish functionally between components which causally influence others and components which are causally influenced. The set of causally-influencing components we call **l_part** and the set of causally-influenced components we call **r_part**. Let us put an object under test, say *aaa*, at the boundary of the division in **r_part** so that it takes the output from **l_part** as its input, as shown in Figure 3.

The rule below forms a simple diagnostic test:

whole_fault: IF INPUT OF *aaa* **OK**
        THEN r_part_fault ELSE l_part_fault.
        l_part_fault.
        r_part_fault.

When called, the rule will send a message to *aaa* to execute its INPUT check and to return a result. Depending on the value returned, other components are checked.

The rule can guide, or be guided by, the inference engine to find one fault at a time. However, there might be some other faults that have not been covered. For instance, given the above rule, if we test INPUT of *aaa* and the result is not OK, we then turn to the **l_part**, but there still might be some faults in the **r_part**. It is the task of the inference engine to generate appropriate diagnostic strategies[6] and to control the diagnostic search. The inference engine in fact dynamically generates a diagnostic tree for a given fault name according to the expert knowledge represented as rules and the nature of the tested objects, and executes the tree[7]. For example, given our experimental circuit and the fault name

---

[5]The test part of a rule can be extended to accommodate complex expressions so that more than one object can be tested in one rule.

[6]For instance, one strategy might be: find one fault; fix it; if the board is still faulty try diagnosing again; find another fault, and so on.

[7]It is important to note that the generation of a diagnostic tree is not the same as the generation of a state-space search: the latter implies an exhaustive search space, whereas the former implies a *controlling* mechanism.

output_abnormal, i.e. output of leds is not correct, the inference engine carries out the diagnosis like this:

1. find the rule named as **output_abnormal;**

2. test the input of the counter, suppose it is OK;

3. find the rule named as **counter_or_buffer_fault;**

4. check the function of the counter, suppose the result is OK;

5. report result: **buffer_fault.**

output_abnormal and **counter_or_buffer_fault** are two rule objects structured in such a way that the former asks for the *input* of the object **counter** to be checked and the later the *function* of the object **counter.** The component object **counter** is therefore called twice in the diagnosis, but each time the component object performs a different check. In this way **counter** presents two different perspectives in the one diagnostic run.

6. Distinguishing features of EXOOD

The approach adopted in EXOOD can be interpreted as a combination of the advantages of two main approaches adopted in current knowledge-base diagnostic systems: the production system approach, and the frame-based approach. As far as production systems are concerned, among the advantages are modularity and naturalness. However, as research continues into production systems, a variety of disadvantages have surfaced. We have already mentioned aspects of shallow reasoning, but other disadvantages are that knowledge, when expressed only as a set of production rules, is not always easy to understand, especially when contextual knowledge must be stated explicitly in the condition part of each rule, and that the search strategy is usually embedded in the code. The advantages of frame-based systems include intuitive appeal, the ability to handle different perspectives, the inclusion of generic values and default values, and 'natural' forms of inference such as the inferring of generic and default properties as well as inferring by analogy (see Frost 1986, pp. 454-455 and pp. 489-490). However, the main disadvantage with frame systems is that causal inference is not well catered for.

The advantages of adopting an EXOOD approach in the domain of electronic troubleshooting can now be seen to lie in the way that the object-oriented approach, as exemplified in frames, is adopted for providing a base-level description of components, on top of which aspects of a production system approach can be included, in object-oriented form, in order to cater for causal reasoning. The advantages include all the advantages of both production systems and frame systems. For instance, the problem of representing contextual knowledge (in production systems) can be solved by storing such knowledge at the object-oriented rule level where individual rules inherit various contextual properties as defined by the class they belong to. Also, the diagnostic strategy is now largely independent of the production rules and can in turn be expressed in terms more appropriate for the domain in question. Whilst we have not so far required diagnostic strategies themselves to be objects. this is implied by the EXOODS approach.

As far as knowledge engineering practice is concerned, EXOOD allows for the possibility of modular construction: the component object base can be designed, implemented and evaluated on the basis of component manufacturers' data and circuit board layout, the diagnostic base on the basis of specific and general experience of hardware diagnosis, and the inference engine on the basis of higher-level diagnostic strategies. Within each module there may also be advantages in terms of portability across domains, since the higher levels of each module, because of their use of object-oriented representations, are typically static (fixed) and may therefore be used as templates in other hardware diagnosis systems.

References

Bobrow, D. G. and Winograd, T. (1985). An overview of KRL, a knowledge representation language. In Readings in Knowledge Representation, ed. R. J. Brachman and H. J. Levesque, pp. 263-286. Los Altos, Ca.: Morgan Kaufman Publishers Inc.

Freiling, M. J., Rehfuss, S., Alexander, J. H., Messick, S. L. & Shulman, S. J. (1986). The ontological structure of a troubleshooting system for electronic instruments. In Proceedings of the 1st International Conference on Applications of AI in Engineering Problems (Volume 1), ed. D. Sriram and R. Adey, pp. 609-620. New York: Springer Verlag.

Frost, R. A. (1986). Introduction to Knowledge Base Systems. London: Collins.

Gordon, M. J. C. (1979). The Denotational Description of Programming Languages. New York: Springer Verlag.

Jones, A. H. & Burge, S. E. (1987). An expert system design using cause-effect representations and simulation for fault detection. In System Fault Diagnostics, Reliability and Related Knowledge-Based Approaches (Volume 2: Knowledge-Based and Fault-Tolerant Techniques), ed. S. G. Tzafestas, M. Singh, and G. Schmidt, pp. 71-80. Dordrecht: Reidel Publishing Company.

Pau, L. F. (1986). Survey of expert systems for fault detection, test generation and maintenance. Expert Systems, 3, no. 2, 100-111.

Tzafestas, S. G. (1987). A look at the knowledge-based approach to system fault diagnosis and supervisory control. In System Fault Diagnostics, Reliability and Related Knowledge-Based Approaches (Volume 2: Knowledge-Based and Fault-Tolerant Techniques), ed. S. G. Tzafestas, M. Singh, and G. Schmidt, pp. 3-16. Dordrecht: Reidel Publishing Company.